GOOD TO
GREEN

Managing Business Risks and Opportunities
in the Age of Environmental Awareness

John-David Phyper and Paul MacLean

John Wiley & Sons Canada, Ltd.

Library and Archives Canada Cataloguing in Publication Data

Phyper, John-David
Good to green : managing business risks and opportunities in the age of environmental awareness / John-David Phyper, Paul MacLean.

Includes index.
ISBN 978-0-470-15942-2

1. Management—Environmental aspects. 2. Business—Environmental aspects. I. MacLean, Paul II. Title.
HD30.255.P49 2009   658.4'083   C2008-907806-3

Production Credits
Cover design: Ian Koo
Interior design and typesetting: Natalia Burobina
Printer: Friesens

John Wiley & Sons Canada, Ltd.
6045 Freemont Blvd.
Mississauga, Ontario
L5R 4J3

Printed in Canada

1 2 3 4 5 FP 13 12 11 10 09

© Mixed Sources
Product group from well-managed forests, controlled sources and recycled wood or fibre
www.fsc.org Cert no. SW-COC-001271
© 1996 Forest Stewardship Council
FSC

ENVIRONMENTAL BENEFITS STATEMENT

John Wiley saved the following resources by printing the pages of this book on chlorine free paper made with 100% post-consumer waste.

TREES	WATER	ENERGY	SOLID WASTE	GREENHOUSE GASES
81	29,418	56	3,778	7,087
FULLY GROWN	GALLONS	MILLION BTUs	POUNDS	POUNDS

Calculations based on research by Environmental Defense and the Paper Task Force. Manufactured at Friesens Corporation

To my wife Christine, for her patience and understanding, and my beautiful daughters, Megan and Madison, for constantly reminding me of the important things in life.

John

To Mariela, for healthy doses of inspiration and support; to Ali and Alexa, for being who they are—and for indulging the old man; and to my friends and colleagues at ÉEM, for the steady stream of ideas and goodwill.

Paul

CONTENTS

List of Figures, Tables and Case Studies

List of Figures

PREFACE

On a sunny day in the spring of 2008, several months before the cataclysmic economic events that will be remembered for decades, we discussed how corporate environmental management had evolved during our twenty years of working in the field, and what lay ahead. We reflected on the many hundreds of projects in which we helped companies to implement environmental management systems (EMSs), to understand sustainable development (SD) and to address corporate social responsibility (CSR) concerns.

Not surprisingly, we both commented that on the spectrum of environmental performance, there are a few key attributes that distinguish "good" companies from truly "green" companies. We noted that companies that demonstrate leadership through sustained action on global environmental challenges and achieve business success in the process also succeed in overcoming two problematic trends that continue to plague the rest of the pack.

The first is "cosmetic environmentalism" whereby companies focus on easy to do activities that provide an aesthetic fix, e.g., recycling program at Head Office or purchasing offsets for CEO travel, instead of digging deeper and developing a good understanding of their business "risks and opportunities" associated with environmental issues. Only by performing that latter can these issues be properly managed at a strategic, tactical and operational level.

The second issue: environmental management is typically fragmented in "silos" of activity—often focusing on SD initiatives, CSR reporting obligations or, more recently, climate change—contributing to further weakening of the approach. Activity in a particular silo may extend from the shop floor to upper management, but an absence of communication and exchange across key functions prevents companies from realizing the true value of management's efforts.

This unfortunately common situation has often left a number of important questions unanswered. Among these are the following:

- Why are companies not assessing the impact of environmental issues on their business models?
- Who has overall responsibility for environmental issues at a company and do they have the authority to make real changes?
- Why do departments that own a business function (e.g., product management, manufacturing, procurement, logistics) not have full ownership/accountability for environmental issues pertinent to their activities?
- What obstacles are hindering companies' shift from a "repair/refine" model for their products to a "redesign/rethink" approach that allows them to capitalize on business opportunities?
- Why are companies not proactively assessing what hazardous chemicals may be in their products and thus pose harm to company's brand (not based upon scientific peer review, but the court of public opinion, with the Internet elevating awareness)?
- What is stopping companies from addressing the environmental/product issues associated with their complex web of suppliers, instead of allowing a "chain of uncertainty" to continue?
- What criteria are companies using to invest in clean technology initiatives? Many clean technologies require long-term subsidies to compete, lack scalability (i.e., declining costs over time) and are solutions to "side issues."
- Why have so few companies automated compliance and risk management activities through their IT systems?

Our discussion led to the idea for this book, and for our choice of title, as Jim Collins (the author of *Good to Great*) also sought to identify distinctive traits of outstanding companies that may serve as guidance to others.

Our goal is to guide managers and executives in making informed business decisions on the management of risks and opportunities related to environmental issues. As IT is now business-critical for companies, we also discuss how environmental issues must be incorporated into IT systems to facilitate compliance and proper risk management. We deliberately avoid describing the impact of humans on the environment, nor do we discuss how to implement standard, well-known environmental programs such as the ISO 14001 EMS standard. There are plenty of good books on these topics.

As noted above, while we drafted the manuscript, dramatic economic and political events were unfolding, which had a profound effect on our writing. Most notable among these were the petroleum price spike (>$140 per barrel) and subsequent crash (<$40 per barrel), the failure of the financial system leading to global recession, and the election of a Democratic president in the United States who supports action to mitigate climate change and promote a green economy. Fortunately for us, they reinforced our basic premise that a shift has begun in which leading companies are starting to focus on business risk and opportunities related to environmental issues and in doing so, they

- assign ownership and accountability to the individuals/groups that manage key business functions and break down the EMS/SD/CSR silos
- redesign and rethink products to ensure the elimination of hazardous ingredients, optimization of energy efficiency and reduction of emissions, while boosting revenue
- seek out mismanagement (inefficiencies leading to elevated energy use, emissions, waste, etc.) in the supply chain to improve the bottom line and prevent environment impact of operations
- identify new business opportunities in both clean technology (clean water, renewable energy) as well as product life cycle management (PLM)

The above coincides with (and in many cases is driven by) a shift in discussion at the board and executive level to the monetary impact on brand, fiduciary duty, renewable energy strategy, cleantech business opportunity and financial reporting obligations related to climate change. No longer are environmental issues viewed exclusively as a cost of doing business but now are seen as opportunities for revenue generation and cost reduction, and in some cases are seen as a way to create new business models with less reliance on carbon energy sources and as a shift from owning things to a service economy. It is important, however, to realize that these changes do not happen overnight and that for real revolutionary change to occur, we need to invent alternative energies and products that strive to be sustainable, are superior to what they are replacing and have a trajectory that allows them to be cheaper within a short period of time.

John-David Phyper & Paul MacLean
Toronto/Montreal
February 2009

ACKNOWLEDGEMENTS

This book represents the efforts of more than the two authors. During its preparation, and even before, many others shared information, experience and opinions with the authors.

To ensure that the material contained in *Good to Green* has been prepared properly and is current, individuals active in each particular area reviewed draft versions of chapters. All of the following people freely gave of their time and ideas and the authors are indebted to each of them for their assistance.

Lino Casalino, Partner in the Advisory Services practice of Pricewaterhouse-Coopers LLP working in the Toronto office, where he is also the Retail and Consumer Advisory practice leader, directing Canada's Supply Chain and Logistics practice. Lino is a member of PwC's global supply chain team that has developed client solutions aimed at reducing cost and managing risk while achieving sustainability goals and objectives. He is a frequent speaker and specialist on the topic of "lean and green supply chain."

Steve Christenson, Vice President of Regulatory Affairs at Ecolab, where he has co-chaired Ecolab's global sustainability programs. Mr. Christenson has practiced law since 1988, working primarily on environmental, health and safety matters. Mr. Christenson previously practiced law at Dorsey & Whitney LLP in Minneapolis, Minnesota. He earned his law degree from the University of Iowa and is a member of the Minnesota bar.

Kevin J. Fay, P.E., Corporate Director, product and supply chain stewardship, for PPG Industries, Pittsburgh. Mr. Fay has over 30 years of international environment, health, safety and product stewardship experience in the coatings, chemicals, glass and fiberglass industries. He is past chairman of the Chlorine Institute board of directors, served on the American Chemistry Council Responsible Care committee and is a member of the Air & Waste Management Association.

Mike Harris, Advisory Services partner in the Toronto office of Pricewaterhouse-Coopers LLP who leads the Canadian Sustainable Business Solutions and Corporate Governance practices. Some 15 years ago, he pioneered PwC's sustainability practice, developing one of the first publicly assured environmental reports in Canada.

Tom Heintzman brings a distinguished record of service to environmental causes along with proven executive leadership experience to his role as president of Bullfrog Power Inc. Tom co-founded Bullfrog Power in 2004. Prior to that, he spent more than 13 years in the private and NGO sectors, including with Zenon Environmental, where he led its global M&A initiatives as director of corporate development, and McKinsey & Company.

Jeffrey Hojlo is a research analyst at AMR who is responsible for research and analysis on trends and developments in product innovation and the product life cycle management (PLM) market. Jeff is a member of the Product Development Management Association (PDMA) and writes on topics such as global product development and launch, integrated product and process development, and the front end of innovation.

Chuck Holt is responsible for the administration of the investment funds at Investeco, which was Canada's first environment sector fund manager. Prior to joining Investeco, Chuck practiced corporate/commercial law at a Toronto-based law firm, and before that he earned an LL.M. from the London School of Economics and an LL.B. from the University of Ottawa.

Colin Isaacs is an environmental and Sustainable Development management consultant with more than 25 years experience. He has been a municipal councilor, provincial politician, Executive Director of the advocacy group Pollution Probe, Chair of the Canadian Environment Industry Association, and, since 1989, CEO of CIAL Group. He is also publisher of the Gallon Environment Letter.

Robert Kendrick is Sun Chemical Corporation Director of Global Regulatory and Product Stewardship North America responsible for product safety. He is a member of both the National Association of Printing Ink Manufacturers and the Flexible Packaging Association Environmental Strategy Committee. He is actively engaged in the collection and analysis of regulatory details, economic data, sustainability metrics, manufacturing indicators and safety statistics. He has extensive experience specializing in IT solutions dedicated to product development and regulatory compliance for the pigment, printing ink, paint, plastics and coatings industries, responsible for the quality and oversight of automated compliance solutions for Sun Chemical Corporation.

David Lavoie, an independent business consultant, was previously Senior Vice President Marketing and Alliances for Atrion International Inc. David has over twenty-five years of marketing, communications and new business development experience as a senior executive in both private and public companies.

Joel Makower, for more than twenty years, has been a writer, speaker and strategist on corporate environmental practices, clean technology and green marketing; he has helped a wide range of companies align environmental responsibility. He is executive editor of GreenBiz.com and other websites, events and research services produced by Greener World Media, of which he is co-founder and chairman. His new book, *Strategies for the Green Economy,* distills his years of watching the green business scene and offers insights and inspiration for understanding and untangling the complexities and controversies of profiting in the growing green economy.

Susan McLean, Manager, Stakeholder Relations for Sustainable Development Technology Canada, was formerly Senior Manager, Business Development, Global Clean Technology at the Toronto Stock Exchange (TSX).

Ron Nielsen, P.Eng, PBAS, is Executive in Residence at the Dalhousie University Faculty of Management and Senior Associate of ÉEM inc. He is former Director of Sustainability and Strategic Partnerships at Rio Tinto Alcan in Montreal. Ron is a Fellow of Tomorrow's Company, on the Board of the Canadian Water Network and Chair of the Canadian Advisory Committee to the ISO Sub-Committee on Climate Change.

Mickey North Rizza brings twenty-three years of global sourcing and supply chain management experience to her role as a research director in the supply management practice at AMR Research. Mickey is a key member of the supply chain team and works to communicate effective supply management strategies to AMR Research's clients.

Dr. Ruud A. Overbeek is Global Director of the Health and Environmental Services Division of Intertek, a leading provider of quality and safety solutions serving a wide range of industries around the world. Due to his contributions in his field, Ruud was last year chosen as member of the HBA Advisory Board and is a well-known author of publications and articles concerning environmental compliance and effective compliance implementation strategies.

Geoff Parsons, Vice President in the PricewaterhouseCoopers Canadian Advisory Practice, specializes in the area of Operational Effectiveness and Performance Improvement within organizational supply chains. His recent focus has been on integrating cost effective initiatives with environmentally sustainable practices to deliver both lean and green supply chain business solutions to address the multifaceted challenges facing organizations today.

Ed Peelen, Professor of (Direct) Marketing at the Center for Marketing and Supply Chain Management at Nyenrode Business University, The Netherlands, has held the Stichting IDEA Chair in Event Marketing and Communication since 2007.

Mike Rose is Vice President, Business Development at DO2 Technologies. DO2 Technologies is the global leader in SaaS (software as a service) electronic invoicing and procure-to-pay solutions. Mike has held senior management positions in a number of organizations focused on business and electronic commerce in the mining, natural resource, manufacturing, energy and utilities industries in North America and internationally.

Diane Saxe is one of the world's top twenty-five environmental lawyers, according to Euromoney's Best of the Best, 2008. Diane Saxe's law firm is the only Canadian environmental firm honored to be a member of the very prestigious International Network of Boutique Law Firms.

Rick Whittaker is Vice President Investments at Sustainable Development Technology Canada (SDTC). During his career in technology investment, Mr. Whittaker has led initiatives in product development and managed several advanced technology investment programs. He has initiated several patents on these technologies, which are in production today.

Errick (Skip) Willis, President and CEO of Carbon Capital Management and former Vice-President of ICF Consulting, is the Chairman of the Board of Directors of the Ontario Environmental Industry Association and he chairs the Technical Advisory Group on Climate Change for CEIA National. He has over twenty-five years of consulting experience in strategic planning, issues management, regulatory affairs, strategic communications and international market development. He has worked at the international level as an industry advisor to the Canadian delegation to the Montreal Protocol starting in 1992.

INTRODUCTION

The environment has finally been given a seat at the boardroom table. Even companies that were once notorious for their exploitation of the environment arc joining the discussion, as they try to cope with the depth and speed of the upheaval environmental issues are having on their business. Some business leaders are coming to terms with this new reality through the following acts:

Humility—as they stand in front of shareholders at the annual general meeting and explain that the strategy of blissfully ignoring hazardous ingredients and the threat of climate change is hurting their profitability, and

"And this little warning light flashes when the outside air becomes too polluted to breathe."

Generosity—as their companies pay significant fines to environmental regulatory agencies or settlements to plaintiffs in class-action lawsuits over product recalls, both of which could have been avoided by adopting more robust programs to protect the environment and by ensuring that products did not contain hazardous materials.

Many companies are caught in a tidal wave of green issues—climate change, alternative energy, scarcity of resources (e.g., looming water shortages) and the explosion of information on the Internet (raising awareness of hazardous materials in consumer products, as well as corporate injustice anywhere in the world). This green wave will force companies to reassess how they do business, by re-evaluating the life cycle of their products and the effectiveness of their supply chains.

Discussion around boardrooms on environmental issues is no longer defined by words like "nice to do" and "early adopters." Instead, one hears the terms "business critical," "crossing the chasm" and "creating competitive advantage"—all giving rise to a new lexicon that is being used at the executive level to identify and exploit opportunities where others see threats.

This green wave will also create a "green rush" that will have a substantial impact on both the economy and environment in the long term. As with the gold rush of the late nineteenth century, some individuals will prosper significantly while others will not for a variety of reasons—inadequate market information, lack of business acumen, timing, access to capital and uncertainty in oil prices. However, unlike the original gold rush, this boom should actually improve environmental conditions, rather than degrade them further. Organizations that fail to consider environmental issues in their business model may find themselves victims of the inevitable bust that awaits those who miss out. The key drivers for change include

- increased public awareness of environmental issues (e.g., global warming, species extinctions, carcinogens, endocrine disruptors) has significantly impacted consumer spending and retention
- growth in the quantity, complexity and enforcement of legislation related to the protection of consumers, workers and the environment around the world
- an increase in the amount of market-based instruments put forward by governments around the globe to reduce emissions and promote alternative energy
- expansion of U.S. disclosure requirements to include environmental costs and liabilities under the Sarbanes-Oxley legislation

- forecasted water shortages in many parts of the globe
- the drive to reduce supply chain costs associated with environmental mismanagement (the Wal-Mart effect)
- increased environmental disclosure requirements from the investment and insurance communities and negative response (i.e., decreased valuation or increased premiums) if environmental, social and governance factors are neglected
- dramatic impacts to the bottom line resulting from the impairment of corporate brand via consumer, worker or environmental issues
- forecasted increase in petroleum prices, which will reinforce activities related to renewable energy and energy-efficient transportation
- elevated security concerns related to the movement and storage of hazardous materials as well as reliance on foreign oil, especially reserves controlled by national oil companies
- improved employee satisfaction and retention following implementation of sustainable development (SD) programs

It is important to note that for true change to occur, companies must alter the way they do business. As Paul Hawken says in *The Ecology of Commerce*:

Environmental protection should not be carried out at the behest of charity, altruism, or legislative fiats. As long as it is done so, it will remain a decorous subordinate to finance, growth and technology.... Recycling aluminum cans in the company cafeteria and ceremonial tree plantings are about as effective as bailing out the *Titanic* with teaspoons.[1]

Industry visionaries have emerged to guide their companies, their sector and, in some cases, industry in general, towards principles of SD and corporate social responsibility (CSR), both of which are discussed in more detail in chapter 1. Key principles that these visionaries have in common are the need to innovate and invest in activities that will provide a strong triple bottom line (TBL)—people, planet and profit. These leaders are turning challenges (such as additional expenditures, process inefficiencies) into opportunities (new products/services) for innovation and success throughout their companies' value chain. They are thinking out of the box and in doing so increasing revenue, reducing expenditures and risk, and creating strong brands. They are decoupling the concepts of "increased production" and "increased environmental impact."

This book does not define the impact or the moral reasons to change—we have left this for other authorities. Nor does it address the cosmetic activities that many companies are undertaking to be green, e.g., purchasing carbon offsets for executive travel and using coffee mugs instead of foam cups. What it does provide is evidence that a green rush is occurring, whereby companies have a unique opportunity to realize greater revenue and profit by seeking real change in how they impact the environment. Companies are shifting attention from concern over legislation (primarily directed at end-of-pipe solutions) to forcing environmental change through the supply chain to ensure brand protection, cost reductions and continuation of the supply of raw materials, all of which are truly revolutionary concepts for business to adopt.

If you have not already assessed and initiated activities to address real environmental concerns associated with your business, you are missing the boat! The key difference between this wave of change and previous green waves—1970s/1980s controls on emissions/discharges from heavy industry and 1990s adoption of management systems (e.g., International Organization for Standardization [ISO] 14001 standard) and CSR standards—is that, this time around, environmental issues are being included in key strategic, tactical and operational planning and decisions. They are not just "add on" or "nice to do" initiatives, but are fundamental components of the business cycle. Wal-Mart's initiatives in energy conservation, the reduction of packaging material and greenhouse gas emissions, and the elimination of hazardous material throughout its supply chain make for nice green reports and press releases, but they are also about getting waste and costs out of the supply chain.

CHANGING CONCERNS

The creation of a product, whether for industrial or consumer use, by its very nature will impact the environment. The extent of the impact can vary significantly depending upon the raw materials, process being utilized, emission control technology, end-of-life practices and the sensitivity of the receiving environment.

Historically, the environmental impact, particularly from industrial emissions, was so significant that local ecosystems suffered measurable harm. Fortunately, in the developed world at least, most facilities have modified their processes and control technology so that emissions now have been reduced, in many cases by orders of magnitude. As an example, with the adoption of Responsible Care, a voluntary program for the safe and environmentally sound management of chemicals, the American chemical industry has reduced emissions by 78%.[2]

Tragically for the environment and the surrounding communities, however, there are still some facilities that continue to emit significant levels of contaminants into the local ecosystem because of the absence of either government legislation or enforcement. Governments, non-government organizations (NGOs) and industry need to work together to change these practices as soon as possible.

As companies overcame the hurdle of "significant local impact," they began to pay attention to the cumulative effect of industrial activity on a global scale. Elevated levels of toxins in animals and humans who inhabit the Arctic confirmed the planetary circulation of contaminants. Alarming thinning of the protective ozone layer in the stratosphere awakened us to the impact of man-made, ozone-depleting substances. Reports of decreased human fertility related to the widespread use of endocrine disruptors (substances that act like hormones and disrupt body functions) alerted us to the potential impact of chronic, low-level exposure to chemicals. And more recently, we now know that the buildup of carbon dioxide in the atmosphere, due to trapped greenhouse gas emissions, can at least partly explain changing global weather patterns.

The focus has shifted from local to global impact—not just related to the transmigration of contaminants and global warming, but also to the quality of goods shipped from developing countries (e.g., concern over lead-based paints on toys shipped from China) to North America and Europe, and the environmental conditions of the manufacturing facilities.

Figure I provides an overview of the changing level of concern associated with different environmental issues from a business perspective. Key trigger events included new/modified legislation, civil lawsuits and awareness campaigns by NGOs. The issues presented are examples only (there are too many to include an exhaustive review) and are plotted against the time period during which they gained the greatest general attention (i.e., in some sectors, certain issues are still front and center).

The concern over lead is a good example of how far the developed world, at least, has progressed. Twenty to thirty years ago, lead was present in the air we breathed and in the paint pigments covering our children's toys. In the United States, lead-based paint was banned in 1978. Lead in plumbing solder and lead solder on food cans was phased out during the 1980s and leaded gasoline was phased out during the early 1990s.[3] A significant amount of lead is still used in lead-acid batteries, but recycling of these batteries is one of the most successful recycling programs ever, with more than 97% of all battery lead recycled.[4]

Figure 1: Examples of Changing Environmental Concerns
(in developed countries)

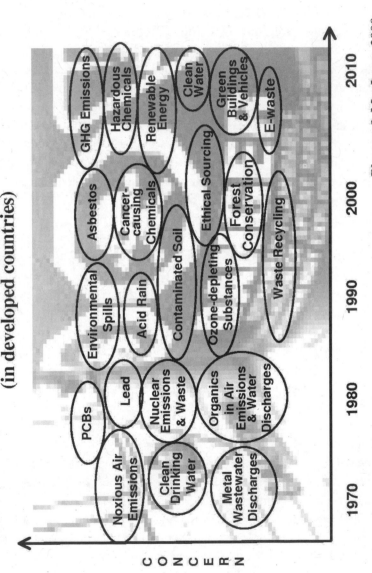

Phyper & MacLean, 2009

Figure II presents information on some key global statistics related to environmental issues.[5] Record amounts of crude oil are being consumed—approximately one thousand barrels of crude every second. More than half of this energy—and this share is increasing—is dedicated to the movement of goods, services and people. We are now entering the twilight of the oil age, but alternatives, such as biofuels from food crops, may also have a significant negative impact on the environment and society.[6]

Note: The values for Chinese CO_2 emissions presented in figure II are derived from the Netherlands Environmental Assessment Agency and do not accord with those produced by the Chinese government. The statement that China has surpasses the U.S. in CO_2 emissions is also supported by other sources, including *National Geographic*.[7]

CHANGING MANAGEMENT OF ENVIRONMENTAL ISSUES

In the 1990s, Paul Hawken wrote two ground-breaking books on business and the environment. In preparation for our book, we revisited these topics to gauge their continued relevance to today's business environment.

His work *Ecology of Commerce: A Declaration of Sustainability*, published in 1994, was a milestone that promoted the concept that businesses must "re-imagine" and "re-invent" themselves as cyclical operations, i.e., from "cradle to cradle." Hawken advised three broad approaches: observe the waste-equals-food (raw products) principle of nature, change from a carbon to a hydrogen-/sunshine-based economy, and create systems that support restorative behavior. Hawken also posed a key question—*who will lead the next industrial revolution, as the first one is not working?*[8]

Natural Capitalism: Creating the Next Industrial Revolution, published in 1999, has been described as the first book to explore the lucrative opportunities for businesses in an era of approaching environmental limits. *Natural Capitalism* describes a future in which business and environmental interests increasingly overlap, and in which businesses can better satisfy their customers' needs, increase profits and help solve environmental problems all at the same time. The four inter-linked principles of natural capitalism are[9]

1. Shifting from the traditional economic focus on productivity per unit of labor to productivity per unit of natural resource use

Figure II: Global Stats on Environmental Issues

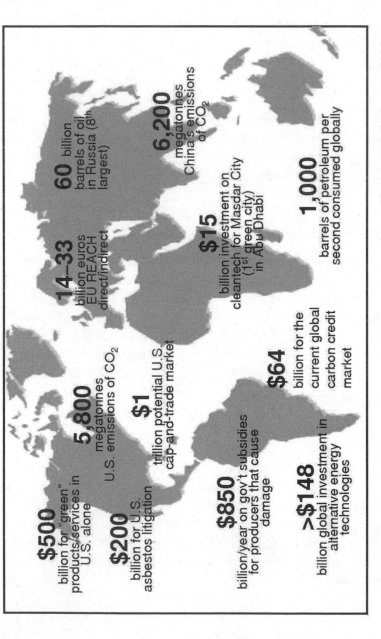

$500 billion for "green" products/services in U.S. alone

$200 billion for U.S. asbestos litigation

5,800 megatonnes U.S. emissions of CO_2

$1 trillion potential U.S. cap-and-trade market

$850 billion/year on gov't subsidies for producers that cause damage

>$148 billion global investment in alternative energy technologies

$64 billion for the current global carbon credit market

14–33 billion euros EU REACH direct/indirect

60 billion barrels of oil in Russia (8th largest)

6,200 megatonnes China's emissions of CO_2

$15 billion investment on cleantech for Masdar City (1st green city) in Abu Dhabi

1,000 barrels of petroleum per second consumed globally

Phyper & MacLean, 2009

2. Building production systems that mimic nature (for example, an agricultural production system that recycles wastes, as nature does, rather than discarding them)
3. Transitioning from a goods-producing, "owning things" economy to a "service and flow" economy
4. Investing in activities that protect or restore ecosystems

So, have companies migrated en masse to natural capitalism? In general, no; however, companies are adopting principle 2—especially the elimination of waste and introduction of "cradle-to-cradle" (c2c) concept, principle 3—in specific sectors, and principle 4—for most, this move forms part of overall philanthropy, while others see protection of raw material sources. The evolution of industrial stewardship of environmental impacts can generally be described as follows, with forward-thinking companies ahead of these timelines (see also figure III):

- Basic EHS systems (early 1980s)—Basic environmental, health and safety (EHS) systems were implemented, primarily at plant level, by industry to ensure ongoing regulatory compliance with legislation. These systems differed dramatically from company to company, as did their effectiveness.
- Costs/risks aversion (early 1990s)—Having mastered basic EHS, industry leaders' focus shifted to tactical discussions of cost reduction and risk aversion, especially when the costs of ongoing compliance were recognized. Other companies adopted this approach when faced with significant liabilities and costs from cleanup of contaminated properties.
- Environmental management systems (EMS) (mid 1990s)—Structured management systems, such as the ISO 14000 series, were introduced. A focus on certification/branding of company operations as being "green," with varied results in terms of actual environmental improvement, began to appear. Activities were still at a tactical/operational level; however, a broader cross-section of companies became involved.
- Sustainable development (early 2000)—Companies adopted SD concepts at the executive level to manage business issues and in doing so viewed environmental issues as opportunity, not just cost. Visionary leaders started to leverage the term/approach to define the direction of their companies and push forward actual change. In many cases, though, SD was used to define cosmetic activities that were less about actual reduction of environmental footprint and more about green branding.

Figure III: Changing Environmental Stewardship

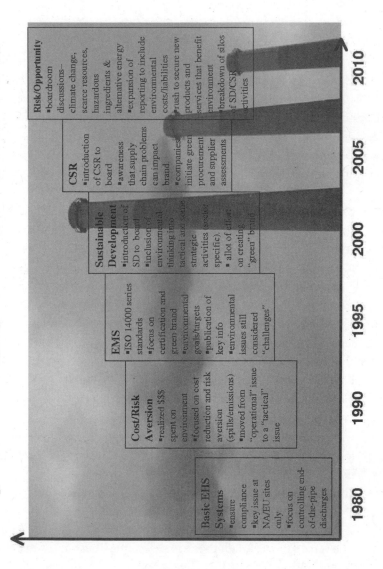

Basic EHS Systems
- ensure compliance
- key issue at NA/EU sites only
- focus on controlling end-of-the-pipe discharges

Cost/Risk Aversion
- realized $$$ spent on environment
- focused on cost reduction and risk aversion (spills/emissions)
- moved from "operational" issue to a "tactical" issue

EMS
- ISO 14000 series standards
- focus on certification and green brand
- environmental goals/targets
- publication of key info
- environmental issues still considered "challenges"

Sustainable Development
- introduction of SD to board
- inclusion of environmental thinking into tactical and some strategic activities (sector specific)
- a lot of effort on creating "green" brand

CSR
- introduction of CSR to board
- awareness that supply chain problems can impact brand
- companies initiate green procurement and supplier assessments

Risk/Opportunity
- boardroom discussions—climate change, scarce resources, hazardous ingredients & alternative energy
- expansion of reporting to include environmental costs/liabilities
- rush to secure new products and services that benefit environment
- breakdown of silos of SD/CSR activities

1980   1990   1995   2000   2005   2010

- Corporate social responsibility (mid 2000)—As ethical sourcing began to dominate discussions, the term "corporate social responsibility" (CSR) began to emerge as the high-level catchphrase to cover a corporation's activities related to the environment, workers, consumers and the adjacent communities in which companies operated. Strategic discussion of supply chain/brand reputation occurred at board level and terms like "triple bottom line" (TBL) began to enter the business vocabulary.

- Risks and opportunities (R&O) (late 2000)—In 2002, the U.S. passed the Sarbanes-Oxley legislation in response to costly revelations of corrupt corporate behavior, such as at WorldCom and Enron, and companies started to put in place systems to ensure compliance—typically referred to as governance, risk and compliance (GRC) tools/processes. In 2007/2008, U.S. organizations started to focus on environment-related costs and compliance risks at the executive level. More advanced organizations saw this as an opportunity to combine SD/CSR and GRC into an approach that balanced both business risk and opportunities related to environmental issues—not at a superficial level, but at a level that truly resulted in change in all components of a product and company life cycle.

A more detailed discussion of SD/CSR and R&O is presented in chapter 1 and chapter 2.

> Historically, the average company's commitment to the environment was tightly aligned to the financial health of the company and the sector in which it operated. During poor economic times, TBL quickly became the "bottom line" through cuts to environmental and social programs. During the current recession forward thinking companies continue to invest in projects that provide environmental benefits, specifically those that significantly reduce business risk or provide opportunity for increase revenue.

An excerpt from a speech by Chad Holliday, former chairman of DuPont, best describes the new direction:[10]

The definition of sustainability has been broadened to include human safety, as well as environmental protection, and it has become a market-driven business priority throughout the value chain. The pace has increased as the synergistic effects of market demand, societal expectations, and product innovation create collaborations up and down the value chain. Sustainability will increasingly become central to the total value proposition and hence every customer and—through their products—every consumer involved in the value chain.

The view of scientists locked away in a laboratory inventing something new and wonderful to spring on the world has given way to a market-back approach. For innovation to be successfully introduced into the marketplace and accepted by society, it must be based on many forms of partnership and continuous dialogue with stakeholders, including governments, NGOs, and academia. Science and innovation that do not address pressing human needs will not advance sustainability. Likewise a vision of sustainability detached from science and technology will not succeed. We need both the commitment to sustainability and the accomplishments of science.

FOLLOW THE MONEY TRAIL

What is driving this current wave of green opportunities and the sale of new products and services?

- increasing amount and complexity of government legislation related to environmental issues, including market-based incentives
- consumer demand for good products that are green/safe
- significant demand for renewable energy and clean water
- greening of the boardroom

Government Activities

Over the past forty years, government regulators enacted legislation to reduce industrial emissions. From 1970 to 1990, command-and-control legislation was primarily related to the reduction of emissions, improved waste management and the cleanup of contaminated sites, and was able to drive contaminant levels down and minimize local impacts. Various emissions trading schemes (ETSs) were employed in the U.S. to phase lead out of gasoline in the 1980s, to contribute to the international effort to stop production of ozone-depleting substances in the 1990s and to reduce SO_2 emissions from electric utilities.

In all cases, the introduction of new legislation triggered significant expenditures/investment by companies affected by the legislation. Examples of these expenditures (and thus opportunities) can be illustrated by recent/proposed legislation:

- Emissions trading schemes (ETSs)—EU ETS 2007 trading volume was $50 billion,[11] this is in addition to money spent on controls. A report released by New Carbon Finance estimates that the U.S. will be home to a carbon market worth in excess of $1 trillion by 2020. The forecast assumes that the U.S. will implement an economy-wide cap-and-trade system within four to five years.
- EU Registration, Evaluation, and Authorisation of Chemicals (REACH)— It will cost industry $12.8 billion to implement the legislation.[12] This legislation is revolutionary as it requires existing products in the marketplace to be reassessed and controlled, and imposed bi-directional communication along the supply chain.
- Renewable energy—The 2008 U.S. Comprehensive American Energy Security and Consumer Protection Act included $18 billion in spending on renewable energy and a requirement that utilities generate 15% of their energy from renewable resources by 2020.
- Electric vehicles/hybrids—Legislation has been enacted in the U.S. to provide a $25 billion loan package to the auto industry as well as mandate higher fuel economy CAFE standards in the 2011–20 model years. The loan package includes a restriction that automakers must only use the funds to retool factories that lead to vehicles that are 25% more fuel-efficient than current models.
- The 2009 American Recovery and Reinvestment Act (ARRA) includes approximately $58 billion in spending and tax cuts to encourage the use of alternative energy and energy conservation. Key components include $20 billion in tax cuts and tax credits for renewable energy, energy conservation and efficiency; $6.3 billion in state energy-efficient and clean-energy grants; $4.5 billion to make federal buildings more energy efficient; $5 billion to weatherize homes for low-income people; $4.5 billion in direct spending to modernize the electricity grid with smart-grid technologies; $6 billion in loan guarantees for renewable energy systems, biofuel projects and electric-power transmission facilities; $3.4 billion appropriated to the Department of Energy for fossil energy research and development, such as storing carbon dioxide underground at coal power plants; and $2 billion in loans to manufacture advanced batteries and components for applications such as plug-in electric cars.

- The 2009 Canadian Economic Action Plan included approximately $2.8 billion of "green" funding—a value significant below the ARRA on a per capital basis. Key components included $1 billion for Green Energy Fund; $1 billion for Green Infrastructure Fund; $351 million for Atomic Energy of Canada Ltd. (significant portion for Advanced Candu Reactor); $300 million for home energy efficiency (extension of ecoENERGY Retrofit Program); and $165 million extension of drinking water and wastewater infrastructure projects for First Nations.

As part of his election platform, President Obama committed to the following investment as part of his New Energy for America plan:[13]

- help create 5 million new jobs by strategically investing $150 billion over the next ten years to catalyze private efforts to build a clean energy future
- put one million American-built plug-in hybrid cars—cars that can get up to 150 miles per gallon—on the road by 2015
- ensure 10% of U.S. electricity comes from renewable sources by 2012, and 25% by 2025
- implement an economy-wide cap-and-trade program to reduce greenhouse gas emissions by 80% by 2050

Consumer Demand

Market forces have resulted in a vastly different competitive landscape than fifteen years ago. "Green products and services" are now a mainstay of business—they have become ubiquitous—and are no longer considered inferior. Consumers are expected to double their spending on green products and services in 2008, totaling an estimated $500 billion annually or $43 billion per month.[14] Companies like GE and Mitsubishi Electric Corp. are betting their future on the growth of this sector. The following are examples of green products that are experiencing significant increase in sales and have become an everyday component of our lives.

Energy Efficient Lighting — Several jurisdictions, including Canada, the United States and the EU, have or are putting in place legislation to phase out inefficient light bulbs by 2009 to 2012.

Compact fluorescent light (CFL) bulbs use 75% less electricity than conventional incandescent lighting and have become something of an icon in the fight against global warming. Wal-Mart set the goal of selling 100 million CFL bulbs by the end of 2007 and exceeded this with a total of 137 million sold.[15] U.S. sales of CFL have been increasing at a rate of 50% per year since 2000, while global sales of CFLs in 2007 were approximately $2.5 billion (based on 1.25 billion units and $2 per fixture).[16] The next generation of lighting—light-emitting diodes (LEDs)—is projected to grow from $205 million in 2006 to $985 million in 2011, according to California-based market research group Strategies Unlimited. When other uses of LEDs are taken into account, such as phones, computers, televisions and signage, the global LED market accounted for $4.2 billion in sales in 2006.[17]

Hybrid Cars — In the United States alone, the sales of hybrid cars grew slowly from their introduction in 2000 to 2004. However, since 2005, sales have accelerated due to both market demand and production increases. Approximately 351,000 hybrid vehicles were sold in 2007—2.2% of the market. Future sales growth will come from the additional models from major automakers. Current projections for vehicle sales and percentage of market are as follows: 2008 (2.4%, 382,000) steadily building to 2012 (6%, 1,007,000).[18]

In its *Annual Energy Outlook 2009* report, the U.S. Energy Information Administration (EIA) predicted that hybrid vehicle sales in the U.S. will jump from current levels to 38 percent in 2030. They also predicted that plug-in hybrids will account for 2 percent of all new car sales.

Green Buildings — The value of green building construction reached $36–$49 billion in 2008, and according to a report entitled *Construction's Green Outlook 2009: Trends Driving Change*, projections are that this value will increase to $96–$140 billion.[19] The U.S. Department of Energy recently awarded $80 billion of contracts covering energy efficiency, renewable energy and water conservation projects at federal facilities.[20]

Increasing Demand for Alternative Energy/Water Purification

Over the last two years, investment and transactions in alternative energy have increased significantly. New global investment in alternative energy technologies, including venture capital, project finance, public markets, and research and development, has expanded by 60% from $92.6 billion in 2006 to $148.4 billion in 2007.[21] Export Development Canada has estimated the global market demand for water purification, solid waste management, and clean energy technologies to exceed $1 trillion per year.

The International Energy Agency (IEA) *World Energy Outlook* for 2008 reports forecasts that the world needs to invest $5.5 trillion (in 2007 dollars) in renewable energy sources between 2007 and 2030 to meet growing demand.[22] The following are summaries of forecasted investment and markets for key components of these markets.

- Biofuels—*A Clean Edge* report predicts that the global biofuels market (global production and wholesale pricing of ethanol and biodiesel) will grow from $25.4 billion in 2007 to $81.1 billion by 2017.[23] Negative press regarding the use of food crops for biofuel has caused many organizations to rethink this approach and shift to biomass and waste-feedstock.
- Wind—*A Clean Edge* report predicts that the global wind market (new installation capital costs) will expand from $30.1 billion in 2007 to $83.4 billion in 2017.[24]
- Solar photovoltaic (PV)—*A Clean Edge* report predicts that the global PV market (including modules, system components and installation) will grow from a $20.3 billion industry in 2007 to $74 billion by 2017.
- Hydroelectric—The IEA forecasts $50 billion worth of investments for added capacity by 2030.[25]
- Fuel cells—*A Clean Edge* report predicts that the fuel cell and distributed hydrogen market will grow from $1.5 billion (primarily for research contracts and demonstration and test units) to $16 billion over the next decade.[26]
- Geothermal—Glitnir, one of Iceland's largest investment houses, projects the annual U.S. geothermal electricity market to grow from $1.8 billion in 2008 to $11 billion by 2025. The industry is expected to draw about $40 billion in financing over the next eighteen years.[27]
- Water treatment—Global Water Intelligence predicts that the market for desalinization plants will reach $95 billion by 2015.[28] A Calvert Research report forecasts that $1 trillion a year is required to meet global water demands (construction and maintenance of infrastructure, conservation, etc.) through 2030.[29]

The 2008 recession has significantly reduced capital expenditures on clean technologies; however, the underlying fundamentals have not changed. There is a need for action on climate change, increasing energy demand and the approach of "peak oil."

Greening of the Boardroom

Major shareholders, chairpersons of boards and CEOs are all getting the green bug and in doing so are investing significant amounts of their or their companies' money in green activities. In some cases, this takes the form of philanthropic activities, like how Google founders Larry Page and Sergey Brin have committed more than $95 million in grants and investments to five initiatives through Google.org. These include[30]

- RE<C—Develop renewable energy cheaper than coal
- RechargeIT—Accelerate the adoption of plug-in electric vehicles
- Predict and Prevent—Use information and technology to empower communities to predict and prevent emerging threats before they become local, regional or global crises
- Inform and Empower to Improve Public Services—Support efforts to provide easily accessible information to people so that they can choose the best strategies for themselves and their community

In other cases, companies were investing (prior to the recession) in environmental projects that may be normally outside of their spheres of influence or commitment but can enhance corporate brand as well as return a reasonable (and in some cases, good) investment.

- In 2006, Richard Branson's Virgin Group has made a commitment to invest $3 billion in renewable energy over a ten-year period to fight global warming. Virgin Fuel's business was the first one off the blocks and invested $400 million in green energy projects, the majority of which are biofuel projects, to further reduce costs/increase return on investment for transportation components of the Virgin Group.[31]
- As a part of Goldman Sachs Environmental Policy Framework, the company committed to make available up to $1 billion for investments in renewable energy and energy efficiency projects. By the end of 2007, Goldman Sachs had surpassed this goal and had invested more than $2 billion in alternative energy projects in the U.S., Europe and Asia.[32]
- Wells Fargo & Company's environmental financing exceeded $3 billion in 2008, hurdling past its goal of providing $1 billion in commitments to Earth-friendly projects and doing so two years earlier than expected.[33]

The price will be high for companies that do not begin to adapt now to the changing reality of the marketplace, among them:

- automobile makers that insist on building large SUVs that have low fuel efficiency
- consumer goods companies that do not recognize changing consumer patterns related to "nasty" chemicals (carcinogen, endocrine disruptors, etc.) as well as the litigious nature of U.S. society
- airlines that do not invest in fleet renewal with new fuel efficient and low-noise aircraft engines
- forestry companies that do not follow sustainable harvest guidelines demanded by their customers, or respond to competing demands for forest land—especially from producers of food and bio-energy

Can companies change? Yes, over the years, numerous organizations faced with significant environmental issues have responded in a manner that has allowed them to regain, maintain or achieve a dominant position in the marketplace. Conversely, many large organizations have faltered and in some cases declared bankruptcy because of mismanagement of environmental issues.

GUIDING PRINCIPLES

The following nine guiding principles should be considered the mantra of companies wanting to minimize environmental impact and maximize revenue:

1. Integrate the environment in all business decisions.
2. Seek the truth (both sides of the debate are spreading misinformation).
3. Eliminate waste throughout the product life cycle (products, packaging, processes, energy use, etc.).
4. Treat stakeholders as you would want to be treated.
5. Eliminate hazardous chemicals (carcinogens, endocrine disruptors, etc.).
6. Switch away from high-carbon energy sources.
7. Promote cultures of innovation (proactive, "out of the box" thinking).
8. Leverage new technologies/disruptions (the playing field is changing rapidly).
9. Don't forget basic business principles.

Integrate the Environment into All Business Decisions

Companies can no longer afford to ignore environmental issues when assessing business risks and opportunities. The vast majority of companies do not discuss environmental issues during the preparation of their corporate strategic plans or the development of business objectives. In those cases, the discussion of environment, SD and CSR are held separately and as such are not fully integrated into a company's activities, nor are key groups allowed to truly take ownership.

Chapter 1, chapter 2 and chapter 9 provide additional guidance on how to include environmental issues in the assessment of business risk/opportunities.

> Bottom line: Failure to properly include pertinent environmental issues when discussing business risks/opportunities may significantly impair profitability.

Seek the Truth

Here are two examples taken from the broad cross-section of information that is being communicated about "global warming." Well-respected individuals who, it is clear, do not share the same political point of view, made the following statements:

- "[Global warming is] the greatest hoax ever perpetrated on the people of the world, bar none. Those who have been fighting against the green agenda have been warning that modern-day environmentalism has nothing whatsoever to do with protecting the environment. Rather, it is a political movement led by those who seek to control the world economies, dictate development, and redistribute the world's wealth."[34]—Tom DeWeese (U.S. advocate of individual liberty, free enterprise, property rights and back-to-basics education)
- "Twenty percent of the economy will disappear. It will cost more than World War I and World War II put together. We'll go into a kind of depression we've never, ever had in all of history."[35]—David Suzuki (well respected Canadian science broadcaster and environmental activist)

According to the research we have reviewed, neither view is correct. The reality is that mankind is having an impact on the temperature of the planet, the magnitude of which is not yet known; however, minor variations can have significant impact, thus justifying a call for immediate, yet balanced, action. No single weather event or a winter's worth of data disproves (or proves) global warming. Al Gore was correct in his characterization of global warming as a crisis. For a balanced review of the impact of global warming, readers are invited to review the *Stern Report*—a study of the economic effects of climate change commissioned by the British government,[36] as well as reports of the Intergovernmental Panel on Climate Change (IPCC), which describe global warming. The conclusion of the IPCC is that "global warming is unequivocal" and there is a 90% chance it is being caused by humans.[37]

Business leaders need to access several reputable sources of information on environmental issues before drawing conclusions or allocating resources, as information is often presented in a manner to solicit responses from key stakeholders. Whether it is an NGO preaching gloom and doom to ensure adequate donations or industries regurgitating the 1970s mantra of "first deny, then delay," remember this next time you read or watch a news report: "The biases the media has are much bigger than conservative or liberal. They're about getting ratings, about making money, about doing stories that are easy to cover."[38]

Bottom line: Get all sides of the issue before making critical business decisions.

Eliminate Waste Throughout the Product Life Cycle

In 2000, Paul Tebo, DuPont's vice president for safety, health and environment, translated the concept of sustainable development into a set of tangible business goals that Wall Street could understand. A key component of these goals was the environmental motto "the goal is zero," which committed the company to impressive stretch goals and cutting-edge metrics. Sustainable growth was defined as creating shareholder and societal value while reducing DuPont's environmental footprint along the value chain. For his efforts, Tebo won the 2000 Environmental Leadership Award and in the process created a silent environmental and social revolution in one of America's largest corporations.[39]

His vision of growth was based on the elimination of all wastes and emissions and the conservation of energy and natural resources. This was a stretch goal for DuPont, as they were nowhere near achieving it, but Tebo had the company set itself concrete targets to incrementally achieve this goal. As a result, four company-wide goals have been adopted for 2010: (1) Using 1990 as a base year, a 65% percent reduction in greenhouse gas emissions from global operations; (2) flat total energy use; (3) sourcing of 10% of global energy needs from renewable energy sources, at a cost competitive with the best fossil fuel alternative; and (4) achieving 25% of revenues from non-depletable resources.

Tebo also pushed for the goal of zero to be extended to what he calls "value partnerships" with customers and suppliers. In a classic product-to-service shift, DuPont Canada struck a deal with one of its major customers, the Ford Motor Company, whereby DuPont was paid for the number of automobiles painted, rather than in gallons of paint sold. As a result, Ford realized cost savings of 35%–40%, while emissions of volatile organic compounds were reduced by 50%.[40]

Chapter 3, chapter 5 and chapter 6 all provide additional insight into eco-design, green procurement and energy conservation.

> Bottom line: Drive for zero! Don't put up psychological barriers before you begin.

Treat Stakeholders as You Would Want to Be Treated

Another way to describe the commitment that needs to be adopted by industry is described below by Lee Scott, CEO of Wal-Mart, in a 2005 presentation to Wal-Mart employees.[41]

> There can't be anything good about putting chemicals into air. There can't be anything good about the smog you see in cities. There can't be anything good about putting chemicals into rivers in Third World countries so that somebody can buy an item for less money in a developed country. Those things are just inherently wrong, whether you are an environmentalist or not.

Companies need to assess the potential impact of their operations and that of their supply chain on the environment, taking into consideration that small, positive changes can collectively have a significant benefit to the world in which we all live.

> Bottom line: Marshall McLuhan had it right: "We now live in a global village." We need to behave accordingly.

Eliminate Hazardous Chemicals

Many regulations around the word prohibit or severely restrict the use of certain chemicals in products, impose significant labeling requirements or require the virtual elimination of them.

Under the European Union (EU) Registration, Evaluation, and Authorisation of Chemicals (REACH) legislation, authorization will be required for substances of Very High Concern (SVHCs). The goal of the authorization system is to ensure that SVHCs are adequately controlled, and progressively replaced with safer substances or technologies, or are only used where there is a clear overall benefit for society. In addition, the EU authorities may impose restrictions on the manufacture, use or placing on the market of substances causing an unacceptable risk to human health or the environment. Additional information on REACH is presented in Appendix A.

In the U.S., by contrast, very few chemicals are prohibited by legislation; rather, the activities of companies are significantly influenced by threat of lawsuits over the presence of a hazard in a product (e.g., asbestos, polyvinyl chloride, lead) and improper labeling (e.g., California Proposition 65) or damage to corporate brand due to environmental/product incidents.

NGOs have successfully used the Internet to quickly raise consumer awareness of corporate impropriety anywhere in the world—facts that are not lost on Mattel and other corporations that have undergone product recalls. EU NGOs recently published an alternative SVHC list called "Substitute it Now" (SIN) that contains over 260 chemicals.

Additional information on what companies are doing related to the elimination of hazardous ingredients is presented in chapter 3 and chapter 5.

> Bottom line: Manufacturers and users of hazardous chemicals need to move towards their elimination—the writing is on the wall.

Switch Away from High-carbon Energy Sources

The switch from high-carbon energy sources to low- and zero-emission technologies is incontrovertible—the question is purely timing. Key drivers include increasing petroleum prices, growing demand for energy in China and India, legislation related to carbon emissions and cap-and-trade programs, avoided costs (e.g., reduced health impact due to air pollution), environmental liability risks, government subsidies/tax credits, system efficiencies, and ongoing cost reductions due to R&D/scalability of facilities for some renewable energy options.

Additional information on clean technology is presented in chapter 6 and chapter 7.

> Bottom line: Track changing technology and invest in new energy sources—they will become the more cost-effective option.

Promote Cultures of Innovation

In order for true change to occur, a company needs a change agent—a senior person who is prepared to be the evangelist and preach the benefits of sustainable development. As mentioned above, Paul Tebo played this role in the early days of the DuPont transformation. Ray Anderson, chairman of Interface Flooring, took on this role. In 1997 he put forward the "Mission Zero" promise to eliminate any negative impact the company may have on the environment by the year 2020, through the redesign of processes and products, the pioneering of new technologies, and efforts to reduce or eliminate waste and harmful emissions while increasing the use of renewable materials and sources of energy. The following quote is from Anderson:[42]

> If we're successful, we'll spend the rest of our days harvesting yester-year's carpets and other petrochemically derived products, and recycling them into new materials; and converting sunlight into energy; with zero scrap going to the landfill and zero emissions into the ecosystem. And we'll be doing well . . . very well . . . by doing good. That's the vision.

An evangelist alone cannot cause true change within a large corporation unless key stakeholders are empowered. In 2005, 3M's Pollution Prevention Pays (3P) program celebrated its thirtieth anniversary. The program has prevented more than 2.6 billion pounds of pollutants being emitted and saved more than $1 billion based on aggregated data from the first year of each 3P project. The 3P program helps prevent pollution at the source—in products and manufacturing processes—rather than removing it after it has been created, through product reformulation, process modification, equipment redesign and recycling and reuse of waste material.[43] When 3P was launched in 1975, the concept of applying pollution prevention on a company-wide basis and documenting the results was an industry first. Who are the change agents—the new evangelists? Chapter 1 presents additional information on individuals who are emerging as leaders in the green rush, while a business summary of 3M's 3P is presented in chapter 8.

> Bottom line: No limits, no boundaries.[44]

Leverage New Technologies/Disruptions

History has shown that people have always made money in times of great change. Many successful companies are already leveraging new technologies to address environmental issues. Funding for clean technology is in place, albeit tight, and there is no shortage of entrepreneurs vying for key positions in the market. An example of a key market undergoing change is the transportation sector—a sector that consumes more than 50% of global crude oil. The following are examples of electric vehicle (EV) companies, many of which may fail unfortunately, while trying to gain a significant foothold in this sector.

- TH!NK is a Norwegian electric car producer that has more than seventeen years of experience in developing and producing EVs. The company recently announced a partnership with leading cleantech investors Rock-Port Capital Partners and Kleiner Perkins Caulfield & Byers to establish TH!NK North America.[45]
- Project Better Place (PBP) raised $200 million from Israel Corp. and VantagePoint Venture Partners for this project, one of the largest and fastest seed rounds in history.[46] PBP's first project will be in Israel and will integrate and deploy a new product, sales and support channel. The cars will be designed and built by the Renault/Nissan alliance.[47]
- Smith Electric Vehicles is the world's largest manufacturer of road-going commercial vehicles. The company is building a plant in the United States that can produce 1,000 vehicles a year and expects to open another by 2009 with a capacity of 5,000 vehicles a year.[48] The company recently launched two new all-electric vehicles that leverage the Ford Motor Company chassis.
- Tesla Motors was started by Elon Musk (founder of Zip2 and cofounder of PayPal). Tesla Motors leverages a team with diverse expertise in electronics, automotive and Internet industries. Their starting point is a high-performance electric sports car—a roadster—but the long-term vision is to build cars of all kinds, including a family sedan.[49]
- Reva Electric Car Co. is an Indian company that has sold approximately 1,800 vehicles and is expanding manufacturing from 6,000 to 30,000 vehicles per year. Its new model will be powered with lithium-ion batteries.
- GoinGreen distributes the fully electric G-Wiz, which has become a London icon. There are currently more than two hundred charging points in London, and special incentives include free parking and exemption from

road tax and the congestion charge. The car was designed in California and is manufactured by Indo-US Reva Electric Car Company.[50]

Chapter 3 provides additional information on design for the environment and the ongoing struggle of the automotive industry, as well as business summaries of TH!NK, Project Better Place and Tesla Motors.

> Bottom line: Continuously monitor or invest in new technology to ensure ongoing competitive advantage. In areas of high risk it may be better to acquire the technology once commercialization is achieved.

Don't Forget Basic Business Principles

There are a great number of well-intentioned individuals who lack business acumen who have created or are in the process of creating green businesses. Key attributes that will apply in this sector, as they do in others, include

- a business model that is both defensible and scalable
- a proven, experienced and committed management team
- financial strength (growth, earnings, liquidity, capitalization, access to funds)
- technology, intellectual property and control/robustness of supply chain
- thorough understanding of current and proposed changes to environmental legislation and government incentives

The latter point is critical as companies often create business plans that do not take into account the risk of changing government (local, federal and regional) policies. Chapter 9 provides insight into business opportunities.

In the corporate world, EHS, SD and CSR executives must understand basic financial terms and be able to translate the benefits/risks of environmental issues using financial metrics, for example:

- lower operating costs due to energy savings, waste diversion and emission reductions at the company's facilities
- increased sales due to introduction of products/services that address environmental issues
- reduced supplier's costs due to environmental improvements, such as energy savings and reduced packaging

- increased shareholder value as new facilities are fast-tracked because of active community involvement programs
- reduced sales and shareholder value due to recall of products containing hazardous ingredients
- increased/decreased cost of operations related to carbon tax or cap-and-trade legislation

They must also leverage existing business systems/workflows and not create silos of information/activities. Key questions that need to be answered include these:

- What is the "business" process—step-by-step activities that are or will be performed?
- How can the business process be modified to address SD/CSR issues and improve company performance?
- What is the best method to do this modification: "design change"— redesign/rethink the product or process; "paper change"—modify policies/procedures; "IT change"—modify existing business information system or integrate specialized software; or "organizational change"—reassign authority or responsibility?

Chapter 2 provides additional information on how to incorporate SD/CSR into existing systems, while chapter 3 provides information on redesigning and rethinking products and processes.

> Bottom line: Business is business. It takes much more than a commitment to environmental causes to be successful.

KEY WEBSITES

http://blogs.wsj.com/environmentalcapital—*Wall Street Journal*'s daily analysis of the business of the environment

http://green.cbc.ca/—CBC and *The Hour* with George Stroumboulopoulos attempt to mobilize Canadians to do One Million Acts of Green

www.cleantech.com—forum for information on the cleantech sector and investments

www.climatebiz.com—business resources for climate management

www.corporateknightsforum.com—forum for information on the business of sustainability www.environmentalleader.com—provides executive daily briefings on the environmental market

www.ethicalcorp.com—CSR and ethical sourcing information

www.gallonletter.ca—twice-monthly letter covering issues of sustainable development

www.globe-net.com—initiative of GLOBE Foundation of Canada. Weekly guide to business of the environment

www.greenbiz.com—update on green initiatives

www.greenwombat.com—update on events in environmental/sustainable development

www.intertek.com—information on product safety and REACH legislation

www.treehugger.com—information on green consumer products

www.zfacts.com—statistical information on many topics, including the environment

RELATED READING

Esty, Daniel, and Andrew Winston. 2006. *Green Is Gold: How Smart Companies Use Environmental Strategy to Innovate, Create Value, and Build Competitive Advantage.*

Makower, Joel, and editors of GreenBiz.com. *State of Green Business*, 2009.

Savitz, Andrew, and Karl Weber. 2006. *The Triple Bottom Line: How Today's Companies Are Achieving Economic, Social and Environmental Success—and How You Can Too.*

Schellenberger, Michael, and Ted Norhaus. 2007. *From the Death of Environmentalism to the Politics of Possibility.*

Speth, James. 2008. *The Bridge at the Edge of the World: Capitalism, the Environment, and Crossing from Crisis to Sustainability.*

NOTES

1 Paul Hawken, *Ecology of Commerce* (New York: HarperCollins, 1993).

2 Anna Lisi, "Chemistry & Sustainability," *American Chemistry*, published by American Chemical Council, March/April 2008.

3 National Safety Council, "Lead Poisoning Happens More Than You Think," not dated, http://www.ncs.org.

4 Battery Council International, "Battery Recycling," not dated, http://www.batterycouncil. org/LeadAcidBatteries/BatteryRecycling.

5 The following sources were used to create Figure 2: CanWest News Service (CNS), "Montreal Climate Exchange Begins Trading in Emission Credit Futures," *Financial Post*, May 31, 2008; James Speth, *The Bridge at the Edge of the World: Capitalism, the Environment, and Crossing the Crisis of Sustainability* (New Haven: Yale University Press, 2008); Angela Logomasini, "Europe's Global REACH: Chemical Regulations in Europe Promise Worldwide Costs," January 4, 2006, http://www.cei.org; Joel Makower, Ron Pernick and Clint Wilder, "2008 Clean Energy Trends," March 2008, http://www.cleanedge.com/reports/ pdf/Trends2008.pdf; Kendall, 2008, World Wildlife Fund; Roger Parloff, "The $200 Billion Miscarriage of Justice: Asbestos Lawyers Are Pitting Plaintiffs Who Aren't Sick Against Companies that Never Made the Stuff—and Extracting Billions for Themselves," March 4, 2002, http://money.cnn.com/magazines/fortune/fortune_archive/2002/03/04/319093/ index.htm; Wikipedia, "Greenhouse Gas," 2008, http://en.wikipedia.org/wiki/Greenhouse_gas; Rowan Challick, "China's Carbon Output Tops US," *The Australian*, June 21, 2007. Values in article derived from the Netherlands Environmental Assessment Agency; Cohn & Wolfe, Landor Associates and Penn, Schoen & Berland Associates, "Consumers Will Double Spending on Green," September 2007; Fred Weir, "Has Russian Oil Output Peaked?", Christian Science Monitor, May 28, 2008, http://www.csmonitor.com; and Andrew Lord, "US Cap-and-Trade Inevitable: Market Could Be Worth $1 Trillion," 2008, http://www.davis.ca/en/blog/Climate-Change-Law-Practice-Group/2008/02/20/US-cap-and-trade-inevitable-market-could-be-worth-trillion

6 World Wildlife Fund, "2009–2010 Post-Doctoral Research Fellowships: Research Plan," 2008, http://www.worldwildlife.org/science/fellowships/fuller/postdoctoral-researchplan. html.

7 Ted Fishman, "King Coal," *National Geographic* (May 2008): 144.

8 Hawken, *Ecology of Commerce*.

9 Paul Hawken, Amery Lovins and L. Hunter Lovins, *Natural Capitalism: Creating the Next Industrial Revolution* (Little, Brown & Company, 1999).

10 Chad Holliday, "An Expanded Commitment: DuPont and Sustainable Growth," speech, 2006, http://www.dupont.com.

11 Katherine Hamilton et al., "Forging a Frontier: State of the Voluntary Carbon Markets 2008" (*New Carbon Finance & Ecosystem Marketplace*: May 2008), 144.

12 BBC, "Q&A: Reach Chemicals Legislation," November 28, 2005, http://news.bbc.co.uk.

13 Barack Obama, "New Energy for America," speech, 2008, http://my.barackobama.com/ page/content/newenergy.

14 EcoAmerica, "53% of Consumers Prefer to Buy from Company with Green Rep," September–November 2007, http://ecoamerica.typepad.com/blog/2007/10/page/2.

15 European Lamp Company Federation, "Industry Commitment to Phasing Out Inefficient Lighting Products in the Home," February 26, 2007, http://www.iea.org/textbase/ work/2007/cfl/Verhaar.pdf.

16 Todd Woody, "PG&E Gives Away 1 Million Energy Efficient Light Bulbs," October 3, 2007, http://www.greenwombat.com.

17 Emma Ritch, "LED Global Market Should Keep Getting Brighter and Brighter," January 14, 2008, http://www.mlive.com/business/ambizdaily/bizjournals/index.ssf?/base/abd-3/120029640599480.xml.

18 Hybrid Car Review, "Slow Down in Hybrid Car Sales Expected for 2008," February 1, 2008, http://hybridreview.blogspot.com/2008/02/slow-down-in-hybrid-car-sales-expected.html.

19 Environmental Leader, "Green Building Could Hit $140 Billion by 2013," November 20, 2008, http://www.environmentalleader.com/2008/11/20/green-building-could-hit-140-billion-by-2013.

20 GreenerBuildings, "DOE Awards Up to $80B for Efficiency, Renewables, Water-Saving at Fed Sites," December 23, 2008, http://www.greenerbuildings.com/news/2008/12/23/doe-awards-80b-contractors.

21 Makower, Pernick and Wilder, "2008 Clean Energy Trends."

22 IEA, "World Energy Outlook 2008, Fact Sheet: Oil Demand. What Are the Prospects for Oil Consumption to 2030?", 2008.

23 Makower, Pernick and Wilder, "2008 Clean Energy Trends."

24 Ibid.

25 IEA, "Renewable Energy Markets: Past and Future Trends," 2005, http://64.233.169.104/search?q=cache:peS3AuVb29YJ:www.iea.org/textbase/work/2005/Biofuels/Biofuels_Sellers_Paper.pdf+IEA+future+hydroelectric+generation+markets&hl=en&ct=clnk&cd=1.

26 Makower, Pernick and Wilder, "2008 Clean Energy Trends."

27 Lawrence Molley, "Glitnir Market Study on Geothermal in North America," December 18, 2007, http://northofthehotzone.com/2007/glitnir-market-study-on-geothermal-in-north-america.

28 ITT, "ITT's Place in the Cycle of Water—Everything but the Pipes, 6th Edition," http://ittfluidbusiness.com/media/ITT_WTRBK_v6_download.pdf.

29 CSR Wire, "Calvert Launches Global Water Fund, Issues Report on Opportunities in $1 Trillion Annual Worldwide Investment in Water Technology and Services," 2008, http://www.csrwire.com/News/13655.html.

30 http://www.google.org, accessed in September 2008.

31 Montreal Gazette, "The Alternative Race Heats Up," February 26, 2007.

32 http://www.goldmansachs.com, accessed in July 2008.

33 Greenbiz, "Wells Fargo Finances More than $3 Billion in Environmental Projects," December 24, 2008, http://www.greenbiz.com/news/2008/12/24/wells-fargo-3-billion-enviro-projects

34 F.R. Duplantier, "Global Warming Is Greatest Hoax Ever," America's Future, week of November 23, 2007. http://www.americasfuture.net/1997/nov97/97-1123a.html

35 CBC News, "Canadians Ready to Pay to Deal with Climate Change, Says Suzuki," April 20, 2007, http://www.cbc.ca/canada/story/2007/04/20/suzuki-baird.html.

The following section is taken from the Executive Summary of the Stern Report where BAU refers to Business as Usual:

"In summary, analyses that take into account the full ranges of both impacts and possible outcomes - that is, that employ the basic economics of risk - suggest that BAU climate change will reduce welfare by an amount equivalent to a reduction in consumption per head of between 5 and 20%. Taking account of the increasing scientific evidence of greater risks, of aversion to

the possibilities of catastrophe, and of a broader approach to the consequences than implied by narrow output measures, the appropriate estimate is likely to be in the upper part of this range."

Clarity on the 20% value is provided by Olivier Goddard "The Stern Review on the Economics of Climate Change: contents, insights and assessment of the critical debate", published in Vol. 1, No. 1, SAPIENS which is available at http://sapiens.revues.org/index240.html

If only gross productive and trade impacts are measured, they total 5%. Taking into account the incidence on human health (induced mortality) and environmental losses (rapid erosion of biodiversity), the cost rises to 11%. Taking on board the risks of overresponse of the climate to concentrations (amplifying feedback) the result is 14%. Finally, since damage would be concentrated in the poorest areas and by taking account of indirect contingent effects, economic, demographic and political (migrations, conflicts) ones in particular, the figure would approach 20%.

36 Nicholas Stern, "The Stern Review," October 30, 2006.
37 International Panel on Climate Change (IPCC), "IPCC Fourth Assessment (AR4)," November 17, 2007.
38 Al Franken, *Lies (And the Lying Liars Who Tell Them)* (New York: Penguin Group, 2003).
39 *Tomorrow*, Number 6, Volume X, November–December 2000.
40 Ecos Corporation, 2006, http://www.ecoscorporation.com.
41 Marc Gunther, "The Green Machine," *Fortune Magazine*, August 7, 2006.
42 Interface, "Who We Are," 2008, http://www.interfaceinc.com/who/founder.html.
43 3M, "Pollution Prevention Pays," http://www.solutions.3m.com.
44 Borrowed from Independent Lubricant Manufacturers Association.
45 Global Warming, "Th!nk Electric Car," 2008, http://www.global-greenhouse-warming.com/THINK-electric-car.html.
46 Kate Fehrenbacher, "Project Better Place Takes On Denmark," March 27, 2008, http://earth2tech.com/2008/03/27/project-better-place-takes-on-denmark.
47 Kate Fehrenbacher, "Project Better Place and Renault-Nissan Charge Ahead in Israel," January 21, 2008, http://earth2tech.com/2008/01/21/project-better-place-and-renault-nissan-charge-ahead-in-israel.
48 Climate Change Corp., "Special Report: The Climate Change Industry Takes Root," November 2008, http://www.climatechangecorp.com.
49 Max Chafkin, "The Companies of Elon Musk: How the Entrepreneur of the Year Does Business and Makes Waves," December 2007, http://www.inc.com/magazine/20071201/the-companies-of-elon-musk.html.
50 GoinGreen, "The New G-Wizi. The Next Level in Performance," 2008, http://www.goingreen.co.uk.

CHAPTER ONE

EXECUTING A GREEN STRATEGIC PLAN

There is a monumental shift occurring from the maxim that the "business of business is business" to the growing belief that business also must address environmental issues, as these are becoming a cornerstone of the value proposition to customers. Numerous companies across a broad spectrum of sectors, ranging from high tech and retail to heavy industry, have successfully included environmental issues in their value proposition. Peter Drucker best describes this role as follows:

> A company's primary responsibility is to serve its customers, to provide the goods or services, which the company exists to produce. Profit is not the primary goal but rather an essential condition for the company's continued existence. Other responsibilities, e.g., to employees and society, exist to support the company's continued ability to carry out its primary purpose.[1]

A comment Paul Hawken made in *The Ecology of Commerce* that is particularly applicable today is that free markets may be superb at setting prices, but they are incapable of recognizing costs.[2] Over time, markets, and more importantly companies, because of the U.S. Sarbanes-Oxley legislation and the input of their insurance providers, have begun to recognize that there are costs associated with not taking environmental issues into account. Examples of real costs incurred by companies include the following:

- government fines and cleanup costs associated with spills and historical releases of contaminants
- lawsuits related to a wide range of environmental issues (spills, discharges, etc.) or the presence of hazardous ingredients in consumer products

- reduction in value of land, sometimes the most significant aspect of a business, due to contamination
- reduced sales due to product recalls (whether attributable to a company's actions or those of its suppliers) and subsequent loss of consumer confidence in company
- higher energy costs than companies that have undertaken energy conservation activities and are leveraging cost-effective (or subsidized) alternative energy sources
- increased operating costs and, in some cases, significant reduction in production, due to water shortage
- higher supply chain costs due to inefficiencies (e.g., energy usage, cost of handling/disposing of hazardous material)
- impact on operations related to unusual weather that may be due to climate change

Worry less about the chemicals that are in the news today and more about the ones that are in your products and may be in the news tomorrow!

Examples of costs that have been incurred by companies, albeit in extreme cases, when they have not adequately put systems in place to ensure protection of the environment, workers or the public are presented in table 1.4 (located at the end of this chapter). As observed in the introduction, those companies not willing to adapt may observe lower revenue/profit margins and in some cases will write their own death sentence.

The elements necessary to prepare a comprehensive strategic plan (discussed further in this chapter) are

- leadership—examples of leaders who pose vision and courage of conviction in these uncertain times
- reference points—information on what sustainable development, corporate social responsibility, and governance, risk and compliance really mean
- strategic vision—activities to prepare company vision statements, as well as departmental documentation that is supportive of the overall vision
- business environment—important elements of strengths, weaknesses, opportunities and threats (SWOT) analysis
- key market influencers—essentials pertinent to environmental issues
- methodology for business risk and opportunity assessment (BR&OA)— guidance on how to conduct a BR&OA related to environmental issues

- putting all the pieces together—translation of above vision statements and findings of SWOT/BR&OA into defined goals, objectives and targets

LEADERSHIP

We are facing difficult times, caused by uncertain financial markets, fluctuating petroleum prices, global warming and the cross-border shipment of goods that pose safety and environmental hazards. Unique leadership skills are required to meet this challenge and are best described in Jim Collins's book *Good to Great*, where he presents a clear hierarchy of leadership styles and what exemplifies exceptional leadership, i.e., the Level 5 Executive (refer to figure 1.1).[3]

In *Good to Great*, Collins claims, "Level 5 leaders want to see the company even more successful in the next generation, comfortable with the idea that most people won't even know that the roots of that success trace back to their efforts.... In contrast, the comparison leaders, concerned more with their own reputation for personal greatness, often failed to set the company up for success in the next generation. After all, what better testament to your own personal greatness than that the place falls apart after you leave."[4]

Figure 1.1: Level 5 Hierarchy

Level 5 Executive
Builds enduring greatness through a paradoxical blend of personal humility and professional will.

Effective Leader
Catalyzes commitment to and vigorous pursuit of a clear and compelling vision, stimulating higher performance standards.

Competent Manager
Organizes people and resources towards the effective and efficient pursuit of predetermined objectives.

Contributing Team Member
Contributes individual capabilities to the achievement of group objectives and works effectively with others in a group setting.

Highly Capable Individual
Makes productive contributions through talent, knowledge, skills and good work habits.

Jim Collins, copyright 2001

Examples of historical leaders in the area of sustainable development who have taken their corporation through significant changes include Paul Tebo, former DuPont vice president for safety, health and environment, and Ray Anderson, chairman of Interface. Below are examples of business leaders/ visionaries who have inspired the current "green rush"—identifying and acting upon opportunities in alternative energy, eliminating hazardous ingredients in products or reducing wastage (costs) at production facilities and across the supply chain, while improving their overall impact on the environment. These leaders were not selected merely for their support of environmental causes or benign impact of operations on the environment.

 **Lee Scott**—The conversion of Wal-Mart's recently retired CEO to green champion began in 2004. Rob Walton, chairman of Wal-Mart, introduced Peter Seligmann, co-founder and CEO of Conservation International (CI) to Scott. CI is a large Washington DC environmental organization whose mission is to protect the world's biologically rich habitats. Scott had just undertaken a review of Wal-Mart's legal and PR woes and was well aware that the company needed to reshape its image. A McKinsey study leaked to the press by Wal-Martwatch.com found that up to 8% of shoppers had stopped patronizing the chain because of its reputation.[5]

Seligmann pitched the stories of how CI had worked with Starbucks to develop coffee-buying methods to protect tropical regions and with McDonald's to promote sustainable agriculture and fishing. The argument put forward was simple: Wal-Mart could improve its image, motivate employees and save money by going green. CI, Wal-Mart personnel and environmental experts spent a year measuring the company's environmental impact. The study was able to identify numerous examples of activities that would both reduce cost and reduce the environmental footprint of Wal-Mart and its supply chain.

The following is an excerpt from a speech by Scott to eight hundred Wal-Mart store employees in 2005, taken straight from the pages of *Natural Capitalism*.[6]

If we throw it away, we had to buy it first. So we pay twice—once to get it, once to have it taken away. What if we reverse that? What if our suppliers send us less and everything they send us has value as a recycled product? No waste, and we get paid instead?

In 2005, Wal-Mart began collecting ideas from everywhere—consultants, NGOs, suppliers and eco-friendly competition—on how to improve its environmental footprint and reduce cost along the supply chain. Based upon this exercise, the company decided to form "sustainable value networks" made up of Wal-Mart executives, suppliers, environmental groups and regulators. The end result was something revolutionary, as described in comments by Glenn Prickett of CI. "The potential here is to democratize the whole sustainability idea—not make it something that just the elites on the coasts do but something that small-town and middle America also embrace. It's a Nixon-to-China moment."[7]

What started out as an intellectual interest has became Scott's passion. What began as a defense strategy was turning out to be the opposite—employees were feeling better and the company was saving its customers money. Scott personally pushed his cause with Fortune 500 CEOs through statements like "There need not be any conflict between the environment and the economy . . . . We will not be measured by our aspirations. We will be measured by our actions."[8]

It is important to note, however, that Scott was not doing this just to please environmentalists. In a conference in California in 2008, he flatly declared, "We are not green. The impetus for the company undertaking these activities is to save money: It really is about how you take cost out, which is waste."[9]

Is Wal-Mart without blemishes? No, of course not. In the past, there have been issues associated with water quality at some of its stores in the United States. Some groups have also criticized Wal-Mart's increasing carbon emissions, despite its publicized efforts to reduce its carbon footprint, and the absence of target dates for achieving goals of zero waste and 100% renewable energy. However, these concerns are minor when compared to the monumental shift that the company has undergone in the last few years on environmental issues, both at its own operations and more importantly along its supply chain.

Jeffrey Immelt—Since beginning his tenure at GE, Jeffrey Immelt has worked to transform the company into a more diverse and customer-driven culture. In doing so, Immelt has twice been named one of the World's Best CEOs by *Barron's*.

During an annual strategic review meeting in 2004, he learned that several GE business units were pursuing environmental initiatives independently of one another.

GE Energy had just acquired AstroPower, the largest American-owned maker of solar panels. The previous year, it had picked up a wind turbine business from

Enron. GE Water & Process Technologies was formulating plans for the largest water desalination plant on the African continent. GE factories overseas were dealing with new regulations on carbon dioxide emissions. GE was also involved in the cleanup of pollutants in the Hudson River that had been discharged there decades ago. It occurred to Immelt that all of these initiatives could be rolled up into a program of green practices and technologies and pushed more aggressively.[10]

To validate the concept, Immelt spoke with the chief executives at thirty of the largest utility companies in the country, some of GE's most important customers. He created an in-house team to study greenhouse gas legislation and conduct customer surveys. He also enlisted New York–based environmental consultant GreenOrder to help create and audit green scorecards—a checklist for measuring the environmental impact of new products developed in the company.[11]

In December 2004, he put his plan to a vote of the top thirty-five executives in the company. The result: The "ecomagination" strategy was shot down dead. "They resoundingly voted no," Immelt recalls. "They said, 'This is stupid.'" Only five or six people in the room sided with Immelt on the idea; the rest argued that ecomagination would cost too much or that it would be undermined by GE's many Superfund sites and other environmental issues that weren't so easy to fix. Immelt overrode the decision of his executive committee, and told them to prepare for the 2005 launch of ecomagination. This was where the company was going, and his team had to trust him.[12] The following quote from Jeffrey Immelt summarizes his vision.[13]

> This is not just good for society, it's good for GE investors—we can solve tough global problems and make money doing it. GE aims to be the partner of choice for our customers around the world—whether homeowners, business leaders or government officials—by offering advanced technology to improve efficiency and reduce pollution in cost-effective ways. We intend to put our global capabilities, technology leadership and market knowledge to work to take on some of the world's toughest problems— and we think we can make money doing it. This is good business.

Since that fateful meeting, his decision to proceed with ecomagination, despite his team's objections, has paid off. According to GreenOrder, GE is on track to reach its long-term environmental goals. Since its launch in 2005, ecomagination continues its explosive growth, generating revenues of more than $14 billion and an order backlog of $70 billion in 2007, along with a robust portfolio of more than sixty energy-efficient and environmentally advantageous products and services.

Is GE's greening activity without problems? No. GE's annual $1 million investment in publicizing the ecomagination initiative has been criticized as a high-stakes branding exercise that amounts to little more than greenwashing. Some environmentalists have concerns about GE's ongoing sales of coal-fired steam turbines, its expansion into oil and gas production, and the fact that it still has not delivered on its promise to clean up PCBs from the Hudson River.[14] (For more information, see the GE case study at the end of this chapter. The case study also includes information on the sizable number of remediation activities that GE is involved in with respect to historical contamination.)

 **Chad Holliday**—The DuPont chairman and former CEO is a member of several organizations furthering research and change in environmental issues, and has been recognized for his actions. Mr. Holliday was commended for improving DuPont's standing on environmental issues, taking steps like pledging to reduce the company's greenhouse gas emissions.

As indicated in the introduction of this book, DuPont was able to translate the concept of sustainable development into a set of tangible business goals that Wall Street could understand. A key component of these goals was the environmental motto "the goal is zero," which committed the company to impressive stretch goals and cutting-edge metrics. His position on these issues is best summarized by the following comment:[15]

> We will never compromise our core values—safety and environmental excellence, integrity, high ethical standards and treating people fairly and with respect. They are our foundation. We must continually strive to find ways to enhance them.

In 2002, he co-wrote a book with Stephan Schmidheiny, the chairman of Anova Holding, and Philip Watts, the chairman of the committee of managing directors of Royal Dutch/Shell Group, entitled *Walking the Talk: The Business Case for Sustainable Development*. In the book, the three corporate leaders outlined their belief that the most successful businesses would incorporate environmental and social aspects into their strategies.

His tenure as the environmental vanguard of business has not been without controversy. Significant concerns have been raised regarding the release of a chemical referred to as C-8 from manufacturing facilities that produce fluoropolymer coated products, which has resulted in the U.S. Environmental Protection Agency (EPA) levying a fine against DuPont. (For more information on the company's environmental performance, including the C-8 controversy, see the DuPont case study at the end of this chapter.)

 **Sir Richard Branson**—In 2005, the Virgin Group faced a bill of about $1 billion to purchase fossil fuels to run its airlines and trains. Sir Richard Branson and the Virgin Group decided that it was their responsibility to combat global warming in a big way. Branson saw an opportunity to improve the bottom line and burnish his brand as a consumer champion. In line with its history of disrupting established markets, Virgin decided to try to overturn the received wisdom that ecological disaster is inevitable.

In 2006, Branson joined the growing ranks of global warming activists by committing $3 billion (£1.6 billion) to tackle climate change. The billionaire pledged all profits from his Virgin air and rail interests over the next ten years to the project. The money, however, will not be going to charities; rather, it will be invested in a new branch of the Virgin conglomerate, Virgin Fuel. Much of the investment will focus on biofuels.[16]

As part of the Virgin Fuel initiative, the Virgin Green Fund (VGF) was established to invest in companies in the renewable energy and resource efficiency sectors in the United States and Europe. The fund is a sector-focused, multi-stage investment firm investing primarily in expansion/growth capital opportunities, with a portion of the funds earmarked for earlier-stage venture capital opportunities. The VGF is committed to helping companies that are about to grow substantially and/or provide disruptive innovation to the marketplace.[17] A total of $200 million was invested by the Virgin Group in the first year and included investments in Virgin Green Fund, Virgin Atlantic Global Flyer and Virgin Atlantic initiatives, as well as companies that build and generate biofuels for both ground transport and aviation.[18]

In 2007, Branson established a $25 million prize, the "Virgin Challenge," for the scientist who comes up with a way of extracting greenhouse gases from the atmosphere. The winner will receive $5 million once judges rule they have succeeded. The rest of the money will be paid out over a ten-year period if the judges decide the goal of removing significant amounts of greenhouses gases has been met over the long term.[19]

The Newcomers

In recent years there has been a steady migration of entrepreneurs from the software industry to the "green rush."

Vinod Khosla—When this cofounder of Sun Microsystems left Sun, he became a general partner at Kleiner Perkins Caulfield & Byers. In 2004 Khosla formed his own firm—Khosla Ventures. *Forbes* magazine estimated his wealth at $1.5 billion in the magazine's 2007 list of the richest Americans.[20] Khosla Ventures considers investments in companies that have[21]

- an attack plan for manageable but material problems
- technology that achieves unsubsidized competitiveness
- technology that scales—if it isn't cheaper it doesn't scale
- manageable startup costs and short innovation cycles
- declining cost with scale—trajectory matters

A key component of this strategy is that energy sources must be adoptable in developing countries in accordance with Khosla's commitment. "Ultimately, new energy sources will only work if they're adopted in China and India—Chindia challenge. They are two of the world's fastest-growing countries, with a nearly insatiable appetite for oil and coal to fuel industries that many scientists blame on rising overall world temperature."

Khosla Ventures's cardinal rules of investing include land efficiency, costs, pragmatics (how realistic and to whom), regulation (permanent versus transient subsidies), and economics and capital formation. Investments are organized into four areas:

1. War on oil—alternatives that will eliminate/reduce fossil oil
2. War on coal—alternatives to coal for power generation
3. Efficiency—improved efficiency of processes using energy
4. New materials—greener building materials

Khosla divides clean-technology investments into two camps: those that can make real but relatively small changes and those that can make huge changes to the world's environmental problems, most notably climate change. The following are Khosla's thoughts on clean technology investments:

- electric cars—need significantly improved battery; possible but uncertain if this will be achieved—a "black swan" event
- biodiesel—limited cost reduction with scale; use of algae provides some hope
- cellulosic ethanol—declining cost with scale; require biomass that has high land efficiency—tons of biomass per acre, and hence gallons of fuel produced per acre (Khosla is also proposing a certification process for biofuels analogous to the LEED rating system for buildings)
- wind and solar photovoltaic—key enabler is energy storage
- geothermal—need engineered geothermal

To date, Khosla Ventures has approximately thirty investments that cover the gamut from green building materials (e.g., carbon-neutral cement), to energy (biofuels, solar, wind and geothermal energy), to water (wastewater treatment and desalination), to electrical/mechanical efficiency. Khosla believes that the technologies he's backing are close to the point where they can compete against oil without the government subsidies now required to make them competitive.[22]

Elon Musk—In 1995, Elon Musk founded Zip2, which was bought by Compaq in 1999 for more than $300 million. In March 1999, he cofounded X.com, an online financial services and email payments company. In February 2001, X.com changed its name to PayPal, and in October 2002, PayPal was acquired by eBay for $1.5 billion in stock.[23] Musk's fortune is estimated at $328 million.[24]

Musk is the chair of the board of Tesla Motors, an electric-car company ($37 million investment), and SolarCity ($10 million investment), a rapidly growing solar-panel installer that was founded by two individuals who sold their software company to Dell. His commitment is best described by the following statement: "[The] motivation behind Tesla is to do as much good as possible for the environment and the electric vehicle revolution."[25]

The focus of Tesla Motors is the Roadster, a $109,000 sports car, with current sales of one thousand to two thousand per year. The company is now working to ramp up production, to ensure the supply chain is secure and to secure good margins by keeping variable costs down and overheads under control. Tesla is also designing a new luxury sedan—Model S. Construction of a manufacturing facility for the sedan will start in early 2009. The car is expected to go on sale in late 2010. Projected sales are in the ten thousand to twenty thousand a year range—not large by major car company standards—and the starting price is about $60,000.[26,27]

SolarCity matches advanced solar power technology with a suite of installation services. SolarCity's SolarLease financing allows residents to achieve "grid parity" with solar power by putting no money down and paying less each month for solar energy than they previously paid for electricity from their utility company. The company serves communities in California, Oregon and Arizona and expects to expand to the East Coast in 2009, taking advantage of state rebate programs. In addition to state programs, the company is also expected to benefit from a provision in the financial bailout package of 2008 that allowed home solar projects to qualify for a 30% federal tax credit, replacing a $2,000 maximum benefit.[28]

Musk has also established the Musk Foundation, which issues grants in support of renewable energy research and advocacy; human space exploration research and advocacy; pediatric research; and science and engineering education. (See chapter 3 for a Tesla Motors case study.)

Larry Page and **Sergey Brin**—Google founders Larry Page and Sergey Brin have committed resources to RE<C—renewable energy that is cheaper than coal—and RechargeIT—to accelerate the adoption of plug-in electric vehicles—through Google.org.[29]

RE<C's mission is to develop electricity from renewable sources that is cheaper than electricity produced from coal. Initially, this project will focus on advanced solar thermal power, wind power technologies and enhanced geothermal systems, but it will also explore other potential breakthrough technologies. The goal is to build one gigawatt of renewable energy capacity that is cheaper than coal. Google expects to spend tens of millions of dollars on research and development and related investments. As part of its capital planning process, the company also anticipates investing hundreds of millions of dollars in breakthrough renewable energy projects that will generate positive returns.[30]

RechargeIT's aim is to reduce carbon dioxide emissions, cut oil use and stabilize the electrical grid by accelerating the adoption of plug-in electric vehicles. Google has a demonstration fleet of plug-in electric vehicles at its headquarters in Mountain View, California, and is collecting and posting data on plug-in performance, investing in innovative technologies and advocating for the passage of important legislation. The vision behind this initiative is that one day, thousands of cars will be plugging into a greener grid.

Shai Agassi—Shai Agassi founded TopTier Software, which was sold to SAP AG, the largest enterprise resource planning software company in the world. In 2007, Agassi resigned his position at SAP and founded Project Better Place (PBP). He was able to raise US$200 million from Israel Corp. and VantagePoint Venture Partners for this project, one of the largest and fastest seed rounds in history.[31]

The business model is defined as engineering transportation as a sustainable service. The issues of range and cost have been resolved by implementing a swappable battery and leveraging a zero emission solution by matching the supply of renewable energy with the demand created by electric vehicles. Shai Agassi succinctly defines it as "Sell Electric Vehicles (EVs) like cell phones—[the] new paradigm shift that will cause a massive disruption to the auto industry."

In its first project, PBP will integrate and deploy a new product, sales and support channel (read "charging stations") that will allow consumers in Israel to drive their own purely electric car with a ±200 km range. It will feature a unique battery design that can be swapped in and out in about the same time it now takes to fill a car with gasoline. A countrywide network of swapping stations is also part of the vision. The cars will be designed and built by Renault Megane and production will begin in 2010.[32]

Similar agreements have been signed for Denmark, Australia, State of Hawaii, Province of Ontario and the Bay Area of San Francisco (which includes Oakland and San Jose). Refer to the case study presented in chapter 3 for additional information.

> Technology is playing a key role in the current stage of cleantech growth and it is expected to accelerate over the next few years.

REFERENCE POINTS

There are numerous definitions for sustainable development (SD), corporate social responsibility (CSR) and governance, risk and compliance (GRC) and to a great extent, confusion over their interaction. In the following section, a very brief overview of each concept is provided along with its impact on a company's strategic decision-making process. A discussion of the tactical/operational inclusion of these concepts is provided in chapter 2 and chapter 5.

Sustainable Development (SD)

Sustainable development is a term that has been thrown about for the last twenty years. Most publications use the definition set out in the United Nations Brundtland Commission Report: "Development that meets the needs of the present without compromising the ability of future generations to meet their own needs." A more business-friendly version was put forward by Accenture, which defines sustainability as "the way a company or organization creates value for its shareholders and society by maximizing the positive and minimizing the negative effects on social, environmental and economic issues and stakeholders to grow revenue, reduce cost, manage risk and build intangible assets."[33]

In recent years, SD has been described in numerous publications as being built on three pillars: economic growth, ecological balance and social progress. These items have always been on the sustainability agenda, but until recently the third—the social pillar—has received less attention. That is changing as greater emphasis is being placed on social progress, with SD linked to CSR. For an example of an SD policy, see the box titled "Bayer SD Policy."

An excellent source of information on SD activities by businesses is the World Business Council for Sustainable Development (WBCSD) website: www.wbcsd. org. The council provides a platform for companies to explore sustainable development; share knowledge, experience and best practices; and advocate business positions on these issues in a variety of forums, working with governments, NGOs and intergovernmental organizations. Members are drawn from more than thirty-five countries and twenty major industrial sectors.

Corporate Social Responsibility (CSR)

More than forty definitions of CSR were identified during a recent Web search. The following definition, put forward by the WBCSD, is used in this book: "Corporate social responsibility is the continuing commitment by business to contribute to economic development while improving the quality of life of the workforce and their families as well as of the community and society at large."[34]

Bayer SD Policy[35]

We at Bayer carefully develop products and services specifically designed to benefit people. In this endeavor, we are committed to achieving the economic, ecological and social responsibility objectives of Sustainable Development. Sustainable Development is a globally accepted approach to sustaining economic growth without harming our planet or exhausting its resources while improving the quality of life for its current and future inhabitants.

We believe that practicing Sustainable Development makes good business sense. In all our operations we consider each of these actions in making business decisions that demonstrate our commitment to the global Sustainable Development effort:

Our business is the means by which we combine human ingenuity and natural resources to benefit mankind. Hence, economic responsibility dictates that we manage our business profitably to help drive economic growth and prosperity. We believe that innovation is essential to achieving sustainable economic success. We also invest extensively in research, development and new technologies as a foundation for future success.

Bayer is committed to continually improving our ecological performance in accordance with the Global Charter Responsible Care as our product lines and related manufacturing operations evolve. We will continue to monitor how our operations impact the environment and strive for continuous improvements. The health and safety of our employees, neighbors, customers, consumers and stakeholders are paramount, as is our continued stewardship of the environment and the quality and safe handling and use of our products.

We will continue to address our social responsibilities through our commitment to help our employees, customers and community neighbors meet their changing personal and professional needs. We also will monitor and address the impact our business has on our plant neighbors, local communities and global society. To this end, we will continue to seek an active, open and honest dialogue with all stakeholders in appropriate forums. The Bayer Values and Leadership Principles are based on preserving and honoring the fundamental rights of every individual. Bayer will continue to seek to promote and protect human rights as defined in internationally accepted humanitarian standards set forth by the United Nations.*

This Sustainable Development approach to conducting our business aligns with Bayer's Mission Statement: "Bayer: Science For A Better Life."† To assure that we continue to demonstrate continual improvement in the Economic, Ecological and

Social Responsibility pillars of Sustainable Development, we have introduced customized management systems to monitor and control progress, document the achievement of objectives, and optimize employee efforts in these areas. And we remain committed to truthfully report on our sustainability performance to all interested parties.

* See "Universal Declaration of Human Rights of the United Nations," December 1948.
† See Corporate leaflet "Bayer: Science for a Better Life," July 2004.

The WBCSD report also goes on to state that "to optimize the long-term value of the company to its shareholders business needs to ensure that its values are aligned with the consensus in society. In this way it can avoid conflict and reap tangible benefits. To do this it has to balance the needs of a range of stakeholders."

The WBCSD report advises that the negative impacts on a company can take several forms and can severely damage corporate reputation. Examples of unwanted outcomes[36] include

- consumer boycotts
- attacks on fixed assets
- failure to attract good employees and loss of employee support
- extra spending to rectify past mistakes
- diversion of management attention from core activities
- restrictions on operations, such as new legislation and regulation
- obstacles in raising finance and insurance
- difficulties with life cycle (customers downstream and suppliers upstream in the supply chain)

Key areas to assess when developing a CSR strategy include the following: human rights, employee rights, environmental protection, community involvement, supplier relations, monitoring, and stakeholder rights.

Note that for the purposes of this book, the focus will be on the environmental component of CSR, including the role of consumers and suppliers. We urge readers to seek out the many excellent publications on the other important aspects of CSR. A good example of a CSR policy can be found in the following box titled "Enbridge Inc. CSR Policy."

Enbridge Inc. CSR Policy (abridged version)

At Enbridge, we have adopted a CSR Policy which covers business ethics and transparency, environment, health and safety, stakeholder relations, employee relations, human rights, and community investment. This policy applies to activities undertaken by, or on behalf of, Enbridge and our subsidiaries anywhere in the world whose operations we manage.

In alignment with our Statement on Business Conduct, Enbridge will ensure that all matters of corporate social responsibility are considered and supported in our operations and are consistent with Enbridge stakeholders' best interests. Our Statement on Business Conduct emphasizes the commitment of the corporation to specific standards of conduct expected of the corporation's directors, officers, employees, consultants and contractors in all countries in which the Enbridge group of companies conducts business.

In January 2002, Enbridge adopted the internationally recognized Voluntary Principles on Security and Human Rights, which deal with responsible corporate action in zones of conflict.

Enbridge has incorporated the Voluntary Principles into its Statement on Business Conduct. In 2003, Enbridge became a signatory to the United Nations Global Compact, an international initiative in support of human rights, labor and the environment.

A variety of other policies provide direction for specific activities that are part of CSR. They are

- Environment, Health and Safety Policy
- Indigenous Peoples Policy
- Climate Change Policy
- Statement of Business Conduct
- Voluntary Principles of Security and Human Rights

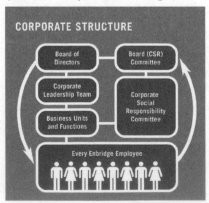

Governance, Risk and Compliance (GRC)

As with CSR, many definitions of GRC exist. The following definition from AMR Research[37] is widely used:

> *Governance* is an oversight role, and part and parcel of setting strategic objectives.
> *Risk management* evaluates all relevant business and regulatory risks, controlling and monitoring mitigation actions in a structured way.
> *Compliance* is the execution of these objectives based on risk tolerance.

In many companies, GRC activities are still limited to the implementation of specialized software. This software typically combines applications that manage the core functions of GRC into a single integrated package that facilitates the use of data between multiple departments. Dashboards and data analytics tools allow administrators to identify the organization's risk exposure, measure progress towards quarterly goals or quickly pull together an information audit. Unless these GRC tool(s) are leveraged into an overall GRC program, however, they tend to remain within the IT department's domain and are not fully integrated into the operations of the company.

According to a 2008 study by AMR on GRC spending, environmental compliance is a top-five risk, and encompasses the following concerns, which are broader than tactical environment, health and safety (EHS) compliance:[38]

- energy consumption and asset management
- greenhouse gas (GHG) emissions management
- product stewardship initiatives

Enhanced CSR/SD initiatives, together with the expansion of GRC programs to cover environmental issues, are driving environmental compliance in organizations from many angles. GRC has moved to the top of the agenda for brand-conscious supply chain companies, as well as the brand owners with whom they do business.

STRATEGIC VISION

At most companies, documentation about the company's direction has two components:

1. Overall company vision statements (vision, mission, core values and broad goals)
2. Business unit or departmental specific policies, guiding principles and objectives/targets

Overall company vision statements define the company's purpose, direction and philosophy and inspire and guide the organization. Typically the mission, vision and values do not change over time, while goals may be assigned on two- to five-year cycles depending on business conditions and direction. At the regional or departmental level, the strategic plans address specific issues the organization currently faces and typically change more frequently.

The number of business opportunities and risks associated with environmental issues is on a scale, in terms of the number of organizations affected, that has not been seen before. No longer is it simply a matter of "greening up" products and processes at the operational and sometimes tactical levels. It is critical that companies also reassess their business strategy. All aspects of a business—business model, technology, human resources, supply chain, new and existing products and markets—will be impacted and need to be reassessed.

Figure 1.2[39] illustrates the business evolution from reactive operational activities that focus on basic protection of an organization to strategic activities that shape its future and create added value.

Four key questions (from an environmental point of view) should be asked at the beginning of the strategic review.

1. Are the company vision statements still pertinent given changing environmental concerns and the company's commitment to its stakeholders?
2. Who has overall responsibility for environmental issues (both historical and new challenges—CSR, climate change, and hazardous ingredients in products)?
3. Do divisional or departmental policies/guiding principles properly express the company's commitment to the environment? For example, are policies/principles in place for eco-design and green procurement?
4. Are division/departmental policies/guiding principles complementary to each other or do they create confusion/conflict? For example, what is the role/interaction of environmental, SD, CSR and GRC programs at the company?

Figure 1.2: Pathway to Strategic Sustainability

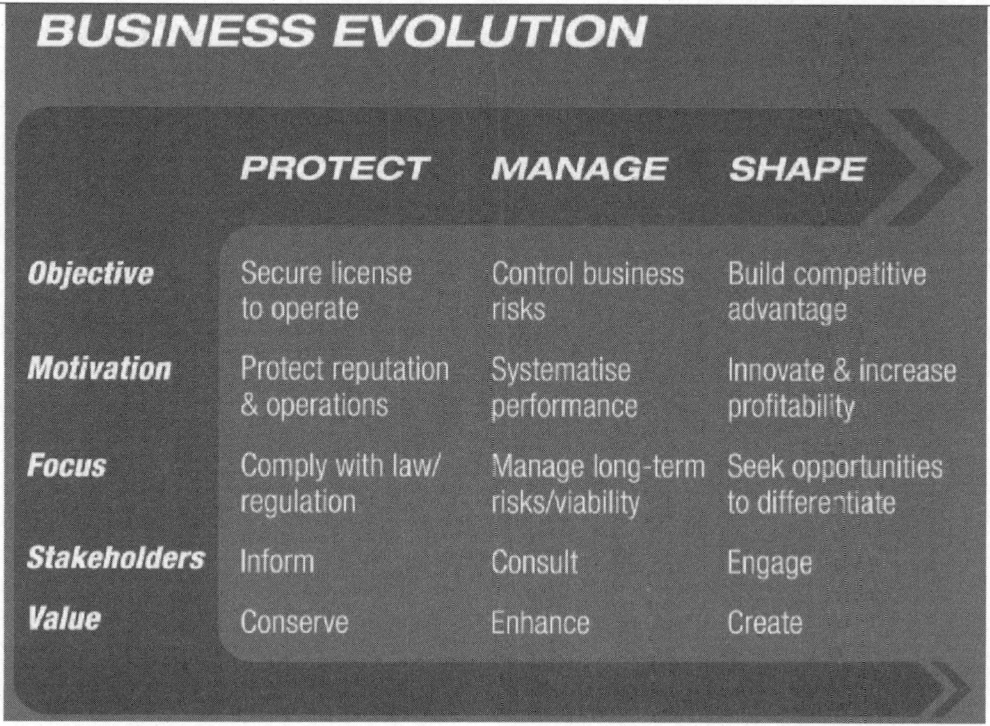

BUSINESS EVOLUTION

	PROTECT	MANAGE	SHAPE
Objective	Secure license to operate	Control business risks	Build competitive advantage
Motivation	Protect reputation & operations	Systematise performance	Innovate & increase profitability
Focus	Comply with law/ regulation	Manage long-term risks/viability	Seek opportunities to differentiate
Stakeholders	Inform	Consult	Engage
Value	Conserve	Enhance	Create

An example of a well-thought-out company vision statement that reflects a commitment to the environment is that of DuPont, which has been included in a case study at the end of this chapter.

It is important to note that numerous versions of environmental, SD, CSR and bioethics guiding "principles" related to corporate governance have been prepared over the last twenty years, many of which address requirements pertinent to specific industrial vertical organizations. Examples include the chemical industry's Responsible Care program, the Canadian mining industry's Sustainable Mining Guiding Principles and the financial sector's Equator Principles.

One commonly used reference, endorsed by many Fortune 500 companies, is the Ceres Principles, formerly the Valdez Principles. Ceres is a national network of investors, environmental organizations and other public interest groups working with companies and investors to address sustainability challenges such as global climate change. The Ceres mission statement is "Integrating sustainability into capital markets for the health of the planet and its people."

Once draft versions of the corporate, business unit and departmental statements have been prepared, it is critical to

- prepare an easy-to-understand document that clearly provides both the statements, rationale for direction and appropriate background information that can be disseminated throughout the organization and to external stakeholders
- communicate this document downward at least two levels, soliciting questions of clarification and suggestions for improvement; this exercise should be face-to-face, with senior executives presenting and listening
- communicate the draft statements to key external stakeholders and carefully document any concerns that are raised; the types of external stakeholders consulted should be a function of the company's business activities and potential risk/opportunity

SCANNING THE BUSINESS ENVIRONMENT

Typically, a three-year horizon is used in the strategic planning process. Futurist Glen Hiemstra recommends something different: using a long-range view of about twenty to twenty-five years because the creative act of thinking strategically this far ahead enables companies to see opportunities that a three-year horizon misses. In his book, *Turning the Future into Revenue,* he puts forward a process called "Preferred Future Planning" that ties together future trends/impacts and strategic planning. Key steps in his process[40] include

Stage 1—develop foresight
Stage 2—choose a future direction
Stage 3—identify web of strategies to shape the future and respond to
         surprises

The following are key components of a scan of the business environment, which should be performed regardless of the size of the organization and can be used as inputs to the Preferred Future Planning process.

Core Business and Affiliates

This typically includes a review of the political/regulatory, social, economic and technical environment in which the organization operates or wants to move into. Planners carefully consider various driving forces (competition, changing demographics, etc.) as well as some specific to sustainable development (impact on brand arising from health/environmental issues associated with facilities/ products and new or proposed legislation, etc.). Planners also look at the various strengths, weaknesses, opportunities and threats (SWOT analysis) of the organization. During this stage, companies should assess how they can turn challenges into opportunities and in doing so create a competitive advantage that results in greater shareholder value.

The elements of a SWOT analysis are outlined below:

Strengths—An assessment of a group's resources and capabilities that can be used as a basis for developing a competitive advantage. A realistic, well-developed listing of strengths should answer a couple of key questions: What do we do well? What advantages do we have over our competitors?

Weaknesses—Internal limitations, faults or defects of the group that may act as barriers to maintaining or achieving a competitive advantage. It is critical that this assessment be done truthfully (which can be difficult because of politics in some organizations) so that the weaknesses may be overcome as quickly as possible. A well-developed listing of weaknesses should answer the following questions: What area(s) of our business can we improve? Which areas put us at a disadvantage vis-à-vis our competitors?

Opportunities—Any favorable current or future situation in the external environment. Information on business opportunities and investment related to environmental issues is presented in chapter 9.

Threats (risks)—External forces that could inhibit achieving or maintaining ongoing competitive advantage or impair future growth. Additional information on risks related to environmental issues is presented in subsequent sections.

Historically, among the first actions organizations have taken (whether consciously or subconsciously) have been to define their mission/objectives according to the line of business to which the organization aspired. That is, do we offer "environment products/services" (e.g., wastewater treatment facilities, pollution control equipment) or "non-environmental" products/services (e.g., consumer products, building materials). More and more, the separation of environmental and non-environmental products/services is disappearing as products/services become intertwined so that any business that manufactures products may be labeled "environmental." This includes, for example, efficient engines for airplanes, cruise ships and locomotives, or turbines for bio gas/coal mine gas and landfill gas.

Business Ecosystems

As is clear from the discussion above about business leaders, it is critical that they clearly articulate their vision of SD/CSR—not just for their organization but also for their "business ecosystems" (encompassing suppliers, customers and even competitors). In essence, they need to translate the concepts of SD/CSR into a set of tangible business goals that apply to their business ecosystem that Wall Street can understand (e.g., "the elimination of environmental mismanagement in the supply chain will reduce costs").

A good example of the impact of a business ecosystem is found in the tight links between the transport and energy sectors. As alternative vehicle technologies take hold, automobile companies and their customers will become increasingly dependent on suppliers and distributors of new fuels. Without the proper infrastructure, the feasibility of bringing alternative fuels to market (e.g., E85 at gas pumps, refueling centers for hydrogen or easy access to recharging centers for electric cars) is questionable. It is important to note that not all of these fuels will be successful and hence investment in infrastructure must be undertaken carefully. ("E85" stands for fuel that contains 85% denatured fuel ethanol and 15% gasoline.)

KEY MARKET INFLUENCERS

Examples of market influencers that may need to be assessed with respect to a particular company's requirements are presented in table 1.1. The examples provided address stakeholders (government, consumer and investment community), technology, raw resources, energy price, environmental degradation, environmental incidents and man-induced impairment. Note that for climate change both mitigation (reduction in GHG emissions) and adaptation (modifying infrastructure/activities) are listed. Other variables may be appropriate to consider depending upon the company and its activities. In the following, two of the more important influencers—government legislation and market-based initiatives—and the price of petroleum are discussed in greater depth.

Table 1.1: Examples of Market Influencers

Market Influencers	Business Opportunities	Business Risks
1. Gov't Initiatives (Examples) - pesticide legislation - California emission control for vehicles - EU Registration, Evaluation, Authorisation and Restriction of Chemicals (REACH) - proposed U.S. cap-and-trade	- introduce "natural" products that comply with legislation - reinforce use of new technology to improve fuel efficiency and sales of hybrids/EVs - large companies increase market share as small to medium-size enterprises (SMEs) face disproportionately high costs - provide services/products related to compliance	- prohibited from providing lawn services in many jurisdictions - drop in sales if automakers do not respond quickly enough to legislation - supply chain disruption as suppliers exit market because cost and significant limitations are imposed on some substances - impose significant additional costs on emitters
2. Consumer Habits/Demands	- provide products and services, which foremost are good, and are not harmful to consumers, workers or environment - reinforce brand	- elimination of products from marketplace, e.g., substances of very high concern (SVHC) - damage to brand and loss of sales if hazardous ingredients are present in products
3. Investment Community Response	- position stock as green via rating/indices or receive favorable debt/equity financing - reduce risk via compliance to Equator Principles	- be branded as high risk because of absence of programs to manage key issues - face shareholder resolutions on climate change
4. Significant Shifts in Energy Prices	- reinforce investment in alternative energy sources as they become more competitive	- increase in cost of petroleum-based products and transportation (which in turn drives up other costs)
5. Depletion of Raw Resources (fish, timber, water, etc.)	- develop sustainable harvest practices to ensure future resources and/or identify environmentally suitable alternatives	- absence of finished product as insufficient resources: fish stocks, clean water, forest, etc.

6. New "Green" Technological Disruptions	- drive advancements in battery technologies for vehicles, white and green biotechnology, green building materials, etc.	- reduce market share due to shift in market - may also experience unknowns related to some gene-tically modified (GM) products and carbon nanotubes
7. Significant Environmental Incidents	- provide either a service to assess and minimize risk for high-risk sectors or alternative products that have much lower risks at comparable price	- devastating impact on company and sector (e.g., failure of nuclear reactor or explosion at hydrogen vehicle refueling station)
8. Man-induced Impairment (Examples) - climate change - ocean dead zones	- offer new products/services to mitigate (e.g., cleantech) and adaptation (e.g., protection of coastal communities) to climate change - new products that reduce nutrients in runoff and use of clean fuels (low NOx), etc.	- rising cost of emissions, damage to brand, increase in cost of water, damage to building and infrastructure due to seawater elevations, etc. - new legislation, degradation of fisheries/crustaceans, loss of tourism, etc.

Figure 1.2 presents the delicate balance between government actions to influence behavior of consumers/citizens and companies' goals of selling product/ services and achieving an appropriate return for shareholders. Tricky questions include what market-based instruments should be used by government agencies and when. Too much government action could hinder market activities or result in the government having a very short mandate of power. Too little and the playing field is no longer balanced; instead, rogue companies will exploit the environment for short-term benefits.

There are numerous examples of what countries, states/provinces and local municipalities/cities have done to influence the greening of their constituents. Two examples worth noting are Sweden and Denmark, which both embarked on programs to reduce emissions via reduction in their reliance on petroleum products. The shift was driven by a complex array of policies with a core component being one of the world's first carbon taxes on fossil fuels. Key lessons learned indicate that this cannot be accomplished with just one policy—e.g., carbon tax—but requires a range of policies that need to be regularly readjusted. One of the common pitfalls for governments is that they tend to tax areas of greatest revenue and not areas that will cause people to change their habits to benefit the environment.[41]

Similarly, Brazilians have been using sugar-based alcohol to fuel cars since the 1920s, although the industry really got off the ground in the 1970s when the government sought relief from the first oil price shock. It is currently the world's second biggest ethanol producer and the biggest exporter. Brazil is trying to repeat the ethanol success with biodiesel by introducing a mandatory 2% biodiesel blend into all diesel pumps in the country. This value will most likely increase to 5% in 2010 based upon the success of the program. The program is not without its detractors, who have concerns about the impact of biofuel production on food production and Amazon deforestation in the next few years.[42]

Additional information specific to legislation-pertinent alternative energy and eco-design/green procurement is presented in chapter 6 and appendix A, respectively.

Directly or indirectly, petroleum greatly influences global energy and transportation sectors. The following table presents a quick overview of some key dates related to the price of both crude and gasoline at the pump.[43,44]

Figure 1.3: Tricky Balance of Government Intervention

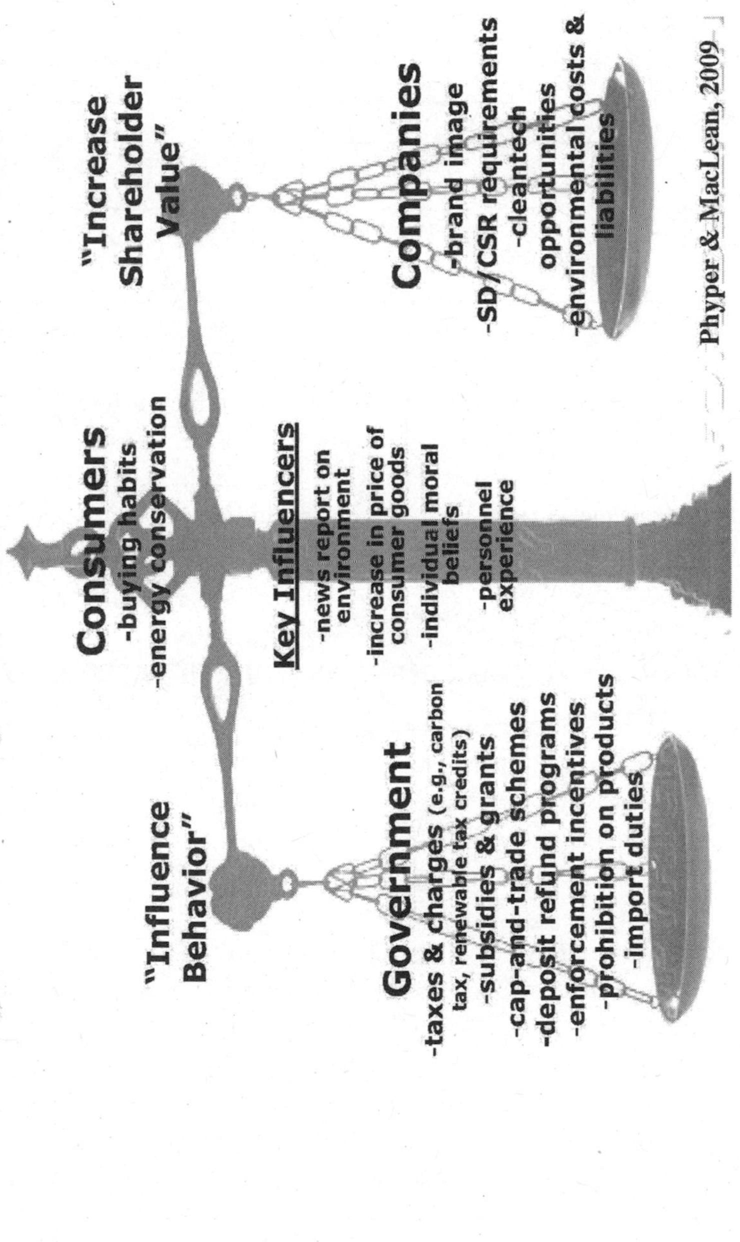

"Increase Shareholder Value"

Companies
-brand image
-SD/CSR requirements
-cleantech opportunities
-environmental costs & liabilities

Consumers
-buying habits
-energy conservation

Key Influencers
-news report on environment
-increase in price of consumer goods
-individual moral beliefs
-personnel experience

"Influence Behavior"

Government
-taxes & charges (e.g., carbon tax, renewable tax credits)
-subsidies & grants
-cap-and-trade schemes
-deposit refund programs
-enforcement incentives
-prohibition on products
-import duties

Phyper & MacLean, 2009

Table 1.2: Spikes in U.S. Crude Imports and Pump Prices*

Date	Triggering Event	U.S. Crude Import $/Barrel*	Avg. Price/Gallon at Pump in U.S.*	Price/Litre at Pump in U.S.
1974	Yom Kippur War, OPEC Oil Embargo	$50	$2.45	$0.65
1981	Iraq-Iran War starts	$92	$3.32	$0.88
1990	Iraq invades Kuwait	$39	$2.20	$0.58
2006	U.S. invades Iraq, Hurricane Katrina	$78	$3.40	$0.90
2008	Asian growth, Iraq war, production issues, weaker U.S. dollar	$116 (April)	$4.00 (July)	$1.06

*Prices are U.S. Department of Energy average prices at "today's dollar" (November 24, 2008).

In addition to the ongoing violence in Iraq, other current destabilizers include violence in Nigeria, the anti-West agenda in Venezuela and Iran, refinery bottlenecks in the United States, marginal increases in output from OPEC, production sluggishness in non-OPEC countries, and the rise of new industrial giants like China and India. (See chapter 6 and chapter 9 for additional discussion of alternative energy and price forecasts.)

METHODOLOGY FOR RISK AND OPPORTUNITIES ASSESSMENT

More and more companies or their institutional investors are realizing that the business risks posed by environmental issues—climate change, hazardous ingredients in products, etc.—can have a significant impact on the bottom line. Historically, approaches that have been used to document the environmental risks and opportunities have yielded mixed results:

- Environmental Impact Assessments (EIAs)—EIAs and financial institutions' "Equator Principles" are required for most new large-scale projects (dams, generating stations, etc.). They provide a good framework for assessing risks, mitigation and alternatives; however, they are narrowly focused on select types of projects.
- International Organization for Standardization (ISO)—ISO 14001 standards require the documentation of aspects/impacts. This provides a good framework for assessing environmental impacts but does not tie them back to business risks or opportunities.

- Sustainable development assessments—More and more companies are assessing their activities from the SD perspective and assigning a senior person to this role. In some cases the outcome is favorable; however, in many cases the results only touch upon portions of the business—e.g., GHG emissions and energy conservation—thereby avoiding key risks areas and do not get the required buy-in from all levels of the organization (top-down, not bottom-up approach).
- Socially responsible investing (SRI)—SRI usually focuses on screening companies for negative criteria such as ethics, social and environmental performance, involvement in tobacco/weapons production and distribution, providing support to political regimes that exploit citizens, etc.
- Governance, risk and compliance—Documentation of significant risks (from a business perspective) should be part of the company's GRC activities. Unfortunately, most organizations limit the assessment to financial risks, which sometimes tie into EPA Superfund activities or asbestos lawsuits. This type of review does not address business opportunities.

The Economist Intelligence Unit (EIU) surveyed 320 executives around the world in March 2008 about their attitudes to environmental risk management. The key findings of the survey included the following:[45]

- Environmental risk management is frequently managed in an *ad hoc* fashion.
- There is no clear consensus about who should be responsible for environmental risk.
- Many companies conduct strategic activities without a formal assessment of environmental risk.
- Respondents see compliance with environmental legislation as a key strength.
- Managing environmental risks associated with suppliers and partners is a key area of weakness.
- Better reputation with customers and investors is seen as the main benefit of environmental risk management.
- Climate change is an opportunity as well as a risk.
- Lack of certainty about the impact of environmental liabilities and the future scope of legislation are the main obstacles to effective environmental risk management.

Instead of asking the usual question—*How do we make our company green?*—
which tends to lead to isolated activities by the EHS group, and cosmetic changes
that may (or may not) assist the brand while doing little to manage true "business
risk," the following types of questions should be asked:

- What are the company's business risks/opportunities related to environ-
  ment/energy issues?
- How can these risks/opportunities be managed to optimize the bottom
  line and improve the brand?
- How can departments take ownership of the management of these issues
  and ensure proper execution? This is a key step that is often overlooked
  once the plan/report is generated.
- What metrics can be used to ensure the tracking and successful completion of the projects related to risk/opportunity within the desired timeline?

More and more financial institutions, shareholders and NGOs are asking for information on environmental risks. Examples include the following:

- U.S. environmental NGOs, joined by state and city financial officers, petitioned the U.S. Securities and Exchange Commission to have companies
  reveal their financial exposure to climate change risks.[46]
- The State of Florida requires managers of the $20 billion treasury fund to
  account for climate change risk in all of their investments.[47]
- Investor Environmental Health Network, a collaboration of investment
  managers representing more than $41 billion in assets, conducted a de-
  tailed review of twenty-five companies' documents and found that company managers "know a lot more about product toxicity risk than they are
  choosing to share with investors" and therefore are not engaging in timely
  investor disclosure of financially important information on product toxicity risks.[48]
- Investors engaging with U.S. and Canadian companies on the financial
  risks and opportunities from climate change filed a record fifty-seven climate-related shareholder resolutions in 2008, of which nearly half were
  withdrawn after the companies agreed to positive climate-related commitments.[49]
- The Toronto Stock Exchange advised firms in 2008 that they must inform
  shareholders of climate change-related financial risks.[50]

In the following section, a business risk and opportunity assessment (BR&OA) approach is proposed that takes into consideration key market influencers, the use of scenarios to better understand potential future events, and stakeholder buy-in and involvement that ensures that activities are supported. The key steps are these:

1. **Compile information.** Collect and review available, high-level information on business processes and environmental impact (e.g., annual environmental, SD or CSR reports). In most companies this is readily available; however, sometimes nuances related to the following need to be documented:

- location and ownership of production facilities and system used to manage suppliers' CSR issues
- available information on composition of hazardous or potentially hazardous chemicals in products (well known for chemical/petrochemical but not for some consumer products)
- energy costs associated with all operations, including IT systems

2. **Identify business risks.** Information collected above is then utilized to assess the areas of the business that may be impacted by key market influencers, the type of impact and its order of magnitude.

- Market influencers—Refer to examples in table 1.1 and table 1.3.
- Type of impact—Does the market influencer create a business risk, opportunity or both? The growing market on environment and energy is too large not to impact organizations in some manner and thus affect future business profitability. Business risk can be subdivided into one of the following categories: financial, reputation, competitiveness, regulatory and litigation.
- Order of magnitude—Will the impact cause a change in the Income Statement (or is it immaterial cost?), equity valuation (if public, the share price), credit risk and/or director and officer liability? Many companies have learned the hard way (e.g., toy companies with hazardous ingredients, automakers focused on gas-guzzling vehicles) that by not properly addressing these market influencers, their business model may be impaired, in some cases beyond repair.

Note: If areas of elevated business risk are identified and validated they must be properly communicated to the company's CFO, VP EHS and, potentially, legal counsel for assessment of appropriate disclosure requirements to the board and regulatory bodies.

3. **Construct and assess scenarios.** Scenarios allow companies to think about the uncertain components of the future that may significantly impact their business—or to discover the aspects about which they should be concerned—and to explore ways in which these might unfold. As there is no single answer to these questions, scenario builders, such as the renowned Shell Scenario team, create sequences of possible events. These scenarios all address the same important questions and include those aspects of the future that are likely to persist, but each one describes a different way in which the uncertain aspects could play out.[51] Ged Davis, managing director of the World Economic Forum's Centre for Strategic Insight, describes the role of scenario building: "At times, the world can look so complex and unpredictable that it becomes hard to make decisions. Scenario building is a discipline for breaking through this barrier."

Scenarios are particularly useful in situations where there is a desire to put challenges on the agenda proactively and where changes in the global business environment are recognized but not well understood (such as those issues associated with climate change and fluctuating energy prices). They help a company prepare for "surprising" change. Good scenarios are ones that explore the possible, not just the probable, providing a relevant challenge to the conventional wisdom of their users. The end result should be healthy discussion (debate) on the issues, which should lead to better policy and strategy, and a shared understanding of, and commitment to, actions.[52] Once scenarios are prepared, the impact of environmental influencers on business can be revisited, leveraging the different scenarios for areas of significant uncertainty.

For example, Shell developed two scenarios that describe alternative ways in which governments may react to climate change.

In the first scenario, called Scramble, policymakers pay little attention to more efficient energy use until supplies are tight. Likewise, greenhouse gas emissions are not seriously addressed until there are major climate shocks.

In the second scenario, called Blueprints, growing local actions begin to address the challenges of economic development, energy security and environmental pollution. A price is applied to a critical mass of emissions, giving a huge stimulus to the development of clean energy technologies, such as carbon dioxide

Table 1.3: Example of Business Risk and Opportunity Assessment for a Consumer Goods Company

Market Influencer	Examples of Issues	Affected Areas	Type	Impact on Business
New Legislation	REACH legislation will require companies to identify Substances of Very High Concern (SVHC) in products. EU NGOs have published their own SVHC list referred to as the "SIN" list with over 260 substances.	EHS, Customer Service and Procurement	Risk: Regulatory/Financial—cost of assessment and need to put systems in place to monitor ingredients on an ongoing basis. Opportunity: Jump ahead of competitors by creating green product and potentially obtain additional information on competitive offerings via new disclosure rules.	Low–Medium: Assessment cost should be relatively low; however, will incur costs for supply chain monitoring system. May also need to reformulate product, which can be costly.
Safe Consumer Products	Suspect that SVHC is present in key product line that is used by children. REACH testing will confirm the absence/presence.	Product Management, R&D, Legal and PR groups	Risk: Reputation/Litigation—consumer response to SVHC, if present, and potential need to reformulate. Opportunity: If possible to reformulate quickly, can reposition product.	Moderate–High: NGOs will be carefully monitoring REACH, especially presence of substances on "SIN" list. Thus, potential drop in sales is very realistic.
New Green Technology	Product: New solar photovoltaic (PV) cells can be added to product to recharge batteries. Facilities: Require substantial amount of energy to heat and provide lighting.	Product Management, R&D and Facility Management	Risk: Competition—if market adopts. Opportunity: To provide more convenient recharging of batteries and reposition product as green. Also, opportunity to reduce facility costs by using alternative lighting and energy (under long-term contracts).	Low–Medium: Savings in energy and increased product market share will assist bottom line.
Changing Price of Petroleum	Increase in petroleum prices will significantly increased shipping cost (from Asian factories, but more importantly, from distribution centers to retailers) and cost of raw materials, as many are derived from petroleum.	Logistics, Product Management, Procurement and R&D	Risk: Financial/Competitiveness—due to increase logistic costs. Opportunity: Reduction of packaging material and use of shared containers with other consumer goods manufactures. Also, opportunity to change some of the raw materials, so less dependency on oil.	Low–Medium: Good opportunity to assess reduction in transportation costs as significant portion of expenditures. Amount of savings is a function of petroleum/plastic prices.

capture and storage, and energy efficiency measures. The result is far lower carbon dioxide emissions.

Additional information on the Shell Scenarios is available at the Shell website.

4. **Determine the current status.** Now that a list of potential business impacts has been prepared, two key questions arise:
   - Are activities underway at the company to address the business impacts?
   - What are competitors doing to manage these business impacts, i.e., are best management practices emerging?

While considering these questions, it is also good to reflect upon the following:

   - Being the leader and developing your company's own approach is good; however, if something is working well at your competitors' shops, borrowing ideas is not a bad thing.
   - It's "nice" to provide funds for a mangrove forest in return for a GHG credit, but if the company is ignoring real environmental risks, many within the organization, especially at the executive level, may develop a false sense of security.

5. **Capitalize on risk transfer opportunities.** Once risks are identified, it is important to assess the opportunity to transfer them through insurance or procurement. Insurance can play an important role in protecting companies if risks are known and tracked in a responsible manner by leveraging appropriate policies, procedures and reporting lines or if related to weather events. The latter may become significant if climate change leads to greater numbers of hurricanes and wind storms, flooding, severe droughts and heat waves. Procurement can also play a critical role in reducing risks, e.g., long-term fixed-rate energy contracts and the requirement that suppliers reduce/eliminate hazardous ingredients in products.

6. **Draft a white paper.** In order to facilitate discussion among the various executive stakeholders and their teams, draft a white paper that contains a summary of the information discussed above. Write the white paper in business language, e.g., provide available estimates or examples on cost or

revenue associated with business impacts, rather than vague terms that may not properly convey the business importance of the issues.

One of the main findings of the EIU survey was that there exists confusion within organizations as to who carries ultimate responsibility for environmental risk management: 25% indicated that it was the CEO, 20% the Chief Risk Officer, 14% no one, and within the remaining organizations, ownership was widely dispersed and often at sub-board level. The end result is that the management of environmental risks remains fragmented.

7. **Obtain executive buy-in.** It is critical that all executives affected by environmental risks be made aware of these risks (within a business context) and that they be given responsibility to put in place plans to proactively manage these issues. The environment should be an agenda topic for executive management meetings. Key issues to discuss include
    - ownership of the overall responsibility for environmental risks
    - the white paper and how it can be used to stimulate both discussion and action
    - operational ownership of the key environmental risks identified in the white paper

Additional discussion of departmental buy-in is presented in chapter 2.

PUTTING ALL THE PIECES TOGETHER

Following careful review of the mission, vision, values and results of the SWOT and BR&OA, planners must carefully come to conclusions about what the organization must do. These conclusions include what goals the organization should strive for, and the overall strategy to achieve these. Goals should be designed as much as possible to be specific, measurable, acceptable to those working to achieve them, realistic, timely, extending the capabilities of those working to achieve them, and rewarding to them. (An acronym for these criteria is "SMARTER.")

In addition to strategic goals, the company should

- Establish strategies to reach goals. The particular strategies chosen depend on matters of affordability, practicality and efficiency.
- Establish objectives along the way to achieving goals. Objectives should be timely and indicative of progress towards goals.

- Associate responsibilities and timelines with each objective. Responsibilities are assigned for the implementation of the plan and for achieving various goals and objectives.

Unfortunately, in many cases, published environmental goals focus too narrowly on impacts (e.g., GHG emissions) without addressing business requirements, like financial issues (cost savings) or employee culture. In the early 1990s, Drs. Robert Kaplan and David Norton developed the Balanced Scorecard (BSC). The BSC approach provides a clear prescription as to what companies should measure in order to balance activities in the following four key areas: financial, customer, internal business processes, and learning and growth. The BSC is a management system (not only a measurement system) that enables organizations to clarify their vision and strategy and translate them into action. It provides feedback about both the internal business processes and external outcomes in order to continuously improve strategic performance and results.

A precondition is that the scorecard is not implemented as a controlling tool but is part of the formulation and realization process of a new business strategy. The BSC suggests that we view the organization from four perspectives, and develop metrics, collect data and analyze these relative to each of these perspectives.

It is common to develop an annual plan (sometimes called the operational plan or management plan) that includes the strategic goals, strategies, objectives, responsibilities and timelines for the coming year. Often, organizations will develop plans for each major function or division, and call these work plans. Strategy sessions within each organizational unit are held to create action plans to accomplish the agreed-upon goals that are aligned with the organization's vision. Critical aspects of these plans include these:

- Corporate goals/objectives need to be aligned with business units (BU) and departmental plans (need top-down and bottom-up review).
- Agreement must be reached on who will do what, when, where, how and with what intent; how results will be tracked; and how the plan supports the realization of the organization's vision all must be documented.
- The plans must be communicated to the senior executive team as commitment statements.

As mentioned previously, the key issue is to ensure throughout the entire process that environmental issues are being addressed according to the degree of business risk/opportunity, and fully integrated into operational systems.

Usually, budgets are included in the strategic and annual plan, and in work plans. Budgets specify the money needed for the resources that are necessary to implement the annual plan and how the money will be spent, for example, for human resources, equipment, materials, etc.

Once the plan is prepared, key activities to perform include

- development of a communications plan that involves all key stakeholders and clearly presents information on the following questions:
  - What business are we in and why?
  - Where we are going and what is the impact on our environmental footprint?
  - What do we stand for as an organization?
- incorporation of responsibilities in policies, procedures, job descriptions, performance review processes, etc. to ensure the following questions are answered:
  - Who has overall responsibility for SD/CSR?
  - What is the interrelationship between SD/CSR and other activities?
- changes in the information, accountability and reward systems. A key question related to the environment includes
  - How do I reinforce green activities that improve the bottom line?
- development of a support system for change management (training, team-building, etc.)
- acknowledgement of success

The last step is critical but is often ignored, which can eventually undermine the success of future planning. The purpose of a plan is to address a current problem or pursue a development goal. It may seem relatively unimportant to acknowledge the solution of a problem or the achievement of a goal, but in fact, skipping this step can cultivate apathy and skepticism—even cynicism—in an organization.[53]

Additional information on reporting and auditing components of a successful management system that addresses environmental issues is presented in chapter 2.

Common pitfalls related to putting in place a robust strategy that takes advantage of changing government, consumer and companies' position on environmental issues include the following:

- Silos of Activity—Fragmented management of environmental issues in "silos of activity"—often focusing on SD initiatives, CSR reporting obligations or, more recently, climate change.

- Tunnel vision—Create a strategy that is based upon a current market niche and conditions (<two years). You need to understand the complete market in which your company operates and potential mid-term/long-term shifts before deciding on what will be done over next few years. As part of the planning process, you also need to assess different market scenarios and their impact on the organization—what if North American gas prices exceed US$8/gallon (which they already did in the EU)?

- Customer mis-expectation—What is the business problem or consumer requirement that needs to be addressed? The days of designing solutions based on high-level feedback from the sales team are gone. A company's product management team needs to be interacting with clients and prospects on a regular basis in order to understand the "business" issues before moving on to potential changes in offering.

- Replication of existing products—Too many companies are focused on product line extensions and not innovative new products or shifts to value-added solutions that contain a combination of products and services. Refer to chapter 3 for additional information on eco-design.

- Supply chain uncertainty—It is critical that companies understand and properly manage their supply chain as it may pose the most significant risks related to environmental issues. Refer to chapter 5 for a detailed discussion.

- Believing that being green sells—Not necessarily. Products that address market requirements and take into consideration environmental concerns at a reasonable price should sell. Being green by itself does not equate to price premium—you need a value-added component that competitors do not address. For more information, refer to chapter 4.

- Succumbing to the mushroom syndrome—Leaving key stakeholders in the dark and feeding them the final version of the strategic plan/key performance indicators (KPIs) is not a great way to get commitment. They need to be involved in the process, albeit in a controlled manner, to ensure the timely preparation of a document that addresses the company's business requirements. Actions and communications must be "real" and not just another management marketing effort or fad to be green, because employees and NGOs will quickly see through these types of activities.

RECENT MISSTEPS?

Will there be problems, missteps and failures in the search for the right solutions? Definitely. Key examples of past problems include the following.

EU Emission Trading System (ETS) Prices

In 2005, more than 320 million allowances under the EU trading scheme, worth more than €6.5 billion, were reported as having been traded over-the-counter. During 2006, the EU ETS was confirmed as the dominant force in the global carbon market, accounting for 80% of monetary value and more than 60% of the total volume of carbon trades.

In 2006 and 2007, the price per tonne of CO_2 fell dramatically on the news that some countries were likely to give their industries such generous emission caps that there was no need for them to reduce emissions. Trading started at approximately €8/tonne, went to a high of approximately €30/tonne in April 2006 and then started to fall to <€1/tonne, reaching €0.10 in September 2007. This reflected the key weakness of the scheme to date: that the cap was not set sufficiently tight to generate a carbon price incentive for real emissions reductions and abatement investment.[54]

The national allocation process for phase 2 (2008–2012) initially suggested that the mistakes of phase 1 would be repeated, with overly generous allocations requested by many member states. The Commission subsequently rejected all but two of the initial National Allocation Plans on the basis that they were over-allocated, and developed a formula to set a maximum level of allowances per member state.[55] This formula embodied levels of emissions; however, its ability to cut emissions and ensure fair pricing is still uncertain. In December 2008, a U.S. Government Accountability office (GAO) report found that EU cap-and-track system had created "a functioning market for carbon dioxide allowances, but its effects on emissions, the European economy, and technology investment are less certain."

Biofuels

Biofuels were once the darling of environmentalists and a great way for governments to get in the headlines, considered a "miracle motor vehicle elixir."

- U.S.—President Bush signed the Energy Independence and Security Act (EISA) in December 2007. The legislation provided for a Mandatory Renewable Fuel Standard (MRFS)—at least 36 billion gallons of biofuel a year will be used by 2022.[56]
- Canada—The Canadian government passed a bill in May 2008 to ensure that gasoline contains 5% ethanol by 2010. The bill also provides for diesel to contain 2% renewable fuels by 2012. In order for this to occur, the approximately 1.5 billion liters of ethanol and biodiesel capacity at Canadian facilities in 2007 must climb to 3 billion liters a year.[57]

- EU—In 2006, following Sir Richard Branson's announcement of a US$3 billion investment to combat climate change, the UK government ordered petrol stations to source 5% of their fuel from renewable energy by 2010. Germany also put in place a law that required a minimum of 10% of petrol be "plant sourced" by 2009 and 17% by 2020. In the last six months, EU lawmakers are reassessing this legislation given the biofuel debate.

An assessment in 2007 by the Earth Policy Institute indicated that if all the planned ethanol plants had been constructed and were on line by September 2008—the start of harvest year—the corn needed for distilleries would be 139 million tons, half the 2008 harvest projected by the U.S. Department of Agriculture.[58]

Recent studies and reports in the news media indicate that crop-derived biofuel may not be the silver bullet in the battle against global warming. In fact, it could make things worse.

- Price hikes in processed/staple foods—If petroleum prices increase significantly, they will drive up the price of biofuels, which in turn will drive up prices for both processed and staple foods (wheat/corn) around the world. In this context, a key supply and demand question to farmers becomes *Do I sell my crop for a lower value to provide bread for bakeries or do I sell it to higher value for biofuel?*
- New agricultural land—Clearing previously untouched land to grow biofuel crops releases long-sequestered carbon into the atmosphere. While planting corn and sugarcane in already tilled land is fine, a problem arises when farmers convert non-agricultural lands (e.g., rain forest, grasslands), as is the case in Brazil, to grow more fuel or food/feed displaced by biofuel crops.

Is all biofuel bad? No, even critics of biofuel agree that ethanol from Brazilian sugarcane produces positive results if grown on existing agricultural lands (i.e., no additional clearing of rain forest). Governments in Europe and the American states are starting to listen to the message that the "type" of biofuel is critical, and instead of granting blanket tax relief they are introducing systems that will waive levies only to biofuels that are certified "low carbon" as compared to conventional gasoline and diesel.[59]

Biofuel is one of several factors that triggers increases in the price of food. Other factors include

- increased transportation costs due to increased petroleum prices
- surging demand for food grains in China and India
- crop failures in some parts of the world

There is also reluctance on the part of oil companies regarding the establishment of infrastructure required for ethanol.[60] "Big Oil is at the top of the list for blocking the spread of ethanol acceptance by consumers and the marketplace," says Loren Beard, senior manager for energy planning and policy at Chrysler, referring to the struggle to get E85 pumps installed

Significant gains have been made in technology related to second-generation biofuels and crop yields, further reducing cost and environmental impact. Chapter 6 provides additional information on biofuels.

Alberta Oil Sands

The Canadian Athabasca oil sands are estimated to contain 175 billion barrels of oil, making it the second-largest oil reserves after Saudi Arabia. Some of the oil sands, however, have very thin and low-grade bitumen, which will be more difficult (i.e., expensive) to extract. Early 2008 projections indicated that at least US$170 billion in investment will occur in the oil sands during the next ten years.[61] Several of these projects have been delayed because of uncertainty over oil prices—the total value of stalled or halted upgraders is at least $45 billion.[62]

The cost of extracting this key resource has increased dramatically in the last few years. Some reports indicate a 55% cost increase for a peak-flowing barrel of oil derived from the oil sands.[63] Forecasts of break-even point for new projects at the beginning of 2008 was close to $85 a barrel (West Texas Intermediate).[64] Chapter 6 presents additional information on changing break-even points.

In addition to rising costs associated with scarce human resources, equipment and energy, environmental concerns are starting to gain public exposure and will translate into increased operating costs and impact political decision. Capital investments in environmental protection by Canadian oil and gas producers, most of which operate in Alberta, totaled $1.7 billion in 2006. Ongoing operating expenses related to environment for this sector were $1.1 billion. According to Statistics Canada these values exceed any other sector.[65]

The label "dirty oil" is being used by U.S. environmentalists and some politicians to describe petroleum from oil sands.

- Land usage—Huge areas of the boreal forest ecosystem have been felled and the underlying peat bogs cleared away to expose the oil sands. Some 5,000 hectares have been destroyed already.[66]
- Resource usage—Massive amounts of water, hydrogen inputs and energy are used to extract the oil from the viscous deposits. Some companies have even sugested that nuclear power be used to address the energy requirements.
- Toxic tailings ponds—Activities to-date have generated approximately fifty-five square kilometers of polluted ponds, with contamination levels significant enough to cause the death of migratory birds that land on them. In ten years, when all planned projects are up and running, these ponds will cover three times this area if additional mitigation is not performed.[67]
- High emissions/barrel—Conventional oil production generates an average of 28.6 kg of carbon dioxide per barrel, whereas oil sands production generates 80–135 kg per barrel.[68]

The death of waterfowl at one of Syncrude Canada Ltd. tailings pond in April 2008 led to charges being filed by both levels of government in February 2009:

> Federal – related to the deposit of substances harmful to migratory birds in waters or an area frequented by birds (maximum penalty of $300,000)
> Alberta – related to proper storage of hazardous substances in a manner that does not allow them to come into contact with animals (maximum penalty of $500,000)

The Ceres investor group—a coalition of pension funds and non-governmental organizations—has also placed two companies operating in the oil sands on a "climate watch list" for their alleged failure to address environmental problems at their sites.

The operators of major oil sands projects have cut back on the energy intensity of oil sands production by 45%, and have made a similar reduction in greenhouse gas, since 1990. The industry is also assessing carbon sequestration—the capture and storage of carbon dioxide emitted during production. The capital cost for sequestration may be in the billions of dollars and the industry is asking for government assistance. Alberta's C$15 levy on a tonne of carbon on specified emissions sources will go into a fund to finance new emission control technologies.[69] The 2009 CEAP also included funding for carbon sequestration projects.

In addition, new rules by the Alberta Energy Resources and Conservation Board require companies to define how they will reduce their tailings production and make their tailings ponds "trafficable"—dried out and ready for reclamation —within five years of being deemed inactive. Several of the key players in the oil sands were already active in assessing new technology for tailings ponds prior to the new rules being put in place.

CHAPTER 1 TAKE-AWAYS

The following take-aways are critical when developing corporate strategy.

Leadership—Ensure that senior people understand the green rush and its impact on the corporation and put forward a bold vision of where they want to take the company. The role cannot be played by anyone other than a believer in sustainable development and the potential corporate value it can bring. This is not about "cosmetic environmentalism" but fundamental change in how a company conducts business.

Unrealistic assumptions—Because you have a green product and want to save the world does not mean that you will have a successful business. Many plans do not adequately take into consideration the business environment or company resources but rely instead on unrealistic assumptions and favor old-school management techniques of adding responsibilities and actions to staff that are already overloaded. It is important to push the organization towards increased productivity and excellence in products and services but it must be done with some semblance of reality.

Right people—It is critical that the right people are involved in the planning process and that both top-down and bottom-up flow of information related to key goals/objectives pertinent to different components of the organization are taken into consideration. These individuals include management, personnel who will be responsible for the execution of the plan, and external experts, if required, who can bring insight into market changes. Corporate strategy development is not an activity to be undertaken within an insular environment.

Execute, execute, execute—A common failure in strategic planning processes is that the plan is never implemented. Instead, the focus is on writing a planning document/PowerPoint presentation that all too often sits unread in the email inbox. Individuals must be assigned objectives that are realistic, provided the resources to achieve these objectives and, yes, be held accountable if they are not met. This means periodic review of performance. It also means that if new information emerges in the rapidly changing business environment, leaders cannot play ostrich; instead, they must assess impacts on the plan and, more importantly, the key objectives.

Ongoing planning—The creation of a strategic plan is not a one-time event. Ongoing monitoring of the business environment must be conducted, especially in areas of technological disruption or reliance on petroleum prices. This information then must be used for ongoing analysis, reflection, discussion, debates and dialogue around issues and goals in the system. Many companies track information about the business environment but do nothing with it.

Table 1.4: Examples of Costs Associated with Environmental/Product Issues

Spills/Contaminated Sites

Spills—There have been some significant spills over the last thirty years. Examples include Seveso, Italy—accidental release of dioxin (1976); Bhopal, India—accidental release of MIC (1984); Basel, Switzerland—warehouse fire and subsequent release of herbicides, fungicides, pesticides and dyes (1986); Chernobyl, Ukraine—failure of reactor and release of radionuclides (1986); Alaskan waters—grounding of *Exxon Valdez* and release of crude oil (1989); Ghislenghien, Belgium—natural gas pipeline explosion (2004); and Buncefield, England—petroleum spill and explosion (2005).

Alabama PCB case—Monsanto, Solutia and Pfizer agreed to pay a $700 million settlement of two Alabama court cases involving thousands of plaintiffs who charged that their homes and lives were damaged by PCB contamination. The problems arose decades ago when the former Monsanto Co. operated a chemical plant in Anniston that made PCBs. In a statement, Monsanto said that under the settlement agreement it would pay about $390 million in cash, while Solutia would pay $50 million "over time" and commercial insurance would provide about $160 million. It also said that Solutia and Pharmacia would also participate in an array of community activities.[70]

Asbestos mine site—In March 2008, W.R. Grace agreed to a record-setting $250 million to reimburse the U.S. federal government for costs of the investigation and cleanup of asbestos contamination in Libby, Montana—site of the Grace asbestos mine. Officials at the Department of Justice and the EPA said the payout was the largest in the history of the Superfund program. Grace now must deal with a ten-count criminal indictment against several senior current and former Grace officials. The U.S. attorney is alleging conspiracy, obstruction of justice and wire fraud for endangering the people of Libby by concealing well-documented hazards of the asbestos.[71]

Fishermen's claims related to the *Exxon Valdez* spill—In 1989, the *Exxon Valdez* supertanker spilled approximately 11 million gallons of crude oil into Prince William Sound, resulting in a significant ecological disaster. The U.S. federal government indicted Exxon on five criminal charges. The company agreed to plead guilty to three counts with a fine of $25 million and $900 million in civil fines to be paid over a ten-year period. In addition, the company paid $2.1 billion in cleanup costs, and several hundred million dollars more to fishermen for their lost summer catch. In all, the company agreed to pay $3.4 billion. At Exxon's request, the federal court in Alaska certified about thirty-two thousand individuals with potentially valid claims to sue as a single group. The jury awarded $5 billion for punitive damages and federal appeals courts reduced the award to $2.5 billion.[72] In June 2008, the Supreme Court further reduced the punitive damage award to $507.5 million.[73]

Product Liability

Lead paint and magnets—In 2007, Mattel Inc. issued a recall for approximately 9 million toys made in China either because they contained magnets that could dislodge and be swallowed, or they contained lead paint[74]; in both cases there was a very low risk of actual harm. During the height of the recall, Mattel's stock plunged as much as 25% from its year-to-date high. Mattel incurred incremental costs of approximately $110 million related to these products.[75] Several class action lawsuits have also been filed for selling toys with lead paint that will further increase the cost of this incident. Chapter 5 contains more details.

PlayStation "cadmium crisis"—In December 2001, the Dutch government blocked Sony's entire EU shipment of PlayStation game systems. More than 1.3 million boxes sat in a warehouse instead of flying off store shelves as they contained legally unacceptable amounts of cadmium in the cables of the game controls. Sony missed the critical Christmas season and has estimated that the total cost of the failure, including rework, at 110 million euros in sales and 52 million euros in profits.[76] Chapter 5 contains more details.

Proposition 65—The State of California enacted this legislation in 1986. The law was supposed to "tell businesses: don't put these chemicals in our drinking water supplies." The list of "chemicals known to cause cancer or birth defects" now includes about 850 substances, many listed as "probable animal carcinogens" with no evidence of causing harm to humans.[77] Proposition 65 is enforced entirely through litigation. To state a cause of action, a plaintiff need only show that a listed chemical is present in a consumer product, and that the defendant business is "knowingly" exposing Californians to that product without proper labeling. Very few shop owners know that lead, a listed chemical, may be present in costume jewelry, poker chips, polyvinyl chloride (PVC) coatings for electrical wires, or brass.[78] In 2007, there were over one thousand Enforcement Filings by "on paper only" organizations through private law firms rather than "mainstream environmental groups." Only a few of these have gone to trial, but the average settlement fee has been $186,000 per litigation.[79]

Asbestos liability—By the early 1990s, more than half of the twenty-five largest asbestos manufacturers in the United States had declared bankruptcy. As of 2008, asbestos litigation is the longest, most expensive mass tort in U.S. history, involving more than six thousand defendants and six hundred thousand claimants. Analysts have estimated that the total costs of asbestos litigation in the U.S. alone will eventually reach $200 billion.[80]

DUPONT CASE STUDY: PART 1

Overview of Company[81]

2007 Revenues: $29.4 billion   **Employees:** 60,000 worldwide

Vision
"To be the world's most dynamic science company, creating sustainable solutions essential to a better, safer, healthier life for people everywhere."

Mission
"To create shareholder and societal value while reducing our environmental footprint along the value chains in which we operate."

The DuPont Commitment (excerpt)
"The core direction of DuPont is Sustainable Growth—the creation of shareholder and societal value while we reduce our environmental footprint along the value chains in which we operate. Through this Commitment to Safety, Health and Environmental excellence, DuPont affirms to all our stakeholders, including employees, customers, shareholders and the public, that we will conduct business with respect and care for the environment. We will implement those strategies that build successful businesses and achieve the greatest benefit for all stakeholders without compromising the ability of future generations to meet their needs. Key commitments that we will make consistent, measurable progress in implementing throughout our worldwide operations include

- ongoing conformance to Responsible Care program
- highest standards of performance business excellence
- goal of zero injuries, illnesses and incidents
- goal of zero waste and emissions
- conservation of natural resources, energy and biodiversity
- continuously improving processes, practices and products
- open and public discussion, influence on public policy
- management and employee commitment and accountability"

2015 Marketplace Goals

Environmentally Smart Market Opportunities from R&D Efforts
By 2015, DuPont will double their investment in R&D programs with direct, quantifiable environmental benefits to customers and consumers along their value chains.[82]

Products that Reduce Greenhouse Gas Emissions
By 2015, DuPont will grow annual revenues by at least $2 billion from products that create energy efficiency and/or significant greenhouse gas emissions reductions for their customers. DuPont estimate these products will contribute at least 40 million tonnes of additional CO_2 equivalent reductions by their customers and consumers.

Examples: DuPont is actively researching and developing a suite of advanced, high-performance fuel and other bio-based energy alternatives; includes advanced biofuels such as biobutanol and ethanol from cellulosic feedstocks. In the field of solar power, DuPont has developed a polyvinyl fluoride used as the backing sheet for photovoltaic modules because of its strength, weather resistance, UV resistance and moisture barrier properties.[83]

DuPont has partnered with Asia Pacific Fuel Cell Technologies to commercialize proton exchange membrane fuel cells for the Taiwan electric scooter market. The company is also working with the Taiwanese government to supply hydrogen for the vehicles.[84]

Revenues from Non-depletable Resources
By 2015, DuPont will nearly double their revenues from non-depletable resources to at least $8 billion.

DUPONT CASE STUDY: PART 2

2015 Sustainability Goals[85]

Greenhouse Gas Emissions

Since 1990, DuPont has reduced global greenhouse gas emissions measured as CO_2 equivalents by 72%. By 2015, DuPont has further committed to reduce greenhouse gas emissions at least 15% from a base year of 2004.

Water Conservation

DuPont commits to reducing water consumption by at least 30% over the next ten years at their global sites that are located where the renewable freshwater supply is either scarce or stressed as determined by the United Nations analysis of river basins globally. For all other sites, DuPont will hold water consumption flat on an absolute basis through the year 2015, offsetting any increased demand from production volume growth through conservation, reuse and recycle practices.

Fleet Fuel Efficiency

Effective immediately, DuPont will introduce fleet vehicles that represent the leading technologies for fuel efficiency and fossil fuel alternatives. By 2015, DuPont will ensure that 100% of their off-site fleet of cars and light trucks meet these criteria. DuPont will continue to ensure these vehicles are safe as well as fuel efficient, and we will track and report on our fuel efficiency improvements.

Air Carcinogens

Since 1990, DuPont has reduced global air carcinogen emissions by 92%, well beyond legal requirements. By 2015, DuPont will further reduce air carcinogen emissions at least 50% from a base year of 2004. This will bring their total reductions since 1990 to 96%.

Cost Savings/Benefits[86]

Carbon Footprint

> 13,550,000 metric tonnes of CO_2 emissions (2005)

Targets (status of 2010 targets)

> 65% greenhouse gas reduction on 1990 levels by 2010
> hold energy use constant at 1990 levels
> source 10% of global energy from renewables

Achievements

> 72% reduction in GHG emissions from a 1990 base (2003)
> 7% reduction in total energy use below 1990 levels
> 6% of total energy from renewables

Benefits

> $3 billion saved through increased energy efficiency

Emissions Trading

DuPont has helped to start up several external emissions trading programs, including the Chicago Climate Exchange and the UK Emissions Trading Scheme. DuPont believes that participation in these markets has enabled it to meet several goals, including generating cash flow to defray the cost of reductions and educating managers on the value of investing in reductions.

Missteps[87]

In December 2005, the EPA reached a $16.5 million settlement with DuPont over the company's failure to report to the agency possible health risks associated with a synthetic chemical, C-8, used in the manufacture of fluoropolymer. Under the settlement, DuPont will pay $10.25 million—the largest civil administrative penalty EPA has obtained to-date—and the company is committing $6.25 million for supplemental environmental projects. DuPont officials said the settlement closes this matter for DuPont without any admission of liability;

Independent Verification
By 2015, DuPont will ensure that 100% of their global manufacturing sites have successfully completed an independent third-party verification of the effectiveness of their environmental management goals and systems. DuPont will make this information publicly available and communicate it to local communities.

their interpretation of the reporting requirements differed from the agency. DuPont representatives have stated that the company has cut perfluoroocta-noic acid (PFOA) emissions from U.S. plant sites by 98%. In February 2007, DuPont committed to no longer make, buy or use PFOA by 2015, or earlier if possible.

Information derived from www.dupont.com unless otherwise stated.

GENERAL ELECTRIC CASE STUDY: PART 1[88]

2007 Revenues: $176,656 million
Employees: more than 300,000 worldwide

Values

Imagine, solve, build and lead—four bold verbs that express what it is to be part of GE. Our action-oriented nature says something about who we are, and should serve to energize ourselves and our teams around leading change and driving performance.

Image. We put imagination to work for our customers, people and communities.

Solve. We help solve some of the world's toughest problems.

Build. We are a performance culture that builds markets, people and shareholder value.

Lead. We are a meritocracy that leads through learning, inclusiveness and change.

Commitment

"We believe that better technology is the answer to our customers' environmental challenges. And we are confident we can find tomorrow's solutions to those challenges, just as we have since the days of our founder, Thomas Edison. Throughout our 127-year history, we have invented solutions to meet our customers' greatest needs. Over many years, we have developed one of the broadest ranges of environmentally advanced technologies. We will build on this legacy of success by researching and developing next-generation clean technologies. Our goal is to be a leader in bringing clean energy, air, and water—and improved quality of life—to all of the world's citizens."

The ecomagination Vision: Welcome to our vision of a cleaner, healthier world.

Revenues from ecomagination Products

The original goal was to grow revenues from ecomagination products from $6 billion in 2004 to $20 billion in 2010. GE achieved $14 billion in 2007 and will cross $20 billion by 2009. Every GE business is participating. GE has created more than sixty ecomagination products that produce cleaner energy and water or improve efficiency. Because of their success the ecomagination revenue target has been increased from $20 billion to $25 billion by 2010.

Water: technology for water/wastewater treatment and desalination

Energy: compressors for re-injecting GHG into petroleum reservoir, goal gasification technology, low NO_x gas turbines and Economic Simplified Boiling Water Rector (nuclear reactor), bio gas/coal mine gas and landfill gas engines, and Roof Integrated Tile photovoltaic system

Transportation: industrial air filtration systems, wind turbines, Capital Solutions for Fleet Services (optimization tools for service, sales and delivery fleets), efficient engines (airplane, cruise ship and locomotive) and hybrid locomotives

Lighting: CFL, efficient halogen lights, efficient LED (refrigerated displays, signage and stoplights) and efficient fluorescent lamps and ballasts

For the Home: "Homebuilder Program," and energy- and water-efficient appliances

Finance: credit card that allows cardholders the opportunity to earn GHG credits that are used to buy carbon offsets.

GENERAL ELECTRIC CASE STUDY: PART 2

KPIs/Initiatives[89]

Double Investment in Clean R&D: GE is growing its research in cleaner technologies from $700 million in 2005 to $1.5 billion in 2010.

Reduce Greenhouse Gas Emissions and Improve the Energy Efficiency of Operations: GE is committed to reducing GHG emissions 1% by 2012, reducing the intensity of GHG emissions 30% by 2008 and improving energy efficiency 30% by the end of 2012 (all compared to 2004).

Waste Site Qualification Program: Add five more countries onto existing thirty-five countries.

Water/Waste: In 2006, GE collected baseline data for water and waste metrics and in 2007 started to use the information to come up with metrics for further reduction opportunities to those already undertaken in past years.

Training: In 2007, GE conducted four plant manager EHS classroom training courses in the developing world that were attended by 132 members of GE's functional leadership teams.

Metrics: Sustain and improve GE's EHS metrics while supporting the company's organic growth and integrating newly acquired operations.

Compliance: Continue focus on EHS compliance, meeting GE's global EHS expectations and developing resources to support capacity in emerging markets. Continue global focus on regulations.

Remediation: GE will continue to work cooperatively with government agencies on remedial issues and at remedial sites for which GE has responsibility.

Customer Business Requirements

Recognizing the role of customers in product development cycle, GE collaborates with customers through "Dreaming Sessions," and through a "Net Promoter" Score.

Dreaming Sessions: GE is committed to holding ongoing dialogues and working with customers in innovative ways. Dreaming Sessions are attended by industry CEOs and experts to better understand customer needs across specific industries and to develop stronger partnerships.

Net Promoter Score: Based on asking customers one simple question: would they recommend or do business with GE again? They are asked to respond on a scale from zero to ten. Customer ratings of a nine or ten are considered promoters, and those with a zero to six are considered detractors. The rest are considered neutral or passively satisfied. Subtracting the detractors from the promoters produces the Net Promoter Score. What is critical is not the actual score, but GE's ability to improve the score over time.

Historical Missteps[90]

GE is involved in a sizable number of remediation actions to clean up historical hazardous wastes as required by federal and state laws. Expenditures for site remediation actions amounted to $0.2 billion in both 2007 and 2006. GE presently expects that such remediation actions will require average annual expenditures in the range of $0.2 billion to $0.3 billion in 2008 and 2009,

Supplier Chain: Find efficient ways to encourage suppliers to improve overall management of EHS; continue to focus on verifiable finding closure; go beyond auditing to consider how capacity building can increase adherence to supplier standards; continue to improve auditor and supplier training and audit closure tracking system; conduct spot checks to assess finding closure; started to identify projects where GE can partner to accelerate capacity development.

Fresh Water Reduction: Company-wide absolute 20% fresh water reduction target by 2012. The new initiative is one of the world's most aggressive corporate water reduction targets to date and is expected to save 7.4 million cubic meters or 2 billion U.S. gallons of fresh water.

respectively. Under a consent decree with the EPA related to historical contamination of the Hudson River with Polychlorinated Biphenyls (PCBs), GE has committed up to $0.1 billion to reimburse the EPA for its past and future project oversight costs and agreed to perform the first phase of dredging. GE also committed that, subject to future agreement with the EPA about completion of dredging after completion of phase 1 and the peer review, they will be responsible for further costs, including costs of phase 2 dredging.

Information derived from www.ge.com unless otherwise stated.

NOTES

1 Peter Drucker, *The Practice of Management* (New York: Collins, 1993).
2 Paul Hawken, *The Ecology of Commerce* (New York: Collins Business, 1993).
3 Jim Collins, *Good to Great* (New York: Collins, 2001).
4 Ibid.
5 Marc Gunther, "The Green Machine," *Fortune Magazine*, August 7, 2006.
6 Ibid.
7 Ibid.
8 Ibid.
9 Jim Carlton, "Walmart: 'We Are Not Green,'" Environmental Capital, March 13, 2008, http://blogs.wsj.com/environmentalcapital/2008/03/13/walmart-we-are-not-green.
10 Douglas MacMillan, "The Issue: Immelt's Unpopular Idea," *Business Week*, March 4, 2008.
11 Ibid.
12 Ibid.
13 Ibid.
14 Lisa Roner, "Runaway Ecomagination Is Not Enough for GE," http://www.ethicalcorp.com/content.asp?ContentID=5935&ContTypeID=37, June 2008.
15 Chad Holliday, International Federation of Automotive Engineering Societies, http://www.fisita.com/about/honorary?id=19.
16 Dan Milmo and David Adam, "Branson Pledges $3bn Transport Profits to Fight Global Warming," *The Guardian*, September 22, 2006.
17 Eco Pragmatists, "Private Energy International," November 2007.
18 Clinton Global Initiative, "Virgin's $3 bill. Commitment to Renewable Energy Initiatives," July 7, 2006 update, http://commitments.clintonglobalinitiative.org/projects.htm?mode=view &rid=42976.
19 Tariq Panja, "British Tycoon Branson Offers $25 Million Prize to Fight Climate Change," USA TODAY, February 9, 2008, http://www.usatoday.com/tech/science/2007-02-09-branson-climate-prize_x.htm.
20 Jim Hopkins, "Venture Capitalist Khosla Joins in Effort to Save the Planet," *USA TODAY*, December 25, 2007.
21 Vinod Khosla, "Biofuels: A Case Study," 2008, available at www.khoslaventures.com.
22 Hopkins, "Venture Capitalist Khosla Joins in Effort to Save the Planet."
23 SEC, *Paypal SEC 10-K*, December 31, 2001.
24 Jennifer Reingold, "Hondas in Space," FastCompany.com, Issue 91, February 2005, http://www.fastcompany.com/magazine/91/honda.html.
25 Max Chafkin, "The Companies of Elon Musk: How the Entrepreneur of the Year Does Business and Makes Waves," December 2007, http://www.inc.com/magazine/20071201/the-companies-of-elon-musk.html.
26 Michael Kanellos, "Elon Musk on Rockets, Sport Cars and Solar," February 15, 2008, http://news.cnet.com/Elon-Musk-on-rockets,-sports-cars,-and-solar-power/2008-11389_3-6230661.html.
27 Mike Monticello, "New & Future Cars: Tesla Builds a 4-Door," RoadandTrack.com, December 2008, http://www.roadandtrack.com/article.asp?section_id=10&article_id=7201.
28 Rebecca Smith, "Lightening the Load," Wall Street Journal Online, October 6, 2008, http://online.wsj.com/article/SB122305854616202945.html.
29 www.google.org, accessed in September 2008.
30 Ibid.

31 Kate Fehrenbacher, "Project Better Place and Renault-Nissan Charge Ahead in Israel," Earth2tech, January 21, 2008, http://earth2tech.com/2008/01/21/project-better-place-and-renault-nissan-charge-ahead-in-israel.

32 Lascelles Linton, "Update: Project Better Place+Renault's Electric Car," January 16, 2008, http://www.autobloggreen.com/2008/01/16/update-project-better-place-renaults-electric-car.

33 Bruno Berthon, Jim Grimsley, Peter Lacey and David Abood, "Achieving High Performance: The Sustainability Imperative," Accenture, 2008.

34 World Business Council for Sustainable Development, "Meeting Changing Expectations," http://www.wbcsd.org/DocRoot/hbdf19Txhmk3kDxBQDWW/CSRmeeting.pdf.

35 Bayer Sustainable Development Policy, http://www.bayer.com/en/sustainable-devclopment-policy.aspx.

36 Ibid.

37 John Hagerty, Jim Murphy and Mark Hillman, "From Tactical to Strategic to Holistic: AMR Research's GRC Maturity Model," December 14, 2006.

38 Simon Jacobson, "Environmental Compliance: Initiatives Broaden, Budgets Up—Complete Apps Still Few in Number," June 14, 2008, http://www.environmentalleader.com/2008/06/14/environmental-compliance-initiatives-broaden-budgets-up-complete-apps-still-few-in-number.

39 ÉEM inc., Sustainable Business brochure.

40 Glen Hiemstra, Turning the Future into Revenue (New York: John Wiley & Sons, 2006).

41 Mitch Potter, "The Low-Carbon Diet," Toronto Star, September 27, 2008.

42 Terry Macalister, "Biofuels: Brazil Disputes Cost of Sugar in the Tank," The Guardian, June 10, 2008.

43 zFacts.com, "Current Gas Prices and Price History," 2008, http://zfacts.com/p/35.html.

44 zFacts.com, "Crude Price in Today's Dollars," 2008, http://zfacts.com/p/196.html.

45 The Economist Intelligence Unit, "Under the Spotlight: The Transition of Environmental Risk Management," 2008, http://www.towersperrin.com/tp/getwebcachedoc?webc=HRS/USA/2008/200805/EIU_Under_the_spotlight_FINAL.pdf.

46 Rob Abbott, "The Risk Universe," March 2008, http://www.green-business.ca.

47 Ibid.

48 Investor Environmental Health Network, "Investor Group Calls for More Disclosure of Market Risk," February 28, 2008, http://www.iehn.org/news.press.MutualNeglect.php.

49 CERES, "Shareholder Action," 2008, http://www.ceres.org//Page.aspx?&pid=428.

50 Carbon Disclosure Project, "Clear the Air on Financial Risks: Report," November 5, 2008, as reported in that day's Globe and Mail.

51 Shell, "Shell Global Scenario," 2008, http://www.shell.com/home/content/aboutshell/our_strategy/shell_global_scenarios/dir_global_scenarios_07112006.html.

52 Ibid.

53 Management Help, accessed August 2008. http://managementhelp.org.

54 OCC, 2008, http://www.occ.gov.uk/activities/eu_ets/analysis-euets-options.pdf.

55 Ibid.

56 White House, "Energy Independence and Security Act Fact Sheet," December 2007.

57 Margaret Munro, "BioFuel Salvation or Perdition?", Montreal Gazette, May 3, 2008.

58 Dana Childs, "Core Ethanol Crisis Looming Says Watchdog," January 8, 2007, www.cleantech.com.

59 Eric Johnson and Russel Heinen, "Biofuels Face a Carbon Certification Challenge," SRI Consulting, April 2008.

60 David Kiley, "Big Oil's Big Stall on Ethanol," *Business Week*, October 1, 2007.
61 Pierre Fournier, "One Way or Another, the Oil Sands Will Play," *Globe and Mail*, October 20, 2008.
62 Norval Scott, "Statoil Deals New Blow to Oil Sands," *Globe and Mail*, December 4, 2008.
63 Chris Nelder, "Tar Sands: The Oil Junkie's Last Fix, Part 1—Tar Sands' Profitability Questionable," *Energy & Capital*, August 24, 2007.
64 Scott, "Statoil Deals New Blow to Oil Sands."
65 Globe-Net, "Oil and Gas Invest Billions in Environment," 2008, www.globe-net.com.
66 Harry Fuller, "Canada caught in its own tar baby. Tar sands investments now a Dead Duck," May 1 2008, http://blogs.zdnet.com/green/?p=1006.
67 Gillian Steward, "It's Not Just About the Ducks," *Toronto Star*, May 11, 2008.
68 Andy Rowell, "Climate Risk Set to Impact Oil Sands Development," Oil Exchange International, 2008, http://priceofoil.org/2008/09/16/climate-risk-might-scupper-oil-sands-development.
69 Peter Hadekel, "Oil Sands Firms Take Heat on Environmental Impact," *Montreal Gazette*, June 27, 2008.
70 Environmental Working Group, "Monsanto Settles PCB Case in Alabama," Reuters staff writer, August 20, 2003.
71 Andrew Schneider, "W.R. Grace to Pay Record Superfund Fine," *Seattle Post*, March 12, 2008.
72 Nina Totenberg, "Supreme Court Weighs Exxon Valdez Damages," February 27, 2008, www.npr.org.
73 "Court Slashes Judgment in Exxon Valdez Disaster," *Juneau Daily News*, June 25, 2008.
74 Renee Montagne and Adam Davidson, "Mattel Recalls 9 Million Toys Made in China," August 14, 2007, www.npr.org.
75 Mattel, "Mattel Reports 2007 Financial Results," press release, 2008, http://www.shareholder.com/mattel/news.
76 Intentblog, 2006, http://www.intentblog.com/archives/2006/11/esty_building_e.html.
77 Lisa Halko, "California's Attorney General Acknowledges Prop 65 Abuse," *Legal Backgrounder*, Vol. 22, No. 29, July 27, 2007.
78 Ibid.
79 Joel Pekay, "Restricted Substances Legislation: Proposition 65," Intertek, presentation, May 2007.
80 Roger Parloff, "The $200 Billion Miscarriage of Justice: Asbestos Lawyers Are Pitting Plaintiffs Who Aren't Sick Against Companies that Never Made the Stuff—and Extracting Billions for Themselves," CNN.com, March 4, 2002, http://money.cnn.com/magazines/fortune/fortune_archive/2002/03/04/319093/index.htm.
81 Climate Group, "Reducing Emission: DuPont Case Study," 2008, http://theclimategroup.org.
82 Ibid.
83 Environmental Protection, "DuPont to Pay Record Fine in PFOA Case," December 1, 2008, http://www.eponline.com/articles/53881.
84 General Electric, "GE 2007 Citizen Report," 2008, http://www.socialfunds.com/csr/reports/GE_2007_Citizenship_Report.pdf.
85 General Electric, "GE Emended Report (10-K/A) SEC Filing, January 19," 2007, http://sec.edgar-online.com/2007/01/19/0000040545-07-000007/Section12.asp.

CHAPTER TWO

(MIS)MANAGEMENT SYSTEMS

In its simplest form, a company's management system can be described as a framework of procedures and processes used to ensure that the organization can fulfill all tasks required to achieve its objectives. Typically this framework covers a four-step process—plan, do, check, act—known as the Deming Cycle.[1] Like any facet of business, management systems can suffer from weaknesses in design, development, implementation and maintenance. They can be crippled by a lack of support or poor infrastructure. In the case of systems designed to ensure environmental compliance, they are often not considered a priority, and consequently become isolated from the other systems used to manage the company and, in some cases, become a hiding place for business risks.

The most common pitfalls related to management systems that companies encounter as they try to align their organizations to address changing environmental issues are

- a failure of management to embed environment within general management processes and to commit resources to it
- absence of a robust framework to ensure compliance with rapidly changing legislation, published guidelines/standards, commitments and customer requirements
- absence of ownership of key issues and collaboration between various functions/departments and with suppliers/customers
- a lack of basic functionality within information systems to ensure proper management of environmental data, reports and risks and product life cycle management (PLM) principles

ENVIRONMENTAL MANAGEMENT SYSTEM SILOS

More than 125,000 companies worldwide have registered their environmental management systems (EMSs) to the International Organization for Standardization (ISO) 14001 EMS standard. The ISO 14001 model is designed to ensure continuous improvement in management and, by extension, in environmental performance. ISO has published several management standards pertinent to environmental issues:

- ISO 14000 series on environmental standards, addressing areas including environmental management, audits, site assessment, performance reporting, greenhouse gas accounting and verification, life cycle assessment, etc.
- ISO/International Electrotechnical Commission (IEC) series on supplier declaration of conformity, conformity assessments and general requirements for laboratories' competence
- ISO 22000 series on traceability in food supply chains
- ISO 26000 standard for CSR (in development; to be published in 2010)

These are all useful standards; however, in many cases, their application within a company occurs in isolation from other components of the business, creating a "silo" of activity and information. It is critical that companies overcome this tendency and integrate their EMS into the company's general management system (e.g., strategic planning, product design, procurement, marketing, manufacturing, logistics) and business information solutions. The latter includes enterprise resource planning (ERP) software and enterprise asset management (EAM) software from vendors like SAP, Oracle and Infor Global Solutions. Additional discussion of the IT role is provided later in this chapter under the section entitled "IT to the Rescue?"

Companies need to document all activities that may result in business risks and opportunities related to environmental issues (refer to chapter 1) and ensure that they are being addressed in either the EMS or general management system and accounted for in the company's information systems where considered business-critical.

Without this integration, the worst mistake a company can make is to label an issue as "green," "sustainability" or "EHS." In doing so, environment and sustainable development (SD) is inadvertently moved out of general business thinking and decision-making. In the process, substandard performance, high costs or failure are almost guaranteed. Environment becomes a "side show" that can be hit or miss, and is often dismissed when company management needs to focus on what it perceives as its critical issues.

The whole purpose of bringing green to the forefront is to make it onto the business agenda as a normal, day-to-day item intimately linked to performance and profitability, in every dimension of the organization. Companies that see value, improved recruitment, employee retention, customer relations, managed risk and enhanced reputation in EMS recognize it as nothing more than a normal consideration in the conduct of business.

This is the optimal way to envision the purpose of a management system: to execute company policy through the systematic deployment of human and technological resources. Green must be given this level of importance for success and it needs to be deployed through a management system that embraces the plan-do-check-act conventions that ensure continuity from the strategic and the tactical, to the operational and the administrative functions of the company.

COMPLIANCE FRAMEWORK

To turn compliance and risk management into a competitive advantage and to strengthen the company brand, companies need to adopt a proactive mode of compliance. This ensures that compliance and risk management are built into the design of products, business processes and each department's business plan. From product life-cycle management to sourcing and supply-chain planning, and from enterprise resource planning to enterprise asset management, continual feedback and integrated compliance ensure that manufacturers do it right every time. To achieve a proactive stance, it's important to embrace compliance as a corporate-wide initiative, from shop floor to top floor.[2] Figure 2.1 presents the key components of a robust framework.

Figure 2.1: Robust Framework for Compliance

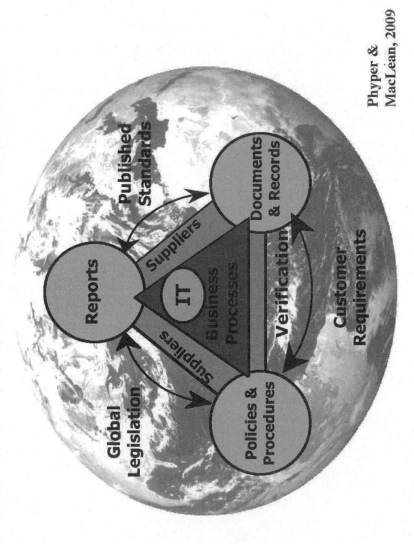

Phyper &
MacLean, 2009

Tracking Changing Requirements

A key component of a robust compliance framework is the presence of processes/ systems to track changing requirements—global legislation, published standards/ guidelines (e.g., industrial associations, NGO initiatives), etc.—that the company has committed to (or may commit to) and customer requirements. These requirements are constantly changing and require vigilance to ensure that all pertinent information is tracked and assessed. No longer is it acceptable to base global compliance systems on U.S. legislation and standards, using them as surrogates for local legislation, because most countries have national and state legislation, much of which is more stringent than that in the U.S.

The key issue becomes how to track these requirements in a cost-effective, timely manner. Increasingly, companies are turning to third-party services to perform this regulatory tracking. It is important to note that the information provided by these companies can take three forms: updates of full legislative text; interpretation of what the text means; and transactional content (data, rules, phrases) that is extracted from the text and used to drive business systems, e.g., change in national toxic substances inventory lists. It is the latter that allows true cost efficiencies.

Part of ensuring proactive compliance means being at the table when new legislation is being drafted. Many organizations rely on their industrial association to track and provide timely updates, as well as to influence government agencies prior to the drafting of the final version of legislation—for example, American Iron and Steel Institute, American Chemistry Council, Canadian Chemical Producers' Association, Canadian Petroleum Products Institute, National Mining Association.

Company Policies and Procedures

Company, business unit and departmental policies, procedures and standard operating practices, etc. are all critical to ensuring that direction is provided to all levels of the organization. They also serve to guide the company in two key ways: (1) by identifying those activities that should be performed beyond compliance (whether for risk management/brand protection, to satisfy corporate standards, etc.) and (2) by clarifying the "grey" areas of legislation where there is potential ambiguity in interpretation.

Two issues arise: how to keep documents up-to-date and how manual components can be replaced with automated processes. Many companies have invested significant effort in preparing detailed policies and procedures that quickly become out-of-date because either insufficient resources have been assigned to update them, the procedures are overly complex or not structured for ongoing updates, or the documents are not managed within a document management software system.

More and more, companies are leveraging content management software to reduce the cost and increase the timeliness of updates. In addition, they are assessing opportunities to automate work processes related to compliance—transactional processing versus manual intervention. An example of this is an automated check to see if a product can be shipped to a company based upon a comparison of chemical ingredients to national inventory lists.

Documents and Records

Most companies have put in place systems to ensure the proper storage, management and retention of documents and records according to both regulatory requirements and ISO standards. Some issues that have emerged in the last few years related to document and record retention are

- centralized data management emerging as a key topic regarding the storage of information for multinational companies; of particular importance is information that is used to generate both internal and external documentation to address global legislation, as the cost and risk of disparate systems is too high
- storage and tracking of information on the compliance activities of multiple suppliers
- communication, including exemptions, between regulatory bodies and the company

All of these can be resolved by a combination of revised processes (workflows) and enhanced IT solutions.

Evaluation, Control and Reporting

Anything that can be measured can be improved. It is thus critical to put in place meaningful metrics, i.e., those that can be used to influence the business. These must be updated on a regular basis by the groups responsible for their execution, validated during periodic audits and tied to executive compensation and bonuses.

Unfortunately this is an area where most companies fail, especially on environmental issues. Some 80% of management effort can be spent collecting data (not always related to the business aspect of environment) and 20%, or less, spent acting upon the results (often focusing on items that may not be business-critical), when in fact it should be the reverse. A formal reporting system must be in place that is partially automated to ensure personnel are focusing on resolving business issues.

Reporting by Suppliers

The monitoring of suppliers and enforcement of key requirements of sourcing programs (both regulatory and voluntary) is still proving to be difficult. Companies can still be found that have either not stipulated what should not be in their products (at a chemical level) or have not put in place processes to assess conformance to these rules. This weakness is exemplified by the recent recalls of numerous consumer products manufactured overseas. Refer to chapter 5 for additional information on programs for suppliers.

Regulatory Reporting

Large multinational companies must prepare hundreds of reports on various environment-related issues. For the most part they have systems to assist with this process; however, many rely on a significant amount of manual intervention and sometimes find themselves being in a situation of non-compliance as they have no mechanism to address changing legislation as mentioned above. Appendix A presents additional information on regulatory reporting that impacts eco-design and green procurement.

In addition to reporting under environmental legislation, there are also reporting obligations under financial legislation. Prior to 2002, the U.S. Securities and Exchange Commission (SEC) rules (Items of Regulation S-K) required the disclosure of environmental costs and liabilities, as follows:

- Item 101 required companies to disclose material effects of compliance (or non-compliance) with environmental laws.
- Item 103 required disclosure of pending, non-routine litigation (with environmental litigation typically being considered non-routine).
- Item 303 required disclosure of business trends or events likely to have a material effect on a company's financial condition, which may include certain environmental "trends or events."

In 2002, the U.S. Public Company Accounting and Reform Act, commonly known as Sarbanes-Oxley (SOX), was enacted. It contained a number of provisions that require publicly traded companies to improve the accuracy of their financial disclosure and establish better internal controls for financial reporting. This expanded requirement is sometimes referred to as "government, risk and compliance" (GRC) as discussed in chapter 1.

The Canadian Securities Administrators (CSA) have introduced a series of national instruments and policies that closely follow Sarbanes-Oxley and the rules and guidelines established by the SEC and U.S. stock exchanges, but strive to accommodate the unique nature of the Canadian financial market. Most provinces have adopted the new rules and regulations.[3] In terms of SOX Section 404 (internal controls), CSA instruments require management to evaluate and report on the effectiveness of the company's internal control over financial reporting (including relevant environmental issues and any weaknesses in design) as of the end of the issuer's financial year in the Management Discussion & Analysis (MD&A). In addition, the Ontario Securities Commission published Staff Notice 51-716 in 2008 on Environmental Reporting. This stated that company disclosure on environmental liabilities, asset retirement obligations, financial and operational effects of environmental protection requirements, environmental policies and environmental risk was inadequate and that a higher standard was required.[4]

Voluntary Reporting

Increasingly, external stakeholders (NGOs, industrial associations, financial institutions and unions) are demanding information on company environmental performance. Over 80% of Global Fortune 250 companies disclose their sustainability performance in sustainability or corporate responsibility reports, according to a 2008 survey conducted by KPMG.[5] Companies are realizing that there are real financial costs to not addressing sustainable development in their operations.[6]

Table 2.1 provides examples of key reporting formats, repositories of reports and sustainability indexes. Additional information regarding interaction with stakeholders can be found in the discussion of collaboration/communications below.

Table 2.1: Examples of Key Reporting Initiatives

Organization	Description
Reporting Formats	
Global Reporting Initiative (GRI)—G3 Reports	Sustainability Reporting Guidelines that are based on triple bottom line, which has become the de facto international standard used by more than 1,200 companies for corporate reporting on environmental, social and economic performance. www.globalreporting.org
Ceres & Tellus Institute Facility Reporting Project	Consistent, comparable and credible economic, environmental and social reporting guidance for individual facilities in the United States. www.ceres.org
World Business Council for Sustainable Development	CEO-led global association of companies dealing exclusively with business and sustainable development, including reporting. www.wbcsd.org
Reporting Repositories	
Corporate Register	Free directory of company-issued CSR, sustainability, and environment reports from around the world. Also manages the GRI Register and AA1000AS Register. www.corporateregister.com
Carbon Disclosure Project	Worldwide, voluntary, annual reporting on GHG emissions, aimed at providing information to institutional investors on how signatory corporations manage risks associated with climate change. www.cdproject.net
SD Indexes	
Dow Jones Sustainability Index (DJSI)	DJSI was the first global index tracking the financial performance of the leading sustainability-driven companies worldwide. www.sustainability-index.com
Corporate Knights Global 100	Global 100 Most Sustainable Corporations in the world as identified by Corporate Knights Inc., a Canadian media company specializing in sustainability coverage. www.corporateknights.ca

The KPMG survey also found that 70% of companies that reported environmental status used the GRI guidelines.[7]

PricewaterhouseCoopers and the Canadian Financial Executives Research Foundation recently conducted a survey of 343 senior Canadian financial executives together with an Executive Research Forum to determine the major issues surrounding CSR. The key findings of the research included:

- Overwhelming majority (90%) of senior financial executives consider reporting on the environmental and social impacts of their companies to be important.
- Large proportion of responding companies (72%) also claimed that their company understood which sustainability issues were most relevant to achieving their business goals; however, when asked if there was an effective strategy for managing these issues, only half of respondents reported that they had one in place.
- Almost all (92%) senior finance executives felt that it was important to communicate sustainability performance to senior management and the Board, while at the same time, over half admitted that they did not have an effective system and process in place for periodically measuring sustainability performance.
- Most agreed that it was important to provide similar information on a periodic basis to shareholders, employees and external stakeholders; however, over half (55%) admitted that their companies did not have an effective system in place to enable this type of reporting. Indeed, most respondents (78%) believe that the average investor does not have enough information about the sustainability performance of Canadian companies.

Two recent reports highlight the benefits of sustainable development:

- Corporate Knights Inc. and Innovest Strategic Value Advisors report entitled "Global 100 Most Sustainable Corporations in the World" concluded that since the inception of their Global 100 List in 2005, companies on the list have outperformed the benchmark (the MSCI World Index) by 480 basis points per annum.
- A.T. Kearney report entitled "Green Winners: The Performance of Sustainability-focused Companies in the Financial Crisis" looked at 99 companies with a strong commitment to sustainability as defined by the Sustainability Index and the Goldman Sachs Sustain Focus List. The report found that companies focused on sustainability outperformed their peers by 15% (average of $650 million in additional market capitalization) during the financial crisis. Key characteristics of these companies included:

- A focus on long-term strategy, not just short-term gains
- Strong corporate governance
- Sound risk-management practices

Company Business Processes

This is a critical component and the one that is undergoing the most change. Five key issues that have emerged in the last few years related to business processes that involve environmental issues are

1. Inclusion of eco-design principles into product management processes (refer to chapter 3)
2. Requirement to have full disclosure of chemicals in a product (including subcomponents) for both regulatory and risk management activities
3. Extraction of costs from the supply chain via "environmental misman agement" approach (refer to chapter 5)
4. Linkage of environment and energy (conservation/sourcing) in strategic planning and goal-setting activities (refer to chapter 6)
5. Reassessment of quality management and verification processes related to components provided by suppliers

Full Composition

Historically, full disclosure of the composition of a product was limited primarily to the chemical and petrochemical sectors with the proviso that information on composition related to "trade secrets" did not have to be disclosed. California Proposition 65 expanded this requirement to other sectors, as all companies were required to label their products, in California only, if they had one of 850 chemicals that were classified as potential carcinogens or the cause of birth defects. Restriction of Hazardous Substances (RoHS) legislation adopted in several countries/states further expanded this requirement to electronic applications, but for only six chemicals.

Recent NGO investigations into a variety of products (refer to chapter 3) along with the new EU REACH (Registration, Evaluation, Authorisation and Restriction of Chemicals) legislation is causing many companies to assess chemicals that are or may be present in their product—a significant undertaking, if leveraging hundreds (in some cases, thousands) of suppliers to produce subcomponents. This legislation requires the registration of both new and existing chemicals in the marketplace. It is the latter that is causing significant impact on companies' business processes—"no data, no market," i.e., if a company fails to register a substance it will not be allowed to sell it in the EU market. Refer to appendix A for additional information.

The consumer recalls of 2007 are prime examples of how compliance and risk management go well beyond internal procedures to span the entire supply chain. Rory Granros, Infor's Director of Industry & Product Marketing for Process Industries, best summarized the key questions which executives are asking or should be: *"Do we have proof of absence or are we at risk from absence of proof by market and regulation? Do our systems help or hinder us?"*[8]

Verification/Audits

The implementation of a verification process (sometimes as part of a quality management system) across a supply chain is a major undertaking.

Product/components—Historically, specifications would be provided to a supplier that would dictate material not to be used in the product (oftentimes referred to as the "company black list" or "hit list"). More advanced companies would put in place sampling protocols to confirm the absence of items on the company list, typically a few metals. Because of pressure from NGOs who actively have been testing consumer products for hazardous materials, company lists have expanded to include many more substances (e.g. proposition 65 List, EU Reach, SVHC List, and EU NGO "SIN" List). However, both companies and their suppliers are finding it more difficult to ensure the absence of these materials as the cost to analyze samples has increased dramatically, especially when organic chemicals are involved.

Facilities—The practice of auditing facilities, both company owned and third party, has been around for more than twenty-five years, with well-established auditing protocols and certification systems in place. During the late eighties, larger companies put in place auditing/verification programs for third party waste disposal and treatment sites, to ensure that their liability under new legislation was minimized. This was extended to suppliers by the chemical industry and consumer goods brands, the latter under pressure from NGOs. (For additional information on verification, refer to the auditing standard ISO 19011 or the audit components of the ISO 9001 or ISO 14001 standards, the Electronic Industry Code of Conduct EICC framework, as well as the case studies on Sony, Mattel and Dell presented in chapter 5.)

In the next few years, a greater emphasis will be placed on preventive actions as companies

- go beyond auditing to consider how capacity-building can increase adherence to supplier standards
- leverage partners/suppliers to find ways to minimize repetitive audits and accelerate adoption of a management system

OWNERSHIP, COLLABORATION AND COMMUNICATION

Five key questions related to ownership and collaboration on environmental issues should be asked of any organization.

1. Who has overall responsibility for environmental issues at the company?
2. What function owns key components of environment programs: SD, CSR, facility emissions/discharges/waste, climate change, energy conservation, or eco-design and green procurement?
3. What is the relationship/overlap between programs established for these key components?
4. How are these programs integrated into general management system processes and procedures, e.g., research and development, procurement, manufacturing and logistics?
5. How is the company collaborating both internally and externally on environmental matters?

Unfortunately, the answers to these questions may not be what some executives expect them to be. Many companies have not assigned owners (assuming someone is taking care of the issue) or, in other cases, are embroiled in turf wars over environmental issues. The result is dysfunctional systems that are inefficient and do not address business risk or opportunities.

The allocation of responsibility is a cornerstone of a good management system. It is also important that "owners" of key components are included in all aspects of plan-do-check-act, including the strategic planning process and assessment of business risk/opportunities, from which they are often excluded.

More and more companies are creating collaborative partnerships with suppliers and environmental NGOs, sometimes called "green alliances," to encourage sharing of ideas that address environmental problems, which result in operational efficiencies, new technologies and marketable "green" products (refer to chapter

4). The particular approach used is dependent upon existing procurement systems, relationships with suppliers, the competitive nature of the business and the willingness of the company to share information with NGOs. (See chapter 5 for additional information on green procurement and collaboration.)

Interactive marketing agency imc2 recently looked at the eighty-six companies on the S&P 100 that have some level of sustainability communication, concluding that companies would benefit from increased stakeholder engagement and transparency. Key areas of improvement that imc2 identified[9] include the need

- to cover environment as well as employees, products and community issues
- for messages to be woven into a company's overall identity, not relegated, for example, to a hard-to-locate portion of a company's website that seems disconnected from its other messages
- to provide constant flow of information to both draw in new stakeholders and keep existing stakeholders informed
- to use a mixed bag of tools: online tools like blogs, newsletters and news releases can provide regular updates, while an annual sustainability report with updates throughout the year can show the big picture of a company's sustainability efforts
- to leverage interactive features on websites to provide more chances for stakeholders to provide input, whether it is adding comments about certain practices or asking questions others might also want to ask

IT TO THE RESCUE?

Information technology (IT) is business-critical for companies and, as such, environmental issues cannot be operationalized without leveraging IT systems. Unfortunately, the following common deficiencies are present at many organizations:

- IT systems lack basic functionality to ensure proper management of environmental data as it relates to both regulatory and voluntary initiatives, and do not promote PLM principles.
- No one in the organization has been assigned a mandate in their portfolio to manage, maintain and improve environmental IT.
- Integration of environmental IT with ERP software is lacking or non-existent.
- Business decisions must be translated into workflow rules and approvals that contain calls to the environmental IT.

- Ongoing investment must be made to update and improve environmental IT systems in order that they address corporate priorities, evolving legislation and changing customer expectation.

These deficiencies are significant sources of risk. As the complexity and number of requirements that companies must comply with increase, manual systems are no longer an option!

Environmental Software

There are numerous software solutions on the market to address environmental issues. Add to these solutions in-house systems that have been constructed over the years to address unique (or not so unique) needs and there is no shortage of solutions. Five steps that companies should undertake to further integrate environmental compliance efforts into their businesses are

Step 1	Consolidate disparate environmental applications and systems.[10] Note that this typically also involves health and safety systems.
Step 2	Ensure systems are seamlessly integrated into, or part of, ERP and EAM software.
Step 3	Automate compliance activities where possible using transactional processing versus manual intervention.
Step 4	Integrate the company's environmental framework with its broader GRC framework.[11]
Step 5	Over time, leverage emerging Manufacturing 2.0 and Enterprise 2.0 constructs into the company's environmental framework.[12]

Manufacturing 2.0 is a new framework that AMR Research created to present a new, more collaborative model for demand-driven manufacturing. Manufacturing 2.0 software lets companies internally collaborate across design, manufacturing and supply chain functions and across corporate boundaries with suppliers, customers, design partners and contract manufacturers.[13]

Enterprise 2.0 uses emergent social software platforms within companies, or between companies and their partners or customers. Emergent means that the software is freeform and as such optional, free of up-front workflow, egalitarian, or indifferent to formal organizational identities and accepting of many types of data. Examples[14] include

- internal company blogs and wikis (websites that allow users to view, remove and edit content)
- enterprise tagging (tagging content located behind a firewall)—very early stage
- R&D departments' use of InnoCentive, an open innovation community that allows participants to earn money while solving tough problems

GRC Solutions

For the last couple of years the focus of most companies' GRC programs, and thus commercial GRC software solutions, has been on policies/procedures, document/records and reporting, leaving many GRC processes to continue "as is." These processes tend to be labor-intensive activities that have high potential for errors and are typically reactive in their nature. The two common misunderstandings are

1. Compliance/risk management activities are viewed as projects, when in fact they are processes that must be monitored and adjusted on an ongoing basis.
2. Reporting is the main line of defense to manage the risks of noncompliance, when in fact the primary line of a proactive defense is the automation/integration of processes.

The assessment of compliance must be performed automatically/semi-automatically using up-to-date legislation/published standards and customer requirements during the

- design of a product or process
- issuance of specifications to suppliers
- receipt of customer orders
- shipment of goods from supplier to company
- verification of supplier conformance
- packaging and shipment of customers orders
- generation of regulatory reports (in local language)

PLM Solutions

One of the biggest barriers to achieving an end-to-end, seamless and integrated PLM process is transitioning to an externally focused organization rather than an

Figure 2.2: PLM Interaction with Key Business Systems

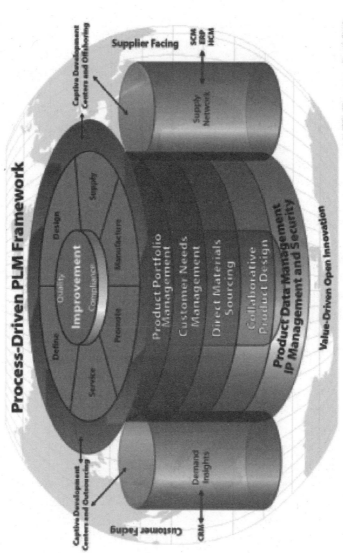

internal one. External-looking companies not only have a consistently good understanding of demand by staying connected with customers, partners, academia and other market sources, but they also work jointly with these entities to create value for the company with new products and supply chain and service enhancements. To get to seamless, value-driven PLM, companies need to understand and adopt a process-driven PLM framework, as illustrated in the AMR Research diagram in figure 2.2.[15]

AMR Research has identified the following key components of a robust PLM framework:[16]

Customer needs management (CNM)—This describes the need to provide a platform for open innovation with customers and partners, linking where appropriate into customers' databases for demand insights, like customer relationship management (CRM).

Direct material sourcing (DMS)—In recent years, DMS has expanded to include request for information, quote process and electronic catalogs. The new trend is to expand this functionality to manufacturers seeking partners as innovators for joint value creation and not simply as suppliers of manufacturing capability or original manufactured product. Manufacturers are taking advantage of global suppliers that bring cost advantage and expertise to regional markets, particularly in fast-moving markets like apparel and consumer goods.

Master data management (MDM)—As manufacturers outsource core product development processes, they will require a stronger form of authentication and authorization, as well as the ability to rapidly link disparate data sources and applications. It is important to note that 30% of manufacturers surveyed by AMR Research currently outsource core new product development and launch activities.

Integration of PLM and DMS—Compliance initiatives like RoHS, REACH, Waste Electrical and Electronic Equipment (WEEE), and the U.S. Code of Federal Regulations (CFR) Section 21 Part II (electronic signatures for Food & Drug Administration requirements) have been behind the integration of PLM and sourcing for the past several years. However, many manufacturers have not put in place systems to address this legislation, nor have they integrated disparate systems allowing the timely and cost-effective exchange of data. The result is increased probability of non-compliant events.

Human capital management (HCM)—This covers core human resource administration automation, investment in employee performance management, talent acquisition, and employee portals/self-service applications.

Strategic service management (SSM)—This is a new customer commitment-centric business strategy that optimizes a company's service business processes through a single, integrated view of post-sale service operations. SSM takes into consideration the planning and forecasting of service parts and resources, and the strategy and management of customer commitments, service partners, and service pricing.[17]

CHAPTER 2 TAKE-AWAYS

Embed environmental management systems (EMSs) into general management systems (GMSs)/IT—EMS must be embedded into general management systems and business software solutions that address key aspects of the business—research and development, procurement, sales, marketing, manufacturing, logistics, etc. Too often EMS becomes a silo of activity/information that is seen as a cost center.

Ownership—The emergence of new environmental issues that touch various parts of a company, e.g., the many business risks associated with climate change (losses, business interruption, insurance rates, carbon finance, etc.), requires that companies ensure clarity regarding both ownership of issues and associated programs, as well as ensure minimum overlap/inefficiencies between groups working on similar activities. Examples of areas requiring clarity include SD, CSR, energy and environmental IT.

Regulatory tracking—It is critical that processes/systems be put in place to ensure proper tracking of draft and final legislation as well as key industrial codes of practice. The system must address the following: tracking changes to legislation/codes of practice, obtaining copies of changed legislation/codes of practice, assessing the changes against the activities of the business, including new requirements in policies/procedures, embedding key requirements into business processes and modifying verification programs to address new requirements.

Integration of business systems—Environmental IT solutions must

- be consolidated into a single instance
- be seamlessly integrated into ERP and EAM software
- allow automation of compliance activities
- integrate the company's environmental framework within a broader GRC framework
- over time, leverage emerging Manufacturing 2.0 and Enterprise 2.0 constructs into the company's environmental framework

As a first step, companies should perform a gap analysis on their environmental IT landscape, i.e., document their current status and compare it against the "ideal" system, as defined by business requirements.

Automate—Companies of almost any size can no longer expect to be in compliance using manual systems, given the rapid pace of changing legislation and its increasing complexity. It is critical that key requirements of legislation be transferred into computer code on an ongoing basis to allow transactional/event processing to occur. Examples include

- generation of supplier specifications using up-to-date legislation
- checking of supplier declaration/composition information against both regulatory requirements, and, where there are potential risks, conducting preliminary hazard evaluation
- ensuring that a substance is registered in jurisdictions in which the customers operate
- quick generation of regulatory documents that are appropriate for transport as well as for the jurisdiction in which the customer is located

Take responsibility—It does not matter to the consumer whether it was your design/facility or that of a supplier. If the product is potentially hazardous or during its production significant environmental impairment occurs, they will blame you! As discussed in chapter 1 and several case studies throughout the book, the real impact to the company is not the government fines or penalties, but the damage to corporate brand.

Verification—In order to "prove absence," companies must either sample a product or component against a significant list of hazardous chemicals or develop statistically sound sampling strategies that take into account raw materials, manufacturing process, history of supplier and other risk factors.

Audits—There is a need to conduct periodic audits, following acceptable protocols using trained auditors; however, there also must be a focus on "capacity building" as a proactive approach to ensure that suppliers "get it" and will respond correctly in a variety of circumstances instead of just putting in a rigid system that only responds to questions on audit checklists.

The following case studies on Wal-Mart and Ecolab illustrate how they are implementing SD principles at their operations and along their supply chains.

Wal-Mart Case Study: Part 1

2008 Fiscal Year Revenues: $374.526 billion
Number of Associates: 1.9 million
Number of Customers: 176 million

Vision: "To improve the lives of everyday people by making everyday things more affordable."

Motto: "Sustainability 360: Doing Good, Better, Together"

Environmental Goals

Simple and straightforward: to be supplied 100% by renewable energy; to create zero waste; and to sell products that sustain our natural resources and the environment.

KPI

Sustainable Buildings: Experimental stores were built to assist Wal-Mart reach three long-term environmental goals:

- to be supplied 100% by renewable energy
- to create zero waste
- to sell products that sustain Wal-Mart's resources and the environment

Wal-Mart has committed to designing a store prototype that is 25%–30% more efficient by 2009, and reducing greenhouse gas emissions in existing stores by 20% by 2012.

Trucking Fleet: Wal-Mart has one of the largest private trucking fleets in the world, and it relies on diesel for fuel. Wal-Mart has committed to reducing emissions from their fleet of trucks and searching for innovative ways to help reduce America's dependence on fossil fuels. Wal-Mart's goal is to make its fleet 50% more energy efficient by 2015. Fuel efficiency innovations will keep 26 billion pounds of carbon dioxide out of the air between now and 2020.

Programs

Sustainable Value Networks: Bringing together leaders inside Wal-Mart along with leaders from supplier companies, environmental groups, academia and government to focus on everything from the energy stores use to the packaging used on products.

Paper Products: Working with suppliers to develop "extended roll life" products that condense several rolls of either toilet paper or paper towels into one thus eliminating the need for extra cardboard centers, reducing the amount of packaging, saving space on shelves and in trucks, and saving customers' time and money.

Seafood: Wal-Mart is offering sustainable harvested seafood (the Marine Stewardship Council's independent environmental standard) at affordable prices, which will impact not only the buying habits of their customers, but shape the industry as a whole. For farm-raised aquaculture products like shrimp, Wal-Mart asks suppliers to obtain certification by the Aquaculture Certification Council, Inc., an independent, non-governmental body established to certify social, environmental and food safety standards at aquaculture facilities around the world.

Organics: Customers shopping in Super Centers and Neighborhood Markets may find organic offerings that include pasta, olive oil, coffee, tea, peanut butter, bread, oranges, tomatoes, lettuce, apples, fresh herbs (thyme, sage, mint, etc.), packaged salads, baby formula, milk, cheese, sour cream, ice cream, cottage cheese, sauces and seafood.

Locally Grown Products: To help reduce the number of miles food travels and help support rural communities, Wal-Mart has introduced a "Food Miles Calculator," which allows their buyers to enter information on each supplier and product, determine product pick-up locations and select which of Wal-Mart's thirty-eight food distribution centers the product will reach.

Wal-Mart Case Study: Part 2

Greenhouse Gas Emissions: Wal-Mart has stated that being an efficient and profitable business and being a good steward of the environment are goals that can work together. They have also accepted that they have a responsibility, as one of the largest companies in the world, to deal with environmental problems, especially climate change. One of their environmental goals is to use 100% renewable energy. One of the ways they hope to achieve this is by establishing a GHG network to study and actively reduce their carbon footprint. Their GHG network works to create business advantages from measuring, reducing and eliminating the use of fossil fuels in their stores and supply chain and by customers.

Zero Waste: Wal-Mart's vision is to reach a day where there are no dumpsters behind their stores and clubs, and no landfills containing their throwaways. They want to create zero waste. Reducing waste saves money for their customers, suppliers and business. It also decreases their reliance on non-renewable resources. In order to assist with their long-term goal, Wal-Mart has set a mid-term goal to reduce waste by 25% by October 2008.

Reusable Bags: Every year, nearly one trillion plastic shopping and grocery bags are used around the world. The vast majority is then sent to a landfill. To help reduce the number of plastic bags that are wasted each year, and to engage customers in helping them reach their sustainability goals, Wal-Mart introduced reusable shopping bags in October 2007. Made from 85% recycled content, the bags hold more than twice the amount of an average plastic bag. Customers can find the black bags near the checkout aisles in Wal-Mart stores and purchase them for $1 each. At the end of the bags' life span, Wal-Mart will recycle them.

Packaging Reduction: Working with suppliers to reduce packaging, in 2007 Wal-Mart announced that by May of 2008, they would only sell concentrated detergent. Wal-Mart estimates that over the next three years, the impact of this effort will save more than 400 million gallons of water, more than 95 million pounds of plastic resin and more than 125 million pounds of cardboard. The potential savings for the entire industry is expected to be four times that much.

Compact Fluorescent Light (CFL) Bulbs: In 2007, Wal-Mart sold 137 million CFLs, surpassing our goal to sell 100 million bulbs. Wal-Mart expects that this will save their customers $4 billion in energy costs and prevent almost 1 billion incandescent bulbs from reaching landfills. They also estimate that this will prevent 25 million tons of carbon dioxide from being released—the equivalent of taking 1 million cars off the road.

Ethical Sourcing: Wal-Mart's Ethical Standards team is composed of more than two hundred associates. The team monitors factories, educates suppliers and buyers, and works with others in the industry to implement effective ethical sourcing programs.

Kids Recycling Challenge: Every year, nearly one trillion plastic shopping and grocery bags are used globally. The vast majority ends up in a landfill. Through the Kids Recycling Challenge, the Wal-Mart Foundation is partnering with elementary school students in twelve states to prevent these bags from ever reaching a landfill.

Misstep

Wal-Mart has received fines over the years for idling of diesel trucks and storm water infractions—the largest was a $3.1 million penalty in 2004, which was related to store construction sites.[18] Note the date of these activities versus the significant awakening that has occurred at Wal-Mart regarding environmental issues. Outside the scope of this book, Wal-Mart is also grappling with issues related to wages, health care and labor relations.

Information derived from www.walmart.com unless otherwise stated.

[18] Aaron Brenner, Barry Eidlin and Kerry Candaele, "Wal-Mart Inc.," conference entitled *Global Companies, Global Unions, Global Research, Global Campaigns*, February 2008.

Ecolab Case Study: Part 1

2007 Revenues: $5.5 billion
Number of Associates: 26,000

Environmental Stewardship

Through continuous improvement and sustainable innovation, Ecolab creates solutions that maximize product performance and environmental impact. The company makes "sound decisions based on good science," and is committed to reducing their carbon footprint, their water footprint and their overall impact on the environment.

Environmental Principles

- "We actively develop products and services that minimize our customers' water and energy use, with innovative packaging and dispensing methods that reduce waste.
- "We make every effort to use environmentally responsible and sustainable resources to meet our needs, and conserve non-renewable natural resources through efficient use and careful planning.
- "We invest in improving energy efficiency in our operations on an ongoing basis.
- "We minimize emissions, effluents and waste caused by our operations, and dispose of all wastes through safe and responsible methods.
- "We review the environmental attributes of raw materials and make environmental sustainability a key requirement in the selection of ingredients for new products and services.
- "We monitor the environmental, health and safety compliance standards of our manufacturing facilities and participate in third-party audits to continuously improve our performance.
- "We promptly respond to situations where our operations have had an adverse effect on people or the environment."

Sustainability—"Cleaner. Safer. Healthier."

"At Ecolab, making the world a cleaner, safer place is our business. We are committed to providing our customers with the most effective and efficient cleaning, food safety and infection control programs available. Sustainability is inherent in our products and services. From concentrated, solid formulations to innovative packaging and dispensing methods, our products are designed to help increase safety, lower the use of water and energy, and reduce the chemicals and waste released to the environment. Strengthened by the expertise of our associates and combined with our dedication to social responsibility, these offerings provide value to our customers and the global economy—and help foster a more sustainable world."

Environmental KPI

- Reduce U.S. GHG emissions to meet target established under U.S. EPA Climate Leaders program.
- Ecolab KPI for other environmental areas include
  - water usage per 1,000 kg production
  - energy usage per 1,000 kg production
  - waste water discharged per 1,000 kg production
  - waste (solid and hazardous) disposed of per 1,000 kg production

After building a baseline of global data, Ecolab plans to establish targets for continuous improvement against these Environmental KPIs in 2009.

Ecolab Case Study: Part 2

Company's Activities

Packaging: Products are designed to use minimal packaging material. Ecolab strives to utilize packaging material that is either recyclable or decomposes to non-hazardous end products. Renewable resource packaging, such as corrugated paper and paperboard, is used wherever safety is not compromised. A return and reuse program for plastic drums and for the collection of smaller packaging for recycling is in place. Every year, Ecolab cleans and reuses more than one hundred thousand 55-gallon drums, resulting in savings of more than 2.5 million pounds of virgin plastic resin. In addition to innovative packaging, Ecolab also provides customers in the janitorial and food processing markets with "packaged" solutions—water-soluble, unit dose packaging of detergents and sanitizers. This eliminates the solid waste generated by other forms of unit-dose packaging such as plastics, foils and paper.

GHG/Energy: Ecolab developed a U.S. GHG inventory of the six major greenhouse gases and reports progress annually based on detailed EPA protocols and guidance during 2007–2008. Ecolab has developed an energy and GHG reduction program for facilities and will be moving towards more fuel-efficient vehicles and vehicle service routes, as well as less GHG-intensive fuels when feasible. Corporate headquarters are heated by renewable resources, and have reduced electricity consumption by 10% over 2005 values.

Audits: A third-party consultant audits EHS performance at Ecolab's North American, European and Asian facilities. Audits are performed when facilities are acquired, and property and casualty insurers conduct fire and worker safety assessments and pressure vessel certifications at Ecolab facilities.

Impact of Products on Customers' Environmental Performance

Restaurant: Using series of Ecolab detergents and rinse aids dispensed through a controlled system that monitors usage and performance, managers were able to track water and energy consumption, detergent usage and waste—and then implement needed changes. Based on the number of racks of dishes washed per day, operational efficiency for the restaurants improved to 55% from 39% in a four-month period. The average annual savings for a single restaurant location using this system is estimated to be

- 27,600 liters of water (7,300 gallons)
- 1 metric ton of CO_2 equivalent greenhouse gas emissions
- 20 kilograms of plastic waste (43.5 lbs)
- 2,100 kWh of electricity

Hotel Chain: An international hotel chain began using the Ecolab laundry system, which reduces the typical wash cycle, water usage and energy needed to heat the water. The system also combines all needed cleaning ingredients into one closed capsule that reduces chemical contact and is easy to transport and load. Using this solution, the chain was able to reduce its hot water usage by 25% and reduce laundry cycle times by between twelve and eighteen minutes. Estimated annual savings from this solution:

- 355 million liters of water (whole chain)
- 12 metric tons of CO_2 equivalent for each location
- more than 26,300 kilograms of plastic compared to 5-gallon liquid containers (across the whole chain)

Poultry: A poultry processing facility (processing two hundred birds per minute) was using 1.4 million liters (384,000 gallons) of water per day—about 7.5 liters (2 gallons) per bird—with its Inside/Outside Bird Washer (IOBW) accounting for about 50%. Ecolab installed

Ethical Sourcing: Their global supply chain initiative requires strategic suppliers to follow their Ethical Sourcing Standard, which addresses forced labor, child labor, health and safety in the workplace, fair pay, harassment in the workplace, diversity, and ethics and environmental policies. Ecolab requires that their suppliers identify and act swiftly to eliminate any unacceptable conditions or practices in their facilities.	one of the lines with its IOBW system that allows the water to be reconditioned and safely reused. The system complies with USDA water reuse standards and also offers savings in energy and labor. By using this Ecolab system the facility will achieve estimated annual savings of 68 million liters (18 million gallons) of water per line.

Information derived from www.ecolab.com unless otherwise stated. |

NOTES

1 Forrest Breyfogle, "Plan Do Check Act (PDCA) as Part of Lean Six Sigma Project Execution Roadmap in Improve Phase," June 23, 2008.

2 Rory Granros, "Risky Business," Quality Digest Magazine, January 23, 2008. http://qualitydigest.com.

3 Tara Gray, "Canadian Response to the U.S. Sarbanes-Oxley Act of 2002: New Directions for Corporate Governances," 2005, http://www.parl.gc.ca/information/library/PRBpubs/prb0537-e.htm.

4 Eric Belli-Bivar and Lana Finney, "OSC Staff Notice 51-716 Environmental Disclosure Must Be Improved Says the Ontario Securities Commission," April 1, 2008, http://74.125.95.104/search?q=cache:4nXCOr1XUmgJ:www.davis.ca/publication/OSC-Staff-Notice-51-716-Environmental-disclosure-must-be-improved-says-the-Ontario-Securities-Commission.pdf+Ontario+Securities+Commission+published+Notice+51-716+in+2008+on+Environmental+Reporting+stated+that+company+disclosure+on+environmental+li&hl=en&ct=clnk&cd=1.

5 Global Reporting Initiative (GRI), "Disclosure On Sustainability Performance Has Become the Norm For Large Companies Globally—New Survey," October 2008, http://www.globalreporting.org/NewsEventsPress/PressResources/Pressrelease_28_Oct_2008.htm.

6 Helen Morris, "Black, White & Green All Over," Montreal Gazette, April 25, 2008.

7 Global Reporting Initiative (GRI), "Disclosure On Sustainability Performance Has Become the Norm For Large Companies Globally—New Survey." Nov. 12, 2008.

8 Granros, "Risky Business."

9 imc2, http://www.greenbiz.com/news/2008/10/16/survey-sp-100-identifies-best-practices-sustainability-communications.

10 Simon Jacobson and Colin Masson, "Laying the Foundation for Sustainability with Environmental Compliance," 2008, http://www.osisoft.com/Resources/Articles/Laying+the+Foundations+for+Sustainability+with+Environmental+Compliance.htm.

11 Ibid.

12 Ibid.

13 Kevin Reilly, "AMR Research Introduces Manufacturing 2.0," July 17, 2007, http://blog.hbs.edu/faculty/amcafee/index.php/faculty_amcafee_v3/enterprise_20_version_20.

14 Andrew McAfee, "The Impact of Business Technology on Business and Their Leaders," 2008, Harvard Business School, http://blog.hbs.edu/faculty/amcafee.

15 Jeffrey Hojlo and Michael Burkett, "PLM Top Business Drivers for 2008," AMR Research, January 25, 2008.

16 Ibid.

17 Wikipedia, 2008, http://en.wikipedia.org/wiki/Strategic_Service_Management.

18 Aaron Brenner, Barry Eidlin and Kerry Candaele, "Wal-Mart Inc.," conference entitled Global Companies, Global Unions, Global Research, Global Campaigns, February 2008.

CHAPTER THREE

"GREEN" OR JUST "GOOD" DESIGN

In the late 1990s, environmental attention shifted away from pollution generated by production facilities and processes to products and their impact on the environment across their life cycle. Product life cycle management (PLM), eco-design, eco-efficiency and eco-innovation are all examples of concepts that emerged during this time. Although all these concepts are different in focus, they have the same aim: to reduce the impact of products and services on the environment.

For many companies, eco-design was an add-on that made for persuasive presentations on how they were "greening" their activities. Meanwhile, such firms were missing opportunities to fully leverage eco-design in development and manufacturing processes. In addition, most of these efforts focused on incremental environmental improvements of existing working methods, products and services at the operational level.

Today, smart companies no longer define activities as eco-this or eco-that for design purposes. Instead, they simply employ "good" design practices, for both products and processes, as a component of PLM. An automobile that has negligible environmental impact but cannot pass crash safety tests or be refilled because there is no infrastructure is of little value to the marketplace. Also, smart industrial processes no longer follow the linear flow characteristic of "take-make-waste"; instead they show "produce-recycle-regenerate" circular industrial systems, such as those proposed by Paul Hawken in *Ecology of Commerce*, which address consumer needs.[1]

Cradle-to-Cradle (C2C) manufacturing is starting to gain traction as companies realize it is more profitable and environmentally beneficial to design and produce chemicals that may be readily recovered as raw materials once a product's useful life has ended. This trend will be accelerated as the cost of feedstock rises, more stringent take-back legislation is introduced, retailers put pressure on their supply chain to eliminate hazardous ingredients and incremental eco-efficiency activities are exhausted as they typically start with the assumption of a one-way, linear flow of materials.

The following quote by Mark Parker, CEO of Nike, best summarizes the change that is occurring: "Corporate responsibility no longer exists on the periphery as a check on our business, but is assuming its rightful role as a source of innovation within our business. Corporate responsibility is no longer a staff function at Nike. It's a design function, a sourcing function, a consumer experience function, part of how we operate."[2]

Manufacturers are beginning to incorporate

- front-end market assessments and ideation to ensure that the voice of the customer is understood
- production process planning to validate that they can manufacture what has been designed

Figure 3.1 presents key PLM business processes that are connected to the supply chain.[3]

Companies also must factor in three important shifts:

- There is increasing demand for information on what is in products, which is being driven by new legislation, NGOs and consumers. This is a significant challenge to many consumer goods companies, as historically they based design on technical specifications related to performance of the device and did not know if hazardous substances were present.
- The above is exacerbated because North American companies now leverage a complex web of suppliers (sometimes numbering thousands) that are geographically dispersed. In many cases, the shift in manufacturing has created a "chain of uncertainty" related to product composition.
- Climate change issues are no longer limited to periodic reporting of emissions related to operations. Business must take into consideration climate change/GHG emissions when designing new products and processes—a complex activity that can have significant implications on all aspects of the supply chain.

A detailed discussion of "green procurement" within a collaborative framework is presented in chapter 5.

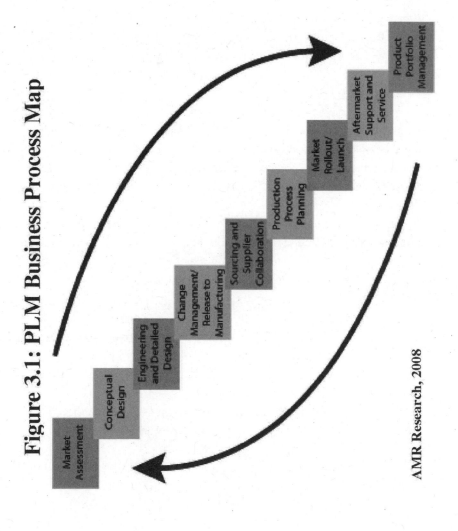

Figure 3.1: PLM Business Process Map

Market Assessment

Conceptual Design

Engineering and Detailed Design

Change Management/ Release to Manufacturing

Sourcing and Supplier Collaboration

Production Process Planning

Market Rollout/ Launch

Aftermarket Support and Service

Product Portfolio Management

AMR Research, 2008

FUNDAMENTALS OF ECO-DESIGN

Successful new products are the lifeblood of a company's growth and profitability. The success of 60% of most new products is determined in the product development phase, as are 80% of costs and 90% of regulatory risks. Supplier collaboration early on can improve a product's capabilities, as well as minimize costs and time to market.[4] Given these values, it is surprising to learn that according to a study by Dr. Robert Cooper, the developer of the stage-gate product development process, 1.2% of product development funds were spent on preliminary market studies and 0.8% on detailed market studies, compared to nearly 30% on the detailed development stage.[5]

Figure 3.2 presents two approaches to product design. The emergence of complex legislation, increased customer requirements and reduced product life cycles are forcing companies to shift to a best practice approach in order to meet market requirements. Most companies, however, have still not developed a systematic, repeatable process that efficiently addresses the complex challenges of global legislation.

The four different levels of eco-design are best described by Charter and Chick's model presented below. The model allows companies to migrate from historical end-of-pipe controls to achieving major environmental benefits in the fourth level, "re-think," and thus generate true breakthrough.[6]

1. "Re-pair" stage—focus is on end-of-pipe solutions
2. "Re-fine" stage—existing processes and products are improved through the implementation of the concept of eco-efficiency
3. "Re-design" stage—existing products are re-designed to incorporate environmental factors
4. "Re-think" stage—significant leaps in thinking are needed, driven by an emphasis on problem solving and opportunity seeking

For any real environmental improvement, the levels of "re-design" and "re-think" must be reached. For the third level, "re-design," product-specific knowledge relating to its environmental impact is needed. The fourth-level, "re-think," calls for new product innovation, which might be another way to provide the function, or a realization that the function is no longer required. The development for re-design needs to be managed differently than projects aiming for re-pair and re-fine. Radical innovation is usually needed and therefore a process specific to managing radical innovation is required.[7]

Figure 3.2: Two Approaches to Product Design

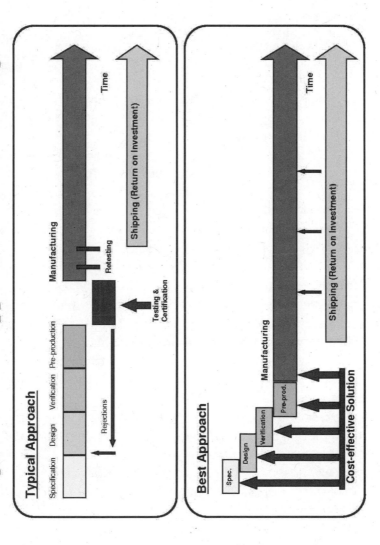

> **During each of the above steps, consider the following simple motto:**
> **"Eliminate hazardous chemicals and wastage of any type."**
>
> The word "wastage" refers to *all* waste—packaging material, material being sent to landfill/hazardous treatment facilities, emissions into the air, discharges into water courses, consumption of natural resources, inefficient use of electricity, etc. VPs of Supply Chain are starting to call themselves "VP of Lean and Waste Removal" as they focus on wastage.

Based upon our review of market conditions, the following realities should be considered when assessing the modification of an existing product/process or design of a new product/process.

- Government legislation—Governments will continue to pass more stringent and complex environmental legislation. Companies therefore need to be aware of draft legislation and influence it where appropriate, in some cases creating a competitive advantage. For very large expenditures, companies need to assess the risks and impact of future government legislation (e.g., cap-and-trade program) via scenarios.
- Green niche—Companies have to be careful about focusing on only "green" product(s) and thus niche markets. Instead, they should define what green or sustainability means to them, then create the connection from those values to the mainstream market.
- Cost and safety—Consumers care about the environment; however, they can also be very price conscious and care deeply about the safety of their family.
- Oil prices—The price of oil will continue to fluctuate in the short term and rise in the long term as we approach peak oil (when production cannot meet demand) and consumerism increases in China and India.
- Electricity prices—Rates will continue to increase over the long term, especially for those regions that are relying on natural gas or coal (if carbon sequestration is required).
- Hazardous ingredients—It is no longer acceptable to be unaware of possible hazardous substances in your product because it is manufactured by third parties overseas. Companies are responsible for knowing the composition of their products, and the market (and in California, the courts) will significantly penalize those that do not.

- Green buildings—The adaptation of green buildings is being driven by reduced operating costs and increasing government action (especially at the state and city level).
- Technological disruptions—Technological disruptions in the environmental area are allowing companies to jump ahead and gain market advantage.

The following quote from Benjamin Heineman, Jr., former GE senior vice president of law and public affairs, highlights the role of legislation in setting a competitive landscape. "Indeed, law and regulation, ironically, can be market enhancing because then all regulated entities face the same obligation under the law and the smartest [corporation] will find a way to comply completely with imagination and less cost."[8]

An example of new stringent government legislation is the EU REACH legislation. Prior to 1981, stringent health and safety tests were not required before a chemical was put on the EU market. The end result is that there are approximately one hundred thousand substances being used in the EU that have not been screened and in many cases there is limited information on their associated hazards. The REACH legislation requires companies that manufacture or import substances that have not been screened and are present in quantities over one tonne per year to register these substances and submit health and safety information. This legislation is expected to cost industry approximately €12.8 billion[9] and was originally anticipated to address thirty thousand substances; however, over one hundred and fifty thousand substances have been pre-registered to date.[10] (Additional information on REACH can be found in appendix A.)

Types of Eco-design Processes

Eco-design processes can be classified into five different categories:

1. analysis of environmental strengths and weakness of products/services
   - life cycle assessments (LCAs)
   - review of regulatory requirements
2. setting priorities and selecting the most important potential improvements
3. providing assistance for design, brainstorming and specifying the details of the proposed products

4. coordination with other important criteria: cost-benefit analysis, economic feasibility studies, etc.
5. collaborative processes that incorporate the customer in building sustainable products

At the end of the chapter, the following additional information is presented:
Table 3.1 (p. 140)—a list of typical tools used in the eco-design process
Table 3.2 (p. 142)—examples of eco-design questions
Table 3.3 (p. 143)—additional sources of information related to eco-design

The eco-design processes presented range from classical—Life Cycle Analysis, Eco-efficiency, Product-oriented Environmental Managements Systems (PO-EMS) and Principles of Green Chemistry to newer approaches like Eco-innovation, Lean Six Sigma and C2C/Green Chemistry. In the latter, C2C is considered the destination whereas Green Chemistry is the "tool box" that facilitates cyclic or sustainable manufacturing systems like C2C.

The checklist in table 3.2 is an important starting point to automating the assessment of key design elements related to environmental issues and should be refined to address the unique attributes of the products being designed.

Examples of a new collaborative process that allows companies to address sustainability issues in design are General Electric's "Dreaming Sessions," at which customers are invited to discuss with senior GE executives the market trends they expect to see over the next five or ten years. Since 2005, GE has been using these sessions to help prioritize R&D project spending. Jeff Immelt, CEO of GE, provides an example of a Dreaming Session at work in the following quote: "We had the railroad CEOs in with their operating people. We spent half a day, grounding ourselves on where the industry is, where we are, what their trends are, and then said, 'Okay, here are some things to think about: higher fuel, more West-East shipments because of imports from China.' And then we'll ask, 'If you had $200 million to $400 million to spend on R&D at GE, how would you prioritize it?'"[11]

GE's approach revolves around picking winners (>$100 million of incremental revenue)—determining the areas where the company should be making major investments so as to have big, new businesses in the near future. Once a project is selected, the best people are assigned and every penny is funded. GE business leaders have no choice but to participate and fund the projects.[12]

Certification

Certification is playing a greater role in substantiating claims about products'/ services' environmental performance. Examples of key certifications programs that may affect eco-design include

- International Organization for Standardization (ISO)
  - 14006 environmental management systems—guidelines on eco-design
  - 14025 environmental labels and declarations—Type III environmental declarations—principles and procedures
  - 14040, 14044, 14047, 14049 life cycle assessment—principles and framework, requirements and guidelines, as well as examples
  - 14062 environmental management—integrating environmental aspects into product design and development
  - 14064 & 14065 greenhouse gases—GHG emissions, accounting, reporting and validation/verification for use in accreditation
  - 17050 (ISO/IEC) conformity assessment—supplier's declaration of conformity
- Ecma International, a European association for standardizing information and communication systems
  - ECMA-341 environmental design considerations for ICT (information communication technology) and CE (consumer electronics) products
- Leadership in Energy and Environmental Design (LEED) Green Building Rating System

The LEED rating system encourages the adoption of sustainable green building development through the implementation of standard tools and performance criteria. Key attributes of LEED[13] include

- third-party certification for the nationally accepted benchmark for the design, construction and operation of high-performance green buildings
- a whole-building approach to sustainability by recognizing performance in five key areas of human and environmental health: sustainable site development, water savings, energy efficiency, materials selection and indoor environmental quality
- architects, real estate professionals, facility managers, engineers, interior designers, landscape architects, construction managers, lenders and

government officials who all use LEED to help transform the built environment to reach sustainability
- state/provincial and local governments across North America that are adopting LEED for public-owned and public-funded buildings

Also, see chapter 4 for additional information on labeling requirements.

Eco-design/PLM Software

Three key trends are triggering a growing demand for PLM and supply chain software:

- increases in the amount, complexity and enforcement of global legislation
- recognition by companies that the presence of hazardous ingredients in a product (regardless of legislation) may significantly damage their brand
- enterprise resource planning (ERP) software becoming the backbone of organizations' IT systems, allowing orders to be processed quickly and low inventories to be maintained

It is no longer possible for a multinational company to ensure compliance using manual systems. They require software, commercially purchased or in-house, that is seamlessly linked to the ERP and addresses the full life cycle of a product, including complex supply chains. The typical rule of thumb is that if a commercial system addresses more than 70% of a company's business requirements it is more cost effective to purchase it than to develop it in-house—especially given changing regulatory requirements.

PLM software assists businesses to maximize profit by optimizing every stage of a product's life, from portfolio management to product development to ongoing maintenance and retirement. Properly leveraged, it integrates product information from design and engineering with sourcing, compliance, suppliers and supply chains to speed product development, ensure quality and mitigate regulatory risks. The software will, as put forward by PLM software vendors,[14]

- improve product innovation
- drive revenue growth with successful new product introductions
- incrementally boost new product profitability

- substantially reduce time to market
- significantly improve on-time product launches

When assessing PLM and supply chain software, there are three important aspects:

1. Integration—The software must ensure a seamless flow of data between various business systems, ensuring both timely update and quality of the data.
2. Collaboration—The software must promote collaboration between customers, suppliers and/or partners to shorten time to market, reduce costs, improve quality, ensure compliance and increase innovation.
3. Content—The software must be easy to update with new content (data, rules, multilingual phrases) that reflects changing regulatory and customer requirements. Refer to figure 3.3 for general requirements.

(Chapter 2 provides additional information on the need to leverage IT solutions to ensure ongoing compliance and cost efficiencies.)

THE ROLE OF GOVERNMENT

The number of requirements imposed by legislation and, more recently, customers, is overwhelming. As noted in chapter 2, companies need to actively track the evolution of legislation affecting their industry as part of their basic management systems. Figure 3.3 illustrates some of these requirements related to PLM once the composition and "use" of a product is known.

The direct impact of legislation on industry is substantial. Examples of new legislation that will significantly impact design of product include the EU REACH legislation, U.S. fuel economy legislation, the EU Eco-design Directive and proposed Canadian legislation on nanotechnology risks. Appendix A presents information on this legislation, as well as others related to eco-design and green procurement.

It is important to note that companies selling their goods globally must comply with the legislation in the countries where they manufacture, as well as the countries to which they are exporting. The days of putting a product on the market that only complies to U.S. legislation with supporting documentation in English and then shipping it around the world are well behind us.

Additional discussion of green procurement is presented in chapter 5.

Figure 3.3: Key Requirements Related to PLM

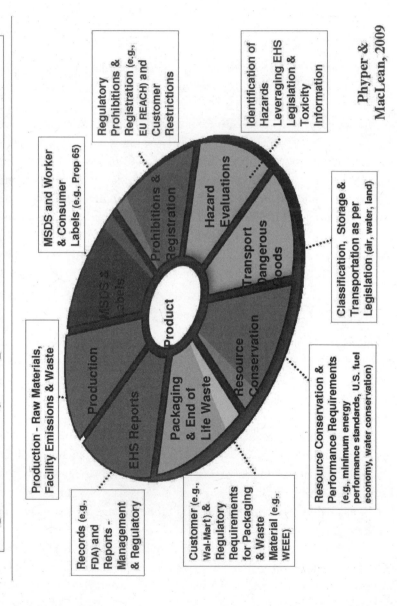

Production - Raw Materials, Facility Emissions & Waste

MSDS and Worker & Consumer Labels (e.g., Prop 65)

Regulatory Prohibitions & Registration (e.g., EU REACH) and Customer Restrictions

Identification of Hazards Leveraging EHS Legislation & Toxicity Information

Records (e.g., FDA) and Reports - Management & Regulatory

Customer (e.g., Wal-Mart) & Regulatory Requirements for Packaging & Waste Material (e.g., WEEE)

Resource Conservation & Performance Requirements (e.g., minimum energy performance standards, U.S. fuel economy, water conservation)

Classification, Storage & Transportation as per Legislation (air, water, land)

Phyper & MacLean, 2009

ADAPT OR DIE

Notable sectors in which environmental issues are driving significant product re-design include the following:

- automotive—reduced tailpipe emissions, improved fuel efficiency, use of alternative fuels, infrastructure for alternative fuels and end-of-life requirements; batteries and fuel cells must be safe, efficient, durable, long-lasting and affordable
- consumer goods—energy efficiency (including improved insulation for appliances), reduction and substitution of toxic ingredients, sustainability of raw materials, and take-back
- biotechnology—seeds for drought-resistant crops, bioplastics, high-yield plants for biofuel and generation of hydrogen from plants
- printing industry—non-toxic inks, recycled fiber content of paper, sustainable forest practices, alternative paper derived from waste material, and, most importantly, the advent of digital media
- buildings—energy and water conservation, non-hazardous/recyclable materials (building material and furniture) and reduction in greenhouse gas (GHG) emissions
- IT hardware—absence of toxic chemicals, recyclable components, energy efficiency and—in the case of server farms—relocation to an area where power is "cheapest and cleanest"

In the following section, brief descriptions of the challenges related to environmental issues faced by companies in these sectors are presented along with the new green opportunities that are emerging.

Automotive

Currently there are approximately 625 million cars and vehicles on the roads globally.[15] In 2008, global sales of cars and other light vehicles will hit 70 million vehicles and within a decade, as India and China embrace the automobile culture, sales will soar to more than 91 million vehicles.[16]

North American consumers want safe, affordable vehicles with a bit of pep that can carry the entire family along with some luggage. Historically, the design focus has been on the gradual reduction of emissions—vehicles produced today are twelve times cleaner than those produced in 1993 and thirty-seven times cleaner than cars produced in 1987. Most of the automotive sector is currently focusing on challenges associated with meeting the exploding consumer demand for fuel efficient and environmentally friendly vehicles as well as the increasingly stringent fuel economy and emission regulations throughout the world. Automakers who have successfully positioned themselves as stewards of the environment, as "innovators in the battle against climate change," have won market share and increased profits.[17]

Ray Lane, a Kleiner Perkins managing partner and chairman of Th!nk North America, best describes the current status of the industry: "The transportation industry is undergoing its largest transformation since Henry Ford built the Model T. Today we are witnessing a seminal event—the first highway-capable electric vehicle intended for mass production, representing a big step toward a zero-emission transportation industry."

Besides responding to the 2008 economic downturn (and in some cases survival of the company), automakers are also faced with critical decisions on what type of engine they should invest in to address changing market requirements—cleaner internal combustion engine, fuel cell or battery technology. Note that fuel cells are different from batteries in that they consume reactant, which must be replenished, whereas batteries store electrical energy chemically in a closed system. Table 3.4 (p. 144) presents a brief overview of the different types of vehicles in the market today and their environmental impact. (Biofuels are discussed in detail in chapter 6.)

Hydrogen Vehicles

Vehicles running on hydrogen fuel cells have been touted as the next great savior of the auto industry and the planet. There exist several significant hurdles that must be overcome before commercialization can occur: the high cost of producing hydrogen (fuel used in cells); infrastructure requirements to distribute hydrogen; cost of fuel cells; and difficulty in storing hydrogen. In addition, hydrogen gas is primarily generated using natural gas as a starting point—a nonrenewable resource whose price may increase substantially.

Currently there are approximately thirty-six hydrogen fueling stations in the U.S. and two-thirds of them are in California. The National Hydrogen Association has estimated that an investment of $10–$15 billion would be required to ensure that the nearest hydrogen station is within 2 miles of 70% of Americans.[18] This figure may be overly optimistic as Royal Dutch Shell, which created a Shell

Hydrogen subsidiary in 1999, has estimated the cost of supplying 2% of American cars with hydrogen by 2020 at around $20 billion. In a publication entitled *How Hydrogen Can Save America,* it is estimated that the switch to a hydrogen economy will cost $100 billion. The current push of the California Fuel Cell partnership is to start small—e.g., forty stations in the Los Angeles area, putting the majority of individuals within five minutes of a hydrogen source.

Electric Vehicles (EVs)

EVs are not new and, over the years, their feasibility has been greatly influenced by legislation, in particular the U.S. 1990 Clean Air Act Amendment, the U.S. 1992 Energy Policy Act, and regulations issued by the California Air Resources Board (CARB), which are stringent air emissions regulations and Zero Emission Vehicle (ZEV) requirements. In 2001, the CARB modified the ZEV mandate to allow manufacturers to claim partial ZEV credit for hybrid vehicles. In response to a lawsuit brought by automakers, CARB removed the requirement for electric vehicles from the ZEV mandate in 2003.

Table 3.5 (p. 145) presents an overview of the history of EVs. Following modification of U.S. legislation in 2001, expenditures on EVs were reduced considerably and some manufacturers cancelled their projects entirely, e.g., GM EV1 and Ford Th!nk EV.

In January 2007, GM surprised the world by introducing its new extended-range electric car, the Chevrolet Volt, at the Detroit auto show. The sedan will require six hours to charge and run for 40 miles (64 kilometers) before a small gasoline engine fires up to extend the range to 600 miles (965 kilometers).[19] The forecasted price is approaching $40,000 with a significant portion—$10,000—related to the battery. The car will be ready in the fall of 2010 (2011 model year), with a first production run of only ten thousand vehicles. GM Vice Chairman Bob Lutz has commented that the Volt is GM's "moon shot", i.e., failure wouldn't kill the company, but success would "be sensational and…have the same sort of symbolism" as Neil Armstrong's giant leap for mankind nearly forty years ago.[20]

Nissan, Chrysler, Mitsubishi and Renault-Nissan also announced in 2008 that they would start selling an EV by 2010. Ford has advised that its target for an electric vehicle is 2012.[21] Add this to several well-backed electric vehicle start-ups (Tesla Motors, Th!nk and Project Better Place—all cases studies at the end of this chapter) and you have a true disruption in the market.

Hybrid/Hybrid Plug-ins

The change in California legislation in the 1990s accelerated the race for hybrids. The Toyota Prius was the first mass-produced hybrid vehicle sold. It went on sale in Japan in 1997 and was introduced worldwide in 2001. By 2005 it allowed Toyota to pull ahead of other automakers and establish itself as the poster boy for the environmental movement. In May 2008, worldwide cumulative sales of the Toyota Prius passed 1 million. Toyota had six hybrids on the market in the U.S. The company plans to lease a limited number of plug-in hybrids by 2010 and put its gasoline-electric hybrid system into more models globally.

Almost all major automakers are currently producing hybrid: Toyota, General Motors, Ford, Honda, Nissan, Volkswagen and BMW. Chrysler recently dropped its hybrid sport-utility vehicles due to a decline in fuel prices and poor sales. The number of offerings varies significantly among the automakers as several (e.g., Mercedes-Benz, BMW and Volkswagen) have chosen to focus on clean diesel.

In terms of plug-in hybrids, several companies have announced vehicle releases in 2009/2010. Honda is bucking this trend as demonstrated by the following statement by its president and CEO, Takeo Fukui: "My feeling is that the kind of plug-in hybrid currently proposed by different auto makers can be best described as a battery electric vehicle equipped with an unnecessary fuel engine and fuel tank. . . . I'm not sure what kind of real advantages they [plug-ins] would have. . . . I don't think that [plug-ins] will contribute to the global environment or to reducing carbon dioxide."[22]

Two other front-runners—clean diesel and mixed fuel (biofuel and gasoline or diesel)—are also important. The first is a modification of existing engines. The latter is discussed in detail in chapter 6.

Government role—Governments around the world are tightening fuel economy standards. The United States Corporate Average Fuel Economy (CAFE) Standard is 27.5 miles per gallon (mpg) for cars and 23.1 mpg for light trucks (starts in 2009) and will be raised to 35 mpg (cars and light trucks) in 2020. This initiative was stalled under President Bush but was quickly moved forward by President Obama. California will require 35.7 mpg by 2016 and 42.5 mpg by 2020 (fifteen other states are putting forward similar legislation). Of important note is that China currently requires 43 mpg and EU currently requires 40 mpg and will move to 48.9 by 2012. Additional information on mileage standards around the world is presented in appendix A.

Figure 3.4: Sustainable Product Design - Automotive

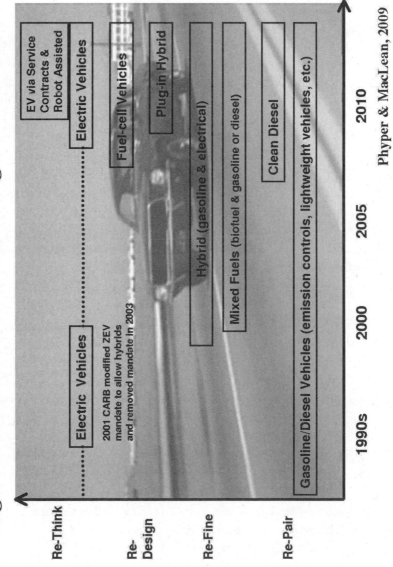

Phyper & MacLean, 2009

The U.S. government has put in place a $25 billion direct-loan program in its 2007 energy law to offset automakers' plant and technology costs to make more fuel-efficient cars. Industry has argued that the loans are not a bailout but will allow them to meet the energy bill's fuel-economy mandate for their fleets to average 35 mpg by 2020. The industry has estimated the cost of the leap needed to meet the standard at $85 billion to $100 billion.[23]

The Future—Figure 3.4 presents an overview of the status of the automobile sector vis-à-vis the concepts of sustainable product design presented earlier in the chapter. The race is definitely on regarding which technology or technologies will emerge to lead the market and thereby influence a $5 to $10 trillion global industry.

Are conventional gasoline cars dead? No, especially not in India and China. In China, approximately seventeen thousand private vehicles are being added daily, while in India passenger vehicle sales are expected to rise by almost 50% over the next three years. In India, Tata Motors' new Nano was designed to bring automotive transportation to the mainstream Indian population. It has a price tag in the US$2,500–$3,000 range and an initial production run of two hundred and fifty thousand cars a year. The car is expected to meet safety standards and pollute even less than motorcycles, passing domestic and European emission standards and averaging about 50 mpg (20 kilometers per liter).

It is interesting to note that the price of gasoline and fuel economy standards will continue to play a critical role in the rate of substitution of conventional gasoline engines with the alternatives listed in figure 3.4. However, a critical review of historical market penetration of transportation systems conducted by Hollinshead, Eastman and Etsell indicates that for real market penetration to occur two things are required: avoided costs and systems efficiencies, examples of which include[24]

- a reduction in air pollution, especially in rapidly growing megacities (*The Economist* has estimated that air pollution costs China the equivalent of 7% of GNP in workdays lost, lives lost and health-care expenditures)
- digitally controlled vehicles that could be slaved in the manner of diesel-electric locomotives and run in high-speed trains with zero head space between vehicles, thereby avoiding the enormously expensive expansion of road infrastructure

- fuel cells that could be used to generate electricity during off-hours (whether in the vehicle, at home or at local stations—analogous to gas stations—especially with new quick-charge technology); several large utilities have already endorsed the concept of distributed generation as it would allow them to avoid the costs of new centralized power plants

Consumer Goods

The number of consumer products in the marketplace has increased substantially over the last ten years, while the average lifespan of a product—especially an electronic one—has decreased. In order to ensure protection of brand and that products are not recalled or held in customs, designers must

- ensure that all hazardous substances present in the product are known and assessed in terms of toxicity, regulatory requirements for "desired" markets (not just North America) and retailer requirements (e.g., Wal-Mart); it also may be appropriate to assess if the substance is on an NGO toxics list (e.g. EU NGO "SIN" list)
- ensure that natural resources used in a product (fisheries, agriculture, forestry, etc.) are sustainable and in many cases certified
- ensure that the product addresses minimum energy performance standards, or water or recycled content, as stipulated in legislation for desired markets
- address both regulatory and retailer requirements related to packaging material and packaging waste
- assess additional direct and indirect costs related to environmental issues, e.g., levies related to take-back and recycling, i.e., extended producer responsibility requirements
- ensure that suppliers involved in the creation of the product understand the regulatory/retailer requirements as well as the need to minimize environmental impact during the production of the product; refer to chapter 5 for additional discussion

In 2003, Greenpeace launched the "Chemical Home" database—a portion of its website devoted to identifying hazardous substances present in household products. The aims of the site[25] were to

- provide information to consumers about the hazardous substances that may be present in consumer products
- encourage manufacturers to give more priority to substituting hazardous substances with safer alternatives
- show that the substitution of hazardous substances is possible by high-lighting companies who were able to substitute for toxic ingredients

Negative publicity on this site resulted in several companies changing the composition of their products. The site was closed as Greenpeace shifted its toxic campaign to focus on the electronics sector to improve its record on chemicals and waste and drafting of EU REACH legislation. A report entitled *Cleaning up Our Chemical Homes: Changing the Market to Supply Toxic-Free Products* provides an overview of the findings of the Chemical Home database. The report indicates that the biggest factor motivating companies to substitute hazardous substances with safer alternatives was increased customer confidence. This was followed by the benefits of being seen as a market leader. A company's core values and ethos, such as commitment to the "precautionary" principle, were also a major consideration for some.[26]

Table 3.6 (p. 146) presents examples of environmental demands on products through pressure from consumers or NGOs, through new or proposed legislation, or through a change in or implementation of company core values and ethos. The substitution of hazardous substances in many cases is not easy as they play a key role in the overall performance of the product.

The following case studies provide information on how consumer product companies and department stores are responding: Wal-Mart and Ecolab in chapter 2, Nike in chapter 3, and Unilever and Mattel in chapter 5.

Biotechnology

The UN Convention on Biological Diversity defines biotechnology as any technological application that uses biological systems, living organisms, or their derivatives, to make or modify products or processes for specific use. Biotechnology has applications in four major industrial areas: health care/medical—sometimes called "red biotechnology"; crop production and agriculture—called "green biotechnology"; non-food (industrial) uses of crops and other products (e.g., biodegradable plastics, biofuels); and environmental uses. The latter two fall into a category sometimes called "white biotechnology." Additional information on biofuels is presented in chapter 6.

One key component of green biotechnology is the design of transgenic plants to grow under specific environmental conditions or in the presence (or absence) of certain agricultural chemicals. An example of this is the engineering of a plant to express a pesticide, thereby eliminating the need for external application of pesticides. An example of this is Bt corn.[27]

The global market for biotech crops in 2007 was $6.9 billion, up 11.5% over 2006. The number of countries planting biotech crops has grown from twenty-one in 2005 to twenty-three in 2007, and includes eight EU countries. The U.S. leads with 142.6 million acres of biotech crops, followed by Argentina and Brazil (47.2 and 37.1 million acres, respectively). The North American corn market is the largest biotech crop market. The higher demand for food crops and limited availability of arable land has heightened the need for increased crop yield and productivity via biotech crops.[28]

Whether or not green biotechnology products are ultimately more environmentally friendly is a topic of considerable debate, especially in Europe where genetically modified (GM) foods and genetically modified organisms (GMOs) are the subject of significant public debate. As indicated in appendix A, the EU has passed legislation governing GMOs that requires risk assessments to be conducted prior to their introduction to the marketplace and stringent labeling to be in place. The legislation also requires all foods containing GM to be labeled accordingly.

White biotechnology, also known as industrial biotechnology, is applied to industrial processes. An example is the design of an organism to produce a useful chemical. Another example is the use of enzymes as industrial catalysts to either produce valuable chemicals or destroy hazardous/polluting chemicals. White biotechnology consumes fewer resources than traditional processes used to produce industrial goods.[29]

Bioplastics is a rapidly growing market that includes vegetable packaging, foil packaging, tire components, biodegradable mulch foils, organic waste bags and biodegradable foils for diapers. A recent report by Helmut Kaiser Consultancy described the bioplastics market as worth 10%–15%, approximately $1 billion, of the total plastics market, which will grow to 25%–30%, approximately $20 billion, by 2020.[30] Jefferies Equity Research 2008 *Cleantech Primer* report estimates that bio-based plastics will account for 11% of the total plastics market in 2009 and 26% in 2013.[31] It is important to note that several issues have emerged: use of GM crops as feedstock; competition with food crops; and when they end up in landfill sites, they degrade without oxygen, releasing methane.

Drinking Water

Water is being called the "blue gold" of the twenty-first century. Thanks to increasing urbanization and population, shifting climates and industrial pollution, fresh water is becoming humanity's most precious resource.[32] More than 1 billion people—one-sixth of the world's population—are without access to a safe water supply. At any given moment, about half of the world's poor are suffering from waterborne diseases, of which more than six thousand—mainly children—die each day by consuming unsafe drinking water. Safe water interventions have vast potential to transform the lives of millions, especially in crucial areas such as poverty eradication, environmental degradation, quality of life, child development and gender equality.[33]

The water industry is broadly defined to include water utilities, desalination companies, water treatment, and companies that manufacture and install pipes, pumps, filters, membranes and turnkey systems. This definition has been expanded in recent years to include infrastructure components, industrial water treatment and agriculture-related products and services (both micro irrigation and more water-efficient crops).[34] The Cleantech Group is predicting that the market for water purification and desalinization will reach $95 billion by 2012.[35]

Consumer costs for water vary widely, mostly due to government subsidies: in the U.S. the average cost is $0.66/m^3$; in Germany, it can be as high as $2.25/m^3$; and in Japan, high-volume users pay more than $3/m^3$. At the opposite end of the scale is California, where farmers use roughly 20% of the state's water and pay only $0.01/m^3$ versus the $0.50–$0.60/m^3$ that consumers pay in Los Angeles.[36]

More and more companies are assessing their water usage from a broader perspective:

- clarifying water risk factors (both the presence of contaminants as well as availability)
- documenting water use and efficiency, water scarcity and community partnerships and putting in place systems to report water usage/conservation
- understanding the business opportunities in improved water stewardship
- applying best management practices to improve water stewardship

Estimates of worldwide bottled water sales are between $50 and $100 billion each year, with the market expanding at the startling annual rate of 7%.[37] Today, one in two Americans drink bottled water while one in six drinks it exclusively. Good marketing has fueled this growth by creating the perception in consumers' minds that bottled water is better than tap water in three ways: it is healthier (i.e., based on purity, perceived health benefits), better tasting and more convenient.[38] In fact, in many developed countries, the standards for both tap and bottled water are the same and hence there is no difference in impact on health.

The National Resource Defense Council (NRDC) and other NGOs are pushing for strict requirements for bottled water safety (including limits on phthalates), labeling, and public disclosure.[39] NGOs also consider bottled water detrimental to the environment (e.g., higher use of fuels to bottle and transport water) and, potentially, municipal supplies (e.g., may divert consumer interest and investment away from public water systems, unsustainable pumping of local aquifers). Brands are facing negative impact as recent anti-bottled water campaigns start to ramp up.[40] Several school districts, universities and cities have banned or are in the process of banning bottled water, setting up "bottle-free zones."[41]

Printing and Publishing Sector

Printing and publishing has undergone dramatic changes over the last twenty years. Historically, the focus was on controlling emissions from printing presses and minimizing worker exposure (refer to figure 3.5). In the late nineties, printers started to pressure ink suppliers to reduce the volatile organic carbon (VOC) composition of their products. This was followed by a renewed interest in both the source of the paper (new growth versus old growth forests), as well as the recycled fiber content. The debate relating to the source of paper shifted forest management practices and the need to use sources that have third-party certification of sustainable forestry management schemes.

Some publishers have assumed leadership positions in the move toward policies related to procurement of more sustainable fiber for books, even forming partnerships with NGOs representing forest protection interests. Transcontinental, a Montreal-based printing and publishing company, and Chapters Indigo, the leading retailer of books in Canada, are but two examples. At the request of Markets Initiative, a leading environmental publishing advocate whose mission is to shift the paper consumption patterns of industry to sustainable options, Transcontinental adopted a paper procurement policy in 2007 that favors recycled fiber and the best in forest management practices. Chapters Indigo CEO Heather Reisman is helping to champion the cause in the Canadian retail book industry by setting similar targets for recycled fiber content and forest management practices.

There are numerous forest certification standards worldwide. Prominent certification standards are:

Figure 3.5: Sustainable Product Design - Printing Sector

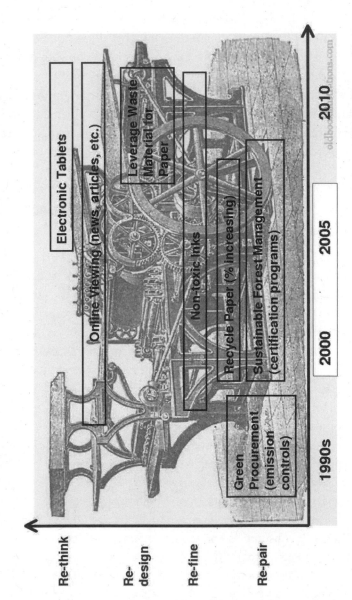

Re-think

Re-design

Re-fine

Re-pair

Electronic Tablets

Online Viewing (news, articles, etc.)

Leverage Waste Material for Paper

Non-toxic Inks

Recycle Paper (% increasing)

Sustainable Forest Management (certification programs)

Green Procurement (emission controls)

1990s   2000   2005   2010

Phyper & MacLean, 2009

- Forest Stewardship Council (FSC)
- Sustainable Forestry Initiative (SFI)
- Sustainable Forest Management standard (Canadian Standards Association)
- Programme for the Endorsement of Forest Certification schemes (PEFC)

Additional changes hitting this sector include

- rise in operating costs due to the prices of natural gas (used to fire VOC oxidizers) and petrochemicals (in solvents)
- extended producer responsibility (in the form of government levies to cover the costs of recycling paper)
- pressure from ethical customers to use paper that is derived from waste material
- online viewing of publications (e.g., recent elimination of catalogues by several large retail chains)
- use of inks made from vegetable oil
- electronic tablets
- emergence of substitutes for conventional paper (e.g., paper made from other types of biomass or from rock powder)

Even though electronic formats for reading have become more readily available, 82% of Americans still prefer to read printed books, according to a recent Random House/Zogby poll. But the survey, which explores the country's reading and book-buying habits, also found that 13% of respondents younger than thirty were open to reading a book online or were already an e-book reader, compared with just 6% of those age sixty-five or older—a potential trend in the future.[42]

This survey notwithstanding, newspaper readership in the west has been in decline in recent years, forcing large media companies to develop and market alternative platforms for their advertisers. Steve Ballmer, CEO of Microsoft, during his conversation with *Washington Post* editors on June 5, 2008, said, "In the next ten years, the whole world of media, communications and advertising is going to be turned upside-down—my opinion. Here are the premises I have. No. 1, there will be no media consumption left in ten years that is not delivered over an IP network. There will be no newspapers, no magazines that are delivered in paper form. Everything gets delivered in an electronic form."[43]

Green Buildings

The green building industry, which has had a fairly strong presence in Europe for two decades, has quickly become worth more than $12 billion in the U.S., according to Green Economy, a Boston-based consultancy. Estimates put forward indicate that green buildings that incorporate energy-efficient and sustainable technologies represent 5%–7% of new commercial building and are predicted to reach at least 10% by 2010.[44]

In 2006, the World Business Council for Sustainable Development (WBCSD) concluded that the cost of building green is not much higher than the cost of building a conventional building—the report estimates the cost differential to be about 5% more versus the perceived 17% in the building industry worldwide. The energy savings that result from building sustainably will help offset some of the initial higher costs—energy efficiency can be increased by up to 35% and heating costs reduced by 80% for the average building, thereby decreasing recurring costs and carbon dioxide emissions considerably.[45]

An example of the adaptation of green buildings is GE Real Estate's commitment, in partnership with the Clinton Climate Initiative, that it will "green" all of its operations, which comprise $72 billion worth of assets and 385 million square feet of property in thirty-one countries.[46]

The LEED Green Building Rating System is a third-party certification program and a widely accepted benchmark for the design, construction and operation of high-performance green buildings. It promotes a whole-building approach to sustainability by recognizing performance in five key areas of human and environmental health: sustainable site development, water savings, energy efficiency, materials selection and indoor environmental quality.[47]

In 2008, there were 850 LEED-certified buildings in the U.S. and more than 6,500 under construction. The Bank of America's headquarters incorporate a range of green technologies and will be the first LEED platinum (>80% score) skyscraper in the U.S. The building is expected to use half as much electricity and potable water as traditional-build commercial office buildings. Two-thirds of the structure's annual energy will be produced on-site.[48]

In addition to overall green building, building materials are gaining significant attention. One of the key areas of research is carbon-neutral cement. Current cement manufacturing processes 5% of the world's CO_2 emissions and work is underway to significantly reduce this via modifications in the process and in some cases use of emissions from coal-fired power plants.

IT Hardware

Two key issues emerge when discussing IT hardware: the presence of toxic chemicals and energy consumption.

Toxic Chemicals

Electronics manufacturing is a complicated assembly of hundreds of materials involving potentially significant discharges. Examples of toxic chemicals in computer components include[49]

- lead and cadmium in computer circuit boards
- lead oxide and barium in desktop monitors
- mercury in switches and flat screen monitors
- polyvinyl chloride (PVC) in plastics used in computers
- brominated flame retardants (BFRs) on printed circuit boards, cables and plastic casing

Semiconductor chips, while containing few toxics, require the most resources and toxic chemicals to produce—more than sixty hazardous acids, solvents, caustics and gases go into making chips.[50]

Pressure on the computer industry has resulted in several manufacturers committing to reducing toxics present in their products. Apple, for example, declared a phase-out of the worst chemicals in its product range—PVC and BVRs—by the end of 2008, which is ahead of Dell and other computer manufactures' pledge to phase them out by 2009. Apple has also committed to U.S. customers that they will be able to return their Apple products for recycling; in the EU this is mandatory for all computer manufacturers. However, they are not making this commitment for customers outside the U.S. and EU.[51]

Energy Consumption

Datacenters require a significant amount of power to meet the energy requirements of the latest high-density hardware, which can draw 30 kW or more per rack. In turn, the datacenter housing this rack requires additional air conditioning, which draws even more power. Recent research from analyst firm Forrester has predicted that the global market for green IT will peak at US$4.8 billion in 2013, and then decline thereafter as businesses reach peak efficiency.[52]

The Green Grid was formed to address green IT issues. This is a global consortium dedicated to efficient IT with members including AMD, APC, Dell, HP, IBM, Intel, Microsoft, Sun and VMware. According to Winston Bumpus, a representative of Green Grid, "In 2006, datacenters consumed 1.5 percent of the entire electricity of the US, and we projected that that would grow to 2.5 percent by 2011. That's several power plants worth."[53]

The average desktop PC wastes nearly half of its power. The Green Grid initiative is setting 90% efficiency targets by 2010 for computer power supplies, which if achieved, could reduce greenhouse gas emissions by 54 million tons per year worldwide and save more than $5.5 billion a year in energy costs. According to Pat Gelsinger, senior vice president and general manager of Intel's Digital Enterprise Group, "Ninety percent of desktops don't use power management [software], even though they could. This is not a technology problem. We can build 90% efficient power supplies today. It's really an industry choice and getting that critical mass over the speed bump, making this a volume proposition."[54]

In order to meet these energy efficiency challenges, a series of innovations has developed, centered on hardware, software and datacentre design. Table 3.7 (p. 148) presents information on these initiatives.

In 2007, Google and Intel and dozens of other partners announced a new computing efficiency effort that is complementary to the Green Grid initiative. The Climate Savers Computing Initiative aims to save energy and reduce greenhouse gas emissions by setting new targets for energy-efficient computers and components, and promoting the adoption of energy-efficient computer components and power management software worldwide. This initiative is based on the U.S. EPA ENERGY STAR goals that many manufacturers are already working towards; however, its goal is to solicit wider participation from vendors, the large organizations that buy desktop PCs, and end consumers.[55]

(For additional information on activities being undertaken by the electronics/computer sectors, see the case studies on Sony and Dell located in chapter 5 and the energy conservation activities listed in chapter 6.)

CHAPTER 3 TAKE-AWAYS

The following take-aways are designed to help ensure eco-design criteria are embedded in a company's processes and IT systems.

Adopt a motto of "zero waste"—The elimination of waste is fundamental to reducing costs and improving the environment. As per Paul Tebo, former DuPont vice president for safety, health and the environment, the environmental motto should be "the goal is zero." This needs to be communicated throughout the organization and reinforced by executives so that it becomes part of the organization's culture. See also chapter 8.

Seek good design—Designs that do not take into consideration all key business and consumer requirements will fail! Environment is just one of many considerations. Consumers will not purchase recyclable paper that falls apart as soon as they touch it or results in smudges because it does not soak up ink properly.

It is easy to get caught up in the "re-pair" and "re-fine" mindset, especially when faced with the shortening product life cycles. Designers must be given the freedom to think outside the box, "re-design" and "re-think"—competitors will!

Avoid toxic chemicals—Virtually any material (including water) can become toxic if we are exposed to it in sufficient quantity. Consumer product companies that have products that contain Substances of Very High Concern (SVHC) need to allocate resources into reassessing or reformulating their product. In general, SVHC include carcinogens, mutagens, reproductive (CMR) toxics; persistent, bioaccumulative and toxic (PBT) chemicals; very persistent and very bioaccumulative (vPvB) chemicals; and endocrine disruptors.

EU NGOs have already published their own list of SVHC—the "SIN" list—and will be advising the public of what products contain these substances. Companies failing to act proactively will find themselves with significant negative press and losing market share. The response of "We follow all appropriate legislation..." (which is very common in the U.S.) or "Our experts tell us that the risk is below a de minimis level" are both reasonable legal and scientific responses. The question is, however, will these responses win over Mr./Mrs. Consumer, who are choosing between your product and that of a competitor? If the components of your product do not fall into these categories, it is important to ensure that you have collected sufficient data to back this up. Remember, it is the court of public opinion, and not a scientific review panel, that will judge your company.

Leverage software—It is critical that companies leverage PLM and supply chain software that automates and integrates their eco-design processes. Failure to do this will result in silos of information leading to resource inefficiencies, as well as significant risk of not complying with customer or regulatory requirements.

Devote the right resources to the re-thinking position—Rapid change is occurring in all sectors. Two key forces—fluctuating petroleum prices and climate change—are causing companies to devote time to re-design and re-think their products, and in doing so, introduce new technical disruptors that may dramatically change markets. It is important to ensure that the right people are assigned time to focus on re-thinking and re-designing following a process that allows innovation (allowing them to think outside their cubicle).

Manage the supply chain—Regardless of whether you produce a product at your own facilities or leverage third parties, you need to take steps to avoid the environmental mismanagement in the supply chain that has the potential to affect your bottom line (via increased costs), as well as impair corporate brand. Companies are morphing into sales/marketing organizations that only assemble their finished products and rely on thousands of suppliers to do their manufacturing and, in some cases, design. Clear rules must be set and adherence to these rules monitored on a regular basis (see chapter 5 for additional information on the supply chain).

Put metrics in place—What gets measured gets managed! Hidden costs must be identified and costs related to environmental issues must be consolidated to ensure that the individuals responsible for managing these areas are aware of the costs. For example, the CIO needs to be made aware of the energy costs associated with datacenters. As indicated in chapter 1, the Balance Scorecard is one approach to ensure key metrics are in place.

Table 3.1: Tools Used as Part of Eco-design Processes

Life Cycle Analysis (LCA)	An LCA (also known as life cycle analysis, ecobalance, and cradle-to-grave analysis) is the investigation and valuation of the environmental impacts of a given product or service caused or necessitated by its existence. The goal of LCA is to compare the full range of environmental damages assignable to products and services and identify the least burdensome one. The term life cycle refers to the notion that a fair, holistic assessment requires the assessment of raw material production, manufacture, distribution, use and disposal, including all intervening transportation steps necessary or caused by the product's existence. The sum of all those steps—or phases—is the life cycle of the product.[56]
Eco-efficiency	Eco-efficiency is a management philosophy that aims at minimizing ecological damage while maximizing the efficiency of a firm's production processes through, for example, the reduced use of energy, material and water; more recycling; and the elimination of hazardous emissions or by-products.[57]

Eco-innovation	Eco-innovation is a term used to describe products and processes that contribute to SD. Eco-innovation is the commercial application of knowledge to elicit direct or indirect ecological improvements. It is often used to describe a range of related ideas, from environmentally friendly technological advances to socially acceptable innovative paths toward sustainability.[58]
Product-oriented Environmental Management Systems (POEMS)	POEMS, or environmental product policy (EPP), encompasses three principles: (1) a sustained improvement process of the product's environmental performance; (2) a cross-organization principle—POEMS can be leveraged across corporate services and processes: sales, marketing, procurement, product management, research and development all have a role to play in order to improve the eco-profile of products; and (3) knowledge management—sustained improvement within the context of a strong innovation must be based on capitalization of corporate experiences.
Integrated Product Policy (IPP)	All products cause environmental degradation in some way, whether from their manufacturing, use or disposal. IPP seeks to minimize these by looking at all phases of a product's life cycle and taking action where it is most effective. This process involves many different actors such as designers, industry, marketing people, retailers and consumers. IPP attempts to stimulate each part of these individual phases to improve their environmental performance by leveraging a variety of tools—both voluntary and mandatory—that can be used to achieve this objective. These include measures such as economic instruments, substance bans, voluntary agreements, environmental labeling and product design guidelines.[59]
Lean Six Sigma	Six Sigma refers to the reduction of errors to six standard deviations from the mean value of a process output or task opportunity, i.e., about one error in three hundred thousand opportunities. In modern practice, this terminology has been applied to a quality improvement methodology for industry. Lean Six Sigma for services is a business improvement methodology that maximizes shareholder value by achieving the fastest rate of improvement in customer satisfaction, cost, quality, process speed and invested capital. The fusion of Lean and Six Sigma improvement methods brings the following benefits: lean cannot bring a process under statistical control; Six Sigma alone cannot dramatically improve process speed or reduce invested capital; together, they enable the reduction of the cost of complexity.[60]
Principles of Green Chemistry	The ground-breaking book entitled *Green Chemistry: Theory and Practice* by Paul Anastas and John Warner, published in 1998, addressed alternative feed stocks, environmentally benign syntheses, the design of safer chemical products, new reaction conditions, alternative solvents and catalyst development, and the use of biosynthesis and biomimetic principles. The key concept of green chemistry is that whenever practicable, synthetic methods should be designed to use and generate substances that possess little or no toxicity to human health and the environment. Chemical products should be designed to bring about their desired function while minimizing their toxicity.[61]
Cradle to Cradle & Green Chemistry	Cradle-to-Cradle (C2C) can be defined as a destination and can be distilled down into two principles:[62] • Materials that are not readily degradable, dubbed "technical nutrients," should only be used in products if they can be fully recovered and reused without any environmental release. An example of this type of nutrient system is the recovery of precious metals used for catalytic converters on automobiles. • Products containing biodegradable materials, or "biological nutrients," should be designed to be readily degradable when composted. An example of this type of nutrient system would be biodegradable t-shirt. Green chemistry plays a significant role as it provides a "tool box" that can facilitate cyclic or sustainable manufacturing systems, including C2C.

Table 3.2: Example of an Eco-design Checklist

1. Hazardous Substances
- Has an inventory of all chemicals in product/subcomponents been taken?
- Are all substances in the product registered for the jurisdictions that you want to sell in?
- Are substances prohibited according to local legislation or industrial codes of practice?
- Has a hazard evaluation* been performed and rating assigned?
- If elevated levels of hazard, do you reformulate? If not, what is the market/brand impact?
- If you do not reformulate, what is the impact on the sales of the product?

2. Use of Product by Customer
- Are all downstream uses understood?
- Have restrictions or risk management methods been identified for each use?
- Will these restrictions impose undue burden on the use of the product and hinder sales?

3. Environmental Releases During Product Use
- What type of chemicals will be emitted into the environment (e.g., GHGs, toxic wastewater discharges) during the product life cycle?
- How much of each chemical will be emitted during the product's life cycle?
- Is there additional cost to minimize the releases of chemicals from the product?

4. Resource Consumption by Product During Use
- Does the product comply with energy and water use legislation?
- What is the energy/water usage of finished product in operational mode/standby mode?
- Do the energy/water use requirements ensure ongoing competitive advantage?
- Are there additional costs to comply with energy/water use requirements?

5. Labeling Requirements for Product
- Are there unique labeling requirements imposed by legislation or consumer groups?
- Does the label impact product sales?

6. Packaging of Product
- Does the packaging conform with regulatory and/or industry (e.g., Wal-Mart) requirements?
- Has an assessment of how to reduce packaging material (especially weight) been conducted?

7. EHS Impact During Manufacturing of the Product
- Are sustainable sources of raw material being used?
- What are the key types of emissions (air, water, waste) during production?
- Are systems in place to minimize emissions during production of the product or its subcomponents—especially minimization of wastage of any type?
- What are the energy requirements and sources of energy to create product?
- Do activities include the conservation of water and energy during production?
- Are there additional costs to minimize releases or maximize use of renewable resources?

8. Take-back/End of Life
- Are requirements of pertinent legislation known?
- Is information on recovery (amount/cost) associated with valuable components forecasted?
- Have rules for disassembly-friendly construction been put in place?
- Have plastic compatibility rules been factored into design?
- What are the end-of-life costs?

* A hazard evaluation typically includes an assessment of ingredients against available hazard data (e.g., toxicity, reactivity, corrosivity), regulatory information (e.g., RoHS-prohibited metals, REACH substances of very high concern, California Proposition 65 chemicals, local occupational exposures limits, and more recently EU NGO "SIN" List.)

Table 3.3: Voluntary Initiatives and Partnerships Related to Eco-design

Carnegie Mellon Green Design Institute—The institute is a major interdisciplinary education and research effort whose goal is to make an impact on environmental quality through green design. The central idea of the institute is to form partnerships with companies, government agencies and foundations to develop pioneering design, management, manufacturing and regulatory processes that can improve environmental quality and product quality while enhancing economic development. www.ce.cmu.edu/greendesign

Centre for Sustainable Design (CfSD)—CfSD was established in 1995 within the Faculty of Design at The Surrey Institute of Art & Design, University College, UK. It has achieved an international reputation for high-quality, innovative, leading-edge work. CfSD facilitates discussion and research on eco-design and environmental, economic, ethical and social (e3s) considerations in product and service development and design. This is achieved through training and education, research, seminars, workshops, conferences, consultancy, publications and the Internet. The CfSD also acts as an information clearinghouse for innovative thinking on sustainable products and services. www.cfsd.org.uk

The Green Grid—The Green Grid is a global consortium dedicated to advancing energy efficiency in datacenters and business computing ecosystems. In furtherance of its mission, The Green Grid is focused on the following: defining meaningful, user-centric models and metrics; developing standards, measurement methods, processes and new technologies to improve datacenter performance against the defined metrics; and promoting the adoption of energy efficient standards, processes, measurements and technologies. www.thegreengrid.org

Journal of Sustainable Product Design (JSPD)—The journal covers economic, environmental, ethical and social issues in product design and development. JSPD is a comprehensive quarterly journal guaranteeing high quality both in content and in presentation. It is a pioneering publication that examines sustainability issues as they affect product and service design and development worldwide. JSPD provides a platform for organizations and individuals to discuss new solutions, although not ignoring the complex issues surrounding sustainability. JSPD's international focus enables business decision-makers and academics to monitor trends as they appear and develop on a global scale, from managing eco-design, life cycle assessment and "design for dismantling," to eco-innovation, systems change and dematerialization. The journal balances practical issues as they affect us today, as well as exploring new ideas. JSPD aims to be the focus for a new vision for product and service development and design that integrates eco-efficiency with social responsibility in the delivery of sustainable solutions. www.cfsd.org.uk/journal

EPA ENERGY STAR—ENERGY STAR is a joint program of the U.S. Environmental Protection Agency and the U.S. Department of Energy, helping companies save money and protect the environment through energy-efficient products and practices. www.energystar.gov

Table 3.4: Types of Automobiles

Gas-powered Vehicles	High-tech features designed to increase fuel economy include cylinder deactivation (also called displacement on demand or active cylinder management), direct fuel injection, automatic idle-off (for red lights or idling in traffic), continuously variable transmissions, lightweight materials and emission control devices that dramatically reduce tailpipe emissions.
Flexible-fuel Vehicles (FFVs) or Dual-fuel Vehicles	Automobiles that can typically use different sources of fuel, either mixed in the same tank or with separate tanks and fuel systems for each fuel. A common example is a vehicle that can accept gasoline mixed with varying levels of bioethanol. Some cars carry a natural gas tank that makes it possible to switch back and forth from gasoline to natural gas.
Clean Diesel	New clean diesel vehicles are anticipated to reduce NO_X emissions by up to 90% and deliver fuel economy gains of 30% over a comparable gasoline engine. These engines are also designed to run on biodiesel. A big question is whether the North American uptake of diesel vehicles will match that of Europe, where diesel accounts for about 50% of all passenger car sales.[63]
Hybrids	A hybrid is a vehicle powered by a gasoline engine plus an electric motor with a small on-board battery pack (charged by the gasoline engine, not externally) to run accessories. The electric motor can move the vehicle for short distances and provide a power boost when accelerating. Key high-tech features include a braking system that charges battery and automatic idle. The key shift is towards plug-in hybrids. Several automakers, including General Motors, Ford and Toyota, are actively working on plug-in hybrids. An important design factor will be the lithium ion batteries, as they need to be safe, durable and affordable.[64]
Fuel Cell (Hydrogen) Cars	A fuel-cell car runs on electricity generated by the chemical reaction of oxygen in the air combining with hydrogen stored in a fuel tank. Hydrogen-powered prototypes are being tested in California and all major automobile companies are investing heavily in the development of fuel cells for future commercial automobile applications. Automakers believe they have developed the technology to an acceptable level for mass production—e.g., Chevrolet Equinox FCEV and Honda FCX Clarity.
Electric Cars	The race is on, with several software entrepreneurs entering this market. The goal is to shift $5 trillion to $10 trillion of expenditures related to the automotive sector to this new energy and transportation system. A key issue will be selling the idea to a wide range of partners, including government officials, the supply chain of the carmakers, technology providers, financial institutions, and the end consumers.[65] Another key issue for the new EV is whether the technology will be able to pass a one hundred thousand-mile warranty test.[66]

Table 3.5: History of Electric Vehicles

Late 1800s—France and Great Britain were the first nations to support the widespread development of EVs. In 1899, a Belgian-built electric racing car called La Jamais Contente set a world record for land speed—68 miles per hour (mph). EVs had many advantages over their competitors in the early 1900s, including the absence of vibration, smell and noise associated with gasoline cars. The decline of the electric vehicle was brought about by several major developments:[67]

- A better system of roads now connected cities, bringing with it the need for longer-range vehicles.
- The discovery of Texas crude oil reduced the price of gasoline so that it was affordable to the average consumer.
- The invention of the electric starter eliminated the need for the hand crank.
- Mass production of internal combustion engine vehicles made these vehicles widely available at an affordable price.

1970s—Two companies, Sebring-Vanguard (U.S.) and Elcar Corp. (distributor of an Italian EV), sold a few thousand EVs in the 1970s in response to problems associated with exhaust emissions from internal combustion engines and the public/government's need to reduce dependency on imported foreign crude oil. Both vehicles had significant issues associated with acceleration, top speed, duration of charge, inadequate braking system and crash safety.[68]

1990s—Several legislative and regulatory actions in the U.S. and worldwide renewed EV development. Primary among these were the U.S. 1990 Clean Air Act Amendment, the U.S. 1992 Energy Policy Act, and regulations issued by the California Air Resources Board (CARB). In addition to more stringent air emissions regulations requiring reductions in gasoline use, several states issued Zero Emission Vehicle (ZEV) requirements. The original mandate of California legislation was 2% of all new cars sold by major automakers were to meet ZEV by 1998 and 10% by 2003. In response to this new legislation, all U.S. automobile manufacturers developed EVs during this period. Many of the EVs were for research and development purposes, while others were available via a lease program. While many of the vehicles satisfied the driving requirements of fleet operators and two-car families, the cost, even with tax incentives, made them expensive.[69]

Early 2000s—In 2001, CARB modified the ZEV mandate to allow manufacturers to claim partial ZEV credit for hybrid vehicles. GM and DaimlerChrysler sued the state of California and CARB, alleging that the new ZEV rules violated a federal law barring states from regulating fuel economy. In response, CARB removed the requirement for electric vehicles from the ZEV mandate in 2003. In January 2003, Ford sold off PIVCO of Norway, the makers of the Th!nk EV, citing lack of U.S. government regulation. They had purchased PIVCO in 1999 to accelerate the development of an updated highway-capable EV for the American market.[70] In late 2003, GM stated that it could not sell sufficient cars to make the EV1 profitable and that to date it had already spent over $1 billion developing and marketing the EV1, though a portion of this cost was defrayed by the government's $1.25 billion Partnership for a New Generation of Vehicles project. GM recalled all of the leased vehicles and donated some to universities.

Table 3.6: Examples of Environmental Demands Put On Consumer Products

Light bulbs—This is an area of significant opportunity to reduce GHG emissions. Incandescent bulbs waste 90% of their energy on heat and will be banned in Canada in 2010 and in the U.S. by 2014.[71] The shift is towards the ENERGY STAR-rated compact fluorescent light (CFL). The Achilles' heel of CFLs is the presence of very small amounts of mercury (a very toxic material), requiring the bulbs to be disposed of at specialized recycling centers (not in the garbage) and any cleanup be done using rubber gloves. Companies are working to reduce the amount of mercury and eventually substitute it with another material. This will be a key breakthrough.

In November 2006, Wal-Mart set a goal to sell 100 million CFLs by the end of 2007; actual sales reached 137 million. Wal-Mart also worked with its CFL suppliers—GE, Royal Philips, Osram Sylvania and Lights of America—to obtain a commitment to achieve a greater reduction in mercury content than the 5 mg standard set by the U.S. National Electrical Manufacturers Association. These suppliers agreed to adhere to clean production techniques that will minimize mercury pollution from factories manufacturing CFLs.[72]

New solid state lighting (SSL), which includes light-emitting diodes (LEDs), are also starting to hit the market. The benefits of this type of light are that it has a much higher efficiency than conventional light bulbs and reduced energy consumption. They also contain no mercury.

Household products (cleaners, shampoo, body and skin care, etc.)—In the mid-1960s, many rivers and lakes in the U.S. and Canada were turning green and choking with aquatic plant growth. A primary reason for these deleterious changes in water quality was the high levels of phosphorus, one of several major plant nutrients, found in domestic and municipal sewage effluents. The principal source of effluent phosphorus was from phosphates used in laundry detergents. Significant debate between government agencies and industry occurred over several years until finally, in 1985, several states enacted legislation limiting phosphate content for detergents. The timing of the release of these products coincided with increased environmental awareness that using cold water to wash clothes could save 1% on national CO_2 emissions, as well as over $3 billion in energy costs.[73]

In response to market demands and/or Greenpeace inquiries, several household product companies are phasing out (over several years) or banning a range of hazardous materials—phthalates, artificial musks, alkylphenols, triclosan and formaldehyde—that have been found in household products. Many retailers are leveraging the absence of toxics to promote their products as being "green" or "naturally" inspired.

Cosmetics/perfumes—Many companies are now starting to eliminate hazardous materials found in cosmetics/perfumes—phthalates, artificial musks, alkylphenols, bisphenol A, nonylphenol ethoxylates and lead (based upon Greenpeace's Chemical Home database and Health Canada's Cosmetic Ingredient Hotlist)[74]. Note that in some cases, companies have substituted phthalates DEP and BBP with the phthalate DEP, which may share some of the same hazardous properties and hence may raise concerns in the future. There is also a shift to "natural" ingredients in skin and face creams.

Clothing—The manufacture of clothing involves numerous steps: manufacturing fibers and yarns, pre-treatment, dyeing, printing, aftercare and preservation. Chemicals are released to the environment during this process, as well as during wear, laundering and final disposal. Greenpeace-commissioned independent analysis found that chemicals found in clothing include alkylphenols, phthalates, organotins, lead, cadmium and formaldehyde. A significant source of hazardous substances in clothing is found in PVC plastic print (plastisol), which is often used in children's clothing to create motifs.

Note: A must-read to understand the flow of raw material related to clothing is *The Travels of a T-Shirt in the Global Economy: An Economist Examines the Markets, Power, and Politics of World Trade* by Pietra Rivoli, which was published in 2005.

Toys—As indicated by the numerous toy recalls of 2007 and the Mattel case study in chapter 5, hazardous substances and choking hazards do sometimes end up in toys. Several types of phthalates were permanently banned from toys and childcare products by the EU in 2005 (temporary ban was in place in 1999), with the result that, over time, most manufacturers phased out of soft PVC for their EU products in favor of alternative polymers to avoid the need for additives altogether. However, some toy companies continue to use PVCs where legislation permits.

Shoes—There has been a shift towards "greening" of products by the major shoe companies. Contaminants previously found in shoes include phthalates, organotins, brominated flame retardants, alkylphenols and triclosan. A case study on Nike's successful effort to eliminate sulfur hexafluoride (SF6) is presented at the end of this chapter.

Paints—During the late 1980s and early 1990s, industrial users of paint often faced strict environmental regulation on their operations because of the large volumes of solvents released in the surface coating process. These manufacturers turned to their paint suppliers, demanding products that not only performed acceptably in all traditional characteristics but also incorporated significantly reduced amounts of organic solvents. Paint manufacturers responded by providing innovative solutions. Where the paint companies successfully developed compliant coatings, their customers were provided with opportunities for compliance at dramatically lower cost than would have been possible through adoption of expensive pollution control equipment.[75]

In recent years, there has been a significant shift to more environmentally friendly paints for the consumer market—products that claim to contain low or even zero VOCs. Some companies have obtained third-party certification, for example, products with the GREENGUARD Environmental Institute (GEI) Children and Schools mark meet the more stringent health-based requirements related to paint for health care and educational environments.

Food—Legislation and voluntary programs have been enacted to promote sustainable agricultural/fishery activities. Examples of these diverse programs include voluntary initiatives like the Monterey Bay Aquarium Seafood Watch Sustainable Seafood Guide; the Marine Stewardship Standard certification program; government programs/legislation initiated by the United States Department of Agriculture's National Organic Program (including certification); and the Canadian Food Inspection Agency's Canada Organic Office.

Table 3.7: Energy Innovations Related to Hardware, Software and Datacenter Design[76]

> **Virtualization**—There are 7 million servers shipped globally every year, with the average server utilization at only 5% to 10%. There is potential for reducing the total number of servers "shipped" through virtualization (i.e., a virtual version of a device or resource, such as a server, storage device, network or even an operating system where the framework divides the resource into one or more execution environments). It is important to remember, however, that in terms of power usage, the more a server is running, the greater the consumed watts, which will offset any reduction in the power footprint.
>
> **Cooling servers**—Cooling servers consumes a significant amount of energy, especially at virtualized, high-density datacenters. New designs are looking at how best to cool the servers and reuse the excess heat for adjacent office areas, or, alternatively, using external cold air, depending on the climate, to cool the datacenters.
>
> **Power utilization**—According to a Green Grid white paper, 35% of the power that reaches a server is lost in power conversion. When combined with an un-virtualized datacenter, this means most power that reaches datacenters does no useful work. One option for mitigating this process involves using more efficient power supplies. The Green Grid notes that typical power supplies used today in datacenters have an efficiency of 65%–70%, whereas power supplies with an efficiency of up to 90% are available. While more efficient power supplies will often pay for themselves over the lifetime of an IT product, IT managers often do not invest in such products as they are unaware of the power cost associated with their datacenter.
>
> **Cost of energy**—Datacenters are moving to locations where power is cheapest and cleanest. Note that global competition resulting from data transfer to more efficient datacenters is still limited by bandwidth.

TH!NK GLOBAL CASE STUDY

Revenues: not available

Vision

Enthusiastic owners with the vision and resources want to make Th!nk "the car company of the 21st century."

Leadership

Dr. Jan-Olaf Willums is the CEO. He is the founding chairman of InSpire Group, a Venture Capital and financial advisory for energy- and socially responsible investments. He is also cofounder of several high-tech companies, including REC (solar power) and Computas (software).

Key Investors

Bought by a consortium of employees and interested parties from Ford in 2003, the company has formed a partnership with clean technology investors RockPort Capital Partners and Kleiner Perkins Caulfield & Byers to establish Th!nk North America. GE is also an investor and announced a strategic partnership with Th!nk.[77]

Why Norway

Government policy promotes the use of EV, through exemption from taxes, free parking, free passes for toll roads, and allowance to drive in the bus lanes.

Market Shift

Wilber James, Managing General Partner of RockPort Capital Partners and acting president of Th!nk North America, provides the following insight into the market shift:[78]

"We believe there is a dramatic shift underway of how people think about mobility. Global consumer demand is forcing the industry to come up with sustainable solutions, including the development of zero emission vehicles."

History

Founded in 1991 as the Personal Independent Vehicle Company. Development took more time and resources than anticipated and finances dried up in 1999. The company then was acquired by Ford, who wanted to accelerate the development of highway-capable EVs. Production ceased in 2002, after 1,005 units had been made. In January 2003, Ford sold the company.

Description

TH!NK city is the fifth-generation EV. It is 95% recyclable and reaches a top speed of 100 kilometers (65 miles) per hour and can drive up to 180 kilometers (110 miles) on a single charge. TH!NK city meets all EU and U.S. federal motor vehicle safety requirements.[79] In 2008 Th!nk announced a strategic partnership with energy giant General Electric. Th!nk has also unveiled its future car, the TH!NK Ox, the first four-/five-seater fully electric vehicle, which is slated to begin production in 2010/11. Th!nk has established partnerships in the U.S. with battery suppliers A123Systems and EnerDel.

Number of Cars Sold

About 1,200 Th!nk EVs are driving on Norwegian roads today. Th!nk's first assembly plant, near Oslo, has increased its capacity to ten thousand cars per year. Th!nk expects to be producing at full capacity sometime during 2009. The TH!NK city is currently produced in Norway, a country with very EV-friendly policies, and international sales are scheduled to begin in Scandinavia, with Switzerland and France also being initial focus areas. Sales, other than initial trial and demonstration projects, will begin for the North American market in 2009.

Information derived from www.think.no unless otherwise stated.

TESLA MOTORS CASE STUDY

Revenues: not available

Mission

Tesla Motors designs and sells high-performance, highly efficient electric sports cars—with no compromises. Tesla Motors cars combine style, acceleration and handling with advanced technologies that make them among the quickest and the most energy-efficient cars on the road.

Leadership

Elon Musk was the founder of Zip2, cofounder of PayPal and more recently major shareholder in SolarCity—a photovoltaics company for residential development. A new management team was brought in during 2007.

Number of Cars Sold/Price

Roadster—In 2007, the company pre-sold six hundred cars at a unit price of $98,000. The entire production of 2008 was sold out. The goal for the future is sales of one thousand to two thousand a year.

Model S (Sedan)—Electric four-door, five-passenger luxury sports sedan, comparable to a mid-range BMW or Mercedes. Currently at the design stage. Anticipated price range of $60,000 with a production goal of ten thousand to twenty thousand vehicles a year. Expected release year is late 2010.

Key Investors

Tesla was launched in 2003 and has raised $145 million in venture capital financing, including a $40 million round that closed in February 2008. Investors include Elon Musk, Valor Equity Partners and Vantage Point. The current plan is to raise $250 million in equity and debt to fund a push into production of the Model S, formerly codenamed the WhiteStar.[80]

Description

The strategy was to enter at the high end of the market where customers are prepared to pay a premium, and then drive down the market as fast as possible to achieve higher unit volumes and lower prices with each successive model. The first vehicle—the Tesla Roadster—was designed to beat a gasoline sports car like a Porsche or Ferrari in a head-to-head showdown.

Roadster: Based on the Lotus Elise. It boasts an impressive acceleration time of 0 to 60 in about four seconds, gets 250 miles per charge, has an efficiency equivalent of 135 mpg, has a top speed of around 130 mph and uses recyclable batteries, which charge in as little as three and a half hours.

Batteries: Tesla Motors' lithium-ion cells are not classified as hazardous and are landfill safe. However, dumping them in the trash would be throwing money away, since the battery pack can be sold to recycling companies (unsubsidized) at the end of its greater-than-100,000-mile design life. Moreover, the battery isn't dead at that point, it merely has less range.

Facilities: The company will begin constructing a new $250 million facility in San Jose, California, in the summer of 2009. This facility will produce the new Model S.[81]

Elon Musk's Unique Rationale

"This is because the overarching purpose of Tesla Motors (and the reason I am funding the company) is to help expedite the move from a mine-and-burn hydrocarbon economy towards a solar electric economy, which I believe to be the primary, but not exclusive, sustainable solution."
Elon Musk, 2006

Information derived from www.teslamotors.com unless otherwise stated.

PROJECT BETTER PLACE (PBP) CASE STUDY

Revenues: not available

Global Progress

In January 2007, Israel and Denmark committed to deploying PBP EV. In January 2008 a partnership between Israel, PBP and Renault-Nissan was signed, making Israel the first nation to commit to an all-electric car infrastructure. Similar agreements have been signed for Denmark, Australia, State of Hawaii, the province of Ontario and the Bay area of San Francisco (including Oakland and San Jose).[82] Renault-Nissan is expected to invest $1 billion into producing nine electric vehicle models that will be available between 2010 and 2014.[83]

Why Unique/Rationale

The business model includes offering customers one convenient plan that includes a car, the battery and access to a charging infrastructure. According to analysts, a typical contract would cost $550 a month and provide 18,000 miles a year. Project Better Place would run the charging infrastructure, allowing consumers to charge their batteries at home or at public charging stations. Batteries also could be swapped out at charging stations. Shai Agassi, CEO of PBP, best defines the shift as:[84]

"We're engineering transportation as a sustainable service. We solve for range and cost by implementing a swappable battery, and we create a zero emission solution by matching the supply of renewable energy with the demand created by electric vehicles."

"Sell Electric Vehicles (EV) like cell phones—[a] new paradigm shift that will cause a massive disruption to the auto industry."

Key Investors

Raised US$200 million for the project from Israeli Corp., VantagePoint Venture Partners, Morgan Stanley and a group of individual investors in one of the largest and fastest seed rounds in history.[85] VantagePoint is also an investor in Tesla Motors.

Description

In its first project, Project Better Place will integrate and deploy a new product, sales and support channel (read "charging stations") that will allow Israeli and Danish consumers to drive their own pure electric (not hybrid) car with a 200-kilometer or so range. The cars will be designed and built by Renault-Nissan.[86]

According to the company, previous attempts at EV failed because they did not create and manage an energy recharge grid (ERG), a network of services for fueling cars. The ERG will provide two ways to recharge. The first is plugging in at the home, workplace or one of many ERG-connected parking lots. With current technology, batteries last about 100 miles, which is fine for most commutes. For longer trips, such as the occasional holiday trip to visit the relatives, users will be able to pull into a switch station, which is similar to a gas station, where spent batteries are exchanged for charged ones.

Efficiency of Vehicle

Deutsche Bank estimates that PBP customers will pay 7 cents per mile for fuel, even after accounting for the cost of the electricity and depreciation of the battery, which is far cheaper than the 24 cents per mile Europeans pay for gasoline and the 15 cents per mile Americans pay.

Information derived from www.betterplace.com unless otherwise stated.

NIKE CASE STUDY

2007 Revenues: $16 billion

Supply Chain
Includes seven hundred factories in fifty-two countries.[87]

Approach to Corporate Responsibility
Corporate responsibility is a catalyst for growth and innovation, an integral part of how they can use the power of brand, the energy and passion of their people, and the scale of their business, to create meaningful change.

Environmental KPI
Waste: Achieve a 17% reduction in footwear waste and a 30% reduction in packaging and point-of-purchase waste by 2011 (baseline of 2007).
VOC in Footwear: Maintain current VOC levels (represents a 95% reduction over 1998 baseline).
Environmentally Preferred Material: Increase use of environmental preferred material by 22%.
Climate-neutral Facilities: Ensure Nike brand facilities and business travel is climate-neutral by 2011, and Nike, Inc. facilities and business travel is climate-neutral by 2015.
Inbound Logistics CO$_2$ Emission Footprint: Deliver a 30% absolute reduction from 2003 baseline.

Nike began a phase-out of PVC in 1998 and has completed the phase-out in shoes for children under three; however, other products for older children and adults may still contain small amounts of phthalates, organotins and alkylphenols.[88]

Business Problem
In 1992, a German environmental magazine wrote an article attacking companies that use sulfur hexafluoride (SF6)—a super potent GHG. The article mentioned Nike's Air Pockets. At the peak of its production (1997), the Nike Air footwear carried a greenhouse gas effect of 7 million metric tons of carbon dioxide—equivalent to 1 million cars. This technology cushioned nearly half of the 200 million shoes Nike sold. The issue arose after Nike had spent considerable resources on ensuring it did not employ sweatshops to prepare shoes.

Solution
Nike committed to looking for alternatives to SF6—an ideal gas as its large, tightly bound molecules rarely leaked after being injected into the Nike Air Pocket. The company missed its first target of 2000 as well as its second target of 2003. The solution finally emerged not in a single breakthrough, but in smaller increments: Nike figured out a way to hold together sixty-five wafer-thin layers of plastic film to keep nitrogen locked in and developed a new technique for thermoforming. Layered plastic is used to trap nitrogen (and hence replaces SF6), which has smaller molecules but is not harmful to the atmosphere.[89]

This new technology allowed Nike to create the Air Max 360—the first sneaker to cushion the entire sole with a bed of air. Matt Banks, World Wildlife Fund, describes the transformation that occurred at Nike as follows:

"This is significant, because [Nike] saw huge cost savings from doing well for the environment."

NOTES

1 Paul Hawken, *Ecology of Commerce* (New York: HarperCollins, 1993).
2 Nike, "Innovate for a Better World," http://www.nike.com/nikebiz/nikeresponsibility/pdfs/color/Nike_FY05_06_CR_Report_C.pdf, . accessed August 20, 2008.
3 Jeffrey Hojlo and Michael Burkett, "PLM Top Business Drivers for 2008," AMR Research, January 25, 2008.
4 Infor, "Product Lifecycle Management (PLM)," http://www.infor.com/solutions/plm, accessed August 20, 2008.
5 Ibid.
6 Martin Charter and Anne Chick, "Welcome to the First Issue of the Journal of Sustainable Product Design," *The Journal of Sustainable Product Design*, April 2008.
7 Johan Tingström, "Product Development with a Focus on Integration of Environmental Aspects," doctoral thesis, Division of Engineering Design, Department of Machine Design School of Industrial Engineering and Management, Royal Institute of Technology, Stockholm, 2007, http://www.sciencedirect.com/science?_ob=ArticleURL&_udi=B6VFX-4HYV040-2&_user=10&_rdoc=1&_fmt=&_orig=search&_sort=d&view=c&_acct=C000050221&_version=1&_urlVersion=0&_userid=10&md5=69abb61ec9be74a1de60dcc39ed39504.
8 "Corporate Social Concerns: Are They Good Citizenship, Or a Rip-Off for Investors?" Wall Street Journal, December 6, 2005, http://online.wsj.com/public/article/SB113355105439712626.html?mod=todays_free_feature.
9 Euroactiv.com, "Chemicals Policy Review (REACH)," updated September 24, 2007.
10 European Chemical Agency (ECHA), "New Alert: ECHA Publishes an Updated Intermediate List of Pre-Registered Substances," ECHA/PR/08/40, November 7, 2008.
11 John A. Byrne, "The Fast Company Interview: Jeff Immelt," the Fast Company, Issue 96, July 2005, http://www.fastcompany.com/node/53574.
12 Ibid.
13 U.S. Green Building Council, http://www.usgbc.org/DisplayPage.aspx?CMSPageID=222.
14 Infor, "Product Lifecycle Management (PLM)." www.infor.com
15 M. Jeanneau and P. Pichant, "The Trends of Steel Products in the European Automotive Industry," http://74.125.95.104/search?q=cache:i1OqgJ7n6xUJ:www.revue-metallurgie.org/articles/metal/pdf/2000/11/p1399.pdf+625+million+cars+and+vehicles+on+the+road+globally&hl=en&ct=clnk&cd=2.
16 "All Roads Lean Toward the Eco-Car," *Globe and Mail*, May 13, 2008.
17 Ibid.
18 Chuck Squatiglia, "Hydrogen Cars Are Here. Now We Just Need a Fueling Infrastructure," March 12, 2008.
19 David Welch, "GM Live Green or Die," *Business Week*, May 26, 2008.
20 Peter Gorrie, "A Dying Industry Turns to Volt," *Toronto Star*, November 22, 2008.
21 Greg Keenan, "GM Could Cut Almost 2,000 U.S. Dealerships," *Globe and Mail*, December 3, 2008.
22 Environmental Leaders, "Chrysler Kills First Hybrids", October 30, 2008. http://environmentalleader.com/2008/10/30/chrysler-kills-first-hybrids/
23 Sharon Silke Carty, "Loans for Automakers Near Approval," *USA Today*, September 25, 2008.
24 Michael Hollinshead, Craig Eastman and Thomas Etsell, "Forecasting Performance and Market Penetration of Fuel Cells in Transportation," 2005.

25 Greenpeace, "Cleaning Up Our Chemical Homes, Changing the Market to Supply Toxic-free Products," 2nd edition, February,
    http://www.greenpeace.org.uk/toxics/chemicalhome, accessed May 2007.
26 Greenpeace, "Tasty News for Apple," May 2, 2007, http://www.greenpeace.org.
27 Wikipedia, Biotechnology, 2008, http://en.wikipedia.org/wiki/Biotechnology.
28 Michelle Bryner, "Agricultural Biotech: Vying for More Ground," *Chemical Week*, June 2, 2008.
29 Wikipedia, Biotechnology.
30 Islem Yezza, "Global Market for Bioplastics," Helmut Kaiser Consultancy, 2008.
31 Jefferies Equity Research, "Clean Technology Primer," June 2008.
32 Chris Baskind, "5 Reasons Not to Drink Bottled Water," June 19, 2007,
    http://lighterfootstep.com.
33 Gizmag, 2008. "The LifeStraw Makes Dirty Water Clean," http://www.gizmag.com/
    go/4418.
34 Jefferies Equity Research, "Clean Technology Primer."
35 Wikipedia, Biotechnology.
36 Jefferies Equity Research "Clean Technology Primer."
37 Baskind, "5 Reasons Not to Drink Bottled Water."
38 Marketing Green, "Bottled Water Backlash," 2008, http://marketinggreen.wordpress.com.
39 Natural Resource Defense Council (NRDC), "Issues: Water, Bottled Water,"
    http://organizedwisdom.com/helpbar/index.html?return=http://organizedwisdom.com/
    Phthalates_in_Bottled_Water&url=www.nrdc.org/water/drinking/qbw.asp#plastic,
    accessed July 2008.
40 Ibid.
41 Tiffany Crawford, "Schools Take Aim at Bottled Water in Vending Machines," *Montreal Gazette*, June 23, 2008.
42 Kristina Cooke, "Americans Pick Print Books Over Electronic Contenders," May 30, 2008,
    http://www.reuters.com/article/vcCandidateFeed2.
43 Peter Whoriskey, "There Will Be No Newspapers in 10 Years: Ballmer," *Washington Post*,
    published in *Montreal Gazette*, June 9, 2008.
44 Climate Change Corp., "Special Report—The Climate Change Industry Takes Root," November 2007.
45 Ecocoach, "The Cost of Building Green Is Less Than You Think," August 22, 2007, http://
    ecocoach.wordpress.com/2007/08/22/cost-of-building-green-is-less-than-you-think.
46 Elsa Wenzel, "Bill Clinton: Green Buildings Key to Fighting Climate Change," November
    7, 2007, http://news.cnet.com/8300-11128_3-54-90.html.
47 U.S. Green Building Council, "LEED Rating System," 2008,
    http://www.usgbc.org/DisplayPage.aspx?CategoryID=19.
48 Ibid.
49 Silicon Valley Toxics Coalition, "Toxics in Electronics," http://www.etoxics.org, accessed in
    August 2008.
50 Ibid.
51 Greenpeace, 2007, http://www.greenpeace.com.
52 ZDNet.com, 2008, http://www.zdnet.com.
53 Ibid.
54 Ibid.
55 Dallas Kachan, "Green Grid Joined by Climate Savers Initiative from Google & Intel,"
    Cleantech Group, http://media.cleantech.com, accessed in May 2007.

56 Wikipedia, "Life Cycle Assessment," 2008,
   http://en.wikipedia.org/wiki/Life_Cycle_Assessment.

57 Business Dictionary.com, 2008, http://www.businessdictionary.com.

58 Wikipedia, "Eco-Innovation," 2008, http://en.wikipedia.org/wiki/Ecoinnovation.

59 Europa, "What Is Integrated Product Policy?", 2008, http://ec.europa.eu/environment/ipp.

60 U.S. Army, "Lean Six Sigma," http://www.army.mil, accessed in August 2008.

61 Paul Anasta and John Warner, *Green Chemistry: Theory and Practice* (New York: Oxford
   University Press, 1998).

62 Alex Scott, "Green Chemistry: Cradle-to-Cradle System Gain Momentum", *Chemical
   Week*, February 2/9, 2009.

63 "Clean Diesels Are on the Way," *Globe and Mail*, May 13, 2008.

64 "All Roads Lean Toward the Eco-Car."

65 Jane Barrett and John Davies, "Building an Electric Car Nation with Shai Agassi,"
   November 2, 2007, AMR Research, www.amresearch.com.

66 David Welch, "GM Live Green or Die," *Business Week*, May 26, 2008.

67 About.com, "The History of Electric Cars," http://inventors.com, accessed in August 2008.

68 Electric Vehicle Discussion List, "Electric Cars Have Been Marketed Without Much
   Success," http://www.evdl.org/docs/cr_ev.pdf, accessed in August 2008.

69 About.com, "The History of Electric Vehicles," http://inventors.about.com/library/weekly/
   aacerselectric2a.htm, accessed in August 2008.

70 EV Finder, http://www.evfinder.com/blog_archive.htm#Th!nk%20Again, accessed
   December 26, 2008.

71 WorldNetDaily, "Congress Bans Incandescent Bulbs: Massive Energy Bill Phases Out
   Edison's Invention by 2014," December 19, 2007, http://www.worldnetdaily.com/news.

72 MSNBC, "Wal-Mart to Reduce Mercury in CFLs. Agreement by Suppliers Reflects a Little-
   known Downside to Light Bulbs," May 10, 2007, http://www.msnbc.msn.com.

73 Orrin Cook, "Energy Tip# 17: Wash and Rinse in Cold Water," October 31, 2006,
   http://www.terrapass.com.

74 Health Canada, "List of Prohibited and Restricted Cosmetic Ingredients (The Cosmetic
   Ingredient 'Hotlist')," 2008, http://www.hc-sc.gc.ca/cps-spc/person/cosmet/info-ind-prof/_
   hot-list-critique/prohibited-eng.php.

75 Management Institute for Environmental Business (MEB), "Competitive Implications of
   Environmental Regulation in the Paint and Coatings Industry," 1994.

76 ZDNET, 2008. www.ZDNET.com

77 Business Wire, "Kleiner Perkins and RockPort Capital, Two Leading U.S. Cleantech
   Investors, Launch Joint Venture with Norwegian Electrical Vehicle Company Think OSLO,
   Norway & PASADENA, Calif.," April 21, 2008.

78 Ibid.

79 Ibid.

80 John Reed, "Tesla to Raise $250m for Electric Cars," *Financial Times*, February 17, 2008.

81 Mike Monticello, "New & Future Cars: Tesla Builds a 4-Door," *Road & Track*, December
   2008.

82 Katie Fehrenbacher, "Better Place to Build First U.S. Electric Vehicle Network in Bay Area,"
   http://earth2tech.com/2008/11/20/better-place-to-build-first-us-electric-vehicle-network-
   in-bay-area, accessed in December 2008.

83 Katie Fehrenbacher, "Shai Agassi: Note to Next President, Better Place for U.S. Would Cost
   $100b," October 17, 2008, http://www.earth2tech.com.

84 Ibid.
85 Alisa Odenheimer and David Rosenberg, "Renault, Nissan Plan Electric-Car Venture in Israel (Update2)," January 21, 2008, http://www.bloomberg.com/apps/news?pid=20601101&sid=aZfe9_PmZrFg&refer=japan.
86 Wired, 2008.
87 Gail Dutton, "How Nike Is Changing the World, One Factory at a Time," Ethisphere, March 26, 2008, http://ethisphere.com/how-nike-is-changing-the-world-one-factory-at-a-time.
88 Greenpeace, "Cleaning Up Our Chemical Homes, Changing the Market to Supply Toxic-free Products."
89 Stanley Holmes, "Nike Goes for the Green," *Business Week*, September 25, 2006.

CHAPTER FOUR

GREEN MARKETING: MOVING GREEN PRODUCTS TO THE MAINSTREAM

Understanding how the natural environment works is not necessarily obvious. Some environmental impacts can be invisible, such as carbon dioxide emissions. In many instances, the most severe impacts are caused incrementally, with damage only becoming visible after many years (e.g., the lethal effects of acid rain on lake ecosystems). Because of this, effective communication is needed to help non-specialists understand the environment. This presents opportunities both for raising general awareness of environmental issues, as well as introducing bias, resulting in misunderstanding and misinterpretation, whether intentional or not.

Likewise, consumers can be persuaded about the environmental qualities of products, whether or not these attributes are real, through communication and marketing strategies. Green marketing is a powerful tool for influencing consumer behavior and, ultimately, the growth of the marketplace for green products.

"Marketing is one of the last domains of commercial enterprise to face up to issues of sustainable development. On both the environmental dimension of resource limits/pollution and the social dimension of well-being, marketing has significant impacts and is deeply implicated in the current challenges of unsustainable consumption and production. Yet at the same time, and I simplify, while marketing got us into this mess, it may be that marketing can get us out. We need to harness the creativity and the sophistication of marketing, and its methodologies, for human health and environmental sustainability."[1]

WHAT IS REALLY HAPPENING?

Shift from Environmental Protest to Engagement

Initial public discourse on environmental issues in the 1970s and 1980s could be characterized as frenzied verbal thrashing by polarized groups, each seeking moral high ground over poorly defined issues. A framework for debate and for information-vetting was lacking and consequently the players, i.e., corporations, NGOs and the media, were ill-prepared to do more than react, or overreact, to discoveries about environmental contamination, impacted populations and product safety. Corporations found themselves on the receiving end of (often justifiable) public outrage, and at the outset, they lacked the tools to anticipate potentially damaging events and to devise appropriate management strategies.

Since the early 1990s, companies have gone to work on both their operations and their communications to prevent and mitigate pollution and to try to shape public discussion on their green performance. In many instances, the latter preceded the former, and corporations could be found making claims about green performance that were partially or wholly unfounded. It was during this period that the term "greenwash" was coined—"disinformation disseminated by an organization so as to present an environmentally responsible public image."[2] A flavor of those times was provided by Greenpeace International in 1992:

> A look at corporate behavior exposes the reality hidden under the green image being created by TNCs (transnational corporations). Despite their new rhetoric, TNCs are not saviors of the environment or of the world's poor, but remain the primary creators and peddlers of dirty, dangerous, and unsustainable technologies.[3]

Where are we today? The situation is more complex for companies as governments (at all levels) put forward a vast array of market-based incentives/prohibitions in response to environmental issues, and as more sophisticated NGOs and the public leverage the power of the Internet and social media to manufacture and influence opinion. These shifts are driven by multiple factors, including climate change and environmental degradation, the cost of energy and the drive for renewable forms of energy, greater understanding of the true costs of pollution and of ecosystem services,[4] and expectations for more regulation. Needless to say, these all have potential and actual impacts on business and have become key ingredients in forming policy.

BRAND CAMP
THE WIZARD OF AD
by Tom Fishburne
PAY NO ATTENTION TO THE COMPANY BEHIND THE CURTAIN – JUST WATCH OUR AD
© 2008
TOMFISHBURNE.COM

The marketplace for green products is disillusioned by the exposure of false claims cynical about the validity of current and future claims, but at the same time is ready for change. It is seeking verifiability of environmental claims and is more interested than before in the genuineness of the companies behind the products, aligning the values attached to a product with those of the product's proponent, i.e., environmentally harmful product = questionable company values.

This is best exemplified by contrasting the current perceptions of IKEA (see the case study at end of this chapter) and General Electric in the United States. While IKEA has, for years, been quietly implementing sustainable business practices through its supply chain and operations (driven by a combination of cost, efficient design and sustainability considerations), it has not showcased these accomplishments in the usual "green" light that has become so fashionable in recent years. Yet consumers ranked IKEA seventh in a 2008 survey of green brands, two positions ahead of General Electric, who had spent $90 million on advertising their new commitment to ecomagination.

It is becoming more and more evident that consumers are increasingly interested in the world that lies behind the product they buy. Apart from price and quality, they want to know how, where and by whom the product has been produced. This increasing awareness about environmental and social issues is a sign of hope. Governments and industry must build on that.[5]

Despite the apparent complexity and a wary marketplace, there has never been greater opportunity for companies who are prepared to stand behind truly great green products. There are a number of straightforward steps that companies can follow to improve their chances of success in green marketing, which we will highlight in this chapter. First, however, let's look at available consumer research.

THE STATUS OF PUBLIC OPINION IN DIFFERENT REGIONS

Clearly, consumers are concerned. Consumer organizations around the world want to play their part. In a recent survey of Consumer International (CI) member organizations in 115 countries, sustainable consumption emerged as the number one international issue.[6] While there is currently no broadly accepted definition of sustainable consumption (sometimes also referred to as responsible consumption), for present purposes, it can be defined as *needs-based consumption, in which a fundamental service is provided by prioritizing activities or harvesting that do not degrade the source materials required to produce the product in the first place, at all phases of the product life cycle. Further, sustainable consumption values items of long-term durability.*

There are potentially a wide variety of issues on the table when discussing green marketing, from environmental performance, climate change and sustainability, to organic products, fair trade and animal rights. Available market survey data on these issues are necessarily fragmented, so it is difficult to address them simultaneously. In the material that follows, we describe the issues surveyed focusing on a broad interpretation of "environment." This not to suggest that any of the other topics are less interesting, relevant or critical to a company's marketing efforts.

It should also be noted that it may be misleading to mention consumer trends in the U.S. and Canada in the same breath, as the markets and consumer preferences are sometimes quite different in the two countries.[7]

In 2006, 2007 and 2008, the multinational marketing firms Landor, PSB and Cohn & Wolfe produced an ongoing survey of American consumers' perceptions of green business practices called Green Brands. In 2006, the survey found an absence of concern among Americans about the concept of green. By contrast, in 2007, green had become an issue for all Americans at a personal level, thereby creating expectations for appropriate behavior from corporations, the media and government. While global warming was the most prominent concern, Americans were also worried about chemicals in products, waste and vehicle emissions.

A dominant group of the sample population (34%)—the "Active Greens"—took an active role in personal environmental gestures and believed that environmental degradation is a societal problem and that the outlook is not positive. They believed that among corporations, appliance manufacturers have done the best job of protecting the environment. A minority group (11%)—the "Muted Greens"—were not convinced that the environment is in trouble, thought that sufficient steps have been taken in the U.S. to address climate change and saw the automotive and oil/petroleum industries as leaders in environmental protection. The personal purchasing and transport habits of this minority group are reflective of this outlook, with little importance attributed to environmental purchases, e.g., avoidance of plastic bags, importance of recycled fiber content of paper products and use of personal vehicle where public transportation is available.

The latest installment of the Green Brands survey in mid-2008 showed a public explosion of interest in green issues, partly due to the U.S. presidential election campaigns, where it was a key plank in the candidates' platforms. Consumers were now expecting to double their spending on green products and services (notwithstanding the economic crisis that descended in the following quarter and into 2009), with 82% thinking it is important for a company to be green. However, as in the findings of a Canadian 2008 survey (see below), cost was a determining factor, to the point that when faced with a choice for a green product or an inexpensive product, a majority would choose the lower cost item.

In 2008, Americans found that corporations were most to blame for having created environmental problems, followed by individuals and politicians in almost equal measure.

> Companies have to be careful about focusing on only green products (and thus the niche market) and instead define what green or sustainability means to them, then try to create the connection from those values to those of the mainstream market.[8]

A June 2008 survey of Canadian attitudes on the environment and the economy by the marketing firm of Bensimon Byrne revealed that the environment ranks third among issues, after the price of gasoline and health care. Three-quarters of Canadians say they consider the environmental impact when they make a purchase decision (with women twice as likely as men to consider it); only 20% of Canadians say they rarely or never do. However, less than 40% of Canadians believe they can afford to pay the additional premium that they believe is associated with environmental products. This price issue notwithstanding, the survey coincides with the findings of the American Green Brands 3.0 survey by Landor, PSB and Cohn & Wolfe (cited above), and can be viewed as a huge leap for the commercial viability of green products and surveys.

Three-quarters of Canadians believe that environmental claims are marketing ploys, revealing a crisis in confidence in company/product claims of being green or environmentally friendly. Companies are the least trusted source of information about the environmental impacts of products. Canadians overwhelmingly want government to regulate this arena and create standards that ensure claims have a basis in fact. Terms like "green" are worn out and viewed with cynicism—consumers don't know what it really means and are therefore cynical about how companies use them.[9]

Table 4.1 reveals the findings of a six-continent 2008 survey of environmental attitudes, performed by BBC and Synovate.

Table 4.1: 2007–2008 Worldwide Survey of Environmental Attitudes

Issue	2007 Survey	2008 Survey
Level of Concern About Climate Change	68%	72%
Location of Respondents Most Concerned		Spain (86%, Brazil (88%)
Country Showing Largest Change in Level of Concern Between 2007 and 2008	U.S. (57% to 80%)	
Countries Considered Responsible for Climate Change (Among All Respondents)	U.S. 66% China 14%	U.S. 61% China 18%
Countries Considered Responsible for Climate Change (Among American Respondents)	U.S. 82%	U.S. 74%
Number of Respondents in Last Year Who Informed Themselves About Climate Change	46%	58%
Man-made Pollution Perceived as Main Factor Causing Climate Change		47%
Number of Respondents in Last Year Who Conserved Energy	76%	81%
Number of Respondents in Last Year Who Bought Energy-Efficient Devices	53%	59%
Number of Respondents in Last Year Who Recycled Waste	65%	70%
Number of Respondents in Last Year Who Reduced Water Consumption	65%	69%
Number of Respondents in Last Year Who Reduced the Use of Packaging and Bags	56%	68%
Number of Respondents in Last Year Who Bought Green Products	53%	61%

When considering the factors most likely to reduce climate change in individual countries, respondents in the survey nominated the changed behavior of ordinary citizens at 45%; technical advances at 20%; government-imposed restrictions and incentives at 29%; and 6% did not know. This implies that while technology and imposed restrictions have support among half of the respondents, there is a very clear voice from the consumer accepting responsibility.

Globally, 2007 and 2008 data confirm a more mature market for green products and services among developed countries than in developing countries, with European nations leading North America in both governance issues and in consumer behavior. Development of the green or "ethical" consumer market nonetheless continues at a brisk pace and shows large growth potential as evidenced by the

- acquisition of "green" companies by multinationals (e.g., Body Shop by L'Oréal for $1.27 billion)
- in North America, growth in sales of hybrid vehicles at the expense of the SUV market
- double-digit growth in organic food and drink in both North America and Europe[10]

Key affected industries are automotive, food, retailing, IT, telecommunications and health and beauty.

It has long been believed that green was a privilege of consumers in developed economies, satiated by consumption levels and guilt-driven to spend on greener products. Also, bigger challenges for the provision of basics such as clean water, sanitation, urban air quality and food have dominated the development agenda of emerging nations for decades.

However, these consumer trends are beginning to cascade onto emerging market turf, despite the frequently cited resentment felt by developing countries towards international environmental initiatives originating in developed countries: "You industrialize, you pollute, now you judge."[11]

There appear to be three key drivers to growth in green consumerism: first, the influence of multinational corporations on local economies. Faced with a myriad of globally applicable requirements and stakeholder expectations relating to corporate governance, scrutiny of the supply chain, EHS performance and disclosure, corporations set standards for internal behavior in these areas that typically raise the bar well above local regulated levels. This informs the workforce, influences government regulatory agendas and places demands for local infrastructure improvements.

Second, a growing number of young "affluentials," "urbs" and visiting eco-tourists are forming target markets in these countries. These are joined by young "creative class" consumers who are in touch with global tendencies and are positive about purchasing locally sourced goods with a traditional element.

The third issue is related to energy demands. As countries recognize that petroleum reserves will not meet future demands and alternative energy sources take time and capital to complete, conservation activities are being viewed as a real opportunity. For example, fuel efficiency standards that are far higher than those in North America have been adopted in China and the Chinese are assessing EU energy standards for new appliances.

A scan of emerging market media and survey reports in 2007 showed the following:

- One of every two business managers in India considers sustainability and environment to be crucial, while this is true of only 26% of managers in China.
- China's health and wellness packaged food industry has grown rapidly with sales of US$4.7 billion in 2006. In 2007, the first Sino-foreign fair for organic food took place in Shanghai.
- Sustainability is becoming cool among high-end Chinese urban consumers; however, it will be at least another generation before sustainability becomes a major consideration for the average Chinese consumer.
- Sensitivity towards the environment is now a fashionable trend in India, and eco-friendly fashion is hip, at least among upper middle-class consumers.
- In Thailand, consumers are seeing through misguided efforts by business to appeal to trendy environmentalism. However, there is an emerging market for locally produced traditional textile products and the government has begun some innovative environmental campaigning.
- More than 110 regional hotels in less-developed Asian economies have been certified to the Green Globe, an international travel and tourism program.
- Today's purchases of green products and services in South and Central America are still limited to a very narrow segment of the marketplace, composed of wealthier consumers with higher living standards. However,

supported by corporate responsibility policies and increasing demands for green articles, sales are increasing. Some observers say that the region is experiencing a revolution in the eco-industry.

- Finally, regional banks in South and Central America are looking to collaborate on greener and sustainable causes, as well as incorporating positive ecological values into their services.

An important caution should be attached to these statistics on consumer attitudes, in that often the reply given to a pollster is a more accurate reflection of what the consumer aspires to achieve (be it buying greener, favoring public transport, eliminating frivolous purchases, etc.) than what they currently do.

The Seriousness of Greenwashing

In some quarters, greenwashing continues to be perceived as a major problem warranting more government regulation to guide environmental marketers on claim integrity. In 2007, the Canada-based TerraChoice environmental marketing company published a report entitled *The Six Sins of Greenwashing*. Their study revealed that greenwashing is pervasive and published statistics in support of their claim. A similar review has been published by Futerra Sustainability Communications of the UK.

While the TerraChoice report draws attention to the greenwash problem, its statistics on the frequency of false claims have been challenged in the marketplace, which raises questions as to their validity. Greenwashing certainly exists, but generalizations as to the extent of the problem are not helpful to the consumer or the product manufacturers.

Nonetheless, TerraChoice's six sins of greenwashing[12] serve to encapsulate some of the more common types false claims:

1. Sin of the hidden trade-off—when the suggestion is made that a product is green, based on a single environmental attribute or an unreasonably narrow set of attributes without attention to other, more important environmental issues.
2. Sin of no proof—any environmental claim that cannot be substantiated by easily accessible supporting information, or by a reliable third-party certification, e.g., shampoos claiming to be certified organic, but with no verifiable certification.

3. Sin of vagueness—every claim that is so poorly defined or broad that its real meaning is likely to be misunderstood by the intended consumer (examples of recurring themes are "chemical-free," "non-toxic," "all-natural" and "green").

4. Sin of irrelevance—when an environmental claim relates to unimportant or irrelevant information about the product being promoted and consequently is distracting to the consumer, however true the claim may be (for example, products claiming to be CFC-free, even though CFCs were banned twenty years ago and are not present in products today).

5. Sin of lesser of two evils—when a claim, however true, risks distracting the consumer from the greater environmental impacts of the product category as a whole, e.g., the use of environmental qualifiers such as "organic" or "green" on products in which the entire product category is of questionable environmental value, such as organic cigarettes or "environmentally friendly" pesticides.

6. Sin of fibbing—when an environmental claim is simply false (examples include false claims to certification).

In the UK, the Advertising Standards Agency (ASA) has disciplined a number of companies in response to complaints by NGOs, such as Friends of the Earth. In 2007, the ASA censured an ad by Shell that claimed, "We use our waste CO_2 to grow flowers." NGOs complained the amount of CO_2 used in the flower project was a tiny proportion of that produced by Shell's global activities—and the ASA agreed.

Public complaints of this type to the ASA have risen sharply: in 2006, 117 complaints about environmental claims in 83 advertisements were received, while in 2007, 561 complaints about 410 ads were received.

As complaints have risen, the ASA has noticed a number of recurring issues. The most common claims being challenged are carbon-reduction claims, cradle-to-grave claims and claims about green energy sources.

In the U.S., overhaul of the Federal Trade Commission (FTC) guidelines on environmental claims is a pressing issue to resolve in light of complaints about real and perceived false claims.

Consumer concerns about suspected greenwashing and confusion over the legitimacy of environmental claims have given rise to advocates, such as the Greenwashing Index website (www.greenwashingindex.com), which claims to be the world's first online interactive forum that allows consumers to evaluate real advertisements making environmental claims.

The intent of the Greenwashing Index is to

- help consumers evaluate environmental marketing claims of advertisers
- hold businesses accountable to their environmental marketing claims
- stimulate the market and demand sustainable business practices that truly reduce the impact on the environment

The Greenwashing Index is an automated tool that provides five simple criteria, essentially the same as TerraChoice's Six Sins, which have been developed by advertising academia and weighted according to their relevance in marketing claims. Subscribers rate claims through a blog.

WHAT IS GREEN MARKETING?

Is green marketing any different than conventional marketing? Yes. Green marketing tackles the complexities of selling a product's benefits (price, quality and environmental compatibility), while addressing consumer expectations about the environmental record of the company behind the product.

Ten years ago, a new paradigm was taking shape that differentiated green marketing from conventional marketing, as illustrated in table 4.2.[13] The essence of this paradigm remains valid today, although the role of communities in consumer behavior, and its implications for marketing strategy, has grown with the Internet's proliferation as a social-networking tool.

Table 4.2: New Green Marketing Paradigm

	Conventional Marketing	Green Marketing
Consumers	Consumers with lifestyles	Human beings with lives
Products	"Cradle to grave"	"Cradle to cradle"
	One size fits all	Flexible
	Products	Services
Marketing	Selling oriented	Educational
Communications	Reactive	Proactive
	Independent	Interdependent
	Competitive	Cooperative
	Departmentalized	Holistic
	Short-term oriented	Long-term oriented
	Profit maximizing	Double bottom line

From Ottman, 1998

Green marketing is about success in driving sales of one or more of the following:

- Corporate virtue/performance—Companies whose activities directly or indirectly impact the environment, including populations near and far, seek to counter or mitigate this perception. These companies have reputations to defend that, if adversely affected, can have financial repercussions. Wal-Mart's proactive drive to green its supply chain (e.g., reduce product packaging, seek certification of forest products) successfully repositioned the firm as a sustainability leader.
- Design/technology—As consumers seek next-generation products that are more and more energy efficient, companies seek to be perceived as

design leaders. For example, in the current competition among the major automobile manufacturers to cleanse motorized transportation, they compete in parallel on communicating their progress to the marketplace.

- Products—Consumers seek products that do not entail massive environmental and social impacts along the supply chain. Companies whose activities are known to impact the environment (e.g., paper-making, oil and gas production, metal mining) seek to be perceived as leaders in preventing, mitigating and compensating for these impacts.

However, the path to achieving success in green marketing is not easy and, as noted above, false claims have led to deep cynicism about green claims among consumers, and apparent general misunderstanding among marketers about the nature of this quickly evolving and young marketplace.

In *The Green Marketing Manifesto*, John Grant provides a useful methodology for understanding the green market.[14] His Green Marketing Grid plots shades of "greenness" (green = setting new standards for environmental performance or green products; greener = developing ideas and experiences collaboratively with clients; greenest = enabling breakthroughs in green design and technology) against three different levels of society at which green marketing functions and brands perform, i.e., public (how a company portrays itself publicly and the alignment of the brand with the reality of the company); social (the association of brand with social groups to achieve identity); and personal (how brands penetrate the realm of personal consumption).

The grid provides a framework for understanding nine key green marketing strategies within a new marketing model, in which sustainability is driving companies to strive for simultaneous achievement of profitability, environmental protection and cultural innovation. The sheer magnitude and breadth of the societal challenges posed by sustainable development, and the extent to which consumers are aware of these challenges, means that increasingly, companies have to live by what they market.

A scan of figure 4.1, left to right across the rows, descending downward from the top row, reveals some familiar green marketing approaches and examples, a few of which are highlighted (shown as shaded squares in the figure).

Setting examples—pointing and framing. Companies can set higher standards for their product categories and gain competitive advantage if they remain factual and avoid unsubstantiated "spin." Pointing can be used to showcase initiatives or products whose value cannot be easily disputed (e.g., the tangible environmental

Figure 4.1: Green Marketing Grid

	Green	Greener	Greenest
Public Company & Markets	**Setting Examples** *Pointing & Framing*	**Developing the Market** *Educating vs. Evangelizing*	**New Business Concepts** *Social Production vs. Property*
Social Brands & Belonging	**Credible Partners** *Eco-labels vs. Cause-related*	**Tribal Brands** *Exclusive vs. Inclusive*	**Trojan Horse Ideas** *Tradition vs. New Cool*
Personal Products & Habits	**Marketing Benefits** *Less vs. More*	**Changing Usage** *Switch vs. Cut*	**Challenging Consumption** *Treasure vs. Share*
	Set New Standards, Communicate	Share Responsibility, Collaborate	Support Innovation, Reshape Culture

Grant, 2008

progress and economic success of GE's ecomagination, or the Toyota Prius[15]). Framing changes the conceptual structures of debate to produce advantage, e.g., giving a progressive policy a comfortable feel, or to disadvantage a competitor, such as by portraying genetically modified (GM) foods as scary.

Credible partners—eco-labels vs. cause-related. Co-opting partners with an existing green brand can be a promotional tactic to build a brand and achieve competitive advantage in green marketing. The choice of partner can serve to neutralize consumer doubts about greenwashing. Eco-labels, discussed in greater detail later in the chapter, are an example of where a product is subjected to independent third-party attestation as to the veracity of the product environmental claims. As long as the certification scheme is itself credible, the partnership between the proponent and the certifier strengthens the product brand. Common examples are Forest Stewardship Council (FSC) (for wood and paper products), ENERGY STAR (for appliances), EcoLogo, European Eco-label and Green Seal (for a wide range of goods). A key advantage of eco-labeling is that it creates a decision opportunity for the consumer where one did not exist. Cause-related marketing occurs when a purchase of a product is automatically linked to a good deed, such as contribution to a charity, an environmental or social cause, or pays for public relations related to such a cause. This type of joint branding has become very commonplace in Europe and North America in the past five years, to the point where it is no longer a differentiator. Offers to provide carbon offsetting from airlines is a recent example of one type of cause-related marketing.

Tribal brands—exclusive vs. inclusive. The concept of style tribal brands is familiar because it evokes images of people wearing clothing that reflects the shared values of their "tribe," e.g., motorcycle gangs = leather jackets + tattoos, or hippie = headband + jeans. The contemporary teenage clothing industry appears to be built on the concept. However, tribal brands are based on value sets that become identifiable through products such as clothes. The societal changes of the 1980s and 1990s brought on by the changing job market, the end of the Cold War, and the rise of the Internet as a social networking tool blurred the lines among "tribes." Whereas "green" used to evoke sandal-wearing, liberal, conservationist and activist images twenty years ago, in some sense those values, driven by more urgent environmental and social crises, have now been taken up by a large cross-section of society, allowing for the possible creation of a new "green cool." Examples include the enlisting of famous people around green issues (e.g., the annual green issue of *Vanity Fair*) and green products (e.g., the Toyota Prius, which is the vehicle of choice for the who's who of Hollywood advocates of the cause of sustainability). But because of its relatively low price tag, and hence its accessibility to many buyers, the Prius is establishing the idea of inverted status—that small is the new big. The epitome of green cool, however, is Global Cool (www.globalcool.org), whose goal is to take a billion citizens carbon neutral through the work of a community that brings together celebrities and causes. At the opposite extreme of exclusive branding, which feeds on envy, elite consumerism and the desire to emulate the rich and famous (in the examples cited), there is inclusive tribal branding, which feeds on giving, sharing and socializing around causes such as climate change. There are several organizations in the UK offering creative products and designs that coincide with green, from sexy clothing to soaps, household products and fragrances. The more successful of these garner support and endorsements from well-known NGOs.

Challenging consumption—treasure vs. share. At the very core of consumerism lie two fundamental barriers to cultural and economic change, which, as they are overcome, will present opportunities for creative entrepreneurs. The first is the status conferred upon individuals who own goods, as opposed to those who share them. Sharing has implied inability to own and, hence, lower social status. However, because individual ownership comes with a heavy environmental price tag that is being shown to be unsustainable, the opportunity lies in discovering the key to making shared use of consumer products socially attractive. Carpooling and communal living, while seemingly ordinary and uninteresting ideas, may hold hidden treasures in that their growth is probably inevitable, given the increasing costs of vehicle ownership and the inevitable burst of the current housing bubble in Europe and North America. The second barrier is the current short life of products. We are slaves to currency—everything has to be new, which leads straight to waste. Changing this will entail creating profit from scenarios where products are "treasured" because of their age or uniqueness. eBay is the outstanding example where secondhand goods have intrinsic value, thereby creating a market, reducing consumption and reducing waste.

What Are Companies Doing to Influence Consumers?

Those challenging the company need to be openly and constructively engaged, instead of confronted. Companies learn from these experiences in ways that ultimately shape their product and service offerings. Engagement comes through proactive, reactive, conventional and new strategies at the corporate and grass-roots levels.

Nearly every big company these days is taking a hard look at its products, processes and operations through the lens of environmental impacts, and many are making changes that reduce their impacts significantly, even though the changes may represent a small, even tiny, part of their operations. They are doing these things for a range of reasons—to cut costs, increase sales, attract and retain employees, reduce risks, and improve their reputations, among other reasons.[16]

There is a business case for this. General Electric indicated in 2007 that it expects to sell $20 billion in ecomagination products by 2010. In June 2008, Peter White, director of global sustainability for Procter & Gamble, indicated that his company has set a goal to sell $20 billion in total sales of "sustainable innovation products."

Predictions by industry gurus suggest that

- more green products will hit the markets in the short term, as retailers demand products with less packaging, less energy use and reduced toxicity (no PVC or heavy metals, for example). Many of these products will put primary benefits—higher performance levels, aesthetics and cost effectiveness—front and center in marketing materials, while green claims will recede, reflecting reticence from potential greenwashing backlash, and a simple growing awareness in good green marketing practice.
- sales of green products will soar, boosted by the marketing heft of major consumer products firms that have been on a green-brand acquisition binge. Examples include Clorox, Colgate, Procter & Gamble and Danone, for health and beauty products, cleaning products and foods.[17]

The market share performance of a selection of green products is shown in figure 4.2.[18]

Note that in figure 4.2, "green cars" includes hybrids and advanced diesel, "green electricity" excludes hydro power, and "SRI" stands for socially responsible investment and only includes investment by individuals.

Are green products priced the same as their non-green counterparts? Market survey data from 2005 suggest a strong premium for a wide range of products from phosphate-free detergents to hybrid cars (figure 4.3[19]). More recent market observations suggest closer pricing between many green and organic/fair trade products and conventional products.[20]

Figure 4.2: Market Share of Selected Green Products (%)

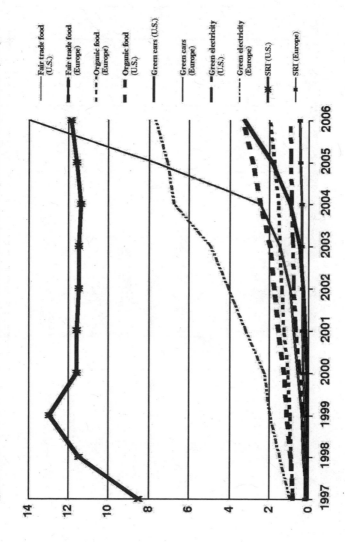

University of Michigan

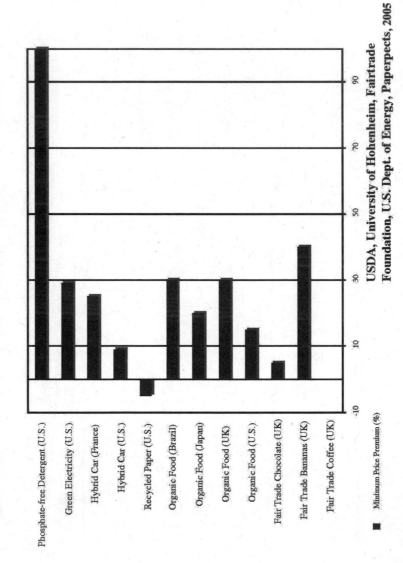

Figure 4.3: Price Premium on Selected Green Products

There is evidence that corporate self-positioning on green products and marketing is evolving as well (figure 4.4[21]).

GREEN MARKETING CLAIMS

The rise in consumer consciousness, as well as companies' interest in promoting the green attributes of their products and services, however real or unsubstantiated these claims are, created a market need for standardization in product labels and marketing claims. The overall goal of creating standards for environmental labels and claims has been to encourage the demand for, and supply of, those products that are less harmful to the environment and society, through communication of accurate and verifiable information that is not misleading. Such standards affect how companies design, package, distribute and market their products.

Standards for environmental labels and claims are intended to reduce costs for the companies that use them, by providing uniform models and approaches that have been adopted internationally. They also can provide greater assurance regarding compliance with a wide variety of consumer protection laws. Ultimately, they should serve to reduce marketplace confusion.

The International Organization for Standartization (ISO) has put forward the following standards, which are all voluntary, meaning that they are not binding on parties making environmental declarations or labels, or the accompanying data sets:

- ISO 14020 general principles of environmental claims and declarations
- ISO 14021 self-declared environmental claims (Type II)
- ISO 14024 Type I environmental labeling—principles and procedures
- ISO 14025 Type III environmental declarations—principles and procedures

Generally, these standards lay out the requirements for achieving consensus on criteria for the creation of labels, prohibit the use of environmental claims as trade barriers, and define requirements on the use of established methodologies and public access to underlying data supporting environmental claims.

Type I labels, or "eco-labels," are those vetted by multiple-criteria-based third-party programs that award a license authorizing the use of the environmental label on products. The labels indicate overall environmental preferability of a product within a particular product category based on life cycle considerations—meaning

Figure 4.4: Evolving Role of Green Products and Sustainable Lifestyles Marketing in Mainstream Companies' Strategy

	Limited Role	Reactive Role	Proactive Role
Inspiration	Copy pioneers	Acquire pioneers	Be pioneers
Target	Opinion leaders	Niche market	Mass market
Attributes to Brands	None	Differentiating	Entry stake (early adopter)
Claims Backed By	No evidence	Green labels	Green labels & product reporting
Connection with Lobbying	Supports defensive lobbying	Disconnected	Supported by positive lobbying
Other Marketing Practices	Opposed/ disconnected	Compliance driven	Aligned with sustainability goals

Utopies, 2005

that there is a measurable difference in environmental impact with other products in the same category.

Eco-labeling programs are operated by a company or a group of companies, industrial sector or trade association, public authorities or agencies, or an independent scientific body. They exist for a variety of products, including office supplies, paper products, electronic equipment, vehicles and fuels, and food. Well-known programs include TerraChoice (EcoLogo) in Canada, Blue Angel in Germany, PC Green Label in Japan and Forest Stewardship Council (FSC).

The general industry consensus on the use of logos is that they should be used with caution. The potential problems stem from consumer confusion and credibility issues. Companies are advised to

- use well-recognized certifications from trusted third parties
- ensure that consumers understand that the eco-logo is based on criteria developed by the manufacturer itself, not an independent verifier
- use transparent processes for measuring environmental footprint
- encourage use of the logo among other players within their industry[22]

Type II (self-declared) environmental claims are those applied to products or services outside of formal third-party programs. The related ISO standard (ISO 14021) sets voluntary rules for the use of thirteen terms commonly found in environmental claims, whether they appear as packaging labels, product literature or advertising. Among these are the terms compostable, degradable, designed for disassembly, extended life, recyclable, recycled content, post-consumer material, reduced resource use and reusable. In 2008, the Canadian Standards Association issued a guidance document, developed in partnership with the Competition Bureau, to accompany ISO 14021.[23] The standard also attempts to rein in the many ways in which claims can be false or misleading, through vague language, incomplete description, ambiguous presentation or the incorrect use of symbols such as the Mobius Loop, shown below.

Type III environmental declarations present quantified environmental information on the life cycle of a product to enable comparisons between products fulfilling the same function. They are based on independently verified life cycle assessment (LCA) data, life cycle inventory analysis (LCI) data or information modules in accordance with the ISO 14040 (LCA) series of standards. Type III declarations are independently verified and used primarily between businesses. While Type I and Type II declarations are about ensuring confidence in claims and labels, Type III declarations are about ensuring quality and integrity of the life cycle data behind environmental declarations.

While the above standards are useful as an auditor's toolbox for what is, and what is not, acceptable, ISO has also published an extensive series of detailed standards on LCA (ISO 14040 series, as noted above) and on integration of environmental aspects into product standards (ISO 14062), which will prove more useful to the businesses interested in how to develop claims.

Despite the impressive international collaboration and consensus behind the publication of the ISO standards described above, there are alternatives available to businesses seeking ways to achieve green product credibility. Beside the need to recognize that this is an endeavor that requires time and management effort (why should the necessary lead time required to get products to market be any different for green products?), there are market-based incentives and other means that can achieve the same end. Among these are procurement policies that stipulate sustainability criteria and thus stimulate change along supply chains, fiscal stimuli by governments and independent verification of claims.

The following five recommended steps are offered to the CEO who is considering introducing green products to his/her company's portfolio. Note that these tasks should be considered alongside conventional marketing techniques, which would apply in any case, whether or not a product has green attributes. The case study on IKEA at the end of this chapter illustrates many of these points.

1. Ask what the company's sustainable development values are and how these align with the proposed product. This may entail reflection on topics as large as the company mission and values, and possibly warrant a review and strategic analysis of the company's position. The internal message that emerges from this analysis must be clear enough to ensure a coherent approach to green products across the organization, i.e., from procurement to sales and marketing to operations.

2. Identify the need for the product (in light of current trends, e.g., low-carbon products); understand the marketplace (e.g., the market understands that reducing GHG emissions is better than offsetting them); and position the product with respect to competing green products (how is it better, e.g., quality, performance or the green value proposition).

3. Ensure the product/product line will meet consumer preferences for quality, performance and price point—independently of the green value proposition.

4. Apply life cycle thinking to ensure the product (and the supply chain) is defensible from the point of view of design; material selection; inputs of energy and natural resources; impacts on society and ecosystem components (air, water, soil and biota) from the production, use and end-of-use phases; and material recovery, reuse and recyclability (see chapter 3).

5. Ensure that life cycle thinking and commensurate sustainability criteria extend to any product packaging.

An additional step, especially for first-time entries into the marketplace, is to identify the areas of weakness in the product, or its development or manufacturing, and explicitly address these through management plans for improvement. The plans need to include objectives, quantified targets, performance indicators, and timelines for achievement.

CHAPTER 4 TAKE-AWAYS

Armed with an understanding of the strategic importance which green has come to assume in all facets of business (chapter 1), including management systems (chapter 2) and awareness of the need to consider it at the design stage of product development (chapter 3), what does the business leader need to remember when preparing a green marketing strategy? Above all else, the market is ready for truly green products, but is now informed and cynical.

Align product with company values—Years of false claims, opportunistic attempts at product positioning followed by accusations of greenwashing and the failure to understand the fundamental need for whole-scale change in how society consumes have moved companies and their products into the spotlight. The successful company will have to be a believer in SD, or at least in how its product offerings contribute to it. And this ethic has to make its way from the boardroom to the product.

Actions speak louder than words—Companies should favor communication of their values through significant action, rather than just talking about it. For example, the conventions used in corporate sustainability or environmental policies, which are carefully scripted texts laden with beliefs, principles and priorities, are less suited to the green product marketplace than direct actions such as credible eco-labels, independent verification, the (collaborative) imposition by firms of wholesale shifts in their supply chain to ensure ethical sourcing of raw materials, and elimination or replacement of products that do not stand up to scrutiny.

The wrong words can speak very loudly—Given what has been said about the need for strong ethical underpinning in corporations, choosing to advertise good deeds or products can inadvertently invite scrutiny and shine the spotlight on the uglier side of one's business. In other words, making a green claim of limited scope (e.g., a narrow range of products, one line, one business location, one material), however true, tends to raise the level of expectation for all parts of the business. Thus, it can become counterproductive to advertise at all. The best approach may be to tone it down. In addition, it is wise to ensure that all parts of the business and key spokespersons are aligned on such messages, lest the right hand be caught saying one thing while the left has already said something else.

Focus on product, not green—As the chapter title suggests, green should become normal. Maturing of the green marketplace will help this happen. Consumers will always be sold on the ensemble of benefits that a product presents, with green being only one of these. It must be part of the thinking from the design stage. Part of a good product is one that meets sustainability requirements. The manufacturer should therefore attempt to join non-green with green benefits in its messaging, e.g., sell the benefits of performance, longevity and cost efficiency, alongside reduced environmental impact.

Think product life cycle—Consumers have become knowledgeable about environmental impacts and their origins, be they related to energy use, carbon emissions, or air/water use and contamination. They also understand why species are endangered. Product manufacturers have to meet customers at the same level.

Sustainability does not equal sainthood—Business leaders should be clear that there should be dual motivation for going green: profit and sustainability. There is no need for pretense to sainthood or being the planet's savior; in fact that position is ill advised, as it can have unintended consequences. Profit and sustainability are necessary and worthy goals when pursued together. Ultimately, companies should be thinking about competitive advantages enabled by taking a leading position on sustainability in their sector, such as the opportunity to drive or influence government regulatory agendas.

IKEA CASE STUDY [24 25 26]

2008 Revenues: $28.5 billion

The Company

IKEA is a privately held, Netherlands-based, international home products and furnishings retailer, founded in 1943.

Stores

IKEA has more than 275, in more than thirty-five countries (mostly developed economies). Stores are colored after the Swedish flag (blue and yellow, in recognition of the company's Swedish founder) and feature walk-through layout from showrooms to self-serve warehouses, free-of-charge play areas for children, inexpensive cafeterias serving Swedish cuisine, and mini food shops.

Products

Based on an approach that leverages environmental design and makes use of economies of scale, the company captures material streams and creates manufacturing processes that hold costs and natural resource use down, such as the extensive use of particle board. The result is flexible, modern-style, utilitarian, assemble-yourself and adaptable home furnishings, scalable both to smaller homes and dwellings as well as large houses. Sold as flat-packs, the concept saves on shipping costs, when compared to pre-assembled furniture. Since 1996, IKEA also offers energy-efficient and environmentally sustainable housing products licenses ("BoKlok") in parts of northern Europe. It also offers mobile phone plans.

Supply Chain

Factories are located in fifty, largely developing, countries.

(Green) Marketing Approach

The IKEA vision is "To create a better everyday life for the many people." The company's market positioning statement is "Your partner in better living. We do our part, you do yours. Together we save money." The marketing approach is to build a relationship with the consumer, using nine key messages. Among these:

- IKEA concept—commitment to product design, consumer value and clever solutions
- IKEA product range—something that appeals to everyone, practical enough for everyday use
- Low price—but represents good value for money (supplier efficiencies, flat pack, etc.)
- Function—practical, attractive, easy to use, and made of the most suitable materials for the purpose
- Right quality—products are subject to rigorous testing to meet international and national safety standards

Remarkably, the terms "sustainability," "CSR," "environment" appear nowhere in these statements, despite IKEA's effective and often controversial marketing techniques.

Environmental Performance

The company developed an action plan in 1992, based on The Natural Step's four conditions for sustainability. Stores designate special parking spots for hybrid vehicles, use reusable cutlery in cafeterias, have low-flush toilets in washrooms and charge for use of plastic bags (the proceeds from which go to planting trees).

Approach to Corporate Responsibility

IKEA's corporate responsibility efforts are achieved primarily through the generation of environmental benefits through efficient design and material used in its products. It partners with UNICEF on various charitable initiatives for children worldwide, as well as with Save the Children and WWF.

Accolades

IKEA was named one of the 100 Best Companies for *Working Mothers* in 2004 and 2005 by Working Mothers magazine. It ranked 96 in *Fortune's* 100 Best Companies to Work For in 2006 and, in 2007, was recognized as one of Canada's Top 100 Employers published in *Maclean's* magazine.

Missteps

The stated intentions of energy and design efficiencies in IKEA stores and products and along its supply chain have been counterbalanced by local impacts associated with at least one construction site, and accidents and car traffic problems around some of its stores.

IKEA parent company (and operator of 207 of the 235 worldwide stores) is INGKA Holding, a private, Dutch-registered company that belongs to the Stichting INGKA Foundation. The structure of the foundation—a tax-exempt, non-profit-making legal entity—has been criticized over the years.

The IKEA Way

"The IKEA Way" is the company's social and environmental responsibility program, which includes posted KPI and performance statistics in several focus areas:

- products and materials (sustainable design and the "e-wheel test" for life cycle considerations)
- suppliers ("IWAY") human rights code of conduct and management system to ensure supplier compliance with IKEA (including forestry requirements from wood sourcing to chain-of-custody tracking to FSC certification)
- energy and transport (distribution, packaging, CO_2 emissions—including customers' use of public transit to reach stores)
- community involvement
- renewable energy

Information derived from www.ikea.com unless otherwise stated.

NOTES

1 Ed Mayo, Chief Executive, National Consumer Council, September 2005 in Anthony Kleanthous and Jules Peck, "Let Them Eat Cake: Satisfying the New Consumer Appetite for Responsible Brands," World Wildlife Fund report, 2007.

2 H.W. Fowler, F.G. Fowler and Judy Pearsall, editors, *Concise Oxford English Dictionary*, 10th Edition revised (New York: Oxford University Press, 2001).

3 Greenpeace, "The Greenpeace Book of Greenwash," 1992.

4 The natural resources and processes supplied by nature and which are in demand from humankind. Services include (1) provisioning, such as the production of food and water; (2) regulating, such as the control of climate and disease; (3) supporting, such as nutrient cycles and crop pollination; (4) cultural, such as spiritual and recreational benefits; and (5) preserving, which includes guarding against uncertainty through the maintenance of diversity.

5 Klaus Töpfer, UNEP Executive Director, in "Talk the Walk: Advancing Sustainable Lifestyles Through Marketing and Communications," UNEP report, 2005.

6 AccountAbility and Consumers International, "What Assures Consumers on Climate Change? Switching on Citizen Power," June 2007.

7 Colin Isaacs, Canadian Institute for Business and the Environment, correspondence, October 2008.

8 S. Bishop, "Don't Bother with the 'Green' Consumer," *Harvard Business Review*, http://www.hbrgreen.org/2008/01/dont_bother_with_the_green_con.html.

9 Bensimon Byrne, "The Bensimon Byrne Consumerology Report: The Impact of Environmental Issues," July 2008.

10 Euromonitor International, "Brands for the Ethical Consumer," 2007.

11 Euromonitor International, "Are Central and South American Consumers Getting Greener?" 2007.

12 Terrachoice, "The Six Sins of Greenwashing: A Study of Environmental Claims in North American Consumer Markets," 2007.

13 Jacquelyn Ottman, *Green Marketing: Opportunities for Innovation in the New Marketing Age*, 2nd edition (Chicago: NTC Business Books, 1998).

14 John Grant, *The Green Marketing Manifesto* (England: John Wiley & Sons, 2007).

15 Judging by sales and informal assessment of its reputation, the Toyota Prius is widely regarded as a successful commercial pioneer in the hybrid automotive market. However, in 2007, an ad it ran in the UK was ruled by the Advertising Standards Authority as being in violation of British advertising codes, including a clause on environmental claims. The ad claimed comparative fuel economies achieved by the Prius and provided evidence to this effect, but was ruled misleading because the bases of comparison were inaccurate.

16 Joel Makower, *Strategies for the Green Economy: Opportunities and Challenges in the New World of Business* (New York: McGraw-Hill, 2008).

17 Jacquelyn Ottman, "Don't Greenwash Your Marketing," *Advertising Age*, 2008.

18 OTA, FTF, IFTA, EISFOM, EFTA, University of Michigan, Observer. 2005.

19 USDA, University of Hohenheim, Fairtrade Foundation, U.S. Dept. of Energy, Paperpects in Stanislas Dupré, "Talk the Walk: Advancing Sustainable Lifestyles Through Marketing and Communications," UNEP/Earthprint, 2005: 30.

20 Colin Isaacs, Canadian Institute for Business and the Environment, correspondence, October 2008.

21 Stanislas Dupré, "Talk the Walk: Advancing Sustainable Lifestyles Through Marketing and Communications," UNEP/Earthprint, 2005.

22 Jacquelyn Ottman, "Eco-logos: A Double-edged Sword?" Sustainable Life Media, not dated.

23 Canadian Standards Association, "Plus 14021 Environmental Claims: A Guide for Industry and Advertisers," 2008: 63.

24 Wikipedia, 2008, http://en.wikipedia.org/wiki/IKEA#IKEA_stores.

25 "Forget About the Gates Foundation. The World's Biggest Charity Owns IKEA—and Is Devoted to Interior Design," *The Economist,* May 11, 2006, http://www.economist.com/business/displaystory.cfm?story_id=6919139.

26 IKEA, "IKEA Marketing Strategy," 2008, http://www.ikea.com/ms/en_GB/about_ikea/press_room/student_info.html.

SUPPLY CHAIN DRIVERS

There has been a significant shift from companies owning and operating manufacturing facilities in North America to leveraging a complex web of suppliers (sometimes thousands of suppliers) that are geographically dispersed and often are small to medium-size enterprises (SMEs). In many cases, this shift in manufacturing has created a "chain of uncertainty" related to the composition of products and the environmental impact of manufacturing facilities.

Key drivers for greening the supply chain include

- ensuring (and, where appropriate, simplifying) compliance with pertinent environmental and product legislation and in the process, demonstrating due diligence
- avoiding costs by eliminating or lowering fees associated with the management of waste, air emissions, water discharges and hazardous materials (e.g., disposal/permit fees, special storage facilities, emission control equipment, reporting)
- minimizing costs associated with take-back, i.e., disassembly and disposal/recycling of goods that are returned where required by legislation or company policy
- reducing costs by conserving water, energy, fuel and other resources
- reducing risk of accidents, insurance costs and health and safety costs
- improving relationships with key stakeholders (government agencies, local communities, customers, etc.) by demonstrating commitment to environmental initiatives

Companies are now faced with four interrelated objectives as they manage environmental issues across their supply chain:

- **Ensure eco-design** criteria for company products are recorded in requirements document and properly communicated (where possible in a collaborative manner) to suppliers (and their suppliers) and a rigid system of checks and balances is in place to ensure compliance.
  - *An example of eco-design criteria is the prohibition on the use of six chemicals that are listed under the Restriction of Hazardous Substances (RoHS) legislation for electronic parts.*
- **Practice green procurement** by developing criteria with proper verification procedures.
  - *An example of a green procurement rule is the purchase of timber that is approved by the Forest Stewardship Council (FSC) or a requirement that suppliers have an eco-label on goods.*
- **Fulfill CSR commitment** by ensuring that supply chain activities conform to the company's CSR policy and objectives.
  - *An example is a commitment to reducing the carbon footprint of both company and supplier operations.*
- **Eliminate mismanagement** of environmental issues throughout the supply chain, placing a strong focus on reducing costs.
  - *An example is working with suppliers to reduce energy and water consumption at their facilities and to pass the cost savings along to the consumer by reducing the price of the product or service.*

Figure 5.1 illustrates some of the different dimensions of a supply chain as they relate to environmental issues, and the degree of control that a company has over them.[1] The key activities for individuals managing their company's supply chain include

- identification of risks related to components that "cannot be controlled" and development of appropriate mitigating measures
- balancing the different business objectives related to eco-design, green procurement and CSR with other business goals, e.g., reduction in inventory, keeping production active, cutting supply chain costs and showing that green decisions can add value to the bottom line

Figure 5.1: Supply Chain Environment Issues

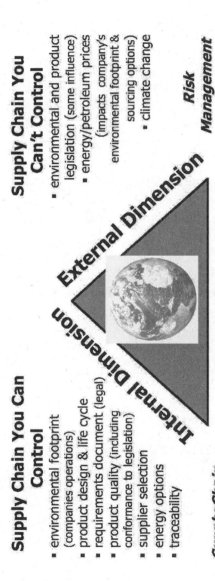

Supply Chain You Can Control
- environmental footprint (companies operations)
- product design & life cycle
- requirements document (legal)
- product quality (including conformance to legislation)
- supplier selection
- energy options
- traceability

Supply Chain Management

Internal Dimension

External Dimension

Customer/Supplier Dimension

Supply Chain You Can't Control
- environmental and product legislation (some influence)
- energy/petroleum prices (impacts company's environmental footprint & sourcing options)
- climate change

Risk Management

Supply Chain You Can't Control, but Can Influence
- customer requirements related to product and suppliers
- product life cycle and development process (in particular, use of hazardous chemicals)
- compliance with relevant legislation pertaining to environment
- environmental footprint related to third-party manufacturing operations
- sustainable use of natural resources by third parties

Phyper & MacLean, 2009

- proactive management of customer/supplier activities that can be influenced by taking into account eco-design, green procurement, CSR and mismanagement (costs) challenges

Note that the term "environmental footprint" refers to the environmental impact associated with manufacturing, distribution and transportation at company-owned or third-party operations: air emissions, wastewater discharges, waste generation, recycling/reuse, water usage, energy usage, presence of hazardous materials in products, reduced discarded packaging material, etc.

This chapter addresses the following key questions related to supply chain management:

- What is the real consequence of having inadequate systems/processes in place to manage environmental issues?
- What are the common pitfalls that organizations fall into that seriously hinder supply chain efficiency?
- What is the impact of government legislation and policy on supply chain management?
- How are sectors and organizations influencing suppliers?
- What is logistics optimization and how is it being applied?

Green programs must reflect the multi-layered and multi-dimensional supply chain to achieve cost efficiencies and avoid cosmetic environmentalism.

SO WHAT? I JUST PAY A LITTLE FINE

More than 71,000 cargo containers enter American seaports daily. In 2006, 467 products were recalled for one or more of the following reasons:

- they contained hazardous materials such as lead
- they were prone to failures such as the separation of treads on a tire
- they contained carcinogenic material or otherwise posed a serious health risk to consumers

In 2007, there was an average of twenty-eight products recalled weekly for environmental and safety reasons.[2]

What is the impact on an organization that does not properly manage environmental issues across their supply chain?

Government response—A full range of responses depending on the type of infraction may be imposed: fines, special one-time fees (e.g., clean-up costs) and even jail time for negligent executives. Fines may be imposed per incident and if the incident persists over a prolonged period of time, the total fine can add up. Government bodies may also ban or significantly restrict the use of a resource (e.g., water, mining rights), prohibit the import/sale of a product, or blacklist a manufacturer or importers. The latter will become easier as the U.S. Homeland Security's Customers and Border Protection (CBP) Automated Commercial Environment (ACE) system is up and running.

Lost revenue—Products may be taken off the market for a period of time, miss a window of opportunity for a launch or require considerable modification. In the long term, the overall sales life of the product may be impaired. The company may also miss the opportunity to lock in buyers if there is a competitive offering released at the same time. Lost market share is generally never regained.[3]

Fixing product—Fixing a non-compliant product is seldom a trivial task and may involve significant redesign effort, including retooling, re-qualification and reliability testing of all new components.[4]

Inventory—Two key decisions must be made concerning non-compliant inventory: one, what to do with units in inventory and two, do you fix or replace units in the field? The company may decide to scrap or redirect non-compliant components or subassemblies for use in other products or markets. The company will also have to ramp up existing suppliers or find new ones.[5]

Lawsuits—California Proposition 65 is enforced entirely through litigation. To state a cause of action, a plaintiff need only show that a listed chemical is present in a consumer product and that the defendant business is "knowingly" exposing Californians to that product without providing an appropriate label. Add on class action lawsuits regarding hazardous ingredients in products as well as sudden drops in share price due to product recalls and you have a very litigious environment in the U.S.

Corporate brand—Newspapers, magazines, blogs and all kinds of media reports have been filled with stories of well-known brands that have failed to ensure that their products or the conditions of their factories (domestically and internationally) are safe and not impairing the environment. Whether the factory is owned or just contracted to by the brand is irrelevant, as most published articles tend to only mention the brand's name. Warren Buffett best describes corporate brand: "It takes 20 years to build a reputation and five minutes to lose it." The link between corporate reputation and product brand is also explored in chapter 4. Case studies on several well-known companies, including Sony and Mattel, and difficulties they have encountered are presented at the end of this chapter.

> Compliance is a must. The key business issue is, how does the company put in place cost-effective systems to ensure ongoing compliance?

COMMON PITFALLS

The five common pitfalls related to the management of suppliers include the following:

1. failure to assign an "owner" to the overall procurement process and activities
2. absence of criteria to properly allow green issues to be factored into purchasing decisions
3. disconnect between accounts payable and procurement regarding fulfillment of obligations by suppliers related to green activities
4. inability to influence/control suppliers because of integrity issues or processes
5. improper management of natural resources that are used as raw materials

Ownership of Procurement

Many companies are appointing chief procurement officers (CPOs) or chief supply officers, positions that have assumed importance in recent years as suppliers outsource manufacturing and look for efficiencies and cost reductions by manufacturing abroad. Key issues facing CPOs include the following:

- Strategic planning—In order to be successful the CPO needs to be a part of the process and must develop a "mental model" to articulate supply chains' role in shaping and fulfilling company strategy.[6]
- Internal collaboration—The supply chain must be made strategically relevant by making connections across company business units and linking

supply chain capabilities to corporate objectives.

- External collaboration—From design to manufacturing to logistics, greater collaboration is a must between stakeholders.
- Criteria—"Green" criteria must be added to existing business criteria to ensure efficiency and consistency in procurement decisions.
- Traceability—Systems must be in place to track who produced each of the subcomponents of a product and the particular batches/lots they prepared.
- Metrics—Proper metrics must be in place and performance tracked in all aspects (including CSR).
- Green procurement—Processes/systems must be in place to promote green procurement and support of the company's overall CSR goals.
- Green logistics—There may be opportunities to reduce cost (and GHG emissions) associated with transport via different modes of transport, co-sharing loads and reducing packaging material.
- Culture—People management, both within the organization and suppliers' operations, is key to building a green culture and thereby shifting to a proactive model versus one dominated by a reactive audit program.

Absence of Green Criteria

Procurement officers are assigned responsibility to meet specific business goals related to reducing inventory, ensuring production is not disrupted, cutting supply chain costs, etc. "Green procurement" is rarely a portfolio mandate, but rather it is a mandated component of procurement execution so that the procurement officer will consider green suppliers as a weighted value in the procurement decision. The key problem, however, is the absence of criteria in most cases to make this type of decision in a manner that takes into account the various objectives of the company on a consistent basis.

Cost, performance, availability, quality and environmental performance all need to be factored into the equation. In many instances, businesses do not know what "green performance" they're demanding from their suppliers. Typically, criteria fall into one of the following categories:

- compliance with government legislation—the key issue is to identify the applicable legislation, as it can be overwhelming, especially for SME suppliers; in most cases, guidance needs to be provided to ensure success

- purchase of eco-labeled products/services (e.g., percent recycled content)—reliance on either third-party certification system or trust in supplier that they are allowed to use a label where no certification is available
- conformance to the supplier's own stated intentions, i.e., supplier tells the company what they are about to do and company follows up to see if it is done
- conformance to company-initiated guidelines/objectives in a variety of areas: e.g., reduction/reuse of packaging, absence of hazardous chemicals in products (e.g. EU NGO "SIN" List), recycled content of paper, low VOC paints, and energy-efficient equipment; the key issue is how to work collaboratively with the supplier to get its buy-in and ensure projects are meaningful
- adoption of government green procurement principles for use with company's suppliers
- green/lean principles developed with industrial association (e.g., Electronic Industry Code of Conduct) or part of the United States Green Supply Network (GSN)

The GSN is a joint effort between the U.S. EPA, the U.S. Department of Commerce, the National Institute of Standards and Technology, and the Manufacturing Extension Partnership Program. GSN has leveraged the proven principles of lean manufacturing and merged them with pollution prevention and the EPA's environmental initiatives.

In an AMR Research publication entitled *Lean and Clean with Green Purchasing*, the following lessons were derived from the integration of GSN's clean initiatives and the principles of lean manufacturing:[7]

- optimizing material use for less scrap yields reduced solid waste
- reducing inventory for less chemical spoilage equates to reduced hazardous waste
- reducing overproduction means less run time and improved energy savings
- less transportation means a reduction in fuel consumption, which reduces air emissions

Companies need to understand what their green objectives (in the form of criteria) are before imposing them on suppliers in order to ensure consistency and value for money.

The Disconnect between Finance and Green Procurement

Unfortunately, companies seldom link poor environmental performance to financial aspects, e.g., should payment for goods be a function of environmental metrics as it is with delivery date, quality of product? The following key elements should be taken into account when including environmental metrics in supplier contracts.[8]

- Companies should request environmental information from suppliers (or potential suppliers) early on in negotiations as it forces them to become more accountable. Suppliers are then able to put more information into a balanced scorecard and measure their performance, creating an incentive for them to improve.
- It is important that realistic targets be included as it is a tricky balance between the company—which wants to get the most for its money—and suppliers—who are eager to please in order to get the contract. If unrealistic conditions are included and the supplier can't meet them, this may cause either significant friction in the relationship or may end it. Contractual points have to be clear, concise and adhered to.
  - *An example of this is "min-max" and just-in-time clauses that can force suppliers to make small, expedited deliveries that drive up energy usage/ GHG emissions.*[9]
- Periodic revisions of the contract should take place, allowing both parties to provide input on the status of activities to achieve targets so that a harmonious relationship is built. This process also allows both parties to build benchmark information.
- Managing suppliers' green strategies shouldn't be revolutionary; KPIs and service level agreements are systems and processes that are already applied to cover non-green elements of procurement contracts.

Influence/Control Suppliers

Typically, companies' relationships with their suppliers involve five activities:

1. Provide specifications to suppliers regarding overall product requirements, indicating what material is not to be used (oftentimes referred to as the "company black list" or "hit list").
2. Provide policies/guidelines on what is expected of the supplier regarding environmental management at its facilities.

3. Undertake a periodic sampling of delivered product to ensure conformance to both specifications and absence of banned material.
4. Audit suppliers, leveraging published auditing protocols, e.g., International Organization for Standardization (ISO) and Electronic Industry Code
   of Conduct (EICC) audit framework.
5. Document problems with supplier environmental performance; where
   control is weak, typically this is done *ad hoc* and isolated from key business systems.

There is a shift towards greater emphasis on collaboration and preventive actions
as companies

- go beyond auditing to consider how capacity-building can increase adherence to supplier standards and understanding of legislation with which
  the company must comply; this could include collaborating on product
  design to reduce weight and packaging material to allow shipping containers to hold more
- leverage partners/suppliers to find ways to minimize repetitive audits and
  accelerate adoption of a management system
- use electronic procurement exchanges to track and flag suppliers with
  spotty environmental records; this allows the full supply chain, including
  suppliers' suppliers, to be monitored—a significant problem for almost all
  companies

According to a report by Business for Social Responsibility (BSR), companies that
work directly with factory managers to help suppliers take ownership of CSR is-
sues have a better chance of effectively addressing concerns about environment.
The report entitled *Pilot Summary Report: Building Capabilities to Implement CSR
Management Systems at ICT Suppliers in China* is based on pilot projects that
sought to break through barriers to improve factory conditions. The World Bank
Group's investment climate advisory service, the Foreign Investment Advisory
Service, the Electronic Industry Citizenship Coalition, the Global e-Sustainability
Initiative and the Shenzhen Electronics Industries Association partnered with
BSR on the projects.[10]

In most cases, companies have limited control over their supply chain and as such,
need to influence behavior in a collaborative manner while ensuring that suppliers
who lack integrity are red flagged and avoided.

Management of Natural Resources Used for Raw Material

Over the last few years, companies are slowly, and sometimes painfully, learning to ask themselves the following five key questions regarding the management of natural resources used as raw materials:

1. Does the consumer want to buy products made from these resources? Well-known examples include products containing asbestos and timber from ecologically sensitive areas.
2. Will consumers boycott the product if the resource is harvested in a non-ecological manner? Examples of significant consumer boycotts that have shifted harvesting techniques include those related to tuna fishing ("Dolphin Safe") as well as forest management.
3. Are the resources readily available or are there limitations on the supply of the resource? Examples include cod stock depletions and the supply of fresh water for food and beverage companies in developing countries.
4. Will subsidies tied to the harvesting of this resource change in the near future? Approximately $850 billion per year of government subsidies are provided for producers that cause damage to the environment.[11] The focus and amounts of subsidies will undergo significant change in the next few years as governments realign their green initiatives. In many cases, the elimination of subsidies will result in marginal businesses closing down operations or switching to other resources.
5. Is the price of the resource (and hence, the product) going to increase dramatically? An example of the competing use of a resource, and associated increase in cost, is the use of corn as a raw material for food products, feedstock for animals, biofuel and bioplastics. The increase in production of the latter two resulted in elevated prices for corn in 2007 and 2008.

As indicated in chapter 4, green products can be desirable to consumers, but if the product fails to deliver on performance or is more expensive, the majority of consumers will choose the lower cost item. Governments must also "selectively" intervene to ensure that there is a level playing field for companies—it makes no sense to put limits on local fishermen when international trawlers and pirate ships can sweep the sea clean of fish stocks, as an example.

Figure 5.2 clearly illustrates the over-exploitation of cod off the coast of Newfoundland, Canada, and the subsequent collapse of the stocks. The economic and social impact of the collapse has been devastating to local communities and companies, never mind the fish. A similar fate awaits other parts of the annual $55 billion seafood industry unless action is taken.

Will resources be available in the future? From 2001 to 2005, more than 1,360 international experts involved in the Millennium Ecosystem Assessment (MA) project assessed the consequences of ecosystem change for human well-being. The report, entitled *Living Beyond Our Means: Natural Assets and Human Well-being*, scientifically appraises the condition of and trends in changes to the world's ecosystems and the services (benefits) they provide, as well as the scientific basis for conservation and sustainability. The four main findings of the report are these:[12]

1. Over the past fifty years, humans have changed ecosystems faster and more extensively than in any period in human history. This has been largely due to rapidly growing demands for food, fresh water, timber, fiber and fuel. The result has been a substantial and largely irreversible loss in the diversity of life on earth.
2. The changes made to ecosystems have contributed to substantial gains in human well-being and economic development, but these gains have been achieved at growing costs. These costs include the degradation of many ecosystem services, increased risks of abrupt changes and increased poverty for some groups of people. These problems, unless addressed, will substantially reduce the benefits that future generations get from ecosystems.
3. This degradation of ecosystem services could significantly worsen over the next fifty years and is a barrier to the achievement of the Millennium Development Goals, which have been commonly accepted as a framework for measuring global development progress.
4. Reversing the degradation of ecosystems while meeting increasing demands for their services is a challenge. This challenge can be partially met in the future under scenarios involving significant changes to policies, institutions and practices. However, the actions required will have to be substantial compared to the actions currently being undertaken.

Carefully select and manage resources that are required as raw materials. If they are no longer available, for a variety of reasons, your company may no longer be able to operate.

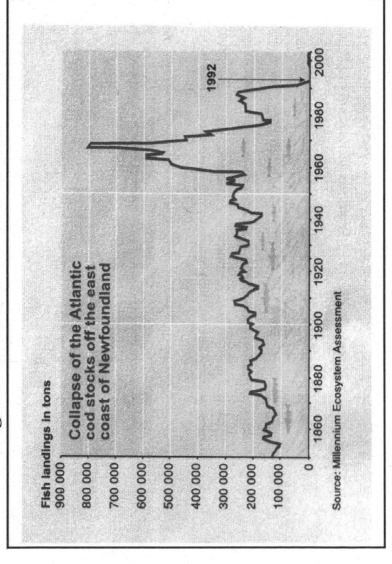

Figure 5.2: Decline of Cod Stocks

Fish landings in tons

Collapse of the Atlantic cod stocks off the east coast of Newfoundland

Source: Millennium Ecosystem Assessment

ROLE OF GOVERNMENT LEGISLATION/POLICIES

Two important trends may significantly influence the ability of a company to ensure that their suppliers comply with legislation:

1. Companies continue to move their manufacturing to offshore locations where suppliers may not have to comply with the legislation that the company adheres to at its operations.
2. The amount and complexity of global legislation related to environmental issues throughout the life cycle of a product continue to increase at a rapid pace.

A partial list of legislation that should be considered as a minimum when assessing supply chain requirements includes

- eco-design requirements
- prohibition of chemicals in products
- registration of substances/chemicals
- hazard labeling and Material Safety Data Sheets (MSDSs)
- energy usage and labeling of products
- fuel efficiency and use of renewable fuels
- packaging materials and amounts
- consumer products safety (including drugs/food)
- releases (air emissions, wastewater discharge and waste) during production of goods
- government green procurement requirements
- take-back and end-of-life

Appendix A provides information on recent legislation/policy related to supply chain activities; however, here is a brief discussion of the new EU REACH legislation, as it is unique in its impact on supply chain activities.

Figure 5.3 presents a high level overview of supply chain connectivity related to the REACH legislation. Manufacturers (M) or companies that import (I) substances into the EU in amounts greater than 1 tonne per year must collect and submit data to the European Chemical Agency (ECHA). A non-EU community manufacturer, who brings a substance into the EU either in pure form or as part of a preparation or an article, may appoint a natural or legal person established in the EU to fulfill, as his only representative (OR), its obligations as an importer.

Figure 5.3: Supply Chain Complexity

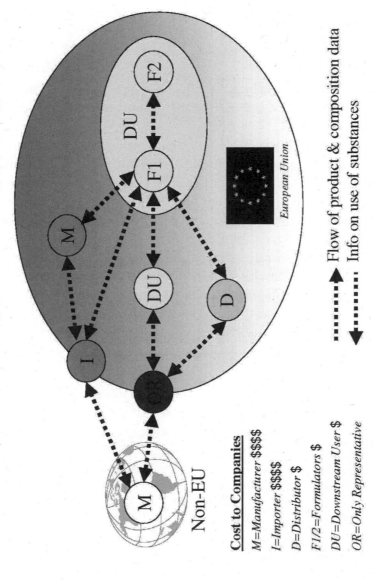

Phyper & MacLean, 2009

Cost to Companies

M=Manufacturer $$$$
I=Importer $$$$
D=Distributor $
F1/2=Formulators $
DU=Downstream User $
OR=Only Representative

The term "article" refers to an object that, during production, is given a special shape, surface or design that determines its function to a greater degree than does its chemical composition.

Downstream users (DU) and formulators in the EU must ensure that they are using registered substances and that they notify suppliers of the intended "use" for the substance. Suppliers need to decide if they will support the "use" or not.

Unique elements of this legislation include the following:

- It targets existing substances in the marketplace. In most countries, this type of legislation is directed at new substances being brought into the marketplace.
- It requires the bi-directional flow of information along the supply chain: in general, a company must provide information to all its customers regarding hazards associated with a particular use and customers must advise on their intended uses.
- All players in the supply chain need to provide full disclosure of supplied formulations if the substance crosses the one-tonne threshold.
- If the material (including articles) contains a Substance of Very High Concern (SVHC) that exceeds 0.1% (by weight), all recipients in the supply chain must, as a minimum, advise users of the name of the substance.

HOW ARE ORGANIZATIONS INFLUENCING SUPPLIERS?

Retailers

There have been a number of government and corporate initiatives to encourage the purchase of environmentally responsible and energy-efficient products, and environmental labeling and eco-logos have been around since the late 1970s. These activities, while admirable, will pale in comparison to the initiatives underway at several large retailers, whose revenues, in many cases, exceed most countries' gross national product.

Wal-Mart

With revenue exceeding $374 billion and a supply chain that is the envy of many companies, Wal-Mart has substantial influence on its thousands of suppliers. Wal-Mart's Sustainable Value Networks (SVNs) bring together internal leaders and leaders from suppliers, environmental groups, academia and government to focus on everything from energy use by stores to the packaging of products. It is important to note, however, that most companies do not have the same level of control over their supply as Wal-Mart does, and hence the ability to mandate green behavior. (See the Wal-Mart case study at the end of chapter 2.)

Tesco

Tesco is a supermarket chain that operates in 13 countries, serving 30 million people on a weekly basis. Tesco sources goods from 5,000 companies across the globe to provide thousands of products. Examples of green components of Tesco's sourcing program include[13]

- Nature's Choice standard—safety, quality and environmental standards for fruit, vegetables and salads
- Organic Product standard—standard for organic products (since June 2006, Tesco has launched more than 250 new organic products)
- Livestock Code of Practice—covers all aspects of animal husbandry, animal welfare requirements, environmental impact and food safety factors, and requires UK providers to be members of an independently audited and certified farm assurance scheme
- Fish Sourcing Policy—is based on four key principles: avoid stocking wild fish from over-fished or vulnerable stocks; support sustainable sourcing initiatives; work with suppliers and the industry to improve sustainability of fishing methods; and promote sustainable fish species
- Genetically Modified (GM) Foods Policy—Tesco does not sell any own-brand GM foods; use of GM feed is prohibited in organic products (including organic animal feed)
- Commitment to Approved Timber—all sources of timber for their garden furniture are either Forest Stewardship Council (FSC)-approved or members of the Tropical Forest Trust (TFT), who are committed to achieving the FSC standard through the certification support programs of ethical auditors

Electronics Equipment

The supply chain in the electronics industry is complex, with multiple manufacturers of finished products sharing the same subcontractors and parts suppliers. In response to increasing interest in CSR, the Electronic Industry Code of Conduct

(EICC) was developed in 2004. This code avoids the introduction of independent, company-specific standards for CSR, as these may cause confusion and constitute a significant burden on companies in the supply chain.

The EICC group comprises more than twenty-five participating companies from the EU, the U.S., Asia and Japan. Members include manufacturers and OEM suppliers and retailers. In cooperation with the Global e-Sustainability Initiative (GeSI) Supply Chain Working Group (formed primarily of EU telecom sector and other electronics industry organizations), the EICC group is currently promoting social responsibility across the global supply chain.[14]

As shown in figure 5.4, the EICC group is working to develop tools, Web-based systems and audit/verification programs to create a framework for ensuring the code is upheld, including[15]

- the formulation of and revisions to the EICC
- the development of common implementation tools
  - *risk assessment tool*
  - *supplier self-assessment questionnaire*
  - *audits*
  - *standardization of audit procedures*
  - *identification of qualified third-party firms to conduct audits*
- the development and administration of a Web-based system
- stakeholder engagement

(Additional information on programs for the electronics industry is presented in the Sony and Dell case studies at the end of this chapter.)

Chemical Industry

One of the first examples of efforts to "de-risk" the supply chain was the Canadian Chemical Producers Association (CCPA) Responsible Care program, which was released in 1985. The program is a unique "ethic" for the safe and environmentally sound management of chemicals. Participation in Responsible Care is mandatory for members, all of which have made CEO-level commitments to uphold the program. The program was adopted by the U.S. Chemical Manufacturers' Association (now referred to as the American Chemical Council, or ACC) in 1988 and more than fifty other national associations around the world since.

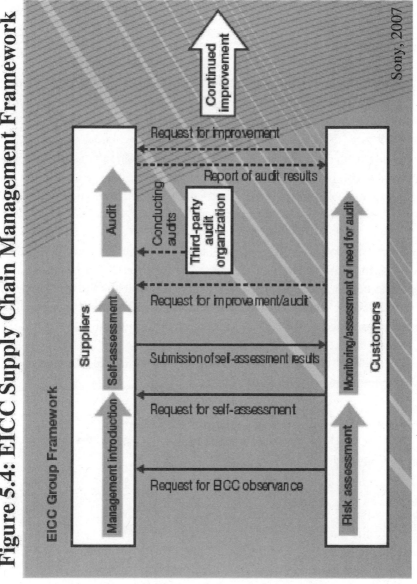

Figure 5.4: EICC Supply Chain Management Framework

Responsible Care fundamental features pertinent to supply chain include[16]

- providing chemicals that can be manufactured, transported, used and disposed of safely
- making health, safety, the environment and resource conservation critical considerations for all new and existing products and processes
- providing information on health or environmental risks and pursue protective measures for employees, the public and other key stakeholders
- working with customers, carriers, suppliers, distributors and contractors to foster the safe use, transport and disposal of chemicals
- supporting education and research on the health, safety and environmental effects of our products and processes
- practicing Responsible Care by encouraging and assisting others to adhere to these guiding principles and practices

Chemical companies live up to their obligations under Responsible Care by allowing verification teams of advocates, industry experts and neighbors to visit every member company. Every three years, repeat visits by the verification team emphasize performance, ascertaining that management systems are delivering the results expected by the public. All verification team reports are posted on the CCPA website.[17]

In addition to the general Responsible Care program, the ACC and the CCPA have also implemented/participated in

- CHEMTREC (Chemical Transportation Emergency Center)
- TRANSCAER (Transportation Community Awareness and Emergency Response)

The national TRANSCAER initiative promotes dialogue and emergency preparedness along chemical transportation routes. CHEMTREC is a public service hotline for fire fighters, law enforcement and other emergency responders to obtain information and assistance for emergency incidents involving chemicals and hazardous materials. Shippers of hazardous materials can comply with American and Canadian legislation by registering with CHEMTREC.

(See the DuPont case study at the end of chapter 1 for additional information on what chemical companies are doing related to supply chain.)

Government Green Procurement

Why include government as a sector of interest? Two key reasons: government procurement accounts for 10% to 15% of gross domestic product in developed countries[18] and government agencies on average have more advanced systems/processes for green procurement than most industry. There are numerous government programs for green procurement, including

- in the United States
  - Affirmative Procurement (also called Green Procurement)—all federal agencies must comply
  - Environmentally Preferable Purchasing Program—Environmental Protection Agency (EPA)
  - Green Procurement Program (GPP)—Department of Defense (DoD)
- in Canada
  - Guidelines for the Integration of Environmental Performance Considerations in Federal Government Procurement—Office of Greening Government Operations

Both countries have green procurement rules that either mandate green procurement, or highly prefer/recommend it. For example, typical procurement rules require the purchase of green products in the following categories (note that this list is not all-inclusive): office products (including electronic equipment and furniture); printing services; fleet vehicles and fleet maintenance products; building construction, renovation and maintenance (including janitorial and landscape services); traffic control; parks and recreation; appliances and lighting.

United States

The Office of the Federal Environmental Executive oversees U.S. federal greening initiatives. These initiatives include the acquisition of recycled content products, environmentally preferable products and services, bio-based products, energy- and water-efficient products, alternative fuel vehicles, products using renewable energy, and alternatives to hazardous or toxic chemicals. Other groups that assist government departments/agencies include the following:

- the White House Task Force on Waste Prevention and Recycling—in conjunction with the EPA and the U.S. Department of Agriculture, assists federal agencies to promote the acquisition of recycled content, environmentally preferable and bio-based products; non-ozone depleting substances; and products containing alternatives to certain priority chemicals

- the U.S. Department of Energy and EPA—assists agencies to implement energy-related purchasing requirements, including the purchase of alternative fuel vehicles and alternative fuels
- General Services Administration and the Defense Logistics Agency—as central sources of supply, assist in the implementation of federal green purchasing programs[19]

The DoD GPP can be used to illustrate the components of a federal policy. DoD GPP objectives include the following:

- Educate all appropriate DoD employees on the requirements of federal green procurement preference programs, their roles and responsibilities with respect to these programs, and opportunities to purchase green products and services.
- Increase purchases of green products and services consistent with the demands of mission, efficiency and cost-effectiveness, with continual improvement towards federally established procurement goals.
- Reduce the amount of solid waste generated.
- Reduce consumption of energy and natural resources.
- Expand markets for green products and services.

The responsibility for implementing DoD's GPP lies not within any single organization, but with every person involved in the procurement process. It should be noted that green procurement requirements apply to the acquisition of both supplies and services.

Canada

The Canadian government's GPP seeks to reduce the environmental impact of government operations and promote environmental stewardship by integrating environmental performance considerations in the procurement process. Green procurement is set within the context of achieving value for money. It requires the integration of environmental performance considerations into the procurement process including planning, acquisition, use and disposal. In this context, value for money includes the consideration of many factors such as cost, performance, availability, quality and environmental performance. Green procurement also requires an understanding of the environmental aspects, and potential impacts and costs, associated with the life cycle assessment of the goods and services being acquired.

> If your company sells to government agencies and you are not aware of government green procurement rules/processes, don't bother bidding.

Outsourcing Sectors

The green procurement wave is also about to hit the outsourcing sector, as more and more companies expect/demand green suppliers. According to an annual study by the Brown-Wilson Group entitled *The Black Book of Outsourcing*, in particular the 2007 edition, more than 21% of U.S. and European companies that already outsource have added green policies and performance indicators to their outsourcing agreements. More importantly, almost every company surveyed plans to add green clauses to outsourcing contracts during renegotiations, and a further 36% have plans to move to a greener outsourcer within the next twelve months.[20]

(Additional information on what companies are doing to green procurements is presented in table 5.1 located at the end of this chapter, p. 215.)

EXAMPLES OF LOGISTICS OPTIMIZATION

More and more companies are optimizing transport and loading efficiency, strategically locating distribution centres, and shifting to more environmentally conscious modes of transport. According to a Deloitte & Touche review of a consumer goods companies' operations, "simply by consolidating shipments—both incoming raw materials and outgoing finished products—and reorganizing deliveries through better communications and customer education on the impact of their shipping preferences, the company estimated it could achieve a 25 percent reduction in annual transportation costs."[21]

Sony—Sony's logistic group (Sony Supply Chain Solutions) recently promoted a shift in long-distance transport to rail and sea transport, which emit less CO_2 than trucks, in a manner that balances lead times and transport costs. Sony also is continuing to use co-transportation by sharing railway containers with other companies to maximize transport efficiency. In addition, Sony is increasing efforts to improve packaging and transport procedures, introducing reusable international shipping containers for shipping parts, to reduce both transportation costs and CO_2 emissions. The use of these reusable containers has enabled Sony to minimize roundtrip shipping costs and at the same time simplified packaging using returnable materials, resulting in the reduction of waste from packaging and transport. Sony has also introduced reusable folding plastic containers for shipping certain digital camera and digital camcorder parts. Sony plans to begin using these containers for semiconductors, LCD panels and other large parts worldwide. Additional information on Sony's activities is provided in its case study at the end of this chapter.

Wal-Mart—Wal-Mart has one of the largest private fleets in the United States, with approximately seven thousand trucks on the road. Examples of Wal-Mart activities include[22]

- Fleet efficiency. Wal-Mart's goal is to increase fleet efficiency by 25% by the end of 2008 and to double it by 2015 (with associated savings of $300 million per year). Wal-Mart estimates that every one mile per gallon increase in fleet fuel mileage results in a savings of more than $40 million per year.
- Auxiliary power units (APUs). In May 2006, Wal-Mart installed APUs—small, efficient diesel engines—on all of its trucks that make overnight trips. Drivers can turn off their truck engines and rely on the APUs to warm or cool the cabin and run communication systems while on breaks. In a single year, this change should eliminate approximately 100,000 metric tons of carbon dioxide emissions and save the company an estimated $25 million per year.
- Truck design. Wal-Mart is working with major truck design companies to develop diesel hybrid trucks and aerodynamic trucks to achieve its efficiency goals. It is anticipated that tests of these trucks will begin in the 2009–2010 time frame.
- Hybrid vehicles. Wal-Mart has been purchasing hybrid passenger vehicles for its corporate fleet since July 2003. It currently has more than 300 hybrid vehicles, and plans to purchase 150 additional hybrids each year.
- SmartWay Partnership. In June 2007, the truck fleet was qualified as a "superior environmental performer" by the EPA's SmartWay Transport

Partnership, an innovative collaboration with the freight industry to increase energy efficiency while significantly reducing greenhouse gases and air pollution.

(Additional information on Wal-Mart is provided in its case study in chapter 2.)

UPS—UPS has undertaken the following key activities:[23]

- retrofitted aircraft, at a cost of several billion dollars, with advanced technology and fuel-efficient engines that reduce noise ahead of regulatory requirements
- developed computer software solution that efficiently dispatches vehicles. (Delivery routes are designed to avoid time-consuming and unnecessary overlaps resulting in a reduction in vehicle emissions and fuel savings. The elimination of left-hand turns alone allowed UPS to take 28.5 million miles off its delivery routes, saving 3 million gallons of gas and reducing CO_2 emissions by 31,000 tonnes per year.)[24]
- runs a fleet maintenance system to minimize environmental impact by ensuring that each vehicle meets and exceeds company standards
- operates the largest private alternative fuel fleet in its industry, which includes more than two thousand compressed natural gas, liquefied natural gas, propane, and electric and hybrid electric vehicles. (Since 2000, UPS's alternative fuel fleet has traveled more than 144 million miles making deliveries to homes and businesses.)

UPS also collaborates with manufacturers, government and nonprofit organizations to promote sustainable product transportation. UPS is a

- charter member of the EPA Smartway Transport Program
- member of Business for Social Responsibility's Clean Cargo Green Freight Working Group, a coalition to develop environmentally preferable transportation practices

There are relatively low-hanging cost savings available to companies related to optimizing their logistics.

CHAPTER 5 TAKE-AWAYS

Define procurement objectives—What is the primary objective of the organization? To be perceived as green? To reduce costs (direct/indirect) associated with environmental issues? To match competitors' green activities? This question needs to be asked before setting and/or refining procurement programs/processes and criteria. The answers are a function of business needs and how best to improve shareholder value. The caveat is that companies who are relying on greenwashing—disinformation disseminated to present an environmentally responsible public image—may find themselves at the center of controversy as NGOs probe their activities, with the potential negative impact on corporate brand.

Ownership—As mentioned in previous chapters, ownership of an issue is key. Procurement touches on many facets of a company's operations and as such processes and systems, with clear accountabilities, need to be put in place to ensure collaboration with both internal stakeholders (e.g., product management, research and development, accounts payable, Environment Health and Safety group) and external stakeholders (industrial associations, government agencies, suppliers and suppliers' suppliers).

Information systems—Global companies can no longer expect to manage their supply chain using disparate IT systems or manual processes. Integrated systems must be leveraged to ensure that green procurement criteria are being used in selection, contract negotiation, generation of specifications, delivery of goods, ongoing facility monitoring and payment processes. No longer is it acceptable to assume that suppliers will track legislation; companies need to perform their own checks, e.g., comparison of supplier declaration/composition information against both regulatory and non-regulatory (hazard assessment) requirements and ensure that chemicals included in the products are registered in the country where they will be used. Companies must also be able to rely on third parties to provide feedback on the integrity of suppliers' suppliers to further minimize business risk.

Collaboration with suppliers—Not every company can influence its supply chain like Wal-Mart can. Most companies must put in place systems/processes to influence the behavior of their suppliers, cooperatively develop realistic joint green criteria, and work with industrial associations to monitor compliance. These are time-consuming activities that must be well thought-out if true change (both cost reductions and improvements for the environment) is to be achieved. It also re-

quires leaders in every vertical to initiate changes in their procurement patterns
and buying decisions in order to alter the vertical's specific buying patterns.

Network Optimization—Need to assess company's entire supply chain focusing
on key logistics areas: materials for products, sourcing and suppliers, manufacturing and production processes, warehousing, and transportation and distribution
(primarily location of distribution centers).[25]

Table 5.1: Samples of Green Procurement Websites

U.S. Government
Alternative fuels and fuel efficiency www.eere.energy.gov/vehiclesandfuels
Alternatives to five priority chemicals under Exec. Order 13148 www.ofee.gov
Bio-based products www.biobased.oce.usda.gov and www.ofee.gov
Energy-efficient production www.eere.energy.gov/
EPA Environmentally Preferable Purchasing (EPP) www.epa.gov/epp/database.htm
EPA WasteWise www.epa.gov/wastewise
EPA-recovered material www.epa.gov/cpg
Non-ozone depleting substances www.ofee.gov/
Office of the Federal Environmental Executive www.ofee.gov/gp/gp.asp
Pennsylvania Department of the Environment Protection www.dep.state.pa.us/dep/deputate/pollprev/
Iso14001/SME.htm

Canadian Government/Cities
City of Toronto GIPPER's Guide to Environmental Purchasing www.ec.gc.ca/cppic/En/refView.cfm?refId=1491
Environment Canada www.ec.gc.ca/default.asp?lang=En&n=FD9B0E51-1
Natural Resource Canada www.nrcan-rncan.gc.ca/com/index-eng.php
Office of Greening Government Operations www.tpsgc-pwgsc.gc.ca/greening/text/proc/decision-e.html
Treasury Board of Canada, Green Procurement Reporting Framework www.tbs-sct.gc.ca/cmp/green-vert/grnproc_e.asp

Other Countries
Australian Green Procurement www.greenprocurement.org
European Commission on Green Public Procurement (GPP) http://ec.europa.eu/environment/gpp/index_en.htm
New Zealand Green Procurement www.med.govt.nz/templates/MultipageDocumentPage____8914.aspx
Norway Green in Practice Purchasing's GRIP Purchasing www.grip.no/Innkjop/English/available_material.htm
Swedish Environmental Advisory Council's Green Headline Indicators www.sou.gov.se/mvb/english/Formeractivities/green_head.htm#Use%20of%20energy

Organizations/Industry
Electronic Product Environmental Assessment Tool (EPEAT) www.epeat.net
Fujitsu General Green Procurement www.fujitsu-general.com/global/corporate/procure/index.html
Green Procurement www.greenontario.org/buygreen/greenp.html
Organisation for Economic Co-operation and Development (OECD) Greener Public Purchasing www.oecd.org/document/21/0,2340,en_2649_201185_37414933_1_1_1_1,00.html
The Canadian Standards Association Environmentally Responsible Procurement Z766-95 (R2006) www.csa-intl.org/onlinestore/GetCatalogDrillDown.asp?Parent=472

SONY CASE STUDY: PART 1

2007 Revenues: $70.3 billion

Environmental Vision

Sony recognizes the importance of preserving the natural environment that sustains life on earth for future generations and helps humanity to attain the dream of a healthy and happy life. Sony is committed to achieving this goal by seeking to combine ongoing innovation in environmental technology with environmentally sound business practices. Sony aims for greater eco-efficiency in its business activities through maximizing the efficiency of nonrenewable energy and resource use and providing products and services with greater added value. Efforts will focus on reducing harmful effects on the environment by ensuring compliance with all applicable environmental regulations and reducing the environmental impact on energy and resource use on a continuing basis. Steps will also be taken to find solutions to complex environmental issues through closer cooperation and enhanced information sharing with the broad spectrum of Sony stakeholders.

Key Environmental Initiatives

Promoting Reduction of Energy and Resources in Products: Promoted energy- and resource-saving measures. Achieved energy savings target for approximately 90% of product categories. Achieved reuse/recycle materials utilization rate of approximately 10%. In Japan, Sony has used the Green Power Certification System since 2001 to purchase electric power generated using renewable energy sources. Sony also received the Sustainable Energy Europe Award, the first consumer electronics and entertainment company to earn this prestigious prize.

Eliminating Specified Chemical Substances from Products: Continuous operation of the Green Partner Environmental Quality Approval Program as part of the effort to manage chemical substances in electronic products.

Building and Operating Product Recycling Systems: Ongoing development and operation of product recycling systems to meet the requirements of different regions. Recovered 36,355 tons of resources from end-of-life products worldwide.

Conduct Life Cycle Assessments (LCAs): Completed for 75% of product

Reducing the Environmental Impact of Sites: Implementing efforts aimed at meeting targets for reducing the absolute environmental impact of Sony's sites. To date the following have been achieved: reduction of GHG emissions—9%; reduction of waste—30%; reduction of water used—16%; reduction of volatile organic compounds released—41% (compared with fiscal 2000).

Establishing Partnership with NGOs to Address the Issue of Climate Change: Participation in the Climate Savers Programme, organized by the World Wide Fund for Nature, under which the NGO partners with companies to implement various initiatives aimed at lowering GHG.

Emissions Trading: Sony Electronics Inc. in the U.S. has joined the Chicago Climate Exchange (CCX), a voluntary GHG allowance trading system. In Japan, Sony is an investor in the Japan Greenhouse Gas Reduction Fund.

Environmental Management Systems: Implemented ISO 14001 across the entire Sony Group.

Promoting Mid-term Environmental Targets: Reinforcement of environmental conservation activities with the aim of achieving Green Management 2010 mid-term environmental targets. Key metrics include

GHG Index = total GHG emissions from sites (in terms of CO_2) + total CO_2 emissions from product use + total CO_2 emissions from logistics – GHG emission offset by GHG reduction activities

Resource Index = waste land filled from sites + product resource input – volume of reused/recycled materials – volume of resource recovery from end-of-life products

Supply Chain

Strengthening Supply Chain Management: Introduction of EICC Supplier Code of Conduct and implementation of self-assessment questionnaires with the aim of encouraging suppliers to comply with the code, with emphasis on environmental preservation, human rights and the work environment.

Participating in Global CSR Procurement Alliance: Involved in the IECC group, an alliance for promoting CSR considerations in supply chain management.

SONY CASE STUDY: PART 2

2001 Cadmium Issue

In October 2001, Sony Computer Entertainment Europe temporary halted shipments of the PlayStation (PS) game console destined for the EU market after Dutch authorities determined that levels of cadmium were above legal limits. PS shipments were resumed after confirming that there was no health risk to users and Sony worked closely with Dutch authorities to replace noncompliant components to meet their standards. After an eighteen-month review including inspections of more than six thousand factories, the company tracked down the source of the problem—a negligent supplier that supplied cadmium-laced cables against Sony's specifications. Sony estimated that the total cost of the failure, including rework, was 110 million euros in sales and 52 million euros in profits.[27]

2001 Response

Concurrent to its response to the PS issue, Sony initiated its own program to inspect all its products and discovered other occurrences. Sony embarked on a company-wide, comprehensive program of measures, including revisions to specific policies and standards and tighter management and control systems, in order to prevent any problems occurring with cadmium and similar chemical substances in the future.[28] Prior to 2001, dedicated teams within Sony were concerned with issues such as product safety and environmental conservation. In 2002, Sony established a separate head office group, Compliance Office, charged with exercising overall control over compliance activities across the Sony Group and initiated an internal hotline system for the entire Sony Group.[29]

Substances Subject to Control by Sony

- heavy metals: cadmium, lead, mercury and hexavalent chromium
- chlorinated organic compounds
- brominated organic compounds
- tributylin compounds, tripheyltin compounds
- asbestos
- azo compounds
- formaldehyde
- polyvinyl chloride (PVC)
- beryllium monoxide and beryllium copper
- phthalate esters
- hydrofluorocarbons and perfluorocarbons

Information derived from Sony CSR Report, 2007 unless otherwise stated.

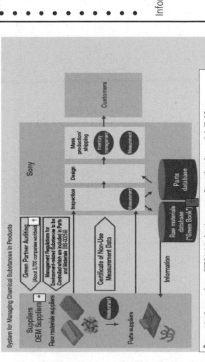

System for Managing Chemical Substances in Products

Sony, 2007

* companies that manufacture OEM (original equipment manufacturer) products on behalf of Sony
† suppliers and OEM suppliers that had completed audits as of March 31, 2007
‡ for direct suppliers the Green Book was made available via its electric procurement system in autumn 2003

MATTEL CASE STUDY: PART 1

2007 Revenues: $5.97 billion

Vision
The world's premier toy brands—today and tomorrow.

Global Sustainability Strategic Plan
The plan promotes a new way of thinking—a sustainability mindset—about providing value to the company by reducing Mattel's environmental footprint. The plan focuses on three spheres, including sustainable products (what), sustainable processes (how) and stakeholders (who). Specific initiatives will be developed around

- sustainable product design and development
- sustainable manufacturing and procurement processes
- creating a sustainability culture at Mattel

Goals are to be identified for each initiative, so that Mattel can track and measure performance over time. The plan emphasizes increasing engagement with stakeholders. Senior leadership will be engaged in both development and review to ensure integration with corporate strategic goals and objectives.

Environmental Stewardship
The focus on Mattel's most recent environmental initiatives includes

- adoption of the LEAN process
- efficiency in their logistical operations
- energy and water conservation
- paper usage related to their American Girl catalogues

LEAN Process: A business model that focuses on promoting efficiencies in the production process, eliminating waste and using time effectively. Mattel believes this approach will also lead to cost savings as the method of thinking and designing is applied not only to manufacturing operations but also across many different business processes. Employee involvement and empowerment are critical to the successful implementation of LEAN processes.

Mattel uses "Kaizen" events, meaning continuous improvement, to form teams of process operators, managers and technical experts—who together identify new ways to reduce the over-production of products, wait time for transport and inventory supply or to simplify a process.

Logistical Operations: A number of programs involving the distribution and transportation operations were recently initiated to reduce fuel consumption and corresponding emissions of CO_2—a greenhouse gas associated with moving manufactured goods from factory floors to store shelves.

Distribution Center Emissions and Recycling Improvements: Focusing on measurements to reduce emissions and improve recycling at distribution centers.

Conservation of Natural Resources: In 2005, Mattel implemented a number of energy and water conservation measures at several facilities.

Packaging: Mattel has been working on environmentally friendly packaging projects during the past ten years and in 2005 adopted a Sustainable Packaging Initiative. It's also working on a Plastics Reduction Program and increased use of post-consumer recycled materials.

American Girl Catalog Paper Usage: The majority of products are sold through direct mail catalogs. American Girl recently implemented several strategies aimed at reducing the volume of paper associated with its catalog mailings, measures that are providing both environmental and cost-saving benefits. In 2006, American Girl surpassed its goal to include a minimum of 10% post-consumer fiber in 50% of the paper used in its catalogue.

Pollution Prevention Program: Improvements made to date include
- reusing most plastic waste from the injection molding processes
- replacing some solvent-based paints and adhesives with water-based products that emit fewer volatile emissions
- replacing some hand spray painting application processes with closed-cup tampo printing systems that reduce emissions and waste

MATTEL CASE STUDY: PART 2

2007 Product Recalls

In 2007, Mattel Inc. issued a recall for nearly 20 million toys made in China. The majority of the toys contained magnets that could be dislodged and swallowed and the remainder had lead paint. A significant consumer backlash occurred against Mattel and all toys manufactured in China. Note that no injuries were reported with any of the products involved. During the height of the recall flap, Mattel's stock plunged as much as 25% from its year-to-date high.[30]

Mattel incurred incremental costs of approximately $110 million related to the product recalls. Of this annual cost, $68.4 million related to the reserves recorded for reversal of sales associated with recalled products, impairment of the affected inventory and other recall-related costs, and approximately $42 million related to incremental recall-related legal, advertising, testing, logistics and administration costs.[31]

Several class action lawsuits were filed for selling toys with lead paint. Mattel has already settled for $12 million a lawsuit brought by 39 states.

2007 Response

The company ordered that all products be pulled off retail shelves and conducted an investigation to discover the source of the problem. According to Mattel, every production batch of toys was tested. Mattel also apologized for blaming Chinese facilities for the recall of the toys as most of the recalls were related to design flaws in the magnetic toys (which have since been redesigned). The lead paint was found to have come from a subcontractor of a vendor that the company had been associated with for twenty years. The subcontractor did not use certified paint.[32]

Supply Chain

Approximately 50% of Mattel products are made in seven manufacturing facilities they own and two joint ventures that they operate. The other 50% are made in facilities owned by others. The following principles/programs apply to Mattel-owned and -operated facilities as well as suppliers' facilities.

Corporate Product Integrity (CPI) Process: This department establishes and documents the requirements of each product. Specifications are based upon regulatory and voluntary internal standards and published standards. Each manufacturing facility tests the products that they produce frequently during production, in addition to performing audits at source. CPI randomly samples products from distribution centers and feeds test data back to quality engineers and manufacturing locations.

Global Manufacturing Principles (GMPs): These form the cornerstone of Mattel's worldwide manufacturing practices and provide the framework within which all Mattel's manufacturing sites (owned and third-party suppliers) must operate. Key components of GMP related to the environment and product safety include

- Management Systems—Facilities must have systems in place to address labor, social and EHS issues.
- Emergency Planning—The facility must have programs and systems in place for dealing with emergencies such as fires, spills and natural disasters.
- Environmental Protection—Facilities must have environmental programs in place to minimize their impact on the environment.
- Audits—All new contractors must submit a Material Compliance Report (MCR). An audit of the MCR against Mattel GMP is conduct by Mattel audit staff.

Independent Auditing Program: An independent monitoring organization performs verification audits to assess the GMP performance and its business partners. In 1998, the Mattel Independent Monitoring Council was formed with experts from academia. The audits are performed by the International Center for Corporate Accountability.

Information derived from www.mattel.com unless otherwise stated.

UNILEVER CASE STUDY: PART 1

2007 Revenues: 40.2 billion euros

Strategy

Unilever's vitality mission sets out its goal to meet the everyday needs of people all around the world for nutrition, hygiene and personal care. Its corporate responsibility strategy seeks to address Unilever's most significant sustainability impacts—greenhouse gases, water, packaging and agriculture.

Approach to Brand and Environment

Anticipating that this would become a major trend, in 2005, the Unilever executive decided that social, economic and environmental factors should be integrated into the development and innovation plans of their brands. This is now a core element of their corporate responsibility strategy. To help evaluate the risks and opportunities presented by this agenda, Unilever developed an approach called Brand Imprint. This provides brand teams with a 360-degree scan of the social, economic and environmental impact that their brand has on the world.

"As one of the world's largest purchasers of fish, it is in Unilever's commercial interest to protect the aquatic environment from fishing methods that will ultimately destroy stocks."

Co-CEO Antony Burgmans

Key Activities

Climate Change: In 2007, the Unilever executive agreed to a new GHG strategy. This has a three-pronged approach. Firstly, they committed to reduce CO_2 from energy in manufacturing operations per tonne of production by 25% by 2012 (against a baseline of 2004). Reaching the 2012 target will mean a total reduction of 43% since 1995. Secondly, they developed a GHG-profiling tool to enable Unilever's R&D teams to assess whether product innovations will improve their greenhouse gas footprint. Finally, they are exploring ways of working in partnership, in particular with suppliers and customers. Unilever is involved in projects with Tesco and Wal-Mart and the Carbon Disclosure Project's supply chain initiative.

Energy Use by Consumers: Unilever's wider carbon footprint shows that across the whole value chain, by far the most CO_2 emissions occur during consumer use. This is most marked with home and personal care brands, which need energy to heat water for showers, washing machines and dishwashers. Unilever believes it can help reduce these environmental impacts through product design and formulation as well as communication with consumers. They have been involved in industry initiatives such as the International Association for Soaps, Detergents and Maintenance Products Washright initiative, which encourages consumers to wash clothes at lower temperatures.

Water Use by Consumers: Unilever has been working on ways to help consumers reduce their water consumption through the design and innovation of products that require the use of less water. Brand innovations include Surf Excel Quick Wash, which aims to save as much as two buckets of water per wash for Indian consumers. Based on assumptions about laundry habits, Unilever estimates the potential savings in the region of 14 billion liters of water a year. The new Easy Rinse Comfort and Vivere fabric softeners also require less water. Based on a technologically complex innovation, these conditioners can be used directly after applying detergent, without the need to rinse in between.

Design Solutions: Unilever has been reducing the amount of packaging in products through innovative design, supported by leading-edge technology. For example, by creating more lightweight plastic containers they can cut down on the overall amount of packaging material used.

Reducing Waste in Manufacturing: Minimizing waste from manufacturing processes has been a core part of Unilever's eco-efficiency program for over a decade. Since 1995, levels of total waste sent for disposal have decreased by 68.9% per tonne of production and 11% of their sites send no waste at all to landfill or incineration. Unilever did not meet their targets for waste reduction in 2007, but have stated that it will continue to work towards them during 2008.

Source: Unilever Sustainable Development 2007[33]

UNILEVER CASE STUDY: PART 2

Supply Chain

Energy Use in Manufacturing: During 2007, Unilever continued to improve energy efficiency and increase the proportion of energy coming from renewable sources. This now accounts for 15.2% of energy use, more than half of which is generated by Unilever, mainly from fuel crops and solid waste biomass. Unilever continues to work towards meeting a 25% CO_2 reduction goal by 2012, by adopting more efficient power and steam generation technology and through the development of more efficient manufacturing processes.

Fish Resources: In the mid-1990s, executives at Unilever saw a big threat to one of their product lines—the frozen fish sticks business was at risk because the world's oceans were running out of fish. Unilever, Dan Esty and World Wildlife Fund set up the Marine Stewardship Council, an independent body to promote sustainable fisheries around the world. Unilever committed to buy 100% of its fish from sustainable sources by 2005 (according to Unilever's website they had achieved 75% by 2005).

Energy Use in Raw Material Stages: Unilever estimates energy use in the supply of raw materials to be around ten times its manufacturing emissions. In the agricultural supply chain it is seeking to minimize this by using more sustainable land practices and reducing the use of nitrogen fertilizers and chemicals.

Distribution: Unilever products get to market via a complex transport network of road, rail and sea, although in most markets they do not own or operate any distribution vehicles themselves. Unilever studies show that the impact of transport and distribution is around 4 million tonnes of CO_2 a year. It is currently working with customers to reduce the number of vehicle movements and continuing a global roll-out of climate-friendly ice cream cabinets.

Water Conservation: There are four elements to Unilever's approach to water sustainability: reducing water use in manufacturing operations, working with agricultural suppliers to reduce their usage, designing products that require less water during consumer use and participating in initiatives that aim to address these challenges through partnerships. Since 1995, Unilever has reduced by 61.7% the amount of water used per tonne of production by minimizing water usage and maximizing water recycling at sites. In 2007, Unilever reduced the total consumption of water in its operations worldwide by 4.9 million m^3 and the load per tonne of production by 7.5%, exceeding its target of 4.7%.

Packaging: In 2007, Unilever created a Responsible Packaging Steering Team to define a revised strategy. This team is building on the work already carried out over the past few years by the Unilever Packaging Group. Unilever's approach consists of five key principles: remove, reduce, reuse, renew and recycle.

Biofuels

Unilever supports the use of renewable energy from sustainable sources to help combat climate change. However, it believes that some first-generation biofuels, made from agricultural raw materials such as rapeseed oil, are neither environmentally efficient nor cost-effective ways to reduce CO_2 emissions. As a major buyer of agricultural and other raw materials, Unilever is also concerned that the use of valuable food crops for energy purposes will increase pressure on availability and cost of food as well as placing increasing pressure on ecosystems and biodiversity. Deforestation, particularly to make way for palm oil and soya beans, could lead to the devastation of the rain forests in Borneo and the Amazon.

Information derived from Unilever Sustainable Development Report, 2007[34] unless otherwise stated.

DELL CASE STUDY: PART 1

Fiscal 2008 Revenues: $61 billion

Dell's Environmental Policy

Dell's vision is to create a company culture where environmental excellence is second nature. Its mission is to fully integrate environmental stewardship into the business of providing quality products, best-in-class services, and the best customer experience at the best value. It has established the following environmental policy objectives to achieve its vision and mission.

Design Products with the Environment in Mind

- Design products with a focus on safe operation throughout the entire product life cycle, extending product life span, reducing energy consumption, avoiding environmentally sensitive materials, promoting dematerialization and using parts that are capable of being recycled at the highest level.
- Set expectations of environmental excellence throughout Dell's supply chain.

Prevent Waste and Pollution

- Operate Dell's facilities to minimize harmful impacts on the environment.
- Place a high priority on waste minimization, recycling and reuse programs and pollution prevention.

Continually Improve Performance

- Use an Environmental Management System approach to establish goals, implement programs, monitor technology and environmental management practices, evaluate progress and continually improve environmental performance.
- Foster a culture of environmental responsibility among employees and management.

Demonstrate Responsibility to Stakeholders

- Act in an environmentally responsible manner through sustainable practices designed to ensure the health and safety of Dell's employees, neighbors and the environment.
- Periodically communicate company progress to stakeholders.
- Engage stakeholders to improve products and processes.

Global Citizenship and Ethical Sourcing

Dell Global Citizenship Program (GCP) employs a variety of self-assessment, auditing and business improvement tools. They integrate supplier performance into procurement decisions. The GCP has been introduced to 75 Tier I suppliers operating a combined 153 manufacturing sites. These Tier I suppliers represent three-fourths of Dell's procurement expenditures. In 2006, Dell introduced Business Performance Improvement (BPI) methodology to help suppliers make meaningful and measurable CSR improvements. The GCP is managed through Dell's Worldwide Procurement Department (WPD) and the Dell Sustainability Council. These groups work with internal and external stakeholders to develop program policy. The GC team administers the program on a day-to-day basis and works directly with the WPD commodity teams and suppliers. Suppliers in the Awareness phase must achieve and maintain ISO 14001 and OHSAS 18001 certification. Suppliers in the Self-Assessment phase must meet the requirements of the Awareness phase and complete a self-assessment questionnaire. Verification phase suppliers must meet the Awareness and Self-Assessment requirements plus receive an independent audit of their facility. Suppliers in the Verification phase work with Dell in using their BPI methodology to address corrective action issues and implement management systems and infrastructure to sustain the changes. In the Sustainability phase, suppliers must sustain the changes implemented in their prior phase and demonstrate continuous improvement, capability building and recognition programs.[35]

Information derived from www.dell.com unless otherwise stated.

Comply with the Law
- Conduct business with integrity and dedicated observance of environmental laws and regulations, and meet the commitments of the voluntary environmental programs in which Dell participates.

16 Years of Environmental Improvements

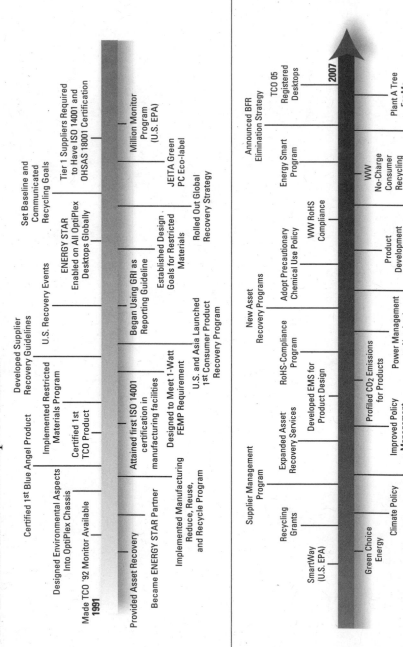

SUSTAINABILITY LIFE CYCLE

CORPORATE ACCOUNTABILITY

» Governance
» Ethical Behavior
» Stakeholder Dialogue
» Global Diversity
» Global Policy for HIV/AIDS
» Global Citizenship and Ethical Sourcing

COMMUNITY ENGAGEMENT

» Company Support
» Dell Foundation
» Employee Volunteerism
» Community Grants
» Healthy Communities
» Connected Communities
» Digital Literacy

DELL

CUSTOMER EXPERIENCE

» Environmental Awareness
» Consulting Services
» No-Charge Consumer Recycling

FACILITIES

» Global Expansion
» Manufacturing
» Regulatory Compliance
» Workplace Health and Safety
» Reduce Emissions from Operations
» Waste Avoidance
» Reduce Tree Fiber Use
» FSC-Certified Paper

EMPLOYEES

» Diversity — Global Values with Local Implementation
» Workplace Health and Safety
» Wellness Programs
» Privacy Policy

PACKAGING

» Packaging Optimization
» Packaging with Environmentally Responsible Materials
» Global Recycling
» Multi-Packs and Vertical Boxes
» Forest Stewardship

SUPPLIERS

» Supplier Global Citizenship
» Electronic Industry Code of Conduct
» Business Process Improvement
» Supplier Diversity
» Human Rights
» Vendor-Partner Audits

PRODUCT

» Energy Efficiency
» Materials
» Climate Protection
» Eco-Labels
» Product Stewardship
» Asset Recovery
» Design for the Environment
» Reduce Greenhouse Gases
» Consumer Recycling and Reuse
» Equipment Recovery and Recycling Programs
» Donations

TRANSPORTATION

» Optimize Shipping
» Reduce Emissions
» Geographic Manufacturing

ENVIRONMENTAL RESPONSIBILITY

NOTES

1 Concept derived from Infor, "How Do Enterprising Manufacturers Stay Ahead of the Compliance Game?", http://www.marketing-intl.com/PDFS/How_Enterprising_Mfgs_Stay_Ahead_of_Compliance_Game_WP.pdf.

2 Bartholomew, 2008.

3 James Fox, "The Cost of Noncompliance: Nine Ways RoHS Can Impact Your Company's Bottom Line," Business Development Manager, Synapsis Technology, August 26, 2006, http://www.greensupplyline.com.

4 Ibid.

5 Ibid.

6 Deloitte, "Making the Difference: Putting Supply Chain Strategy to Work," 2007.

7 Mickey North Rizza, "Lean and Clean with Green Purchasing," AMR Research Alert Article, April 17, 2008.

8 Martyn Hart, "Green Outsourcing Changes IT for All," October 8, 2008, http://www.zdnetasia.com/insight/business/0,39051970,62046723,00.htm.

9 Paul Brody and Mondher Ben-Hamida, "12 Steps to a 'Greener' Supply Chain," Environmental Leader, November 30, 2008, http://www.environmentalleader.com/2008/11/30/12-steps-to-a-greener-supply-chain.

10 "Building CSR into the Supply Chain," GreenBiz.com, August 5, 2008, http://www.greenbiz.com/news/2008/08/05/building-csr-supply-chain.

11 James Speth, *The Bridge at the Edge of the World: Capitalism, the Environment, and Crossing the Crisis of Sustainability* (New Haven: Yale University Press, 2008).

12 Greenfacts, "Conclusions and Main Findings of Millennium Ecosystem Assessment Report," http://www.greenfacts.org/en/ecosystems/#10.

13 Tesco, http://www.tescoplc.com, 2008.

14 Sony, "CSR Report 2007," 2007, http://www.sony.net/SonyInfo/Environment/issues/report/2007.

15 Ibid.

16 American Chemistry Council, "Responsible Care," http://www.americanchemistry.com/s_responsiblecare.

17 Canadian Chemical Producers Association, "Responsible Care," http://www.ccpa.ca/ResponsibleCare.

18 Wikipedia, "Government Procurement," 2008, http://en.wikipedia.org/wiki/Government_procurement.

19 Office of the Federal Environmental Executive, 2008, http://www.ofee.gov.

20 Martyn Hart, "Green Outsourcing Changes IT for All."

21 Johanne Gelinas, "Corporate Environmental Responsibility – Good Governance, Plain and Simple", September, 2007, www.green-business.com.

22 Wal-Mart, "Wal-Mart Is Taking the Lead in Logistics," 2008, http://walmartstores.com/media/factsheets/fs_2314.pdf.

23 UPS, 2008, http://www.ups.com.

24 Paul Brody and Mondher Ben-Hamida, "12 Steps to a Greener Supply Chain, Environmental Leader," November 30, 2008.

25 Green Biz, "New IBM Consulting Service Finds Savings throughout Supply Chains", January 23, 2009

26 Sony, "20-F SEC Filing," June 28, 2002, http://sec.edgar-online.com/2002/06/28/0000950109-02-003508/Section4.asp.

27 Jim Dills, "Supply Chain Data Exchange for Material Disclosure Solving One of the Most Difficult RoHS-related Problems for Small-to-medium-sized Enterprises," presentation to NIST, October 6, 2005.

28 Sony, "20-F SEC Filing."

29 Sony, "CSR Report 2003," 2003, http://www.sony.net/SonyInfo/Environment/issues/report/2003.

30 Renee Montagne and Adam Davidson, "Mattel Recalls 9 Million Toys Made in China," August 14, 2007, http://www.npr.org/templates/story/story.php?storyId=12778928.

31 Mattel, "8-K SEC Filing," January 31, 2008, http://sec.edgar-online.com/2008/01/31/0001193125-08-015787/Section9.asp.

32 CNN.com, "Mattel CEO: 'Rigorous Standards' After Massive Toy Recall," November 15, 2008, http://www.cnn.com/2007/US/08/14/recall/index.html.

33 Unilever 2008, Sustainable Development 2007: An Overview, www.unilever.com

34 Ibid.

35 Dell, "Values in Action – Dell Sustainability Report & Fiscal Year 2007 in Review," 2007.

CHAPTER SIX

WHAT ARE THE ALTERNATIVES TO PETROLEUM?

To understand the opportunities related to alternative energy sources, it is important to understand the current state of affairs:

Increasing demand—In the short term, the 2008 global recession has significantly reduced demand, but in the mid and long term, demand for petroleum will increase as China and India industrialize. The International Energy Agency (IEA) *World Energy Outlook for 2008* report has forecasted a 25% increase in global demand for oil by 2030 to 106 million barrels/day, from current levels of approximately 86 million barrels/day.[1]

The approach of peak oil—Many experts believe we will reach peak oil (when maximum rate of global petroleum extraction is reached.) within the next ten to fifteen years (though the 2008 recession may push this date out), because of geological limitations, insufficient investment in exploration/production activities, environmental concerns and political instability. Other experts believe that peak oil is further away because of new technology, which increases extraction efficiency at existing sites and the identification/development of new reservoirs. A recent IEA report stated that the global peak oil capacity of conventional oil is just shy of 90 million barrels/day, i.e., well below future demand.[2]

Increasing cost to extract—The cost to extract new reservoirs for both smaller conventional oil fields and non-conventional sources such as oil sands is much higher than for large conventional fields. Add proposed fees related to carbon sequestration, carbon taxes or cap-and-trade programs, and the economics start to become questionable unless there is a significant rise in the price of oil. Figure 6.1 presents information on the production costs of various sources of oil.

Speculators—In 2000, the U.S. deregulated trading in energy markets and allowed speculators to trade relatively freely in oil futures. Prior to 2003, there was plenty of spare oil capacity and OPEC could influence the price by turning the taps on or off. Post-2003, growing consumption in China and India and increased production by non-OPEC countries created significant uncertainty and thus a unique opportunity for speculators. In 2008, however, speculators exited the market when it became clear that the cost of oil had risen so high that demand was collapsing. The actual impact of speculators on the 2008 oil spike is debatable—ranging from culprit to scapegoat—and proposed legislation initiated by Congress was put on hold in 2008 because of the credit crunch.[3]

Tipping point for renewable energy sources—We are approaching the tipping point for renewable energy. The point at which development of a particular renewable energy source becomes feasible is very much dependent upon the cost of non-renewable alternatives (petroleum, natural gas, coal or nuclear power), avoided cost (e.g., reduction of air pollution in urban areas), system efficiencies and government incentives. Note that government incentives may apply to both renewable and nonrenewable energy sources, and include indirect assistance (e.g., farm subsidies).

Multiple solutions—There is no one "magic bullet" alternative energy source that will replace oil within the next twenty years. Instead, a combination of conservation initiatives and multiple renewable and nonrenewable alternative energy sources will be required. It would be nice to be able to move to a renewable energy economy as many individuals have proposed; however, it is not feasible given foreseeable energy demand. Chapter 9 provides additional information on the potential future energy mix.

Investment opportunity—According to Clean Edge in 2008, revenues from the four leading clean technologies (wind, solar, biofuels and fuel cells) have grown to $77.3 billion in 2007 from $55.4 billion in 2006, and are expected to grow to $254.5 billion within a decade.[4] The IEA has estimated that the world needs to invest US$5.5 trillion (in 2007 dollars) in renewable energy sources between 2007 and 2030 to meet growing demand.[5]

Figure 6.1: Products Costs as a Function of Source

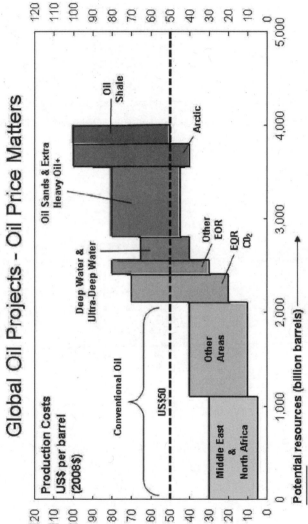

Global Oil Projects - Oil Price Matters

Costs include exploration & development, lifting costs and typical return on capital employed, but exclude royalties and income taxes, which usually loom large. EOR: Enhanced Oil Recovery. +Mostly in Alberta and Venezuela. Based on information from the "World Energy Outlook 2008", International Energy Agency and Scotiabank estimates.

Government energy (and security) policies—The specific market-based instruments (MBIs) that governments decide to use to promote alternative energy and energy independence (from imported oil) will greatly affect both the feasibility of and return on these projects. The recently launched International Renewable Energy Agency mandate is to promote renewable energy sources by informing and advising countries on regulations, financing and technology expertise.

Global warming—Mankind is having an impact on the temperature and weather patterns of the planet, the full magnitude of which is not yet known. However, in the meantime, minor variations in temperature can have a significant impact, justifying a call for immediate, balanced action that makes business sense and meets other critical demands (e.g., poverty and disease alleviation).

"No, THEY LEFT THE MONEY, BUT, THEY SIPHONED ALL OUR GAS..."

So when will oil reserves be exhausted? The forecast for remaining reserves is highly controversial, because of uncertainty about how much oil remains underground and our ability to recover the large reserves of unconventional oil in a cost-effective way.[6] Examples of new reserves include fields off the coast of Brazil (50 billion to 70 billion barrels) and oil trapped beneath the Arctic pack ice (estimated to be in excess of 400 billion barrels), amounts far in excess of Saudi Arabia's proven reserves. In the case of the reserves under the Arctic Ocean, the ownership of these reserves, the costs of extraction and the environmental impact of extracting the oil, as well as political considerations, are not yet fully understood, and therefore it is too early to assess their impact on meeting demand.

Lehman Brothers Holdings Inc. estimated that Exxon Mobil Corp., Royal Dutch Shell PLC, BP PLC, Chevron Corp., Total SA and ConocoPhillips spent a record $98.7 billion in 2008 on exploration and production. These costs have more than quadrupled since 2000, as exploration targets more challenging reservoirs and the demand for labor and material rises.[7] In the latter part of 2008, many companies curtailed spending on exploration and production (especially oil sands projects).

Additional discussion of the forecast price of a barrel of oil is presented in chapter 9.

> The real issue is not the amount of available oil reserves; it is the cost to extract new reserves versus alternative energy sources. Add potential fees associated with cap-and-trade or carbon taxes, and many believe we are approaching the tipping point for alternatives.

Once the tipping point is exceeded, alternative, "cleaner" energy sources will become more cost-effective. Eventually, though it may be several decades away, petroleum's role in energy production (including for transportation) will substantially diminish. Whales are no longer hunted for whale oil—it just became uneconomical to continue the harvest given the rise of an alternative cheap fuel supply.

The fact that future energy needs will need to be met by alternative sources has been recognized by many leaders in the petroleum sector.

Jeroen van der Veer, the chief executive officer of Royal Dutch Shell, has acknowledged that the end of the oil era may be upon us sooner than we realize, in this extract from an email he sent out to all Shell employees in January 2008: "Regardless of which route we choose, the world's current predicament limits our maneuvering room. We are experiencing a step-change in the growth rate of energy demand due to population growth and economic development, and Shell estimates that after 2015 supplies of easy-to-access oil and gas will no longer keep up with demand. As a result, society has no choice but to add other sources of energy—renewables, yes, but also more nuclear power and unconventional fossil fuels such as oil sands. Using more energy inevitably means emitting more CO_2 at a time when climate change has become a critical global issue."[8]

James Mulva, the chief executive of ConocoPhillips, expressed his doubts that world oil producers will be able to meet forecast long-term energy demand growth, at a New York financial conference in 2007. "Demand will be going up, but it will be constrained by supply. I don't think we are going to see the supply going over 100 million barrels a day and the reason is: Where is all that going to come from?"[9]

Christophe de Margerie, the chief executive of Total, stated the following during a media briefing in London on February 2009 that "the capacity that the oil industry has to go to 93 to 95 million barrels per day is already over." He predicts peak oil production at about 89 million barrels a day—far less then the IEA projection of global demand for 2030 of 106 million barrels a day. Mr. Margerie's forecast was based upon delays and cancellation of oil projects as prices fall and production declines at many of the large oil fields.[10]

CONSERVATION—YOU MEAN WE HAVE TO BEHAVE LIKE EUROPEANS?

In his book *A Thousand Barrels a Second*, Peter Tertzakian describes four evolutionary phases that society experiences when undergoing a fundamental realignment, such as we are now experiencing with energy:

1. complaining and paying up
2. conserving and being more efficient
3. adopting alternative energy sources
4. making societal, business and lifestyle changes

As a society, where are North Americans on this spectrum? Most likely at step 2: conserving and being more efficient. The EU, on the other hand, has been at the forefront of energy conservation and adoption of alternative energy sources for a variety of reasons: limited supplies of petroleum, the green ethic of citizens and the viability of European transportation systems. Unlike North America, where most large cities are designed around cars, Europe has a radically different urban development history that is typically based on higher density of buildings and well-developed public transportation systems. Many EU cities are not car-friendly, with narrow streets, limited parking and major traffic congestion. In 2008, European gas prices were in the US$2.10-$2.60 per liter (US$8–US$10 per gallon) range, whereas in North America, even at their peak, prices were in the US$0.80–US$1.40 per liter (US$3–US$5.3 per gallon) range.

The developed economies use oil much more intensively than developing economies, and Canada and the United States stand almost alone in their consumption of oil per capita at almost 11.4 liters (3 gallons) per day. Per capita oil consumption in the rest of the OECD is 5.3 liters (1.4 gallons) per day, and outside of the OECD, 0.76 liters (0.2 gallons) per day.[11]

Unfortunately, North Americans have been used to low oil prices for several decades and, save for a few high price spikes (the Yom Kippur War and OPEC oil embargo in 1973–1974, the Iran-Iraq War of 1981) and melee of activities in 2008, there has been no financial necessity to conserve energy. In recent years, the American and Canadian federal governments, as well as many states and provinces, have imposed energy efficiency standards for a wide variety of products, including appliances and automobiles (see appendix A for additional information).

A 2007 McKinsey & Company report found that improving energy efficiency in buildings, appliances and factories could offset almost all of the projected demand for electricity in 2030, largely negating the need for new coal-fired power plants. The report indicates that one-third of the U.S. greenhouse gas reductions by 2030 could come from electricity efficiency and be achieved at negative marginal costs.[12] The IEA estimates that the application of proven technologies and best practices on a global scale could save between 1.9 and 3.2 gigatonnes of CO_2 emissions per year.[13]

A key first step along this path will be to ensure that the correct metrics are in place to improve efficiencies in energy generation. A good example of inappropriate metrics can be seen in the U.S electrical utility industry. Historically, a utility made more money the more power it sold, and the only way a utility could lose money was if demand dropped. If demand increased, the utility could build a new power plant with a guaranteed profit, with the consequence that not a lot of serious effort was put into strategies that reduced consumption.[14]

President Obama has recently stated that he wants to see the system changed whereby the utilities have greater incentives to promote conservation and allow decentralized renewable energy sources to "plug-into" the grid.

So what should a company do to reduce the risks associated with increasing energy costs? A proposed plan of action, in order of priority, is

1. Assign an owner—A key starting point for organizations is to assign a C-level owner of the energy issue, for example, a chief sustainability/energy officer (CSO). A recent survey by Hill & Knowlton showed that most companies did not in fact have an overall owner at the C-suite for sustainability/energy issues, yet the impact of decisions in this area are critical to a company's business.[15] It is important to note that unless the person has the authority and a clear mandate to reduce costs and emissions, they will not be taken seriously.

2. Develop an energy/sustainability strategy—Similarly, most companies surveyed by Hill & Knowlton did not have an energy/SD strategy, and those that did have one did a poor job of communicating it to employees. It is important that companies understand and evaluate the impact changing markets (in particular, petroleum prices and emergence of cleantech) will have on their business. In many cases, there is an incredible business opportunity, but the key questions that have to be asked are: what role does or should your company play in the cleantech value chain, and how will changes in the market affect this position?

3. Before developing an energy/SD strategy, senior personnel in a company should understand the company's areas of significant energy usage and its carbon footprint (see item 7 below), as well as undertake a risk/opportunity assessment (see chapter 1).

4. Track/influence government policy—Tracking changing government policy/legislation related to energy and petroleum is key, as it will have a significant impact on a company's products/services (directly or indirectly through increased cost of raw materials, including electricity).

5. Implement energy conservation strategy—As a general strategy, successful companies eliminate waste and in doing so, improve the efficiency of operations and the bottom line. Companies already should be vigorously executing energy conservation strategies, with a key metric being the reduction in energy costs from all activities (e.g., manufacturing, buildings, IT servers).

6. Drive cultural change—In order for true conservation to work, all key stakeholders must be involved and be allowed to attack the problem creatively. A cultural change may be required so that individuals feel comfortable coming forward with good ideas and are allowed to execute them. This type of change cannot be mandated and must reflect the cultural nuances of the organization.

7. Determine carbon footprint—Determine the carbon footprint of company's activities, i.e., the impact that company activities have on the environment, measured in units of carbon dioxide produced. The term activities may include company's own operations, indirect emissions from company's supply chain and potentially emissions linked to the use of a company's goods and services. A plan to reduce company's carbon footprint should be integrated into its overall energy strategy. Many companies are currently participating in the World Wildlife Fund (WWF) Climate Savers program, U.S. Climate Action Partnership or the Global

Roundtable on Climate Change to establish targets to voluntarily reduce their GHG emissions.

8. Purchase green power where possible—Where appropriate and supportive of overall energy/SD strategy, purchase green energy. But be aware that the definition of "green energy" is very much open to interpretation, and hence should be carefully defined by the company.

> Energy/SD strategy should not be developed in isolation or as an "add-on." It must be an integral part of the company's overall business strategy and the company's culture. The primary business goal should be real cost reductions both in the short and long term while preserving/enhancing the environment.

What are companies doing to reduce energy use and, more importantly, operating costs? The following are examples of significant cost savings that companies have achieved through energy conservation. These examples highlight both corporate-driven initiatives and employee-generated activities.

Dow

In 1982, the energy manager of Dow Chemical's Louisiana division, Ken Nelson, began an annual contest to identify and fund energy-saving projects. Some were simple, while others involved more sophisticated activities. In the first year, twenty-seven winners were selected, requiring a total capital investment of $1.7 million with an average annual return on investment of 173%. The momentum did not stop in the second year, when thirty-two winners were selected, requiring a total capital investment of $2.2 million and a 340% return. Even after ten years, and nearly seven hundred projects, the contest continued to generate great ideas. In 1991, 1992 and 1993 each had in excess of 120 winners with an average return on investment of 300%. Total savings to Dow from these projects exceeded $75 million a year.[16]

Russel Mills of Dow Chemical recently told the U.N. Climate Change Conference in Poland that "if you want to follow your wallet, remember energy-efficiency." He indicated that Dow Chemical has saved four times more than expected through energy-efficiency measures—about $7 billion—and avoided the emissions of 70 million tons of CO_2 along the way. He also indicated that energy accounts for half of the $55-billion corporation's costs.[17]

DuPont

In 1999, DuPont pledged that by 2010, it would reduce its GHG emissions to 65% below its 1990 levels, and to obtain 10% of its energy and 25% of its feedstocks from renewables. The plan, in part, was to diversify the product line—shedding divisions such as nylon and pharmaceuticals to focus on materials that reduce GHG, such as Tyvek house wraps for energy efficiency.[18] It made this announcement in the name of increasing shareholder value and delivered on that promise: during the same period, the value of DuPont stock increased 340% as the company reduced global emissions by 67%, for a savings to date of $3 billion.[19] (See chapter 1 for a corporate summary of DuPont's green initiatives.)

Wal-Mart

In 2006, the world's largest retailer, Wal-Mart, announced the following goals:

- reduce energy use at its stores by 30% over three years
- become carbon neutral
- be 100% powered by renewable energy
- double the efficiency of its vehicle fleet
- build hybrid-electric long-haul trucks
- sell millions of compact fluorescent light (CFL) bulbs

In 2007, Wal-Mart created its own electricity company in Texas, called Texas Retail Energy, to supply its stores with cheaper power bought at wholesale prices. This saves the company about $15 million annually in Texas and gives the company control over its utility bills.[20] Also in 2007, Wal-Mart sold 137 million CFLs, surpassing its goal to sell 100 million. It estimates that these units will save its customers $4 billion in energy costs. Wal-Mart's High-Efficiency prototype stores have energy savings of $25 million over five years when compared to 2005 levels at traditional stores. The cost reductions will be achieved by using waste energy from refrigerators to help heat the stores, cutting lighting costs and covering roofs with white membranes to reflect sunlight and reduce summer cooling costs.[21] (See chapter 1 for additional information on Wal-Mart's green initiatives.)

BP

BP estimates that between 1998 and the end of 2001, when the company fulfilled its commitment to reduce GHG emissions to 10% less than the 1990 level, emissions reductions created savings with a net present value of $650 million. BP now estimates that the total savings generated from GHG reduction since 1998 has a net present value of $2 billion, with projects and interventions from the start of 2002 to the end of 2007 accounting for three quarters of that.[22] Examples of significant reductions in 2007 include the following: reduced flaring and venting, improved gas transport infrastructure at key sites, and energy efficiency and operational improvement projects.[23]

3M

In 1973, 3M established an energy management department to drive continuous improvement in energy management. The company achieved an 80% improvement in energy efficiency at its U.S. operations and 37% improvement in energy efficiency at worldwide operations. The 3M energy department's new goal is to improve energy efficiency by 20% between 2005 and 2010. In 2006, 3M reduced energy use by 11% from its 2005 base year and achieved annual energy savings of $25.6 million by means of 278 employee-inspired projects. 3M's new product development teams take into account energy efficiency in the choice of raw materials, product formulations and manufacturing processes.[24] (See also chapter 8 for a case study on 3M.)

PepsiCo

Key elements of PepsiCo environmental sustainability strategy are to

- reduce water usage through conservation, reuse and replenishment
- reduce GHG emissions through energy conservation and use of clean energy sources
- reduce, recycle and reuse packaging and solid waste

PepsiCo Green Team activities have allowed the company to make its facilities and manufacturing processes more energy efficient. Savings since 1999 total $179 million and include a decrease in the purchase of 20 trillion BTU of natural gas and 3 billion pounds less of CO_2 emissions.[25] PepsiCo was honored with the EPA's 2008 ENERGY STAR Partner of the Year Award for its commitment to reduce GHG emissions through energy efficiencies. Key actions by PepsiCo facilities include[26]

- putting in place measures to reduce the amount of energy used to produce food and beverage products. These measures include the installation of ENERGY STAR-rated equipment, energy-efficient motors and energy-efficient windows and skylights to enhance natural lighting.

- installing variable frequency drive systems, which allow efficient energy use and thermal regeneration systems to capture waste heat. The company performs periodic energy audits to find opportunities to continuously improve its energy efficiency.

IBM

The following is a summary of IBM activities related to energy savings and CO_2 emission reductions.[27]

- From 1990 to 2006, IBM avoided nearly 3 million metric tons of CO_2 emissions, equal to 44% of the company's 1990 global CO_2 emissions, and saved more than $290 million through its annual energy conservation actions.
- In 2006, the company set a new goal to reduce CO_2 emissions associated with its energy use by 12% between 2005 and 2012 through energy conservation, the use of renewable energy and/or the funding of an equivalent CO_2 emissions reduction by the procurement of Renewable Energy Certificates (RECs) or comparable instruments.
- IBM's procurement of renewable energy and RECs increased from 11 million kilowatt-hours (kWh) in 2001 to 368 million kWh in 2006, which accounted for 7.3% of IBM's total 2006 global electricity purchases. Between 2005 and 2006 alone, IBM's purchase of renewable energy grew by more than 180%.
- IBM is redirecting $1 billion per year across its businesses, mobilizing the company's resources to dramatically increase the level of energy efficiency in IT. Called Project Big Green, the plan includes new products and services for IBM and its clients to sharply reduce data center energy consumption.

Johnson & Johnson

Johnson & Johnson joined WWF Climate Savers in 2000 with an undertaking to reduce emissions to 7% below 1990 levels by 2010. By 2006, the company had reduced its emissions to 16.8% below 1990 levels, despite more than tripling revenue over the same period. Although initially Johnson & Johnson undertook some of its early renewable energy investments despite relatively low returns on investment, it now reports that its GHG and energy use reductions make good business sense for the company. "The energy efficiency program has resulted in an estimated $30 million annualized savings over the last 10 years and our GHG reduction projects are achieving an average 16% internal rate of return," the company reports.[28]

Greening IT

A recent study by Aberdeen Group entitled Going, *Going, Green: Planning for the Green IT Ecosystem* four key performance criteria to distinguish Best-in-Class companies:

- Decrease in power consumption in the data center
- Decrease in floor space occupied by data center
- Decrease in data center cooling requirements
- Decrease in data center operating costs

Firms enjoying Best-in-Class performance shared several common characteristics:

- 81% use energy efficient components to decrease power consumption in the data center.
- 78% include sustainability principles in the design or acquisition requirements for new product and system acquisition or development
- 71% use a software solution that integrates facilities and IT management
- 67% have both formal green or sustainability policy and documented data center energy efficiency policies
- 61% have facilities staff reporting directly to IT management
- 31% IT has budget responsibility for IT energy use

Key questions that companies should be asking are these:

- Are we doing enough to reduce energy costs and improve the bottom line?
- Are we seeking out ways to improve the efficiencies of our processes and supply chain?
- Do we have employee buy-in or is this a top-down directive?

ENERGY VALUE CHAIN

Before getting into the different alternatives to petroleum, it is important for a company to identify their role in the "energy value chain." The following are examples of roles:

- owner/investor in energy or transport sectors (more and more companies are assessing on-site power generation and, in some cases, their role in the retail power market)
- supplier of raw material/equipment to the energy (e.g., pipelines, turbines, inverters) and transportation (e.g., biofuel, batteries) sectors
- involved in the design and construction in the energy and transport sectors
- involved in the maintenance activities in the energy and transportation sectors
- consumer of large amounts of energy or fuel for transportation
- provider or user of insurance/weather derivatives (a growing number of insurance companies are offering a variety of agreements to address changing risk related to weather)
- financial institution provides loans to companies in this sector

The particular role that a company plays (or wants to play) may significantly influence its activities at a strategic, tactical and operational level.

WHAT ARE THE ENERGY OPTIONS?

The U.S. ranks seventh in per capita energy consumption after Canada and a number of small countries. In 2007, the majority of U.S. energy (electrical) was derived from fossil fuels: coal—32.8%, natural gas—31.0%, crude—15.9%, nuclear—11.7%, biomass—5.0%, hydroelectric—3.43%, geothermal—0.49%, wind—0.44% and Solar/PV—0.11%.[29] The U.S. is the largest producer of coal and has significantly increased its capacity for wind and solar energy over the last few years to the point where it will be catching up with key EU players.

Figures from 2005 show that Canada relied predominantly on the following power production sources: hydroelectric—57%, thermal—26% and nuclear—15%.[30] Canada is a net exporter of electricity, has the second-largest oil reserves (when oil sands are taken into consideration), is the second-largest producer of hydroelectric energy and is the leading producer of uranium for nuclear power generation.

In 2007, the U.S. national average price of electricity increased 2.7% to 9.14 cents per kWh. The price of electricity varies greatly by state, with 2006 data showing a range from 4.92 cents per kWh in Idaho to more than 20 cents per kWh in Hawaii.[31] In Canada, the price of electricity ranges from approximately 5 cents to 6 cents/kWh in Ontario, Quebec, British Columbia and Manitoba, to between 9 cents and 11 cents/kWh for other provinces. Rates in the Canadian north are considerably higher as diesel fuel must be flown in—rates range from 39.39 cents/ kWh in Ikaluit to 81.72 cents/kWh in Kugaaruk.[32] Note that several jurisdictions are introducing time-of-use pricing to reduce load during peak hours.

As the demand for and prices of petroleum and natural gas increase over the next several years and governments impose stringent requirements on emissions to control GHGs, alternative energy sources will play a dominant role in addressing domestic energy demand and energy security concerns. Table 6.1 summarizes the average costs associated with the different forms of electric power generation (excludes transmission) and may vary significantly depending upon numerous factors. Note that the values listed are primarily for energy sources connecting to a grid. For off-grid power, such as solar power in the range of 15 cents to 30 cents per kWh, it is better to compare to the average retail rates for electricity set out above.

Table 6.1: Comparison of Generation Costs (Excluding Transmission)

Type	Generation Cost (U.S. cents/kWh)
Coal	U.S.: 3.5–4.1, Canada: 4.5, EU: 4.7–6.1d
Natural Gas	U.S.: 6–10e and 6.3–8.9f, strongly dependent on gas price
Nuclear Power	France: 3.7, U.S.: 4.2–4.6, Canada: 5, EU: 5.4–7.4d
Hydro	Canada: 1.6 (older) and 4.1–7.4a, g (newer)
Wind—Onshore	U.S.: 6–9e, 7–9h, 7.9h, 7.5–10i, Canada: 8.6b,j UK: 7.4, EU: 4.7–14.8k
Solar—CSP	U.S.: 15.7e, 15–22l, 14–16m
Clean Coal	U.S.: 10.1e, 14–16c
Tidal Power	U.S.: 8–16n (small-scale project)
Geothermal	U.S.: 5–8o

a Based upon Hydro-Québec historical rates (C$0.02/kWh), Eastman 1A Rupert (C$0.05/kWh) and proposed La Romaine (C$0.09/kWh), and exchange rate of 0.82.
b Based upon Hydro-Québec actual cost if C$0.105/kWh and above exchange rate (C$0.087 for the wind energy, C$0.013 for transmission, and estimated C$0.005 for network balancing services).
c Value of $0.101/kWh is based upon $25/ton CO_2 price. Value of $0.14–$0.16/kWh is based on production cost of $0.09–$0.11s/kWh and an additional $0.05/kWh for capturing and transporting carbon.
d World Nuclear Association, 2008.
e Arvizu, 2006.
f Invest in Canada Bureau, 2007.
g Moore, 2007.
h Jefferies & Company Inc., 2008.
i Climate Progress, 2008.
j Melnbardis, 2008.
k World Nuclear Association, 2008; Energy Justice, 2008.
l Wikipedia, 2008.
m Del Chiaro, Payne and Dutzik, 2008.
n Bedard, McGinnis and Klure, 2005.
o Everything2, 2008; Arvizu, 2006.

Why are the costs of alternative energy sources so high when wind and sunlight are free? The capital cost of solar panels and wind structures is still high relative to the amount of power they can produce. Nuclear plants produce electricity with such high efficiency and with quite low operating costs that returns negate the high capital input costs.[33]

> Prices for alternative energy sources will become more cost effective when petroleum prices rise, more stringent requirements for emissions from coal-fired generating plants are put in place and new technological advancements become commercially available. Currently they require government incentives to be economically viable.

According to a 2008 report entitled *Cleantech: Current Status and Worldwide Outlook*, the renewable energy market is expected to grow from $104 billion (2007) to approximately $467 billion by 2017.[34] Clean Edge research estimates that four benchmark technologies (biofuel, wind, solar and fuel cells) will grow from $77.3 billion in 2007 to $254.5 billion by 2017.[35]

Table 6.2 presents a list of key alternative renewable energy sources for large-scale generation and assesses the potential market.

Wind Power

In 2007, 19.7 gigawatts (GW) of wind capacity were installed (for a cumulative capacity of 94.1 GW), which represented 14.8% of the total new (all sources) generation capacity installed worldwide.[36] A report from BTM Consult ApS, a Danish wind power consultant, entitled *World Market Update 2007: International Wind Energy Development,* predicts new installation will rise to 50.7 GW by 2012 (cumulative installed capacity of 287 GW). Global Wind Energy Council forecasts a final installed capacity 240 GW in 2012.[37] These predictions were made prior to the 2008 credit crunch and fall far short of what the IEA is estimating as necessary to address energy demands while reducing GHG emissions—which is that 17,500 wind turbines will be need to be installed every year until 2030.[38]

The United States currently leads the world in new installations of wind turbines (total of 16.8 GW). The U.S. Department of Energy believes that wind power could play a significant role in future energy requirements, supplying 20% of the nation's total electricity needs by 2030 (304 GW), requiring $43 billion to implement (including new transmission lines).[39]

Canada has increased its wind capacity from 137 MW in 2000 to 2,400 MW in 2008, with another 100 MW expected to come on line in 2009.[40]

Table 6.2: Alternative Renewable Energy Sources

Source	Description	Market and Investment Estimates
Wind Power—electricity	Large scale on/offshore wind farms in areas of high wind. Require nearby grid infrastructure that can handle the inevitable surges as well as provide an alternative source during calms.	• growth from $30.1 billion to $37 billion in 2007, to $83.4 billion in 2017, to $111 billion in 2012*
Solar Power—electricity	Scalable concentrated solar plants that either collect and store heat (day/night) and turn it into electricity or allow direct transfer of sunlight to electricity using photovoltaics (PVs).	• solar thermal investments of $85 billion by 2020† • PV market is expected to grow to $74 billion by 2017 from $20.3 billion in 2007‡
Biofuel—transportation	Once considered a key solution to global warming, energy security and farm policy. As demand has increased, several issues have emerged that have caused investors to reassess both type of biofuel and associated economics.	• $25.4 billion in 2007 to $81.1 billion in 2017‡
Hydroelectric—electricity	Reliable, proven source of electricity. Key issues include number of untapped rivers and environmental/social impact on creating dams.	• IEA—$50 billion worth of investments for added capacity by 2030a
Fuel Cells—transportation	Significant progress is being made on the design of fuel cells. A key issue is fuel source, as the majority of cells rely on hydrogen, which is currently expensive to generate and store.	• growth to $16 billion by 2017‡ from $1.5 billion in 2007 (primarily R&D and test units) • six-fold expansion in commercial demand to $2.5 billion by 2011 and $8.5 billion by 2016a
Geothermal—electricity	Provides base-load of 24/7, 365 days/year—average plant uptimes (i.e., facility producing energy) of 98%.	• IEA—$5.2 billion worth of investments for added capacity by 2030§ • anticipated $11 billion in investment in coming years as doubling of current installed base in North America#
Tidal Power—electricity	Tides are predictable and produce 24/7, 365 days/year. Limited number of commercial installations.	• at time of print, no published information was available on projections for market size

Note: All of the above predictions were made prior to the October 2008 credit crunch and may be adjusted for short-term fluctuation.

* Makower and Pernick, Wilder, 2008; Milford, 2008.
† Chang, 2008.
‡ Makower and Pernick, Wilder, 2008.
§ IEA, 2005
a Cleantech, 2007.
Glitnir Geothermal Research, 2007

The EU continues to be the largest market for wind power, at 8,285 MW of installed capacity, accounting for nearly 42% of the global total. Germany and Spain combined account for over half of the EU capacity. There is also significant growth in France, Italy, Portugal and the UK. China installed 3,287 MW of wind power in 2007, more than doubling the total installed capacity to 5,875 MW. India also installed significant new capacity—1,617 MW, a 26% increase.[41]

Pre-2008, the cost to construct a wind farm ranged from $1.40 to $2.20 per kilowatt (kW) excluding transmission costs. Table 6.3 provides information on recent costs for large-scale wind projects. The price of offshore turbines increased by 48% in the past three years, according to BTM Consult ApS, causing investors to rethink this option.[42]

Table 6.3: Cost of Wind Power Project (Excludes Transmission Costs)

Company	Type Location	Size (megawatts)	Cost in US$ (billions)	US$ per kW
BTM Consult ApS‡	Onshore Offshore	— —	— —	2.12 3.65
Hydro-Québec§	Quebec Onshore	2,004	3.6*	1.80
BP Capital (T. Boone Pickens)a	Texas Onshore	4,000 (2,700 turbines)	10†	2.50

*   Total price is C$5.5 billion and includes C$1.1 billion for transmission infrastructure.
†   Additional $2 billion is required for transmission lines. Current projections are for a 15%–25% profit assuming wind production tax credit is renewed (Gulyas, 2008).
‡   Milford, 2008.
§   Melnbardis, 2008.
a   Sassoon, 2008.

In the last few years, there has been significant consolidation in the market by very large global generators of wind power, examples of which include

- Energias de Portugal (Portugal) acquired Horizon Wind Energy from Goldman Sachs in 2008 for $2.15 billion. The company's goal is to increase installed capacity over the next four years to 7,600 MW by the end of 2010.[43]
- Iberdrola (Spain) acquired three U.S. wind development companies in 2006, completed two buyouts in 2007 ($22.5 billion for ScottishPower and $73.8 million for U.S.-based CPV Wind Ventures) and then created an IPO spinoff named Iberdrola Renewables. The company plans to invest $8 billion in U.S. renewable energy sector between 2008 and 2010.[44]

Figure 6.2: U.S. Wind Resources

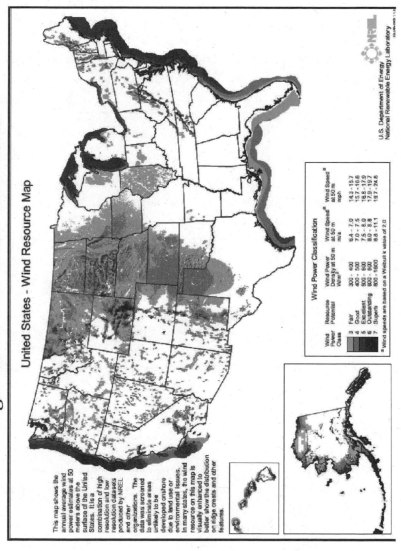

United States - Wind Resource Map

This map shows the annual average wind power estimates at 50 meters above the surface of the United States. It is a combination of high resolution and low resolution datasets produced by NREL and other organizations. The data was screened to eliminate areas unlikely to be developed onshore due to land use or environmental issues. In many states, the wind resource on this map is visually enhanced to better show the distribution on ridge crests and other features.

Wind Power Classification

Wind Power Class	Resource Potential	Wind Power Density at 50 m W/m2	Wind Speed[a] at 50 m m/s	Wind Speed[a] at 50 m mph
3	Fair	300 - 400	6.4 - 7.0	14.3 - 15.7
4	Good	400 - 500	7.0 - 7.5	15.7 - 16.8
5	Excellent	500 - 600	7.5 - 8.0	16.8 - 17.9
6	Outstanding	600 - 800	8.0 - 8.8	17.9 - 19.7
7	Superb	800 - 1600	8.8 - 11.1	19.7 - 24.8

[a] Wind speeds are based on a Weibull k value of 2.0

U.S. Department of Energy
National Renewable Energy Laboratory

- Scottish and Southern Energy (SSE, Scotland) has almost 1,500 MW of onshore wind farm capacity in operation, in construction or with consent for development in the UK and Ireland, up from a level of 875 MW when it acquired Airtricity (Ireland) in early 2008. SSE plans to invest £2.5 billion in renewable energy in the UK and Ireland over the next five years.[45]

Note that the growth projections above were all made before these companies experienced the full impact of the 2008 global recession.

WIND

Benefits

- competitive with natural gas under current government tax incentives, and will be competitive with coal if a cap–and–trade program or carbon tax (of sufficient value) are implemented
- technology is relatively straightforward and proven; research is focused on ways to improve efficiencies
- significant areas of North America have elevated areas of constant wind—for example, strong winds in central U.S. and coastal regions (see figure 6.2)
- can be used as a decentralized power source or connected to the grid
- ongoing government market based incentives (refer to section of chapter entitled Government Influence or Meddling)
- benefits financially from the carbon trading market—many companies sell tax credits, emission credits or depreciation streams to offset upfront cost[46]

Issues

- majority of sites are intermittent and there exists no cost-effective technology (although it is getting close) to store electricity in large quantities; work is underway on ultra capacitors, hydraulic accumulators and cheaper lithium-ion batteries for both off and on grid
- not in my backyard (NIMBY) opposition is increasing because of visual/noise pollution and associated impact on wetlands, farmlands, property values and tourism
- rising material cost (turbines and steel used for blades/structure) and installation costs for wind farms; need to reduce these costs to be competitive
- need to improve performance and reliability and advance rotor development[47]
- supply chain issues related to large bearings, gearboxes and blades, especially carbon fiber blades[48]

- problems with offshore wind farms: shortage of construction vessels, skilled workers and high-voltage cables.
- if onshore, large areas of land are required (roughly 0.1 square km of unobstructed land per MW of design capacity) at increasing rental/acquisition fees
- perceived impact on birds and real impact on bats in some areas—studies show that the number of birds killed by wind turbines is negligible compared to the number that die as a result of other human activities, but the number of bats killed has caused alarm in some communities; more research is needed[49]
- local utility may provide transmission lines (within the timeline of the project) or there may be the need to construct infrastructure as part of the project (and hence incur cost). The U.S. alone may need more than 19,312 km (12,000 miles) of additional transmission lines.
- rules on curtailment, i.e., restriction of the output of wind generation to maintain system security (prevent system overload)
- availability of funding, as it is capital intensive and requires project/debt equity
- restrictions imposed by financial institutions (e.g., Equator Principles)

Note: Equator Principles are a financial industry benchmark for determining, assessing and managing social and environmental risk in project financing.

A Canadian map is available from Environment Canada's *Canada Wind Energy Atlas* (www.windatlas.ca).

Wind power makes economic sense provided there exist constant winds of sufficient strength, the community accepts the installation, there is access to transmission lines, and there is a long-term agreement to purchase electricity that reflects cost structure and ongoing government incentives (which may not be required if petroleum/natural gas prices increase substantially).

Key issue: If wind is to provide 5% of world electricity demand, a robust system is required to store energy when there is insufficient wind power available.

Solar

In general terms, there are three types of solar power sources: concentrated solar power (CSP), solar thermal and photovoltaic (PV). According to the Global Solar Center, world solar cell production reached a consolidated figure of 3,436 MW in 2007, up from 2,204 MW a year earlier.[50] The United States is the fourth largest market for solar power behind Germany, Spain and Japan. This market is expected to grow from an installed capacity of 230 MW in 2007 to 450 MW in 2008, with California (which already accounts for 80% of the market) responsible for most of this growth.[51] According to a report by JP Morgan, the United States will surpass Germany and become the largest market for solar power in the world by 2011, with an installed capacity of 1.6 GW compared to Germany's capacity of 1.35 GW.[52]

According to the Canadian Solar Industries Association, solar capacity across Canada is a mere megawatt.[53] Current forecasts indicate that solar capacity will grow at a much slower rate than other countries, and far behind wind. It is interesting to note that while much of Canada's populated regions have similar solar intensity as Germany, the latter has significantly higher installed capacity because of government market based incentives.

Concentrated Solar Power (CSP)

CSP power plants generate heat by using lenses to reflect concentrated solar energy to heat a fluid or PV solar panels. The heated fluid then is used to drive a conventional generator to create electricity. Newer designs allow the heat to be transferred to a thermal storage medium in an insulated reservoir during sunlight hours so that the heat can be withdrawn for power generation when there is no sunlight. This allows the use of solar power for base-load generation as well as peak power generation, and increases the utilization of the generator, which reduces cost. Prior to the global recession, the capacity of CSP was expected to double every sixteen months over five years, so that worldwide installed CSP capacity would reach 6,400 MW in 2012—fourteen times the current capacity. In 2008, more than a dozen new CSP plants were planned in the United States, with some 3,100 MW expected to come online by 2012. Some impressive CSP projects in the planning stages include the 553 MW Mojave Solar Park in California (Solel Solar Systems), the 500 MW Solar One and 300 MW Solar Two projects in California (Stirling Energy Systems), and the 400 MW Ivanpah Solar Electric Generating System (BrightSource Energy Inc.).[54]

Solar Thermal

Solar thermal turns sunlight into heat. Solar thermal collectors are categorized by the U.S. Energy Information Agency as low, medium or high temperature collectors. Low-temperature collectors are flat plates generally used to heat swimming pools. Medium-temperature collectors are also usually flat plates but are used for creating hot water for residential and commercial use. High-temperature collectors concentrate sunlight using mirrors or lenses and are generally used for electric power production. See the discussion of Concentrated Solar Power above.

Photovoltaic (PV)

PV solar panels are really just large semiconductor chips that convert solar energy directly into electricity. Currently a race is on to develop low cost/high efficiency cells. Current options include concentrated PV (CPV), wafer silicon, film silicon, copper indium gallium selenide (CIGS), cadmium telluride (CdTE) and next generation PV (organics, dye-sensitized solar cell [DSSC] and multiple exciton generation [MEG]). Photovoltaic production has been doubling every two years, increasing by an average of 48% each year since 2002, making it the world's fastest-growing energy technology. At the end of 2007, according to preliminary data, cumulative global production was 12.4 GW.[55]

Roughly 90% of this generating capacity consists of grid-tied electrical systems. Such installations may be ground-mounted (and sometimes integrated with farming and grazing) or built into the roof or walls of a building, known as building-integrated photovoltaic.[56]

Several large players have announced significant manufacturing capacity increases in the PV market and will be applying their expertise to reduce cost across the supply chain and improve conversion efficiency (i.e., sunlight to electricity) of cells. Examples of planned expansion (pending impact of 2008 recession) include the following:

- Sharp Corporation (Japan) is currently constructing a new "Manufacturing Complex for the 21st Century" in Japan to support its vertically integrated business model. The facility has capacity to manufacture 1 GW of thin-film solar cells.
- Renewable Energy Corporation (Norway) is the world's largest producer of silicon materials for PV applications and PV wafers, as well as a significant producer of cells and modules. It has agreed to construct a US$1.2 billion silicon materials manufacturing complex in Quebec that will employ more than three hundred people. The deal included a twenty-year power supply agreement with Hydro-Québec. REC was able to secure a stable supply of relatively cheap renewable electricity, allowing it to make silicon—and, up the value chain, solar cells and panels—with a low carbon footprint.[57] REC also agreed to spend close to US$1.84 (NOK13 billion) in the first phase of

an integrated manufacturing complex for production of wafers, cells and modules in Singapore. Production is expected to commence in the first quarter of 2010, and reach full capacity of 740 MW of wafers, 550 MW of cells and 590 MW of modules before 2012.[58]

SOLAR

Benefits

- vast majority of southwestern U.S. has exceptional solar intensity (see figure 6.3)
- significant amount of land in this area is desert and not being used for other activities
- utilizing 1% of the earth's deserts can allow the production of clean solar electric energy equivalent to current global energy requirements[59]
- PV cost is falling because of mass production, new technologies and supply chain efficiencies; next generation dye-sensitive thin film (DSC) and organic PV (OPV) solar cells are showing significant promise; can be used as a decentralized power source or connected to the grid
- ongoing government market-based incentives (refer to "Government Influence or Meddling")
- benefits financially from carbon trading market—many companies sell tax credits, remission credits or depreciation streams to offset up-front costs[60]

Issues

- requires energy storage systems to offset limitations of generating during only sunny daytime hours (key technology issue to overcome)
- availability of direct sunshine on a consistent basis (solar intensity key)
- requires significant amounts of land (ideal location is in desert)
- high construction costs for new facilities—typically in the range of $5–$10 per kW
- relatively high cost for solar PV panels; costs are falling because of mass production, new technologies (e.g., thin film PV, which does not use traditional crystalline silicon wafers) and supply chain efficiencies
- if linking to the grid, access to transmission lines—cost of approximately $1 million per mile of transmission line
- availability of funding, as capital intensive and requires project/debt equity

Figure 6.3: Solar Intensity

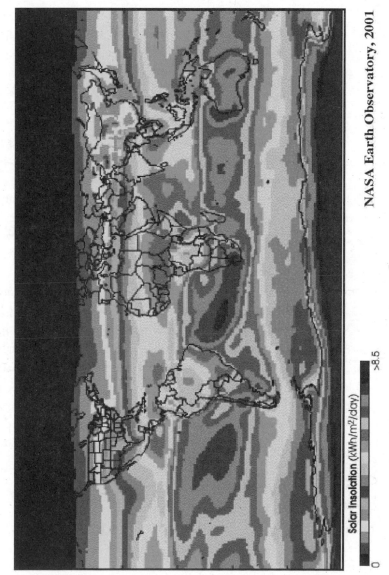

Solar Insolation (kWh/m²/day)

0   >8.5

NASA Earth Observatory, 2001

As the price of PV modules drop because of mass production and new technology it will become ubiquitous—a low-cost add-on to any device that requires power (buildings, residences, vehicles, electronic devices, etc.).

For a more detailed map of U.S. intensity, refer to Solar Energy Industries Association's website (www.SEIA.org), and for Canada, refer to Canadian Solar Industries Association's website (www.cansia.ca).

Biofuel

In 2007, the global biofuels market comprised more than 49.2 billion liters (13 billion gallons) of ethanol and 7.57 billion liters (2 billion gallons) of biodiesel.[61] The U.S. market for biodiesel grew from approximately 94.6 million liters per year in 2004 to approximately 1.7 billion liters in 2007.[62] U.S. ethanol production was expected to reach 2.46 billion liters in 2007. The United States renewable fuel standard (RFS) discussed below guarantees a market of 28.4 billion liters per year for ethanol by 2012.[63] Global ethanol production is projected to reach about 125 billion liters in 2017.[64]

The Brazilian government began investing heavily in ethanol infrastructure and research and development more than thirty years ago. The country currently produces 45% of its own transportation fuel and is aggressively looking beyond both first-generation biofuels and its domestic market. Current annual production is 4.7 billion gallons of ethanol and the government estimates that number will double by 2015.[65]

As indicated in chapter 1, there have been some "missteps" regarding biofuel, in particular the use of corn as a raw material. Because of this debate, discussion of biofuels has been separated into two parts: biofuel from crops and biofuel from waste/non-crop sources referred to as "other."

Biofuel from Crops

In 2007, biofuels accounted for more than 30% of the U.S. corn harvest.[66] Numerous studies and media reports have raised concern over the generation of biofuel from crops. Key concerns include

- price hikes in processed/staple food due to redirection of crops for ethanol, with the amount of the price hike a contentious issue between ethanol supporters and the food industry

- the actual carbon output or energy use once the entire production cycle is taken into account
- clearing previously untouched land to grow biofuel crops releases long-sequestered carbon into the atmosphere

Governments in Europe are starting to listen to the message that the "type" of biofuel is critical and, instead of granting blanket tax relief, are introducing systems that will waive levies only to biofuels that are certified "low carbon" as compared to conventional gasoline and diesel.[67]

"Other" Biofuels

Due in part to the food for fuel debate, environmentalists, government and industry are taking a look at the carbon footprint of various types of biofuels. The lowest biofuel carbon footprint will be from waste products, algae and plants grown on wasteland or through very high-efficiency cultivation systems.[68] The current focus of many companies is on "next generation" biofuels: second-generation cellulosic ethanol technologies that rely on the non-edible parts of plants and third-generation biofuel derived from algae. Key benefits of algae include high yields and flexibility of location and feedstock (e.g., uses sewage).

A second trend in this area is the significant increase in the size of commercial scale biofuel facilities as companies construct both first generation—Ineos Scotland and Natura Spain—and second generation—Nestle Oil Singapore and Tyson-Conoco Texas facilities—in excess of 450,000 MT/year.[69]

BIOFUELS

Benefits

- provide safe alternative to gasoline, leveraging some of existing infrastructure
- biodiesel reduces tailpipe emissions of particulate matter (in particular carbon black—a major contributor to global warming)[70]
- cost-effective where raw material is plentiful, as seen in Brazilian market
- supported by RFSs and relief from EU excise tax
- emerging technology related to second-generation (cellulosic biofuel) and third-generation (algae fuel) biofuels and crop yields will further reduce costs
- potentially contribute to cooling of atmosphere due to release of aerosols during combustion

Issues

- carbon footprint for different types of biofuels varies significantly and has started to impact government policy and excise taxes
- supply of raw materials, because of prices and potential restrictions if using a staple food
- clearing previously untouched land (especially rain forest) to grow biofuel crops releases long-sequestered carbon into the atmosphere
- capital cost to set up and maintain systems
- an 85% ethanol/gasoline mix (E85) has only 72% of gasoline's energy content[71]
- ethanol is hydrophilic and hence tends to separate from gasoline over time so it cannot be shipped in the same pipeline and must be blended at distribution terminals rather than refineries[72]
- reluctance on the part of some oil companies to establish infrastructure for ethanol as it requires separate pumps, trucks and storage tanks
- availability of funding as capital intensive and requires project/debt equity
- untreated biodiesel emits roughly 10% more nitrogen oxides (NO_x) than regular diesel and hence requires fuel additives and a catalytic converter
- restrictions imposed by financial institutions (Equator Principles)

It is critical to take into consideration changing government subsidies, raw material (carbon footprint, availability and price fluctuations), emerging technology and transportation costs to ensure the ongoing feasibility of biofuel facilities.

Hydroelectric

Hydroelectric facilities have been a source of energy in North America for more than one hundred years, with most of the good sources already developed. The technology is relatively unchanged, except for the introduction of newer, more efficient turbines that allow the safe passage of fish. There has also been renewed interest in "run of the river" sites, i.e., instead of damming a river, a portion of the water is diverted via a pipeline, allowing it to travel downhill to a small powerhouse and then be returned to the stream.

Table 6.4 presents the top five hydroelectric energy-producing countries in the world. China is significantly expanding its hydroelectric capacity—approximately

83 GW of hydroelectric projects are currently under construction (a similar size to the total capacity in Canada) with several additional projects planned.

Table 6.4: Top Producers of Hydroelectric Energy (2007 data)

Country	Annual Hydroelectric Production (TWh)*	Percentage of Global Hydroelectric Power*	Installed Capacity (GW) †
China	483	15.4%	145
Brazil	372	11.9%	69
Canada	368	11.7%	89
United States	251	8.0%	80
Russia	179	5.7%	45

* BP, 2008.
† Answers.com, accessed January 9, 2009.

Several Canadian provinces generate most of their electricity from hydro-electric projects: Manitoba—98%, Quebec—95% and Newfoundland—95%.[73] Hydro-Québec is the world's largest hydroelectric generating company, with a total installed capacity (2005) of 31.5 GW. Work on the lower Churchill River in Labrador will begin in 2009, bringing the province of Newfoundland and Labrador's combined total hydroelectric generation to 18 GW upon completion of the project. Manitoba will have three new hydro plants: a 220 MW project in Wusk-watim is expected to come on-line in 2011, and on the drawing board is a 650 MW plant at Keyask and a massive 1,350 MW plant at Conawapa.[74] Forecasts of untapped rivers indicate an additional 34 to 100 GW of technically feasible power available in Canada, with 10% to 15% made up of comparatively small-scale sites of less than 50 MW capacity.

The U.S. Electric Consumers Protection Act (ECPA) of 1986 increased the focus on non-power issues in the hydroelectric licensing process. The end result was an increase in development costs and lengthening of the time period required to obtain a license. Due to increased environmental awareness, the construction of new dams is often viewed more negatively than in the past. Between 1991 and 2000, only six hydroelectric projects were constructed in the U.S. with new dam or diversion structures, and all of these structures were less than 30 feet (10 meters) in height. In Canada, dam construction has continued, albeit under significantly increased scrutiny related to environmental impact.

HYDROELECTRIC POWER

Benefits

- plants tend to have much longer economic lives than other types of generation; some plants now in service were built fifty to one hundred years ago
- automated operation, resulting in low labor requirement and costs
- hydroelectric facilities are only installed at about 2% of U.S. dams; hydroelectric plants may be added to the remaining dams (potentially 30 GW) at relatively low construction costs, as well as low environmental impact
- "run-of-the-river" (i.e., no dam) hydroelectric plants are gaining popularity because of reduced impact on the environment
- reservoirs often provide facilities for water sports and become a tourist attraction
- in some countries, fish farming in reservoirs is common
- benefits financially from carbon trading market—many companies sell tax credits, emission credits or depreciation streams to offset up-front costs[75]

Issues

- the number of untapped rivers that can provide reasonable amount of energy is limited in North America
- significantly impacted by rainfall in watershed; reduction in generation may occur if there is prolonged reduction in rainfall or snowmelt
- hydroelectric facilities requiring dams can have the following impacts:
  - impacts on fish migrations and on other aquatic organisms; research is underway on turbine blade configuration to allow safe passage of more than 98% of fish
  - loss of wildlife habitat as land is flooded
  - if forested land is not cleared during development, especially in tropical regions, GHG emissions from reservoirs may be high
  - displacement of communities due to flooding of lands
- potential run-of-the-river sites must offer a significant gradient (elevation drop) and sufficient annual precipitation
- opposition from environmental groups, recreational associations and tourism groups—especially to sites where dams will be constructed
- increase in licensing cost and time for site studies (hydrological studies and environmental impact assessment) due to changes in regulatory process
- access to transmission lines if part of the grid, as typically sites are far from population centers (cost of approximately $1.5 million for each kilometer of high

voltage line necessary to carry the massive power flows that come out of large hydroelectric facilities)
- availability of funding as it is capital intensive and requires project/debt equity
- restrictions imposed by financial institutions (e.g., Equator Principles)

There is good opportunity to add hydroelectric plants that leverage new technology at existing dam sites as well as new "run-of-the-river" sites that have significant gradient. Electricity may be for localized use or to connect to the grid, depending upon access to transmissions lines.

Fuel Cells

A fuel cell is an electrochemical conversion device. Fuel cells are different from batteries in that they consume reactant, which must be replenished, whereas batteries store electrical energy chemically in a closed system. Historically, fuel cells have been used as power sources in remote locations as they are compact and lightweight, and have no major moving parts.[76] Recently, several Japanese corporations began investing in methanol fuel cells for high-capacity batteries for laptops and other relatively energy-demanding portable devices.[77]

During the last decade, a significant amount of investment has been made in using fuel cells as a primary source of energy for transportation. To date, fuel cells running on hydrogen fuel dominate this research. While this type of cell is an especially clean method of meeting power requirements, emitting only water as waste, large amounts of energy are required to produce the hydrogen fuel. Additionally, greenhouse gases are emitted during the extraction of hydrogen from hydrocarbons. Proponents of this approach have argued that more than 40 billion kilograms per year of hydrogen are produced globally for industrial purposes, enough to fuel 130 million fuel cell–electric vehicles. The problem is that the majority of hydrogen is generated from natural gas, which is a nonrenewable resource that is increasing in price.

The cost to provide hydrogen fueling stations for 70% of the U.S. population has been estimated to be in the area of $20 billion. Additional discussion on these costs were provided in chapter 3.

FUEL CELLS
Benefit

- provide zero emission vehicles that can be quickly refueled and can travel long distances between refueling
- public perception of a simple, futuristic solution
- gaining market share in specialty applications, e.g., forklifts as zero emissions and more consistent power for lifting/movement (vs. lead-acetate batteries)
- positive results emerging on use of methanol fuel cells for high-capacity batteries for laptops and other relatively demanding portable devices
- can benefit financially from carbon trading market—many companies sell tax credits, emission credits or depreciation streams to offset up-front cost[78]

Issues

- cost of fuel cell is dropping, but still has a way to go to be economical; key component in many cells is platinum catalyst
- most fuel cells require hydrogen as the fuel, which is currently expensive to generate and difficult to store
- need to ensure commercial versions are reliable, in particular to ensure correct water balance, temperature management and avoidance of carbon monoxide
- if used in transportation vehicles, infrastructure is required to deliver and store fuel at substantial cost
- also requires (simultaneously with infrastructure) automakers to commit to producing this type of vehicle and hence key issue of economic viability of mass-producing hydrogen cars that the market will accept
- if hydrogen fuel cell, there is risk of explosion as it is a very flammable material

Fuel cells are currently limited to specialty applications; however, if an economic solution to hydrogen generation is found and the cost of the fuel cell is reduced, it could be a major source of fuel for transportation.

Geothermal

In general, there are two types of geothermal resources: geo-exchange heating and cooling, which are low temperature (e.g., heat pumps), and high temperature geothermal resources. The latter is often called Enhanced Geothermal Systems (EGS) and involves electricity generated from heat extracted with an engineered fluid-flow path in hot rocks. Taking into consideration ground source heat pumps, the nonelectric generating capacity of geothermal energy is estimated at more than 100 GW and is used commercially in over seventy countries.[79] Iceland generates 17% of its electricity and 87% of its heating from geothermal energy.[80]

According to a 2008 report by Glitnir Geothermal Research, a consulting firm with headquarters in Iceland, the U.S. is a global leader in geothermal energy, with total installed capacity of some 2,800 MW; annual electricity generation of approximately 16,000 GWh; and projects underway that, when completed, will increase U.S. installed capacity by a further 2,500 MW. The report also indicates that a total investment of $16.9 billion will be required to develop available resources over the next eight years, with a further $22.5 billion over the next ten years.[81]

In a 2006 report by MIT that took into account the use of EGS, it was concluded that it would be affordable to generate 100 GW or more by 2050 in the U.S. alone. Some of the key findings of the study include these:

- The U.S. has largely ignored the geothermal option and government policies and incentives have not favored growth in this area.
- Geothermal can provide base-load electric power and heat at a level that can have a major impact on the United States, while incurring minimal environmental impacts.
- A reasonable investment ($1 billion) in R&D is required for EGS to provide 100 GW or more of cost-competitive generating capacity in the next fifty years.
- Most of the key technical requirements to make EGS work economically over a wide area of the country exist, with remaining goals easily within reach.

GEOTHERMAL ENERGY

Benefits

- predictable source of energy
- offers degree of scalability
- emissions of undesirable substances are low
- unaffected by changing weather conditions
- reliable source that works continuously (24/7) making base-load power

- good potential for electricity production via EGS in the western states and provinces as well as Hawaii (see figure 6.4)
- ongoing government MBIs (refer to section of chapter entitled Government Influence or Meddling)
- price competitive where there is access to high temperatures at shallow depths.
- can benefit financially from carbon trading market—many companies sell tax
  credits, emission credits or depreciation streams to offset up-front cost[82]

Issues

- geo-exchange heating and cooling:
    - start-up capital is high and ROI is typically four to eight years
    - many jurisdictions in North America do not provide MBIs or they are insuf-
      ficient
    - to accelerate adaptation, needs to be part of building codes
- Enhanced Geothermal Systems (EGS):
    - proven systems; however, R&D is required to increase the overall competitive-
      ness
    - government tax credits/subsidies need to be increased in a manner similar to
      Australia to accelerate development
    - need significant increase in capacity of drilling equipment and related human
      resources (currently in conflict for human and equipment resources with oil
      industry)
    - geothermal fluid is corrosive and contains trace amounts of mercury and
      heavy metals (e.g., arsenic, antimony), which may cause toxicity in rivers
    - geothermal fluid is relatively low in temperature (compared to steam boilers)
      and lower efficiency
    - preferred locations are limited
    - potential impact on land stability of surrounding region in areas where previ-
      ously there was no water at the depth of injection
    - emissions of low levels of carbon dioxide, nitric oxide, and sulfur (roughly 5%
      of a fossil fuel plant)
    - some opposition from environmental groups, recreational associations and
      tourism groups depending upon use of energy (refer to recent issues regard-
      ing Iceland's use of geothermal for smelters)
    - access to transmission lines unless used off-grid

Figure 6.4: Subterranean Temperatures*

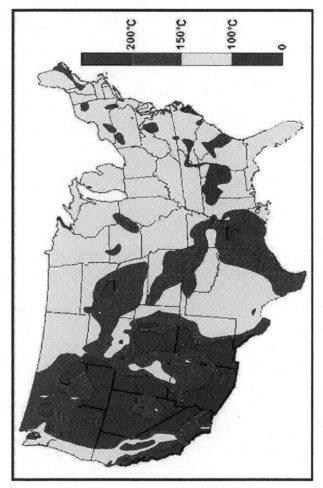

* Depth of 6 km

Geothermal Energy Association, 2007

For additional information on the United States, refer to http://nationalatlas.
gov/articles/people/a_energy.html#three. For information on Canadian geothermal sites, refer to www.cangea.ca.

Geo-exchange heating and cooling are proven and economical. EGS has potential to
address future energy needs. However, additional government and industry investment is required to move this rapidly forward.

Tidal Power

Tidal power can be classified into two main types:[83]

- barrages systems, which make use of the potential energy of the difference
  in height between high and low tides
- tidal stream systems, which make use of the kinetic energy of moving water to power turbines, in a way similar to how windmills use moving air;
  this method is gaining in popularity because of the lower cost and lower
  ecological impact compared to barrages

Several countries have committed to significant investment in tidal power,
e.g., Scotland has committed to 10% of its power from tidal generation. Both
Spain and the UK have established successful supporting mechanisms for wave
power by putting in place marine energy tariffs and R&D funding.

The first U.S. pilot tidal generator was launched in New York City's East River
in late 2006. The first utility-scale wave project, off Oregon beaches, won preliminary U.S. federal approval in 2007. Numerous preliminary permits have been filed
and cleared by the U.S. Federal Energy Regulatory Commission for wave and tidal
projects, largely off the West Coast and shores of Florida and New England.

Barrage Tidal Power

These systems are similar to a hydro dam that produces static head (a height of
water pressure). When the water level outside of the basin or lagoon changes relative to the water level inside, the turbines are able to produce power. The largest
such installation is located St. Malo, France, and was installed in 1965 with peak
power of 240 MW. The second commercial-scale tidal barrage was put in service
at Annapolis Royal, Nova Scotia, in 1982.[84]

Tidal Stream Generators

This type of system needs to be located in areas with fast currents where natural flows are concentrated between obstructions, for example at the entrances to bays and rivers, around rocky points, headlands, or between islands or other land masses.

In April 2008, the first commercial prototype, called SeaGen, was installed in Strangfor Lough in Northern Ireland. The turbine is expected to generate 1.2 MW and is being connected to the grid.[85] A $50 million pilot project is set to begin in the fall of 2009 or spring 2010 in the Bay of Fundy. The Nova Scotia government has chosen three companies to participate in testing three types of systems for overall capacity of about 4 MW.[86] Other large-scale projects include an Ocean Power Technologies unit off the coast of Spain, Pelamis Wave Power project off the coast of Portugal and SDE Energy & Desalination project in Africa. The latter will cost approximately $100 million, have capacity of 100 MW and generate revenue of $1 billion from electricity sales according to DSE representatives.[87]

TIDAL POWER

Benefits

- predictable source of energy
- offers degree of scalability
- works continuously (24/7) making base-load power
- new U.S. tax credits for wave and tidal projects
- can benefit financially from carbon trading market—companies may sell tax credits, emission credits or depreciation streams to offset up-front costs[88]

Issues

- number of locations with appropriate tides
- biofouling can occur over time
- barrages—block navigation, impede fish migration, very high civil infrastructure costs, change size and location of the intertidal zones, change the tidal regime downstream[89]
- tidal stream—absence of sites that have been running for any significant period of time; new technology (e.g., shrouded tidal turbine) is also emerging with significantly higher power output
- access to transmission lines if connecting to grid
- restrictions imposed by financial institutions (e.g., Equator Principles)

The early stage of development in tidal stream projects shows promise but requires additional history. It has potential to become a significant source of energy.

Table 6.5 presents a summary of nonrenewable energy options to meet increasing demand. As indicated by the prediction of growth, all three are seen as key sources of energy to meet future demand.

Table 6.5: Alternative Energy Using Nonrenewable Resources

Alternative Energy	Description	Market
Nuclear Power (fission)*—electricity	• very efficient and consistent—24/7—source base-load energy for utilities with very little GHG emissions (related to maintenance activities) • does not allow for fluctuating loads, issue of storage/disposal of spent nuclear fuel, or impact and public response if an accident occurs	• IEA estimates that thirty-two new nuclear power plants (individual cost $1.5 billion) must be constructed per year (between 2010–2050) to meet global demand ($1.92 trillion) • Ontario is proposing two new reactors and will be upgrading existing ones—worth $26 billion
Liquefied Natural Gas (LNG)—electricity and fuel	• natural gas, primarily methane that has been converted to a liquid form for easier storage and transport	• a total of $106 billion is projected to be spent on export terminals, LNG carriers and import terminals from 2008–2012†
Clean Coal Technologies—electricity	• include chemically washing minerals and impurities from the coal, gasification, treating flue gases with steam to remove sulfur dioxide and other proposed technologies to capture the carbon dioxide from flue gas	• IEA estimates that thirty coal-powered and twenty-five gas-powered stations with carbon capture and storage must be constructed per year (between 2010–2050) to meet global demand

* Nuclear fission occurs when a massive nucleus splits into smaller nuclei with the simultaneous release of energy. Nuclear fusion is the combination of two nuclei to form a heavier nucleus with the release of energy. The commercialization of fusion is still some distance in the future and hence beyond the scope of this book.
† Subsea World, 2008.

Nuclear Power (Fission)

Significant renewed interest in nuclear power has emerged—a "nuclear renaissance"—in the last two years, as the nuclear industry repositions itself to be a green alternative to oil. Backers of this movement include U.S. and Canadian political leaders as well as several icons of environmental causes like Stewart

Brand (author of *Whole Earth Catalogue*), James Lovelock (propagator of the Gaia theory of the Earth as a comprehensive living organism) and Patrick Moore (Greenpeace co-founder). Moore summarizes his position by saying, "When I do the math, it's very clear to me that renewables (solar, wind and hydro) can't do the job themselves. That's why nuclear has to be in the mix. As an environmentalist, I choose nuclear." The backers' support of nuclear was prompted by the realization that the threat to humanity from climate change induced by carbon-emitting energy production outweighs the inherent dangers of nuclear power.[90]

According to the IEA, 16% of global energy production comes from approximately five hundred nuclear facilities operating worldwide. The IEA report calls for approximately 1,400 new nuclear facilities by 2050. The following table presents the generating capacity of the top nuclear generating countries.

Table 6.6: Top Producers of Nuclear Energy (2007 data)

Country	Annual Nuclear Production (TWh)	Percentage of Global Nuclear Power
U.S.A.	849	31%
France	440	16%
Japan	279	10%
Russia	160	5.8%
South Korea	143	5.2%
Germany	141	5.1%
Canada	93	3.4%

BP, 2008

The U.S. has some one hundred nuclear reactors providing about nearly 100 GW of capacity, which accounts for less than 14% of the total electricity generation capacity (note: not energy production); however, because they operate at high levels of efficiency and reliability, these plants produce almost 20% of the total annual electricity supply of the U.S.[91]

In Canada, Ontario leads the way, with 14 GW of nuclear generating electricity (88.2 TeraWatt hours [TWh]). Two new reactors have been proposed with combined capacity of 3.2 GW. Construction of the new reactors is anticipated to begin in 2012 with electricity being generated by July 1, 2018. The addition of the new reactors to the grid will result in more than 60% of peak power demand coming from nuclear-generated electricity. The price tag for the new reactors and upgrades to existing nuclear facilities is within the province's budget of $26.3 billion to increase nuclear capacity over the next twenty years.[92]

More than thirty new nuclear reactors were being considered in the United States prior to the 2008 recession.[93] In addition, in 2006 the U.S. rescinded a 1976 ban on nuclear cooperation with India. Some estimates indicate that India's significant expansion of nuclear power will bring $100 billion to American companies.[94] In January of 2008, MidAmerican Energy Holding, a Berkshire Hathaway owned company, suspended plans to build a nuclear plant in Idaho as it did not make economic sense.[95]

There are significantly different viewpoints[96] on the feasibility of new nuclear sites in the U.S.:

- Adrian Heymer, Nuclear Energy Institute senior director of New Plant Deployment, says, "If the first few plants can be built on time and within budget, nuclear capacity in the United States will soar. If we do that, I think you could see 20 new plants by 2020."
- Michael Morris, CEO of American Electric Power Co., isn't planning to build any new nuclear power plants because delays will push operational starts to 2020. Builders would also have to queue for certain parts and face realistic costs of about $4,000 a kW. "I'm not convinced we'll see a new nuclear station before probably the 2020 timeline."

NUCLEAR POWER (Fission)

Benefits

- extremely efficient conversion of fuel to electricity
- operates 24/7 with minimum maintenance time
- near zero GHG emissions
- number of direct/indirect deaths is significantly below those related to air pollution from carbon-burning sources
- supply of uranium (proven uranium reserves total 4.74 million tons worldwide, enough for more than fifty years of global consumption)
- studies have shown that the number of deaths associated directly/indirectly with nuclear power are significantly below the 3 million that the World Health Organization reports are killed each year from air pollution from carbon-burning sources[97]

Issues

- significant capital cost to construct a nuclear facility ($3 billion–$6 billion per 1,000 MW facility)
- cost to refurbish a facility and thereby extend its life (a significant number of reactors are coming to the end of their normal life)
- selection of locations for construction of new facilities (NIMBY syndrome has not gone away)
- anti-nuke opposition from mainstream environmental movement: Greenpeace, Sierra Club, Friends of the Earth, etc.
- cost and availability of key portions of reactors because of demand and limited number of providers (e.g., conventional reactor containment vessel)
- absence of track record with new third-generation reactors
- restrictions imposed by financial institutions (Equator Principles)
- time required to build a facility; six to ten years in some cases in North America and four to five years in Asia
- disposal of spent nuclear material, which remains hazardous for a significant number of years (more than ten thousand) contributes significantly to operating costs
- accidental release of radiation into the environment and surrounding community; the issue is less about impact, which has historically been small because of response systems, and more about public response and restrictions on new facilities
- ongoing cost for security and threat of terrorist activities
- significant money to decommission nuclear facilities once they reach end-of-life; however, when amortized over the life of the facility, at a discounted rate, it's only a few percentage points of the capital cost

Liquefied Natural Gas (LNG)

Liquefied natural gas played a key role in both Japan and UK in rebalancing their national energy mix following the 1973 oil crisis. Japan had no domestic natural gas and hence all of the gas was brought in by newly constructed LNG tankers, which required significant effort to construct an infrastructure for this new fuel type. Many other countries are now following suit, resulting in a significant rebalancing in the LNG supply chain in Asia, the Middle East, Europe and Africa as indicated by the surge of LNG tanker construction in the last few years.[98]

Expenditures on export terminals, LNG carriers and import terminals are expected to total $106 billion from 2008–2012 according to energy analyst Douglas-Westwood. Asia has the largest proportion of global LNG expenditure—43%—followed by the Middle East at 15%. Examples of ongoing expenditures include these:

- Qatar has one of the largest natural gas fields and is constructing a facility to convert the gas to liquid. The $7 billion project is being built in conjunction with ExxonMobil, Shell and others and is slated to start to deliver 154,000 barrels per day (including 75,000 barrels of clean diesel per day) in 2011.[99]
- In Russia, Gazprom has signed an agreement with a Canadian company for deliveries of LNG from the Shtokman field in the Barents Sea. This is the first large investment by Gazprom in the North American market, which is a vital part of its global strategy on exports of LNG. Gazprom plans to start production at 3.8 trillion cubic meters from the Shtokman field in 2013. The gas will be exported partly by pipeline to European buyers and partly as LNG. The production of liquefied natural gas will start in 2014.[100]

LIQUIFIED NATURAL GAS
Benefits

- cleaner than coal plant emissions
- relatively large supply of natural gas left
- potential fuel for both electricity generation and transportation
- good experience in offsetting coal and oil demand in several countries, including the UK and Japan
- several large producers are shifting resources to produce LNG
- new pipeline being constructed from field in Barents Sea to North America

Issues

- rising demand and hence price as utilities shift from coal-fired generating plants to natural gas
- ability of supply chain to keep up with demand, e.g., number of available LNG tankers
- current production is negligible relative to amounts required to offset gasoline consumption for transportation

- cost for carbon sequestration will be high
- infrastructure investment required to store, transport and distribute natural gas
- restrictions imposed by financial institutions (e.g., Equator Principles)

Clean Coal

As indicated in table 6.7, the United States has the largest proven coal reserves and is second (behind China) in terms of production. There is a significant push by numerous organizations, including American Coalition for Clean Coal Electricity, a partnership of the industries involved in producing electricity from coal, to ensure that coal plays a key role in resolving U.S. energy demands. Clean coal is a term used to describe methods and technologies intended to reduce the environmental impact of using coal as an energy source. These efforts can include chemically washing minerals and impurities from the coal, gasification, treating the flue gases with steam to remove sulfur dioxide, and other proposed technologies to capture carbon dioxide from the flue gas.[101]

Table 6.7: Coal Reserves and Production (2007 data)

Country	Coal Reserves (million tonnes)	% of Global Reserves	Coal Production (million tonnes)	% of Global Production*
U.S.	242,721	28.6%	1,039	16.2%
Russian Federation	157,010	18.5%	314	4.9%
China	114,500	13.5%	2,537	40.0%
Australia	76,600	9.0%	394	6.2%
India	56,498	6.7%	478	7.5%

BP, 2008.

Note: Canada's coal reserves are 6,578 million tonnes, less than 1% of global reserves.
* The % of Global Production numbers include a correction in their calculation.

China currently plans on adding another 800 GW over the next eight years and 90% of it is expected to be coal-generated. China is currently building one coal-fired power station per week. Because the life of a thermal power plant that uses coal is relatively long (up to fifty years), it will be financially difficult to close them down before the end of their economic lifetime, and thus they will be a major source of GHG emissions.[102]

According to Clean Edge's 2008 report, the U.S. obtains approximately 50% of its electricity from coal-fired plants.[103] The U.S. Clean Coal Power Initiative (CCPI) was providing government co-financing for new coal technologies that can help utilities meet President Bush's Clear Skies Initiative to cut sulfur, nitrogen and mercury pollutants from power plants by nearly 70% by the year 2018 and will be assessing new funding under the recent U.S. stimulus package. CCPI is actively involved in a few projects that cover Integrated Gasification Combined Cycle (IGCC), advanced multi-pollutant control by means of optimization and carbon sequestration (discussed below) technologies and/or beneficial reuse of carbon dioxide. An IGCC plant does not directly burn coal as traditional plants do, but pressurizes it, thereby producing a gas from which smog-causing pollutants can be filtered before the gas is used to power a jet-engine-style turbine (similar to natural-gas power plants). The pressurizing process also releases a stream of carbon-dioxide emissions that can be captured for underground sequestration.[104]

Carbon capture and sequestration (CCS) refers to the provision of long-term storage of carbon in the terrestrial biosphere, underground or the oceans so that the buildup of carbon dioxide (the principal GHG) concentration in the atmosphere will reduce or slow. In some cases, maintaining or enhancing natural processes accomplishes this; in other cases, novel techniques are developed to dispose of carbon. Key areas of research include

- sequestering carbon released from energy production in underground geologic repositories
- enhancing the natural terrestrial sequestration cycle through CO_2 removal from the atmosphere by vegetation and storage in biomass and soils
- carbon sequestration in oceans by fertilization of phytoplankton with nutrients, and injecting CO_2 to ocean depths greater than 1,000 meters
- sequencing genomes of microorganisms for carbon management

A recent study by MIT indicates that carbon capture can increase the initial capital cost of a coal-fired power plant by between 30% and 60% and decrease plant efficiency. The study also indicated that current coal-fired plants can use CCS projects for 60% of their emissions to optimize economies of scale. Additional carbon capture would require significant additional capital investments.[105]

For additional information on carbon sequestration, refer to the IEA study entitled *Prospects for CO_2 Capture and Storage* or recent projects: e.g., Shell and Statoil projects in Norway, which will provide carbon capture for offshore oil and gas fields, and the Alberta Saline Aquifer Project (ASAP) for oil sands projects.

The ASAP is led by Enbridge Inc., is the largest project of its kind in North America, and will play a major role in advancing industry and government's knowledge of carbon dioxide sequestration.

In addition to CCS, there is also a push for co-firing coal with biomass. The UK's largest power station, Drax, launched a £50 million project in 2008 aimed at replacing 10% of the coal it uses with biomass (e.g., wood chips, sunflower husks or grasses). Dorothy Thompson, chief executive of Drax, said that the co-firing technology would deliver 2 million tonnes of CO_2 savings from coal and take the power station towards their overall target of a 15% reduction in carbon emissions by 2012.[106]

CLEAN COAL

Benefits

- the U.S. has an abundance of coal (29% of known reserves globally)
- control of emissions will allow the use of coal resourced even if cap-and-trade or carbon taxes are introduced
- research is proceeding on carbon sequestration; however, most of the sites are related to petroleum exploration

Issues

- environmental impacts of coal extraction (e.g., stripping of mountains, hillsides and natural areas)
- uncertainty in the technical feasibility for IGCC and sequestration of GHG emissions on a large scale
- requires substantial government funding to offset technical risks
- having systems in place in the short term is unlikely, as current estimates are predicting commercial systems in 2018–2025
- estimates for carbon capture for coal-burning plants range from $40–$70/ton of CO_2 for the current plants; additionally, the process could absorb as much as 25% of the energy output of the plant[107]
- transportation of high-pressure CO_2 requires new investment in pipe networks
- limited number of Grade A reservoirs for carbon sequestration as well as degree of risk of leakage
- even with sequestration, still relatively large amounts of pollutants when compared to solar and wind power

- public response to clean coal: environmental groups maintain that it is green-wash
- restrictions imposed by financial institutions (e.g., Equator Principles)

No single alternative energy source is emerging as a clear winner for large-scale projects. Instead, several may fulfill regional niches:

- onshore wind power for the backbone of the U.S. and Canada
- onshore/offshore wind as well as tidal power for northern coastal areas of North America
- CSP for southern western U.S. (primarily in deserts)
- ESG geothermal along west coast of U.S./Canada
- hydroelectric at existing dam sites (U.S.) and a few untapped rivers (Canada)

GOVERNMENT INFLUENCE OR MEDDLING

As indicated in chapter 2, governments can significantly influence (for better or worse) markets in environmental issues. The following is a list of key areas of government (federal, state/provincial and municipal) legislation/policy related to conservation, emissions (related to energy production) and alternative (renewable and nonrenewable) energy sources. Additional information on eco-design and green procurement is presented in appendix A.

Manufacturers of Consumer Goods
- energy efficiency standards for consumer goods
- automotive fuel efficiency standards
- rebates to consumers buying electric or hybrid vehicles

Energy Consumers
- rebates to retrofit dwellings to make them more energy efficient
- grants and incentives to small- and medium-sized businesses and industry that encourage energy and pollution-saving upgrades

Electricity/Alternative Fuel Producers
- federal subsidies and R&D grants to alternative energy providers
- state/province grants, loans and rebate programs
- state sales tax exemptions

- accelerated depreciation
- investment tax credits (ITCs)
- renewable energy production tax credits (PTCs) (large scale-utility projects)
- small wind system tax credits
- state and federal renewable energy certificates (RECs)
- renewable fuel standards (RFSs)
- emission limits (SO_x, NO_x, CO_x, radionuclides, etc.) for coal and petroleum extraction, processing and use to generate electricity
- mandatory and voluntary carbon trading (also refer to chapter 7)
- carbon taxes for coal and petroleum extraction and use
- guarantees for loans and capping insurance payouts because of extreme failure
- property tax incentives

Electricity Generator/Retailer Companies
- increased openness to allow connection to the grid
- renewable portfolio standard (RPS) requires utilities to either purchase a set amount of renewable energy or pay providers feed-in-tariffs (FITs), which are of higher value than nonrenewable sources
- allowance for "net metering" based upon buy-down payment ($ per kWh installed) or performance based incentive (PBI) payments ($ per kWh generated)
- time-of-use (TOU) rates and installation of smart metering
- increased capacity for transmission lines for decentralized energy production

The result in many cases, especially for generators, is that there are substantial monies available from various levels of governments and/or government-directed utilities if a company understands the complex maze of government legislation/incentives. As an example, when the various subsidies, net metering, tax relief (including accelerated depreciation) and state RECs are taken into account, two-thirds of the total costs of a new solar power system may be subsidized in some states, e.g., California, New Jersey, New York.[108]

In the following section, examples of some key market based instruments (MBIs) related to energy are provided for the U.S. and Canada. Incentive schemes for alternative energy can be classified into one of the following two types:

1. Subsidy/Tax Relief Model—Legislation that provides either an upfront subsidy on the initial cost of a system through direct payment (usually state/province or local level) or through a tax credit to offset owner's income tax liability. Examples of the latter include ITCs for solar and fuel cells and renewable energy PTCs.

2. Feed-In Tariff (FIT) Model—Also called Advanced Renewable Tariff (ART) in the U.S., this places a legal obligation on utilities to purchase electricity from renewable energy installations. The tariff rate is guaranteed (retail price of electricity or greater, as is the case of EU and Canada) for a set period of time—up to twenty years in some jurisdictions. This approach was initiated in Germany and has worked quite well to stimulate the development of renewable energy.

Detailed information on all of the listed government MBIs can be accessed via the websites listed in table 6.9 (p. 295) at the end of this chapter.

United States

President Obama's New Energy for America Plan contains the following provisions related to energy:[109]

- Help create 5 million new U.S. jobs by strategically investing $150 billion over the next ten years to catalyze private efforts to build a clean energy future.
- Within ten years, save more oil than the U.S. currently imports from the Middle East and Venezuela combined.
- Ensure 10% of U.S. electricity comes from renewable sources by 2012, and 25% by 2025.
- Implement an economy-wide cap-and-trade program to reduce greenhouse gas emissions 80% by 2050.

The National Renewable Energy Laboratory of the U.S. Department of Energy has stated the following United States national goals:

- biofuels: reduce gasoline usage by 20% in ten years
- wind: provide 20% of total energy by 2030
- solar: be market competitive by 2015 for PV and 2020 for CSP

The 2009 American Recovery and Reinvestment Act (ARRA) includes the following key components related to renewable energy and energy conservation.[110]

> **Tax Cuts/Credits for Renewable Energy**—$20 billion in tax cuts for renewable energy providers and tax credits for research and development in renewable energy, energy conservation and energy efficiency (including credit for purchase of plug-in electric vehicles).
>
> **Conservation/energy efficiency**—$6.3 billion in state energy-efficient and clean-energy grants; $4.5 billion to make federal buildings more energy efficient, and $5 billion to weatherize homes of up to 1 million low-income people.
>
> **Renewable energy, smart grid and transmission lines**—$4.5 billion in direct spending to modernize the electricity grid with smart-grid technologies, $6 billion in loan guarantees for renewable energy systems, biofuel projects, and electric-power transmission facilities, and $2 billion in loans to manufacture advanced batteries and components for applications such as plug-in electric cars.
>
> **Reduction of coal plant emissions**—$3.4 billion appropriated to the Department of Energy for fossil energy research and development, such as storing carbon dioxide underground at coal power plants.

The U.S. employs a complicated mix of federal, state and municipal incentives to promote energy conservation and the development and commercialization of new, lower emission technologies. In the following sections examples are provided.

Grants for Alternative Energy

In response to economic conditions, which severely undermined the effectiveness of both the Production Tax Credits (PTC) and Investment Tax Credits (ITC), the ARRA also allows taxpayers to receive a grant from the Treasury Department in lieu of tax credits—of significant benefit when a company has no taxable income. The grant operates like the current-law investment tax credit. The Treasury Department will issue a grant in an amount equal to thirty percent (30%) of the cost of the renewable energy facility within sixty days of the facility being placed in service or, if later, within sixty days of receiving an application for such grant. An applicant will qualify for a grant if an application is received by September 30, 2011.

Investment Tax Credits (ITCs)

Investment tax credits are available for residential and business.

Residential Renewable Energy Tax Credit—Originally created in the Energy Policy of Act of 2005, this 30% credit was extended to 2016 by the Energy Improvement and Extension Act (EIEA) of 2008. Eligible renewable technologies include: solar water heat, photovoltaics, wind, fuel cells, geothermal heat pumps and other solar electric technologies. The maximum incentives are as follows: Solar electric–no maximum (previously had limit of $2,000), solar water heating–$2,000, fuel cells–$500 per 0.5 kW, small wind–$500 per 0.5kW up to $4,000 and Geothermal heat pumps–$2,000.[111]

Note that there is also a "energy efficiency tax credit" for improvements in the building envelope of existing homes and for the purchase of high-efficiency heating, cooling and water-heating equipment.

Business Solar Tax Credit and Fuel Cell Tax Credit—extended a 30% business credit, established in the Energy Policy Act of 2005, for the purchase of fuel cell power plants, solar energy property, and fiber-optic property used to illuminate the inside of a structure; once it expires, the credit reverts to a permanent 10% level

The ARRA allows investors, with projects that begin operations in 2009 and 2010, to claim the investment tax credit (ITC) rather than the PTC (see below), giving potential investors more flexibility. The PTC is payable over a 10-year period while the 30% ITC for solar facilities can be taken the year the facility enters commercial operation. [112]

Renewable Energy Production Tax Credit (PTC)

PTC was originally enacted as part of the Energy Policy Act of 1992 and covers large-scale utility projects. Since its establishment, it has undergone a series of one- or two-year extensions, and has been allowed to lapse in three different years: 1999, 2001 and 2003. Under present law, an income tax credit is allowed for the production of electricity from qualified wind energy facilities and other sources of renewable energy. The current value of the credit is 2 cents/kWh of electricity produced.[113] The 2008 EIEA has extended the PTC for wind projects by one year (the industry is already lobbying for longer-term extension of credits) and two years for geothermal, biomass and other alternative sources.[114]

The ARRA extends the PTC for wind energy projects through 2012 and for biomass, geothermal and other renewable energy through 2013.

Small Wind Systems Tax Credits

A handful of states provide some incentives for small wind facilities, but the federal government has not provided any assistance since 1985. The federal PTC covers only large utility-scale wind projects, not individuals who want to install their own wind power systems for on-site power. In 2005, Congress passed an energy bill that included an investment credit for residential solar energy applications, but did not include small wind systems. In 2007, a small wind tax credit was included in farm policy legislation. The Farm Bill contains a provision that would provide a new investment tax credit of $500 per half kW of capacity, capped at $4,000, for the purchase of small wind systems used to power homes. The credit lasts through 2012.

Renewable Energy Certificates (RECs)

RECs, or "green tags," are transferable rights for renewable energy within some American states. A provider of renewable energy is issued a REC for each 1,000 kWh of produced energy, which can be sold on the open market for additional profit. The RECs are used like offsetting schemes and allow an individual or company to show commitment to the environment. However, RECs are currently unregulated and there is no national registry to prevent double counting.[115]

Renewable Portfolio Standard (RPS)

RPS, also known as Renewable Electricity Standard (RES), uses market mechanisms to ensure that a growing percentage of electricity is produced from renewable sources. The RPS provides a predictable, competitive market, within which renewable generators will compete with each other to lower prices. Numerous states (more than twenty-five) and the District of Columbia as well as many provinces have adopted RPS requirements. There is currently no RPS legislation pending at the federal level in Canada or the U.S. Figure 6.5 presents a summary of state RPS. The 2008 U.S. Comprehensive American Energy Security and Consumer Protection Act included a requirement that utilities generate 15% of their energy from renewable sources by 2020.

An updated version of figure 6.5 is available at the Database of State Incentives for Renewables & Efficiency—www.dsireusa.org.

Figure 6.5: U.S. Renewable Portfolio Standards

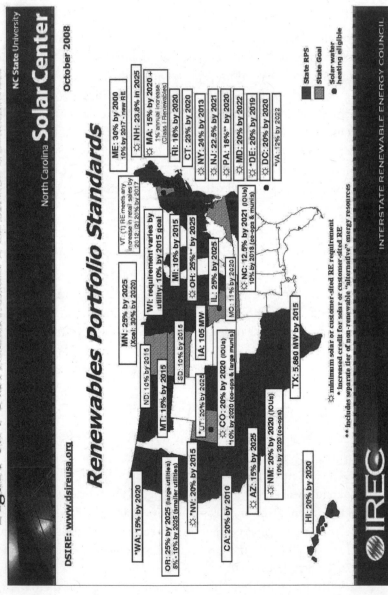

Renewable Fuel Standard (RFS)

Under the RFS program introduced by the Energy Independence and Security Act (EISA) of 2007, refiners are obliged to process minimum quotas of renewable fuels that must achieve at least a 20% reduction in life cycle GHG emissions, compared to 2005 baseline for conventional fuels.[116] The legislation provided an expanded mandate to the Renewable Fuel Standard (RFS)—from 7.5 billion gallons of renewable fuels per year by 2012 to at least 36 billion gallons of biofuel/year by 2022.[117]

The ARRA extends/expands upon the existing tax credit to businesses that install alternative fuel pumps, such as fuel pumps that dispense E85 fuel, electricity, hydrogen, and natural gas.

Carbon Capture

The Emergency Economic Stabilization Act (ESSA) of 2008 provides new credits for coal-fired plants that capture and store carbon dioxide, including pumping it into depleted oil fields to extract the remaining oil. The 2009 ARRA includes $2.4 billion for carbon capture and sequestration technology demonstration projects that aim to reduce the amount of carbon dioxide emitted from industrial facilities and fossil-fuel power plants.

Net Metering

Under Net Metering, installers of renewable systems have an incentive to match the electricity generation by their solar installations with their use of electricity. If they produce more electricity they either receive a credit on their electricity bill, get paid an amount equal to the utility's cost to produce electricity (primarily used in U.S. and maybe one-third of the retail price) or receive monies equivalent to utility retail prices (Canada and EU).

Buy-down Payments

One approach that a few states have adopted, and others are considering, is a "wires charge" used for a "buy-down" program. A small charge is levied on every kilowatt-hour of electricity sold. The money is used to "buy down," or subsidize, the purchase of renewable energy systems, e.g., a homeowner or small business might pay only 50% of the cost of a new small wind turbine, for example, and the state's wires charge fund (may be called a "public benefits fund") would pay the rest (by means of a rebate).

Performance Based Incentives (PBI)

PBIs include the payment of monies based upon actual generation of electricity for renewable energy. Beginning January 1, 2007, a ruling by the California PUC establishes PBI of up to 50 cents/kWh over five years for solar energy systems greater than 100 kW in size installed in businesses and other large facilities. For systems smaller than 100 kW, incentives will be based on each system's estimated future performance although projects can opt in for PBI payments. The level of PBI and the up-front payments decline in ten steps based on how much solar power is added to the state's electricity system.

California's Million Solar Roof Bill (SB1)

The goal of the legislation is to create a million solar roofs in the next ten years. The main components of the bill include[118]

- increasing the cap on net metering—a program that allows solar customers to get a credit on their electric bill for excess power generated by their solar system
- mandating that solar panels become a standard option for all new homebuyers, enabling new homebuyers to choose to add solar panels to their new home while it is being constructed
- requiring that the state's municipal utilities create their own solar rebate program, totaling $800 million in rebate funds to drive municipal utility ratepayers towards solar power

In 2007, the Million Solar Roofs Initiative's first full year in operation, California saw more interest in solar power among California consumers than in all previous years in which the state had a solar rebate program, 1996–2006, combined. The state went from having 200 MW of installed solar power throughout the state at the end of 2006, to potentially adding more than this amount in 2007 alone.

Transmission Line Expansion/Smart Grid

In an effort to support the expansion of decentralized power—in particular wind— several states and provinces are expanding their transmission systems. Texas has given preliminary approval for a $4.9 billion plan to build transmission lines to carry wind power from West Texas to urban areas such as Dallas. Texas is already the national leader in wind power and the plan will add enough transmission lines to move 18 GW. The plan will result in an additional \$3–\$4 per month on residential energy bills.[119]

The new ARRA allocates \$4.5 billion in direct spending to modernize the electricity grid with smart-grid technologies and \$6 billion in loan guarantees for renewable energy systems, biofuel projects, and electric-power transmission facilities. Smart-gird technology/infrastructure helps consumer monitor their electricity consumption and adjust during peak hours of usage and allow greater access by decentralized power sources, in particular renewable energy sources.

Nuclear

In order to promote nuclear power, the U.S. Congress is offering loan guarantees and tax credits to electricity providers. The energy bill conference report (*The Energy Policy Act of 2005*) negotiated between the House and Senate contains billions for the following:[120]

- authorization of \$2 billion in "risk insurance" to pay the industry for any delays in construction and operation licensing for six new reactors, including delays due to the Nuclear Regulatory Commission or litigation
- unlimited taxpayer-backed loan guarantees for up to 80% of the cost of a project, including building new nuclear power plants
- reauthorization of the Price-Anderson Act, extending the industry's liability cap to cover new nuclear power plants built in the next twenty years
- weakening constraints on U.S. exports of bomb-grade uranium
- production tax credits of 1.8 cents for each kWh of nuclear-generated electricity from new reactors during the first eight years of operation for the nuclear industry
- changes in the rules for nuclear decommissioning funds that are to be used to clean up closed nuclear plant sites by repealing the cost of service requirement for contributions to a fund and allowing the transfer of pre-1984 decommissioning costs to a qualified fund

A potentially telling sign of what may be to come is the elimination of \$50 billion in federal load guarantees from the ARRA that could have been utilized by the nuclear and coal industries as well as for renewable energy projects. Called Title 17, the Innovative Technology Loan Guarantee Program, the provision would have put aside \$50 billion to guarantee loans under the Energy Policy Act of 2005 for eligible projects, to remain available until committed.

City Initiatives

Mayors of nearly eight hundred U.S. cities have pledged to reduce greenhouse gases to Kyoto Protocol targets to upgrade the energy efficiency of city-owned buildings by between 20% and 50%. The initiative, launched in 2007 with the Clinton
Foundation, is funded with $1 billion each from ABN Amro, Citi, Deutsche Bank,
JPMorgan Chase and UBS.[121]

Security Risk

The U.S. crude oil reserves peaked in 1970 and the country currently relies on foreign oil for 60% of its demand—up from less than 40% at the time of the 1973 oil
crisis.[122] The U.S. imports approximately 43% of its oil from countries it regards as
close allies, including Canada, Mexico and Saudi Arabia, while the remaining 57%
is from countries where relationships are a bit more tenuous. Canada provides
approximately 20% of U.S. oil imports, approximately 90% of natural gas imports,
and approximately one-third of the uranium used in U.S. nuclear power plants.
Canada and the United States supply each other with almost all of their electricity
imports.[123] The development of the Alberta oil sands should allow a significant
source of petroleum for both Canada and the U.S. The Canadian Association of
Petroleum Producers is forecasting oil sands production to surpass 693,000 cubic
meters (4.36 million barrels) of oil per day, or 82% of total Canadian crude oil
production, by 2020.[124]

   Even with the increased rates of oil sands production, however, Canada will
not be able to offset the projected increase in U.S. demand for oil imports. Mexico
has approximately 12 million barrels of petroleum and thus is not seen as a significant source of future oil by the U.S. This leaves Saudi Arabia, Kuwait and United
Arab Emirates as potential sources of oil to fill the gap in demand as well as a
group of countries that have not always had the best relationship with the U.S.

   In terms of natural gas, Russia, with 44.7 trillion cubic meters (tcm); Iran, with
27.8 tcm; and Qatar, with 25.6 tcm, have 70% of the proven gas reserves. Canada
is not even in the top ten, with 1.63 trillion cubic meters of proven reserves; however, production in 2007 was 184 billion cubic meters—third highest in the world.
The U.S., which only has 3.4% of the proven reserves, also boasts production at a
level similar to the Russian Federation, which has 25% of the proven reserves.

   Based upon forecasts for increased U.S. and global demand (especially India
and China), the shrinking size of U.S. petroleum reserves, and the questionable
ability of low-risk countries (Canada, United Arab Emirates and Qatar) to fill U.S.

import demand, it is reasonable to conclude that the U.S. security risk related to future energy supplies is high.

As oil prices rise, "resource nationalism" begins to raise its head, as evidenced by both rhetoric and actions in Venezuela, Russia and a few African countries. Some countries with key reserves are seeking increases in their "cut" of oil revenue, restricting investment opportunities (as they decide to develop resources themselves), and in some cases seeking outright change in control. Examples of the latter include the Russian government taking control of BP's position in the Kovykta gas field and Venezuela's seizure of four oil ventures from multinational companies.

Over the last ten to twenty years, national oil companies (NOCs) have emerged as key global players yielding significant power, and the influence of independent oil companies (IOCs) like Exxon/Mobil, Chevron, Shell and BP has waned. New IOCs have also emerged, including China National Petroleum, Oil and Natural Gas Corporation, Sinopec, Petrobras, LUKOIL, Petronas and many others. Note that CSR guidelines that have been agreed to by most, if not all, western IOCs may not be followed by NOCs.

NOCs owned by high-growth nations like China, Malaysia and India have a vision to secure access to long-term oil supplies. As indicated in *A Thousand Barrels a Second*, for NOCs, serving their energy-hungry countries is their crucial shareholder objective, i.e., security of supply trumps near-term profitability for state-owned oil companies representing large consuming nations.[125]

With more players and fewer opportunities, the price for the right to explore, develop and bring oil to the market will increase significantly in places like Libya, Kazakhstan and Canada—a new real estate boom for petroleum reserves.[126] The net result is that the cost and associated risk related to foreign oil will most likely continue to increase, especially if China and India go on buying binges to secure petroleum supplies.

As indicated in Tertzakian's book entitled *A Thousand Barrels a Second*, "A high concentration of the world's oil supply is not only buried under rock, ocean, or sand, it is buried under layers of corruption, political risk, and capricious authoritarianism."

Canada

Canada is emerging as a global energy superpower because of its rich supply of hydroelectric power, uranium, conventional oil and gas and non-conventional—oil sands potential and strong tides. There is also the potential for untapped oil reserves in Canada's far north (however, there is significant public opposition to their development). This stature on the energy stage is at odds with the country's performance on climate change.

As of 2008, Canada's GHG emissions were more than 25% higher than they were in 1990, i.e., 32% above the national Kyoto target (which was 6% below 1990 levels by 2008–2012), revealing a serious disconnect between federal policy and action on GHG emissions in Canada. See also chapter 7.

Under the "Turning the Corner" federal climate change action plan, the government of Canada established a new national target of an absolute 20% reduction in GHGs from 2006 levels by the year 2020. Key regulatory initiatives under the plan include[128]

- new oil sands plants and coal-fired power plants that are coming into operation in 2012 or later will face tough requirements: effectively, new carbon capture and storage technologies to prevent the release of greenhouse gases into the atmosphere
- legislation that will address
  - mandatory renewable fuel content in gasoline, diesel and heating oil
  - new fuel consumption standards for cars, light trucks and sport utility vehicles
  - new energy efficiency requirements for a wide range of commercial and consumer products, such as dishwashers and commercial boilers
  - new national performance standards that will ban inefficient incandescent lightbulbs

The overall goal of these initiatives includes[129]

- putting in place large-scale carbon capture and storage and other innovative green technologies
- generating 90% of Canadian power from sources that do not emit greenhouse gases
- increasing electricity from renewable sources like wind and wave power by twenty times
- cutting greenhouse gas emissions from coal by more than 50%
- increasing average fuel efficiency in new cars by 20%
- improving Canada's energy efficiency by some 20%

Many of the general statements regarding U.S. legislation and funding also hold true in Canada—e.g., Investment Tax Credits (ITCs), Renewable Portfolio Standards (RPSs) and net metering.

EcoEnergy Fund—In 2007, the Canadian government introduced the ecoENERGY Initiatives—included investment of $3.2 billion in four key initiatives to make clean, low-impact renewable energy and biofuel more available in Canada and less expensive.

- ecoENERGY for **Renewable Power**: a $1.48 billion investment in renewable sources like wind, biomass, small hydro and ocean energy with a goal of an additional 4,000 MW of clean energy. An incentive of one cent per kilowatt-hour for up to ten years, for power produced by low-impact renewable energy sources, will be offered to eligible projects constructed over the next four years.
- ecoENERGY for **Renewable Heat**: a $36 million program that will provide incentives and industry support for the use of renewable energy for heating. In addition, projects for residential solar heating technologies will be explored with partners such as utilities and community organizations. In March 2009 the maximum payment for solar hot water projects incresed from $80,000 to $400,000.
- EcoEnergy for **Technology Initiatives**: a $230-million investment in science and technology to accelerate the development and market readiness of technology solutions in clean energy.
- ecoEnergy **Retrofit Grants and Incentives**: provides financial support to homeowners and small and medium-sized businesses, public institutions and industrial facilties to help them implement energy saving projects that reduce energy-related greenhouse gases (GHGs) and air pollution. This program received an additional $300 million under the 2009 Canada Economic Action Plan.
- EcoEnergy for Biofuels: a $1.5 billion investment over nine years (started in 2008) in support of biofuel production in Canada. Recipients are entitled to receive incentives for no more than seven consecutive years.

The 2009 "Canada's Economic Action Plan" (CEAP) did not extend the ecoEnergy Program for Renewable Power that will expire on March 31, 2011—a program that will most likely run out of money at the end of 2009 due to its popularity. This program was considered by many to be critical to the success of Canada's fledging clean tech sector.

As indicated above, the 2009 CEAP did allocate $300 million in funding for energy-saving home retrofits—second wave ecoEnergy Retrofit Program but changed funding model to spending based tax credits from energy audits.

Technology Fund—The federal government also established a technology fund. The fund will be used primarily to finance investments in technology and infrastructure deployment that have a high likelihood of resulting in GHG emission reductions. Companies could contribute to the fund at a rate of $15 per tonne of carbon dioxide equivalent from 2010 to 2012, and $20 per tonne in 2013. Thereafter, the rate will escalate yearly at the rate of growth of nominal GDP. This rate structure will be reviewed every five years as part of the general review of the regulatory system.[130]

Sustainable Development Technology Canada (SDTC)—Provide funds to finance and support the development and demonstration of clean technologies to deliver economic, environmental and health benefits to Canadians. SDTC operates two funds: $550 million SDTech Fund - supports projects that address climate changes, air quality, clean water and clean soil and $500 million Next Gen Biofuels Fund—first of a kind large demonstration scale facilities for the production of next generation renewable fuels.

Federal Green Energy Fund—The 2009 CEAP included $1 billion over 5 years for green energy—$150 for research and $850 for clean-energy demonstration projects, including Carbon Capture and Storage (CCS).

Federal Green Infrastructure Fund—The 2009 CEAP included $1 billion over 5 years for green infrastructure to support projects such as "sustainable energy." Funding will be allocated based upon merit to support green infrastructure projects on a cost-shared basis.

Provincial Programs

At a provincial level, the following targets have been put forward:

- Alberta: 1,000 MW of renewable energy by the end of 2008
- British Columbia: 50% of new generation from clean energy sources by 2020
- Manitoba: 1,000 MW of wind energy by 2014
- New Brunswick: 400 MW of wind energy by 2016
- Nova Scotia: 380 MW of wind energy by 2014
- Ontario: 2,700 MW of renewable energy by 2010
- PEI: 200 MW of wind energy by 2010
- Quebec: 4,000 MW of wind energy by 2015

Examples of key provincial funds for "green" activities include:

Alberta Funds—Alberta has allocated $4 billion over five years for carbon capture and sequestration, primarily oil sands projects, and energy-saving public transit in Alberta. The province has also allocated $239 million over five years to support the production and marketing of bio-energy and biofuels.

Ontario Funds—Ontario has expanded the $650 million Next Generation Jobs Fund to $1.15 billion to secure the next generation of high-paying jobs for Ontarians by supporting the use and sale of clean and green technologies and the development of green businesses. The development of new green technology is also nurtured through the $527 million Ontario Research Fund.

In addition to the funds mentioned above, Ontario has put forward a historical "Green Energy and Green Economy Act 2009". Key components of the proposed legislation (according to version put forward for first reading):

- Address local bylaws and regulations that are used to delay or stop proposed renewable energy projects—a streamlined, one-stop approval process.
- Green energy proponents will have a "right to connect" to the electricity gird and government commitment to establish new generous "Feed-in Tariff" that guarantees specific rates and spurs adaptation of renewable energy generation.
- Develop a smarter electricity grid better adapted to renewable energy projects.
- Allow conservation standards to be built into the Building Code Act and requires energy audits prior to home sales or leases (for longer than a prescribed period).
- Requires a range of household appliances to meet Energy Star standards for energy and water efficiency.
- Sets forth a series of "guiding principles" for the construction, acquisition, operation and management of government facilities related to efficient use of energy and renewable energy suppliers.
- Provides assistance to First Nation and Métis communities in building, owning and operating their own renewable energy projects.
- Support and expand economic investment, thus building a stronger, greener economy with an estimated 50,000+ direct and indirect jobs over the next three years.

Proposed Ontario Feed-in Tariffs for 20-year contract include the following: Solar PV—53.9 (>500 kW) to 80.2 cents per kWh (10 kW rooftop); wind—13.5 (onshore) to 19 (offshore) cents per kWh; biomass—12.2 cents per kWh; and water-power—12.9 (<50 MW) to 13.4 cents (community based and <2MW) per kWh.

Wind

Under an RPS-type approach, several provinces are entering into agreements, via their publicly owned utility companies, to secure power from wind projects. The Quebec government announced in 2008 that $5.5 billion of new wind projects had been awarded by Hydro-Québec. The contracts were to produce 2,004 new MW of wind power. Note that the tender calls put extra weight on vendors who manufacture wind turbines in Quebec therefore supporting the cleantech sector.

Also in 2008, the province of British Columbia declared its intention to seek proposals from power producers for the installation of 1,600 MW of generation capacity at an expected price tag of close to $4 billion.[131] The Ontario Power Authority currently has 471 MW of commercial wind power, with another 789 MW in development and construction as per 2008.

Solar

In 2007, the Ontario Power Authority signed 145 contracts for future construction of more than 250 MW of solar power systems (note that proponents have three years to construct the system or the deal is dead). The deals fall under Ontario's feed-in tariff (FIT) system called "Standard Offer Program" for renewable energy—the only one of its kind in Canada—which guarantees a set price over twenty years for alternative energy the province buys. Ontario pays 42 cents a kWh for solar-generated electricity, roughly seven times the price of conventional power, and almost four times what it pays for electricity generated by wind or biomass projects.[132] The Ontario government also announced a $3 million "community power fund" to help establish community-owned renewable energy projects.

Nuclear

Ontario Power Authority's current development plan calls for the refurbishing of older nuclear stations and adding two new reactors at one of its sites. The 2006 cost estimate for the reactors and refurbishing existing ones was $26 billion.[133] Once the two new reactors are on line, 70% of Ontario's annual consumption will be supplied through nuclear power. This level is approaching France, which generates 77% of its energy from nuclear energy.

Carbon Capture and Storage

Alberta has set up a $2 billion fund to advance carbon capture and storage (CCS) projects. The CCS fund will support projects that reduce emissions up to 5 million tonnes a year. Funds will be allocated to encourage construction of Alberta's first large-scale CCS projects. The province has indicated that it wants CCS proposals that can be built quickly and provide the best opportunities to significantly reduce greenhouse gas emissions.[136]

For a more global perspective it is recommended that information on legislation in other jurisdictions, in particular Europe and Brazil, be reviewed. Europe continues to strongly promote alternative energy via MBIs; however, the values for some of the incentives have been reduced in the last twelve months (still significant when compared to North American MBIs).

> Government initiatives related to alternative energy are numerous and complex. They greatly influence the economic viability of most, if not all, alternative energy projects.

SHOW ME THE MONEY

The following table presents a cost comparison of average prices for different energy sources, which will vary significantly depending upon government incentives and cost of resources (labor, building materials, etc.).

Table 6.8: Cost Comparison of Different Energy Sources

	Natural Gas	Coal Plant	Wind	Nuclear	Solar
Construction ($ billion for 1,000 MW)	$0.9†	$0.75–$1.4‡, $2†	$2.13–$2.5 (see table 6.3), $2†	$2–$6‡ $4–$6§ $6–$7a $2.5†	$5–$10‡ $6.5†
Operational (cents/kWh)*	$97.94†	$96.42†	$40.4†	$40.8†	$265†

* Natural gas and coal are based upon a "fully loaded" emission cost of $25/MT, and government subsidies of $20/kWh and $84.6/kWh have been applied to wind and solar, respectively.
† Jefferies & Company Inc., 2008
‡ Makower and Pernick, and Wilder, 2008
§ Moody's Investors Service, 2008
a Nuclear Energy Institute, 2008

In terms of solar power, table 6.8 is appropriate when comparing the cost of concentrated solar power (CSP); however, it may not be appropriate when assessing off-grid solar power. A more appropriate comparison, as proposed by Jefferies & Company, is the average rates of electricity. Currently solar power is still well above the U.S. national average of approximately \$0.10/kWh; however, it may start to make economic sense in some regions where electricity is \$0.15–\$0.30/kWh.[137]

It is imperative that a company understands all of the key costs associated with an investment in alternative energy. The following equation lists the key components that need to be taken into consideration when assessing net revenue from a project that will generate electricity. The selection of an appropriate inflation rate and interest rate to support the capital costs as also critical.

Revenue = Power Purchase Agreement (PPA)

Costs = amortized capital cost for facility
+ financing cost (key is interest rate)
+ amortized cost of transmission system (if required)
− government subsidies and R&D grants (all types)
+ property rental fees
− property tax exemptions
+ raw material cost (primarily fuel if coal, natural gas, co-gen, or nuclear facility)
+ operations and maintenance costs
+ retrofit costs
+ security cost
− ongoing tax credits
+ carbon tax or extra cost of additional pollutant control equipment
− carbon tax credits
+ decommissioning costs (primary nuclear facility)

A PPA is a contract involving the generation and sales of electricity—which is normally developed between the owner of a power plant generating the electricity and the buyer of the electricity—commonly a utility company in the case of large-scale alternative energy projects. A PPA can also be between a utility that generates electricity and host site owner or a lessor who is purchasing the energy.

PPAs play a critical role in the financing of electricity generating assets. PPA typical include:

- **PPA provider** (the electricity generator)—assumes the risks and responsibilities of ownership when it purchases, operates, and maintains the turnkey facility. It also provides secure funding for the project, maintains and monitors the energy production, and sells the electricity to the host at a contractual price for the term of the contract (commonly 5–25 years).
- **PPA host**—agrees to purchase the generated electricity for agreed upon price and time period. In some renewable energy contracts, the host has the option to purchase the generating equipment from the PPA provider at the end of the term, may renew the contract with different terms, or can request that the equipment be removed. The host may also allow an inflation rate to the purchase price or contract can be at fixed rate for term.

CHAPTER 6 TAKE-AWAYS

The following take-aways are considered critical to companies that want to minimize business risk due to changing petroleum demand as well as to take advantage of new opportunities in the marketplace.

All companies should do the following:

SD owner and strategy—A key starting point for organizations is to assign a C-level to oversee energy and sustainability development (SD) issues. Companies must also prepare an energy/SD strategic plan at the same time as they prepare their business plan—not as a separate add-on exercise—as it is fundamental to most companies' growth.

Track/influence government policy—Systems must be put in place to track and influence, where appropriate, government MBIs that will impact business. As indicated in the section entitled "Government Influence or Meddling," changes in government direction/MBI can significantly influence ROI.

Implement energy conservation—A repeating theme in this book is that it is critical to "eliminate waste" in order to improve the bottom line. As part of this activity to determine the carbon footprint of operations, i.e., the GHG emitted directly and indirectly over the full life cycle of the operations (including supply chains), and leverage this information when preparing and executing the energy/SD strategy plan.

Purchase green power where possible—Where appropriate and supportive of the overall energy/SD strategy, purchase energy that minimizes environmental impact.

An investor in or owner of alternative energy should do the following:

Understand the financial model—It is critical that the true revenues and costs of investing in alternative energy are understood. Key factors to thoroughly research include

- government MBI, which are complex and changing; their impact on the bottom line of most alternative energy operations may be substantial
- the ability to connect to the grid (and associated rules) as well as distance to transmission lines (including who pays if there is a shortfall)

Respect the supply chain—Alternative energy supply chains are not well developed in most cases and hence provide both risks and opportunities.

Watch technological changes—Track key changes that may alter the cost equation of alternative fuels. Examples include

- work being performed on a low-cost process to produce hydrogen for use in fuel cells
- more cost-effective batteries that recharge more quickly and retain charge longer
- alternative sources of biomass for fuel production (e.g., second- and third-generation biofuels)
- advancements in energy storage for CSP facilities
- nanotechnologies for desalination, solar power and recyclable materials

And remember Vinod Khosla's statement during an interview with Mother Jones website: "We are reminded of Arthur C. Clarke's quip that any revolutionary tech goes through three stages: 'It's completely impossible—don't waste my time'; 'it's possible, but it's not worth doing'; and 'I said it was a good idea all along.'"

Table 6.9: Sources of Information on Government Legislation/Incentives Related to Alternative Energy

United States

American Wind Energy Association (AWEA) www.awea.org

Database of State Incentives for Renewables & Efficiency (DSIRE) www.dsireusa.org

Energy Bible www.energybible.com/default.html

Geothermal Energy Association www.geo-energy.org/

Solar Energy Industry Association (SEIA) www.seia.org

U.S. Department of Energy—Renewable Energy Certificates www.eere.energy.gov/greenpower/markets/certificates.shtml?page=1

U.S. Energy Information Administration (EIA) (note: provides information on both domestic and international energy production/consumption) www.eia.doe.gov/emeu/mer/overview.html

Canada

Canadian Wind Energy Association (CanWEA) http://canwea.ca/media/release/release_e.php?newsId=26

Government of Canada ecoACTION programs www.ecoaction.gc.ca/ecoenergy-ecoenergie/faq-2-eng.cfm

Natural Resources Canada (NRC)—Energy Sources www.nrcan-rncan.gc.ca/com/eneene/sources-eng.php

Natural Resources Canada (NRC)—Office of Energy Efficiency www.oee.nrcan.gc.ca

Sustainable Development Technology Canada www.sdtc.ca

Global

Clean Edge—Clean Energy Trends 2008 report www.cleanedge.com

Cleantech Forum—ongoing updates on sector www.cleantech.com

Investeco—ongoing updates on sector www.investeco.com

Jefferies & Company. Clean Technology Primer June 2008 www.jefferies.com/cositemgr.pl/html/Industries/CleanTech/CleanTechReview/index.shtml

International Energy Agency www.iea.org

World Nuclear Association (WNA) www.world-nuclear.org

World Wide Energy Association (WWEE) www.wwindea.org

NOTES

1   Robert Rapier, "The 2008 IEA WEO – Renewable Energy," The Oil Drum, December 3, 2008, http://www.theoildrum.com/node/4798.

2   Matt Simmons and Aage Figenschou, "A Peak-Oiler, but Still in the Closet? IEA's 2008 Report," ASPO-USA, November 17, 2008, http://www.aspousa.org/index.php/2008/11/a-peak-oiler-but-still-in-the-closet-iea.

3   Tyler Hamilton, "Earful on Oil," Toronto Star, August 29, 2008.

4   Joel Makower, R. Pernick and C. Wilder, "Clean Energy Trends," 2008, http://www.cleanedge.com.

5   Rapier, "The 2008 IEA WEO—Renewable Energy."

6   Paul Roberts, "Tapped Out," National Geographic, June 2008.

7   Grant Smith and Jim Kennett, "There's No More Easy Oil," Montreal Gazette, May 19, 2008.

8   Jerome Paris, "Shell Energy Futures," The Oil Drum, January 25, 2008, http://www.theoildrum.com/node/3548.

9   Jerome Paris, "Peak Oil: BP, Conoco CEOs Say It's Here—Also IEA's Fatih Birol Really Freaks Out," The Oil Drum, November 11, 2007, http://www.theoildrum.com/node/3226.

10   Eric Reguly, "Total Sticks to Oil Investment Strategy," Globe and Mail, February 18, 2009.

11   EIA, "Demand," http://www.eia.doe.gov/pub/oil_gas/petroleum/analysis_publications/oil_market_basics/demand_text.htm.

12   Joseph Romn, "Why We Never Need to Build Another Polluting Power Plant. Coal? Natural Gas? Nuke? We Can Wipe Them All Off the Drawing Board by Using Current Energy More Efficiently. Are You Listening, Washington?", Salon.com, July 28, 2008, http://www.salon.com/news/feature/2008/07/28/energy_efficiency.

13   IEA, "Worldwide Trends in Energy Use and Efficiency," 2008, http://www.iea.org/Textbase/publications/free_new_Desc.asp?PUBS_ID=2026.

14   Romn, "Why We Never Need to Build Another Polluting Power Plant."

15   Neil Boyd, "Opening the C-Suite: Chief Sustainability/Energy Officer—Key to a Defined Energy Strategy," presentation to Energy Matters Summit, April 1, 2008.

16   Romn, "Why We Never Need to Build Another Polluting Power Plant."

17   Valerie Davis, "Dow Chemical Ties Energy-Efficiency to Cash Savings," December 10, 2008, Environmental Leader, http://www.environmentalleader.com/2008/12/10/dow-chemical-ties-energy-efficiency-to-cash-savings.

18   Erik Assadourian et al., "State of the World 2008," Worldwatch Institute.

19   Hunter Lovins, "The Economic Case for Climate Action," 2007, Presidential Climate Action Project, http://www.natcapsolutions.org/publications_files/PCAP/PCAP_Economic CaseForClimateProtection_04xii07.pdf.

20   Elizabeth Souder, "Will Wal-Mart Sell Electricity One Day?", RedOrbit, January 28, 2007, http://www.redorbit.com/news/science/817594/will_walmart_sell_electricity_one_day/index.html.

21   "Morning Briefing—Retail, 2008. Stores to Reduce Energy Use," Toronto Star, August 27, 2008.

22   BP, "Greenhouse Gas Emissions—Detailed Data from 2007," www.bp.com/sectiongenericarticle.do?categoryId=9023665&contentId=7043739.

23   Ibid.

24 Brad Kenney, "Green Spot: 3P at 3M," 2008, http://www.industryweek.com/ReadArticle.
    aspx?ArticleID=16131.
25 Pepsico, "Environmental Sustainability Report," 2007, http://www.pepsico.com/PEP_
    Citizenship/sustainability/environmental_v11d.pdf.
26 Pepsico, "Environmental News," 2008, http://www.pepsico.com/Purpose/Environment/
    Articles/PepsiCo-Honored-Energy-Partner-Of-Year.aspx.
27 IBM, "Climate Protection," 2008, http://www.ibm.com/ibm/environment/climate.
28 Climate Savers, "2008 Update: Highlights from Climate Savers Companies," February
    2008, http://209.85215.104/search?q=cache:8UG9MgYoG1cJ:generazioneclima.wwf.it/
    pdf/cs_update08_final.pdf+Sony+savings+in+energy+consumption+due+to+logistics+
    optimization&hl=en&ct=clnk&cd=1.
29 EIA, "Energy Overview," 2008, http://www.eia.doe.gov/emeu/mer/overview.html.
30 APEC, "Energy Overview 2007," APEC Energy Working Group, January 2008.
31 Dennis Markatos, "What Can Record Coal Prices Do to US Electricity Prices?", May 26,
    2008, http://www.igloo.org/dmarkatos/whatcanrec.
32 National Energy Board, "Current Market Conditions October–November 2008," http://
    www.neb.gc.ca/clf-nsi/rnrgynfmtn/prcng/lctrct/crrntmrktcndtn-eng.html.
33 Cosmos Voutsinos, "Using Nuclear Energy to Get the Most Out of Alberta's Tar Sands.
    A White Paper for Discussion," January 2007, http://www.computarc.org/Support%20
    documents/Guests/Cosmos%20Voutsinos/Getting%20the%20most.htm.
34 Fuji Keizai, "Cleantech: Current Status and Worldwide Outlook," February 2008 Report
    Linker, www.reportlinker.com/p077393/2008/02/Cleantech-Current-Status- and-
    Worldwide-Outlook.html.
35 Clean Edge, "Clean-Energy Trends 2008," http://www.cleanedge.com/reports/reports-
    trends2008.php.
36 Jefferies & Company Inc., "Clean Technology Primer," June 2008.
37 Edward Milford, "Record Growth for Wind: What Comes Next?", Renewable Energy
    World, August 27, 2008, http://www.renewableenergyworld.com/rea/magazine/
    story?id=53436.
38 IEA, "Energy Technology Perspectives," 2008, http://www.iea.org/Textbase/techno/etp/
    index.asp.
39 David Enrlich, "Another Cellulosic Powerhouse Formed," May 14, 2008, http://media.
    cleantech.com.
40 Shawn McCarthy, "Renewable Power Firms Weather the Storm," Globe and Mail,
    October 27, 2008.
41 Milford, "Record Growth for Wind: What Comes Next?"
42 Lars Paulsson and Paul Dobson, "Offshore Wind Projects Hit the Doldrums," Globe and
    Mail, May 15, 2008.
43 Peter Wise, "EdP Buys Horizon for $2.9 bn," Financial Times, March 28, 2008.
44 Clint Wilder, "Our New Greatest Generation Opportunity," Clean Edge, http://www.
    cleanedge.com/views/index.php?id=5382.
45 Makower, Pernick and Wilder, "Clean Energy Trends."
46 Jefferies & Company Inc., "Clean Technology Primer."
47 Dan E. Arvizu, "Alternative Energy: Solar, Wind, Geothermal," Milken/Sandia Energy
    Workshop for Financial and Capital Market Leaders, October 23 2006, http://www.nrel.
    gov/director/presentations_speeches.html.
48 Jefferies & Company Inc., "Clean Technology Primer."
49 Wikipedia, "Environmental Effects of Wind Power," http://en.wikipedia.org/wiki/
    Environmental_effects_of_wind_power.

50   Global Solar Center, http://www.globalsolarcenter.com/solar_industry_statistics.html.

51   Ibid.

52   Jennifer Kho, "U.S. Solar Could Surpass German Market by 2011," 2008, Greentech-media, http://www.greentechmedia.com/articles/us-solar-market-could-surpass-germany-by-2011-1148.html.

53   Energy Refuge.com, 2008, http://www.energyrefuge.com/archives/Solar_panel_subsidy.htm.

54   Jonathan Dorn, "Solar Thermal Power Coming to a Boil," Earth Policy Institute, July 22, 2008, http://www.earth-policy.org/Updates/2008/Update73.htm.

55   Wikipedia, "Solar Thermal," 2008, http://en.wikipedia.org/wiki/Solar_thermal_energy.

56   Ibid.

57   Tyler Hamilton, "Quebec Lands New Silicon Plant," August 26, 2008, http://www.thestar.com/comment/columnists/article/485413.

58   REC, "REC ASA – Invest NOK 13 Billion in Singapore," press release, 2008, http://www.recgroup.com/default.asp?V_ITEM_ID=611&xml=/R/136555/PR/200806/1228877.xml.

59   Solar Development, "Solar Energy Fact Sheets," obtained on December 10, 2007, http://www.solardev.com/SEIA-makingelec.php.

60   Jefferies & Company Inc., "Clean Technology Primer."

61   "Morning Briefing—Retail, 2008. Stores to Reduce Energy Use."

62   Biodiesel 2020, "Global Market Survey, Feedstock Trends and Forecasts," http://www.emerging-markets.com/biodiesel.

63   EIA, "Biofuels in the U.S. Transportation Sector," 2008, http://www.eia.doe.gov/oiaf/analysispaper/biomass.html.

64   Sybille La Hamaide, "Global Biofuel Output to Soar in Next Decade: Report," May 29, 2008, http://www.reuters.com/article/GCA-Agflation/idUSL2930418620080529.

65   Craig Rubens, "Primer: What You Need to Know About Brazil Biofuels," 2008, Earth2tech, May 7, 2008, http://earth2tech.com/2008/05/07/primer-brazilian-biofuels.

66   Investeco, 2008, quarterly newsletter.

67   Eric Johnson and Russel Heinen, "Biofuels Face a Carbon Certification Challenge," *Chemical Week*, April 2008.

68   Rubens, "Primer: What You Need to Know About Brazil Biofuels."

69   "Morning Briefing—Retail, 2008. Stores to Reduce Energy Use."

70   National Biodiesel Board, 2008, http://www.biodiesel.org/resources/reportsdatabase/reports/gen/20040321_gen-332.pdf.

71   Peter Tertzakian, *A Thousand Barrels a Second* (New York: McGraw-Hill, 2006).

72   Jefferies & Company Inc., "Clean Technology Primer."

73   Shawn McCarthy, "Global Warming: Province Against Province?", *Globe and Mail*, March 14, 2008.

74   "Energy Rich Western Provinces Boost Conservation and Clean Power Efforts," *Globe and Mail*, A Special Information Supplement, December 10, 2008.

75   Jefferies & Company Inc., "Clean Technology Primer."

76   Wikipedia, "Fuel Cells," http://en.wikipedia.org/wiki/Fuel_cell.

77   Jefferies & Company Inc., "Clean Technology Primer."

78   Ibid.

79   U.S. Department of Energy, "Energy Efficiencies and Renewable Energy," 2008, http://www1.eere.energy.gov/geothermal/powerplants.html.

80   Canadian Geothermal Energy Association, 2008, http://www.cangea.ca.

81   Glitnir Geothermal Research, "United States Geothermal Energy Market Report," September 2007, http://docs.glitnir.is/media/files/Glitnir_USGeothermalReport.pdf.

82   Jefferies & Company Inc., "Clean Technology Primer."
83   Wikipedia, "Tidal Power," http://en.wikipedia.org/wiki/Tidal_power.
84   Tidal Electric, "Technology: History of Tidal Power,"
      http://www.tidalelectric.com/History.htm.
85   Jefferies & Company Inc., "Clean Technology Primer."
86   Grant Buckler, "Clean Power Comes In with the Tide," Globe and Mail, October 20,
      2008.
87   Cleantech, "Israel's SDE Plans 100MW of Wave Energy for Africa," November 13, 2008,
      www.cleantech.com/news/3871/israels-sde-plans-100mw-wave-energy-africa.
88   Jefferies & Company Inc., "Clean Technology Primer."
89   Tidal Electric, "Technology: History of Tidal Power."
90   Hubert Bach, "Nuclear Power Gets Green Sheen," Montreal Gazette, June 15, 2008.
91   Brant McLaughlin, "Nuclear Power Rise to the Occasion," August 28, 2007, values de-
      rived from Nuclear Energy Institute, http://www.associatedcontent.com/article/360531/
      nuclear_power_rises_to_the_occasion.html.
92   Robert Benzie and Debra Black, "Darlington to Get Two New Reactors," Toronto Star,
      June 17, 2008.
93   Tom Rand, "Forget the Russians—The CANDU Can Do It," Globe and Mail, April 10,
      2008.
94   Tim Harper, "Bush Signs Nuclear Deal with India," Toronto Star, December 19, 2006.
95   Konrad Yakabuski, "McGuinty Is Wrong-headed on Nuclear," Globe and Mail, July 10,
      2008.
96   Climate Progress, "McCain Calls for 700+ New Nuclear Plants (and Seven Yucca Moun-
      tains) Costing $4 Trillion," 2008, http://climateprogress.org/2008/05/04/mccain-calls-
      for-700-new-nuclear-plants-and-7-yucca-mountains-costing-4-trillion.
97   Bach, "Nuclear Power Gets Green Sheen."
98   National Biodiesel Board, 2008.
99   Ibid.
100   "Gazprom to Sell Shtokman LNG to Canada," Barents Observer, May 16, 2008,
      http://www.barentsobserver.com/gazprom-to-sell-shtokman-lng-to-canada.
      4482345-91228.html.
101   Wikipedia, "Clean Coal Technology," http://en.wikipedia.org/wiki/Clean_coal.
102   National Resources Defense Council, "Coal in a Changing Climate," February 2007,
      http://www.nrdc.org/globalwarming/coal/coalclimate.pdf.
103   Makower, Pernick and Wilder, "Clean Energy Trends."
104   Amanda Griscom Little, "Coal Position," December 3, 2004,
      http://www.grist.org/news/muck/2004/12/03/little-coal.
105   Emma Rich, "MIT Unlocking Carbon Capture and Storage," Cleantech, November 17,
      2008, http://www.cleantech.com/news/3888/mit-carbon-capture-research-shows-green
      house-emission.
106   Alok Jha, "Drax's £50m Renewables Project Throws Biomass into the Coal Mix," Guard-
      ian, May 19, 2008, http://www.guardian.co.uk/environment/2008/may/19/biofuels.
      fossilfuels.
107   Jefferies & Company Inc., "Clean Technology Primer."
108   Ibid.
109   Barack Obama, "New Energy for America," 2008, http://my.barackobama.com/page/
      content/newenergy.
110   Martin LaMonica, "Obama Signs Stimulus Plan, Touts Clean Energy", February 17th, 2009.
      GreenTech, http://news.cnet.com/8301-11128_3-10165605-54.html?tag=mncol;title

111 DSIR, "Federal Initiatives for Renewable Energy", http://www.dsireusa.org/library/includes/incentive2.cfm?Incentive_Code=US37F&State=federal&currentpageid=1&ee=1&re=1

112 Environmental Finance, "US Stimulus Package Proposes $54 Billion of Clean Energy Spending", January 22, 2009. http://www.environmental-finance.com/onlinews/0122uss.html

113 American Wind Energy Association, "Legislative Affairs," 2008, http://www.awea.org/legislative.

114 Solar Energy Industry Association, "Congress Extends Federal Solar Energy Tax Credits Through End of 2008."

115 Wikipedia, "Emissions Trading," 2008, http://en.wikipedia.org/wiki/Emissions_trading.

116 Johnson and Heinen, "Biofuels Face a Carbon Certification Challenge."

117 The White House, 2008, http://www.whitehouse.gov/infocus/environment.

118 California, "Million Solar Roofs," Environment California, 2008, http://www.environmentcalifornia.org/energy/million-solar-roofs.

119 Energy Bible, "Renewable Energy News," http://www.energybible.com/default.html, accessed July 31, 2008.

120 Public Citizen, "Nuclear Giveaways in the Energy Bill Conference Report," 2008.

121 Makower, Pernick and Wilder, "Clean Energy Trends."

122 Barrie McKenna, "The Oilman's New Stripes," Globe and Mail, July 10, 2008.

123 Canadian Embassy, "Canada-US Energy Relations," 2008, http://geo.international.gc.ca/can-am/washington/trade_and_investment/energy-en.asp.

124 David Cohen, "What's New at the Tar Sands," January 2, 2008, http://www.aspo-usa.com/index.php?option=com_content&task=view&id=291&Itemid=91.

125 Ibid.

126 Ibid.

127 Ibid.

128 Environment Canada, "Turning the Corner: Taking Action to Fight Climate Change," March 2008, http://www.ec.gc.ca/doc/virage-corner/2008-03/brochure_eng.html.

129 Ibid.

130 Government of Canada, "Canada's New Government Announces Targets to Tackle Climate Change and Reduce Air Pollution," April 2007, http://www.ecoaction.gc.ca/news-nouvelles/20070426-9-eng.cfm.

131 Canadian Wind Energy Association, 2008, www.canwea.ca.

132 Richard Blackwell, "Solar Power Heats Up with New Ontario Projects," Report on Business, Globe and Mail, January 22, 2008, http://www.theglobeandmail.com.

133 Yakabuski, "McGuinty Is Wrong-headed on Nuclear."

134 Margaret Munro, "Biofuel Salvation of Perdition," May 3, 2008, Green Line, http://www.canada.com/montrealgazette/features/greenlife/story.html?id=fde9f701-9002-4c1f-ada1-e1722be7e6d5&p=2.

135 Agriculture Canada, "ecoAgriculture Biofuel Capital Initiative," http://www4.agr.gc.ca/AAFC-AAC/display-afficher.do?id=1195672401464&lang=e.

136 Alberta Government, "Alberta Surges Ahead with Climate Change Action Plan," July 8, 2008, http://www.alberta.ca/home/NewsFrame.cfm?ReleaseID=/acn/200807/23960039FB54D-CC21-7234-31C3E853089A1E6C.html.

137 Jefferies & Company Inc., 2008.

CHAPTER SEVEN

EMISSIONS TRADING

Can global ecosystems remain viable under the imperatives of economic growth? For decades, ecologists have been arguing that traditional economic valuations ignore the significant cost of "services" provided by the environment, in the form of fresh water, air and biota—all of which are essential to business and society.[1] In the absence of associated values for many of these natural resources, they have been deemed to be free and exploitable by all. Recently the costs associated with services, such as climate change and water shortage, have begun to appear on the balance sheet.

The combined weight of physical evidence, damage claims, scientific consensus and international cooperation has made the climate change phenomenon a very real business issue. As the business community comes to grips with climate change, economic principles of valuation and exchange are being applied to components of the environment, with the emergence of opportunities as well as risks. The atmosphere, in particular the collection of Greenhouse Gases (GHGs), is becoming a widely commoditized component.

Fast-forward these fundamental concepts to Europe in 2008, where the European Union Emission Trading Scheme (EU ETS) saw the value of trade in GHGs exceed US$90 billion, with projections for global trade in carbon reaching US$150 billion in 2009. A 2008 report released by New Carbon Finance estimated that the U.S. will be home to a carbon market worth in excess of $1 trillion by 2020, more than twice the size of the EU ETS. The forecast assumed that the U.S. would implement an economy-wide cap-and-trade system within four or five years and that the system will be confined to domestic trading only.[2] The call to Congress for cap-and-trade legislation on carbon emissions by U.S. President Obama in late February 2009 may help to realize this forecast even sooner.

Governments in North America and Europe are struggling with the fundamental policy shifts needed to accommodate the challenges of energy supply, quality, cost and carbon content. The resultant policies, which are more developed in Europe and still nascent in North America, all include market based instruments (MBIs) such as emissions trading as options available to reduce GHG emissions.

What does this all mean to business? Depending on the industry sector, the implications of climate change policy and the importance of emissions trading vary. The best place to begin is by briefly describing the larger climate change context in which business finds itself in 2009. (Note that many related issues have been discussed in preceding chapters, especially the introduction, chapter 1 and chapter 6.)

THE BUSINESS CASE FOR ACTION ON CLIMATE CHANGE

Climate change will directly or indirectly affect all businesses. Industries most immediately impacted are those affected by changing weather patterns or increased storm events, such as agriculture, tourism, insurance/underwriting and banking/finance. The energy sector, and energy-intensive industries, will also be hit heavily by market shifts arising from both the environmental price of carbon and the desire (of individuals, companies, cities and countries) to switch to renewable energy sources. Industries with heavy carbon footprints will be first in the line of fire of legislators—and they know it. Executives of energy-intensive industries in Europe have cited the EU ETS as one of the primary factors affecting their long-term investment decisions.[3] Secondary effects will be felt along the supply chains of product manufacturers, through price adjustments, the disappearance or transformation of product lines and the arrival of new products.

Opportunities to protect the environment from further man-induced change will be just as abundant, as the race to develop and deploy low-carbon energy products continues, as other products and processes evolve to match the modified climate, and as new suites of services emerge to guide business.

Climate change presents risks and opportunities for business that can be summarized under the following five headings:

1. Physical risks
2. Investor/shareholder concerns
3. Price of energy and raw materials
4. Impending policy and legislation
5. Energy efficiency and new market opportunities

Physical Risks

Climate change is altering the face of disaster risk, not only through increased storms, rising sea levels and localized temperature changes, but also through increased societal vulnerabilities, because of stresses on water availability, longer exposure to vector-born diseases, the changing geography of food-producing regions and risks to ecosystems.[4] A World Health Organization assessment, taking into account only a subset of the possible health impacts, concluded that the effects of climate change that have occurred since the mid-1970s may have caused more than one hundred fifty thousand deaths in 2000. It also concluded that these impacts are likely to increase in the future.[5]

Any business in the extractive industries, or whose operations rely on stable climatic conditions on land or at sea, in the middle latitudes or the tropics, is at risk. Extreme weather phenomena of the past decade, many of which may be directly related to climate change, have been the subject of media attention. Notable examples are the following:

- Hurricane *Katrina* in 2005 was the costliest weather catastrophe on record, with 1,300 deaths, $40 billion in insured economic losses and over 1 million people displaced. Hurricane *Ike* in 2008, while not as destructive, idled one-fifth of U.S. oil production as it passed over the Texas Gulf coast in September.
- The European heat wave of 2003, during which average temperatures were 2.3°C higher than average, caused thirty-five thousand deaths.[6]
- Over the past several decades, the area of Canadian boreal forest affected by fire and insects has doubled. One study of a current pine beetle outbreak in British Columbia concluded that 374,000 km² of forest will have been converted from a small net carbon sink to a large net carbon source.[7]
- Arctic sea ice thickness is more than a meter thinner than three decades ago.[8] Following a record rate of ice loss through August 2008, the extent of the Arctic sea ice stood as the second-lowest on record, further reinforcing conclusions that it is in a long-term state of decline.[9]
- The predicted rise in sea level associated with climate change has begun and will become a significant challenge to countries with extensive infrastructure and investments in low-lying lands. The IPCC's (Intergovernmental Panel on Climate Change) *Fourth Assessment Report* shows that between 1993 and 2006, sea levels rose by 3.3 mm a year on average, while the 2001 IPCC report had predicted an annual rise of less than 2 mm. In

addition to coastal flooding and storm damage, eroding shorelines, saltwater contamination of freshwater supplies, flooding of coastal wetlands
and barrier islands, and an increase in the salinity of estuaries are all predicted effects of sea level rise.

It should be noted that the changes to the Arctic sea ice might also herald a
new marine transportation corridor (the Northwest Passage), which will entail
commercial benefits for the east-west movement of goods and, possibly, some environmental benefit from the shortening of itineraries.

Investor/Shareholder Concerns

Investors in American and Canadian companies filed a record fifty-seven climate-
related shareholder resolutions in 2008, of which nearly half were withdrawn after
the companies agreed to positive climate-related commitments. The resolutions,
which sought emission reductions and greater disclosure from companies on their
strategies to address climate-related business trends, were filed by state and city
pension funds and labor, foundation, religious and other institutional shareholders who collectively manage more than $300 billion in assets.[10]

Climate resolutions were filed with the Canadian-based Bank of Montreal,
Scotiabank, Russel Metals and EnCana. Among those petitioned in the U.S. were
Ford for a detailed plan on how it will reach the goal of reducing by at least 30%
the GHG emissions from its new vehicle fleet by 2020; ConocoPhillips and Chevron, for disclosure on the risks associated with oil extraction from tar sands in
Alberta; and ExxonMobil, for a commitment to adopt quantitative goals for reducing GHG emissions from its products and operations.

If climate change is on the minds of investors, it is because risks and opportunities are readily apparent, as shown in table 7.1.

Price of Energy and Raw Materials

The physical risks of climate change described earlier, which can result in losses
to business from storm damage and temperature extremes, also imply that there
will be periodic energy supply shortfalls and higher prices, particularly when oil
producing or refining regions, such as the Gulf of Mexico and Texas Gulf coast,
are affected. These price spikes will be superimposed on the general medium- and
long-term rise in the price of oil, which will occur for a number of reasons, as
detailed in chapter 6.

Table 7.1: Climate Change-driven Risks and Opportunities

Type of Business	Risks	Opportunities
Hydroelectric Power Generation and Transmission		
	Higher transmission infrastructure and equipment maintenance costs due to more extreme weather events	Increased reservoir storage due to higher precipitation
	Decreased reservoir storage due to lower precipitation	• increased conservation due to electricity supply shortages • increased consumer interest in renewable energy
Engineering and Construction		
	Loss of contract opportunities for infrastructure projects due to changing weather patterns, e.g., new areas of drought or flooding	Creation of contract opportunities for infrastructure projects due to changing weather patterns, e.g., new areas of storm damage and flooding
Corporate Banking and Project Financing		
	• higher energy costs for consumers • price volatility in carbon markets • reputational risk due to investments in controversial energy projects • increased credit risks by affected clients	• cleantech investments • civil engineering project financing in coastal regions
Insurance		
	Losses from: • extreme weather events (e.g., hurricanes, ice storms) • business disruption coverage • impacts on human health	• new insurance products • carbon-neutral insurance coverage • insurance for emissions trading • carbon as an insurable asset
Tourism and Recreation		
Ski Operator	Revenue decline due to decrease in precipitation or higher temperatures	Revenue growth due to increase in precipitation or decrease in temperature
Beach Vacation Operator	Revenue decline due to lower temperatures or more frequent precipitation	Revenue growth due to higher temperatures or less frequent precipitation
Agriculture		
	• decreased crop yields due to water stress • increases in type and variety of pests	Introduction of crop varieties to regions where climate was previously too harsh

Adapted from Labatt & White, 2007

As consumers of oil, businesses are already preparing for this more costly energy future through a range of measures from energy conservation (e.g., energy audits, retrofitting older facilities, designing new facilities with energy efficiency in mind) to switching or supplementing energy supplies and "de-carbonizing" (where possible). While such measures may represent important costs in the short term, the flipside presents medium-term returns on investment and avoided energy costs.

Oil is not the only energy source susceptible to climate-related risks. The impact mechanism of energy price increases is the same for businesses located in jurisdictions supplied with energy from other sources, such as hydro. Climate-related fluctuations in reservoir levels might impact upon supply (and costs).

Raw materials whose cost to produce and transport may be impacted by climate change include petroleum derivatives, plastics, wood and other forest products and agricultural products.

Impending Policy and Legislation

Early recognition of the risks and opportunities related to climate change, anticipation of policy changes and readiness to respond to legislation or to participate in market mechanisms have been shown to be critical to maintaining profitability through periods such as the present, in advance of a regulated regime.[11]

In Canada, there are both carbon taxes and GHG emission control legislation at the provincial level; however, there will not be federal regulations in Canada until sometime in 2009. At the provincial level are

- recently deployed carbon taxes in the Canadian provinces of Quebec and British Columbia
- a suite of emissions-control regulations at the provincial level, some framing cap-and-trade schemes (British Columbia), others favoring technology-based emissions intensity standards (Alberta)

On the other side of the equation are government incentives, such as the California Million Solar Roofs Bill (SB 1) and Ontario's Standard Offer Program for Renewable Energy. Through guaranteed energy pricing, the latter has succeeded in attracting more proposed projects than anticipated, totaling 1,400 MW of new generating capacity in that jurisdiction.

As noted earlier, carbon-intensive industries, such as fossil fuel-powered power generation, oil and gas, petrochemicals and metal smelting, are already targeted by GHG emissions reduction legislation and regulation in Canada and are coping with technology changes, operational and pricing adjustments, relocation, lobbying and communication strategies. The most common response is to start looking at building portfolios of compliance units. Private and public entities in the transport sector, a major contributor to national GHG emission inventories, are targeted by federal legislation in Canada and the U.S., through rising fuel efficiency standards and minimum biofuel targets. Players in the transport sector will need to improve and enhance logistics, in addition to seeking greater combustion efficiencies and reductions in fuel burn.

In all of these instances, the fundamental driving force is recognition of climate change and the need to reduce GHG emissions. As much as these examples illustrate the financial risks of overexposure to carbon in energy and raw material sourcing, they also represent opportunities for competitive positioning, if the risks are managed early.

In January 2007, seeking clarity in government policy, the United States Climate Action Partnership, a group of leading companies—including Alcoa and Pacific Gas and Electric—called for the rapid enactment of mandatory, economy-wide regulatory programs to support a 10% to 30% reduction of GHGs over fifteen years in the U.S. At a Senate hearing in 2006, representatives of companies like General Electric, Duke Energy and Exelon made the case that it was time to move forward with legislation because they would rather know the rules soon, they said, than be surprised by a sudden change to the political agenda.[12] Their greatest concern is not to have to face a patchwork quilt of regional plans in the absence of federal action.

As part of its effort to guide international and national efforts, and in the interests of presenting a unified business position on climate change action, the World Business Council for Sustainable Development has posited four policy priorities to stabilize the global GHG environment in 2050 by[13]

- managing emissions
- decarbonizing the world's energy mix
- using resources more efficiently
- developing zero- and low-GHG technologies

These policy proposals, listed below, point the way for government action:

1. A quantifiable, long-term (fifty-year) global emissions pathway for the management of GHG emissions established by 2010 will help build

confidence to support technological development, deployment and business action.

2. Using the existing international framework as a basis, and modifying it to build up from local, national, sector or regional programs, will close the gap that would otherwise exist after 2012 (see further below on the Kyoto Protocol).

3. At the national level, and in support of the international pathway, robust programs to encourage energy efficiency should be developed
   - in new and existing buildings and in the small and medium enterprise sector
   - by targeting process improvements at industrial and manufacturing facilities
   - through the deployment of high-efficiency vehicles
   - by targeting consumer goods and services.

4. The range of fuels in the transport sector should be broadened to include biofuels, hydrogen and electricity.

5. A number of low- and zero-GHG technologies (e.g., nuclear, renewables, fuel cells, clean coal and carbon capture and sequestration [CCS]) must be developed and commercialized over the coming decades. These will require supporting policies and programs to address technical and cost challenges.

In the European Community, climate change policy and the enabling legislation based on ratification of the Kyoto Protocol are already in effect, with a viable emissions trading market at work. In North America, steps towards effective climate change action are less advanced. The Canadian federal government has made it clear through the release of its policy framework in 2007 that it is not going to try to meet its Kyoto commitments as an Annex I country, though it ratified the Protocol in 2002. As the U.S. never ratified Kyoto, attempts are being made to reduce GHG emissions through a patchwork of regional emissions trading schemes, none of which are yet in force. Domestic development of policy and legislation had been proving to be a slow process until February of 2009.[14]

Strong endorsement of market-based mechanisms by the U.S. President and a call for Congress to pass cap-and-trade legislation holds promise for change to take place in the U.S., if not all of North America, in the near future. In Canada, the federal government stepped back from its original Kyoto commitments and in April 2007 released its "Turning the Corner" Regulatory Framework favoring a technology-based, emissions-intensity approach towards control legislation with less aggressive cuts than would otherwise be dictated by its share of the Kyoto plan. Emitters have several mechanisms at their disposal to meet regulated emission levels, including a domestic emissions trading scheme to begin in 2010.

The real advances in North America in 2008 were made at the state/provincial and regional levels. The current status of emissions trading regimes in the EU and in North America is detailed further below.

Energy Efficiency and New Market Opportunities

For more than two decades, achieving energy efficiency has been the single most promising and cost-effective solution to meeting the growing demand for energy at all levels of government, industry and society in North America. It is a risk mitigation strategy and major business opportunity at the same time, with net environmental benefits. Legislation in both the U.S. and Canada aimed at improving product energy efficiency, as well as fiscal incentives for industry and the public to invest in energy efficiency, has provided some relief to the supply side. Additional good news is that the end to the gains that can be achieved through energy efficiency is not yet in sight, as a significant portion of national GHG emissions remains bound to energy losses from buildings, industrial processes and heating and air conditioning systems.

For society at large, climate change is fundamentally a challenge to decarbonize the economy and extract more productivity out of every tonne of GHG emitted. Estimates of the magnitude of the change required at a global scale are in the order of a tenfold increase in global GDP per tonne of carbon dioxide equivalent (CO_2e).[15] While much of this increase must come from energy efficiency and more reliance on low-carbon energy sources, business is now presented with a range of opportunities, some more challenging than others, to re-think strategy (as discussed in chapter 1) and to achieve intelligent design (as described in chapter 3) in pursuit of low-carbon versions of what they already do and make. For most industries, this implies finding superior technologies to achieve greater energy efficiencies. For others, it may entail a technology switch and wholesale change in the business model.

So where does trading in GHG emissions fit into this mosaic of risk and opportunity? To understand its potential role for any business, it may be appropriate to cover some of the basic concepts.

EMISSIONS TRADING FOR DUMMIES

Emissions trading was just a promising theory in the U.S. until the mid-1970s, when regulators tested it for the first time as a means of improving ambient air quality in certain areas to meet the requirements of federal legislation without impeding economic growth. Excess emissions reductions below regulatory limits were certified by the EPA (as credits or "offsets") and made available to new industry, provided the latter purchased 120% of the emissions credits they would need to offset their own emissions. The excess 20% then was retired.

Various emissions trading schemes have since been used in the U.S. to phase lead out of gasoline in the 1980s, to contribute to the international effort to stop production of ozone-depleting substances in the 1990s, to reduce sulphur dioxide (SO_2) emissions from electric utilities, and in regional initiatives in California and the northeast states.

What Exactly Is Emissions Trading?

Emissions trading is an environmental policy instrument based on market economics. On the continuum of instruments available to government, it sits alongside market-oriented regulations, such as Renewable Portfolio Standards (RPSs) in the energy sector and vehicle emissions standards (figure 7.1). It is an alternative method of pollutant emission control to taxation and regulation, which are the exclusive responsibility of government authority, because it transfers the burden of identifying the appropriate control technologies to the polluter and allows flexibility (and lower cost) in how specified emission reduction targets can be met through either direct reduction of emissions at facilities or acquiring emissions reductions from other facilities.[16]

Role of Government

As stewards of the "commons," which includes the environment, governments can exercise control to prevent or minimize environmental impact through either regulation or taxes. North Americans are all too familiar with the so-called command and control regulatory approach, by which governments usually effect control over activities with environmental impact. The problem with this approach is that it is not necessarily the most cost-effective. Emissions trading is an approach designed to allow GHG emission reductions (or reductions of other pollutants) to be made in an economically efficient way.

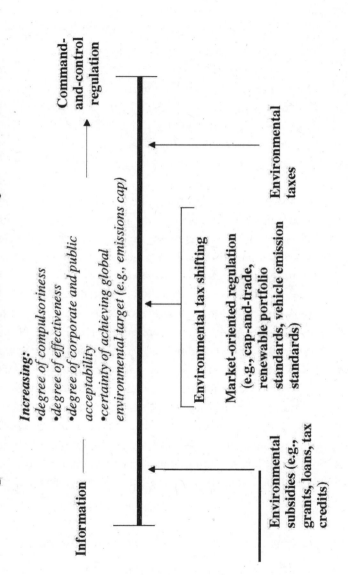

Figure 7.1: Environmental Policy Instruments

Increasing:
• degree of compulsoriness
• degree of effectiveness
• degree of corporate and public acceptability
• certainty of achieving global environmental target (e.g., emissions cap)

Information ————

Command-and-control regulation

Environmental taxes

Environmental tax shifting

Market-oriented regulation (e.g., cap-and-trade, renewable portfolio standards, vehicle emission standards)

Environmental subsidies (e.g., grants, loans, tax credits)

Adapted from Jaccard et al., 2002

Emissions trading refers to the buying or selling of permits to pollute. The trading takes place within regulatory frameworks set by government. The trading provides an incentive for reductions beyond what is specified by the regulation. In an emissions trading scheme, an overall emissions reduction target is set for a group of organizations, and those participants then decide, in a flexible way, how to achieve their own target by either

- meeting their target by reducing their emissions
- reducing their emissions below their target and selling or banking the excess emission allowances or
- letting their emissions remain above their target, and buying emissions allowances from other participants

In emissions trading schemes involving pollutants such as CO_2, the market assigns the pollutant a price, and quotas (in the form of allowances or permits) are made available as part of the government compliance strategy. The scheme is based on either an overall emissions "cap" established by government regulation that applies to all emitters, or upon "baseline" emissions levels that are measured based on a specified methodology (such as that established in ISO 14064 Part 2 Greenhouse gases—Specification with guidance at the project level for quantification, monitoring and reporting of greenhouse gas emission reductions or removal enhancements). Capped trading entities then calculate their marginal costs of abatement to achieve target reductions and determine the best abatement method, i.e., capital investments in pollution control equipment, process alterations, etc., or by buying permits. These methods all carry different costs for the emitter, which vary over time. The marginal cost of abatement refers to the incremental cost per unit of emission reduced. Any regulated entity, or emitter, under a specific set of circumstances, should establish how its marginal cost compares to other available options in order to achieve the economically optimal solution (figure 7.2).

Difference Between "Cap-and-Trade" and "Baseline and Credit"

In a cap-and-trade scheme, the regulatory authority establishes an overall "cap" on emissions, which is the total amount of a pollutant that the participants in the scheme are allowed to emit in a given period. Allowances equal to all of the emissions permitted under the cap are then distributed, either for free or by auction (the latter is generally viewed as more efficient).[17] Once the allowances

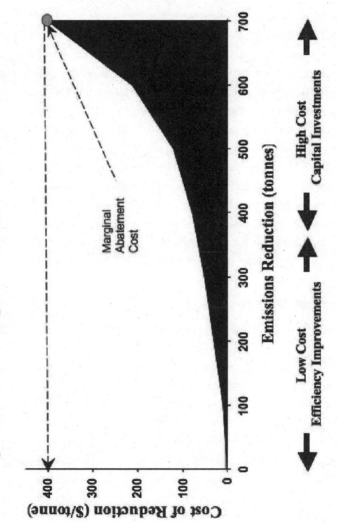

Figure 7.2: Marginal Cost of Abatement

Adapted from Pollution Probe, 2003

are distributed, they may be traded freely. During the compliance period, each participant must monitor or calculate its actual emissions using specified procedures. At the end of the period, it must hand over to the regulatory authority allowances that are equal to its actual emissions during the period. Examples of cap-and-trade programs include U.S. programs for ozone-depleting substances and SO_2 emissions by electric utilities.

The participants in a baseline and credit scheme have to earn credits before they can begin trading. The methodology for calculating the baseline is determined by the regulator (e.g., ISO 14064 Part 2) and may or may not require third-party verification. Each participant then makes reductions and monitors or calculates its actual emissions using specified procedures.

At the end of the compliance period, verifiers compare the baseline calculation with the actual emissions from the source during the period. Participants whose actual emissions are lower than their baseline receive "credits" equal to the difference. Credits then can be traded freely. A participant whose actual emissions exceed its baseline must purchase credits equal to its excess emissions to achieve compliance. The U.S. trading scheme to eliminate lead in gasoline and the heavy-duty engine emission standards programs are baseline and credit schemes, as is Canada's current Regulatory Framework for Greenhouse Gas Emissions.

What Are Offsets?

An offset represents the reduction, removal or avoidance of GHG emissions from a specific project that can be used to compensate for GHG emissions elsewhere. While offsets are often used outside of regulated trading systems as potentially cost-effective MBIs to achieve GHG reductions, they can be an additional compliance mechanism available on a project basis in most trading systems, including national and regional systems established to meet Kyoto Protocol goals. In Canada, for example, the federal government's climate change plan allows for 10% of the compliance obligations of targeted industries to be met through the use of the Clean Development Mechanism (Kyoto Protocol—see further below) offsets. The use of offsets by GHG emitters is the subject of much debate, as it is said to deflect attention from the real challenge of global emissions reduction, which can be directly achieved through emissions avoidance, reduction and replacement strategies.

Offsets are typically generated from emissions-reducing projects, such as methane abatement, energy efficiency, reforestation and fuel switching. However, they may also be generated through renewable energy projects. Key features of offsets are the year in which the emissions reduction was achieved (the so-called vintage), the type of project and how it was certified. The Clean Development Mechanism and the Chicago Climate Exchange (both described further below) have set standards to approve offsets. Recognizing the need to establish credible offsets, in late 2007 six nonprofit organizations in the U.S. (The Climate Trust, Pew Center on Global Climate Change, California Climate Action Registry, the Environmental Resources Trust, Greenhouse Gas Management Institute, and The Climate Group) established the Offset Quality Initiative to lay out the principles and criteria for offsets in the emerging U.S. carbon emissions trading market. In August 2008, the federal government in Canada released its own set of rules for developers of offset protocols in Canada.

Carbon capture and sequestration (CCS) is a set of new technologies aimed at removing CO_2 from industrial gas streams, either before or after combustion, transporting it to suitable deep geologic formations, and injecting it for permanent storage. It also refers to the practice of injecting CO_2 into hydrocarbon reservoirs as a means of improving yields from these reservoirs and storing the CO_2.

Although some CCS technologies have been developed, deployment has slowed because of the significant installation and operating costs, the lack of a widespread cap-and-trade scheme to put a price on GHG emissions, uncertainty regarding the actual cost of CCS at a commercial scale, and the need to reach agreement among stakeholders on an appropriate regulatory system for carbon storage, including siting and determination of liability. These factors mean that geologic sequestration offset projects accounted for only 1% of all over-the-counter trades in GHG offset credits in 2007.

Notwithstanding these current drawbacks, much rides on the potential success of CCS and it will likely become a necessity where no viable alternatives exist to reduce emissions for major generators of GHG, such as the Canadian oil sands. It has been effectively mandated in Canada's federal Turning the Corner regulations.

Common Characteristics of Emissions Trading

There are several common characteristics of successful emissions trading schemes:[18]

- A limit is set on emissions, which is usually lower than the "business-as-usual" emissions of the sources participating in the programs.

- The participants must face divergent clean-up (i.e., abatement) costs so that there will be cost savings from trading. The number of participating sources must be sufficiently large to constitute a competitive market.
- Accurate monitoring of actual emissions and reductions by each participant is essential.
- There must be effective enforcement to ensure that each participant holds enough emission entitlements to cover its actual emissions.

Emissions trading schemes are developing or being proposed in several regions and countries. While some have designed their schemes and defined rules (e.g., EU ETS, Japan, Norway, certain North American regional trading initiatives), others have not yet finalized their options (e.g., United States, Canada, New Zealand). Schemes already in operation also provide "lesson learned" that can be used to design new emissions trading schemes. When deciding which design options best address the countries' emission levels, policymakers obviously account for national circumstances; hence, schemes differ in their size, scope, target, credit allocation mode, etc.

Kyoto and the Flexible Implementation Mechanisms

The Kyoto Protocol is an important step on the international community's path of response to the climate change threat. Scientific work on climate change and human activities has been ongoing since 1979 under the auspices of the World Meteorological Organization. In 1988, the Intergovernmental Panel on Climate Change (IPCC) was established and GHG reduction targets were drafted. The IPCC has provided the scientific consensus on man-induced climate change in its four assessment reports since 1995.

Born of the United Nations Framework Convention on Climate Change (UN-FCCC), which was signed at the Rio de Janeiro Earth Summit by 165 countries in 1992, the Kyoto Protocol was negotiated in 1997 and committed 37 countries and the European community to aggregate GHG reductions of 5.2% below 1990 levels by 2008–2012. The protocol came into effect in 2005 following ratification by 55 countries that collectively account for 55% of the total emissions from Annex I.

Each of the Annex I countries have been assigned a specific reduction target (expressed as assigned amount units—AAUs), Canada's being 6% below 1990 levels. The U.S. was assigned 7%, but did not ratify the treaty. The mechanisms by which signatory countries can achieve their targets are by domestic emission reduction (e.g., fuel switching, energy efficiency), augmentation of domestic carbon sinks (e.g., enhanced forest and agricultural practices designed to capture and store more atmospheric carbon) and through the three Kyoto market-based mechanisms.

A key attribute of the UNFCCC's work has been the acknowledgement that climate change has been attributable to industrialization within the developed world. Developing countries took the position that their industrialization should not be hampered by commitments to tackle climate change. Hence the concept of "common but differentiated responsibilities" was developed, meaning that developed countries would take the lead. These are the so-called Annex I countries and include, notably, Canada, the U.S., the U.K., the EU Member States, Japan, the Russian Federation, New Zealand and Australia. Of these, only the U.S. has not ratified the Kyoto Protocol.

The distinction between developed and developing economies has enabled the deployment of the following three key Kyoto market-based mechanisms by which developed countries can supplement their direct emissions reductions efforts to meet the targets assigned to them under the Kyoto Protocol.

Joint Implementation (JI)

JI allows a country with an emission reduction or limitation commitment under the Kyoto Protocol to earn emission reduction units (ERUs) through investment in an emission-reduction or emission removal project in another Annex I country. Each ERU is equivalent to 1 tonne of CO_2.[19] A critical element of JI is that the host country must cancel AAUs equal to the ERUs created.

The Clean Development Mechanism (CDM)

CDM allows a country with an emission-reduction or emission-limitation commitment under the Kyoto Protocol to implement an emission-reduction project in a developing country. Such projects can earn saleable certified emission reduction (CER) credits, each equivalent to 1 tonne of CO_2. The mechanism stimulates sustainable development and emission reductions, while giving industrialized countries some flexibility in how they meet their emission reduction or limitation targets.

A CDM project must provide emission reductions that are additional to what would otherwise have occurred (e.g., a project to capture gas leaking from a natural gas pipeline may not be considered "additional," as there is a case for doing this work anyway and selling the gas profitably). Additionality is proving to be a challenging concept for the CDM, resulting in numerous rejections of project applications. CDM projects must qualify through a rigorous and public registration and issuance process. Approval can be given by Designated National Authorities (DNA) at the country level to ensure that the projects conform to the sustainable development priorities of the country. CER issuance by the CDM Executive Board is based on verification reports from Designated Operational Entities (DOEs, which are essentially accredited professional verifiers).

Operational since the beginning of 2006, the mechanism has already registered more than one thousand projects and is anticipated to produce CERs amounting to more than 2.7 billion tonnes of CO_2 equivalent in the first commitment period of the Kyoto Protocol, 2008–2012.[20] (For an appreciation of the size of the carbon market from 2006 to 2008, refer to table 7.3, p. 326).

Emissions Trading (ET)

As described earlier, ET allows countries that have emission units to spare—emissions permitted but not "used"—to sell this excess capacity to countries that are over their targets. Figure 7.3 depicts the flow of carbon trading among the various entities implicated in the Kyoto Protocol. Countries with developing economies (to the right of the figure) generate excess credits through the mechanisms described above and have the opportunity to sell these to the developed economies of the European Community or other Annex I countries.

The fundamental significance of emissions trades between developed and developing economies is that a significant portion of global GHG emissions reduction opportunities lies in developing economies.[21]

> The EU ETS is the largest cap-and-trade carbon emissions trading scheme in the world, responsible for roughly half of the EU's total emissions of CO_2.

Emissions Trading Schemes
European Union ETS

The EU ETS, the largest cap-and-trade carbon emissions trading scheme in the world and responsible for roughly half of the EU's total emissions of CO_2; it began on January 1, 2005. The EU ETS is linked to the European Member State Obligations under the Kyoto Protocol to enable credits generated through the

Flexible Mechanisms to be traded. Emissions reduction obligations are imposed upon operators of installations carrying out energy activities (e.g., combustion installations, coke ovens, mineral oil refineries), iron and steel processing, mineral industries and pulp and paper. The obligations are imposed through National Allocation Plans (NAPs). Together the more than ten thousand affected installations trade more than ten million reduction credits per week.[22] Most of the trades take place on the European Climate Exchange. The first phase of the EU ETS was marked by significant carbon price volatility (with prices per tonne varying from €0.1 to €30 in 2006–2007) owing to over-allocation of allowances, i.e., more allowances were allocated than actual emissions.

The EU ETS is evolving on two fronts. First, the second phase of the NAPs running from 2008 to 2012, in line with the first trading period of the Kyoto Protocol, is now complete. The total cap for these countries represents a 6.5% reduction from verified 2005 emissions, while the coverage of the system has increased in terms of gases/sources. The second area in which the EU ETS is evolving is the scheme's design post-2012. The European Commission presented its proposals for a revision of the ETS in early 2008. The commission also intends to include the aviation sector in the ETS by 2011.

When compared to the EU ETS, the emergence and implementation of GHG emissions trading schemes in North America are lagging, having been delayed in part by lack of political will. While there has been considerable experience with emissions trading in the U.S., the presidential election in 2008 and the presence of a minority government in Canada, followed by elections late in 2008 in both countries, effectively delayed federal government action on climate change.

Situation in the U.S.

Between mid-2006 and mid-2008, a number of events relevant to GHG emissions trading had nonetheless taken place in the U.S.:

- the passage of California's Global Warming Act (AB 32)
- Democrats taking control of Congress in November 2006 was also significant, if not symbolic as evidenced by statements by representatives: the outgoing Republican chair, James Inhofe of Oklahoma, had once called global warming "the greatest hoax ever perpetrated on the American people," while in 2007, Senator Sheldon Whitehouse, a Democrat, called global warming "the single greatest threat to the world's natural environment"

Figure 7.3: Carbon Credit Flows Under the Kyoto Protocol

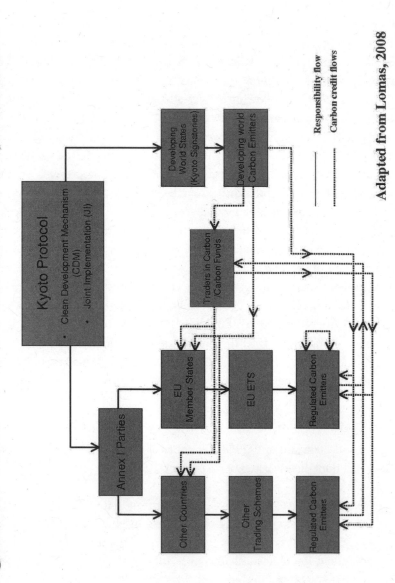

Adapted from Lomas, 2008

- on April 2, 2007, the Supreme Court ruled that the EPA has authority to regulate carbon dioxide and other GHGs as "pollutants" under the Clean Air Act, and the EPA is now required to assess whether GHG emissions pose a threat to public health (*Massachusetts v. EPA*)
- several comprehensive climate change bills worked their way through Congress, principally:
  - the House Appropriations Bill, which will require mandatory reporting of GHG emissions across the U.S. economy
  - the Lieberman-Warner cap-and-trade bill, which would have imposed mandatory emissions reductions across the U.S. economy; however, in June 2008, the Republicans mounted a filibuster against the bill and the Democrats lacked the votes to override, so it never came to a vote

In late 2008, President-elect Barack Obama pledged to reduce GHG emissions 80% below 1990 levels by 2050 and endorsed a CO_2 emissions cap-and-trade scheme to help accomplish this goal. His election platform called for $150 billion over ten years in new investments to achieve U.S. energy security, including fast-tracking of green energy business. Since assuming the presidency, he has maintained these commitments.

Situation in Canada

Canada's 2007 Regulatory Framework for Greenhouse Gas Emissions (revised in 2008 following stakeholder consultations) aims to achieve a 20% reduction in GHG emissions from a 2006 baseline (with an absolute reduction of 150 Mt by 2020). The government has proposed to cap GHG emissions intensity in the electricity generation, oil and gas, forest products, smelting and refining, iron and steel, cement, lime, potash and chemicals, and fertilizer sectors. Beginning in 2010, facilities in some of these sectors will face facility-specific targets, whereas others will be part of sector-wide targets. In both cases, an 18% reduction in emissions intensity will be mandated, followed by 2% reductions every year thereafter. Application thresholds (the emissions levels above which the targets apply) ranging from 10 Mt per year to 50 Mt per year apply to some sectors. The potash, natural gas pipeline, upstream oil and gas, oil sands and electricity sectors will be subject to a cleaner fuel standard.

Emitters will be able to comply with their emission targets through six channels:

1. Internal reductions
2. A domestic, baseline and credit, inter-firm, emissions trading scheme, which includes banking
3. Access to a domestic offsets system outside the regulated framework; off-set credits are expected to begin to be issued in 2009
4. Access to Clean Development Mechanism (10% of total reduction target)
5. Contributions to a technology fund
6. A pool of early action credits (15 Mt of CO_2 for all of industry, for actions undertaken between 1992 and 2006)

Draft regulations are expected for publication in the first quarter of 2009 at the earliest. While awaiting final federal regulations for industrial emitters, offsets are the only trading tool available to fill the market void in the current period. Environment Canada projects carbon prices to rise from C\$25/tonne in 2010 to C\$65/tonne in 2018.

By 2012, there is expectation for emissions trading in Canada to have evolved to a cap-and-trade system and for the Canadian market to link to a U.S. counter-part scheme.[23]

Regional Initiatives in North America

More significant than federal action in either country have been regional and state/provincial initiatives to control GHG emissions. While all of these are sig-nificant because they advance the design and knowledge base required to bring about emissions reductions and each participating jurisdiction has the regulatory authority to bind emitters, actions by the U.S. states can be pre-empted or en-dorsed by the federal government. This has left some uncertainty as to the final framework by which GHG emissions control will be deployed in the U.S. at a national level. Announcements by the U.S. President in February 2009 suggested that the federal government, likely through the EPA, will actively develop a na-tional cap-and-trade emissions scheme.

The most significant of these regional initiatives, all of which profess cap-and-trade emissions trading and openness to linkages among them, are listed below:

- California Global Warming Solutions Act (AB 32)—In September 2006, California governor Arnold Schwarzenegger signed into force precedent-setting AB 32, or the California Global Warming Solutions Act, which combines regulatory and market mechanisms to reduce GHG emissions in that state to 1990 levels by 2020, and a further 80% reduction by 2050. The main strategies of the law include direct regulations, recognition for early actions, mandatory emissions reporting, a cap-and-trade scheme, monetary and non-monetary incentives and alternative compliance mechanisms. Application is being phased in between 2008 and 2012.

- Western Climate Initiative (WCI)—Formed by seven western U.S. states and four Canadian provinces (Arizona, California, Montana, New Mexico, Oregon, Utah, Washington, British Columbia, Manitoba, Quebec and Ontario), WCI aims to achieve a 15% reduction below 2005 levels (baseline year) by 2020 through a cap-and-trade emissions trading scheme (see table 7.2).

- Midwestern Greenhouse Gas Reduction Accord—Formed in 2007 by six U.S. states (Iowa, Illinois, Kansas, Michigan, Minnesota and Wisconsin) and the province of Manitoba, this pact represents the most coal-dependent region of North America (60% of electricity generated from coal). The accord aimed to have a multi-sector cap-and-trade emissions trading scheme in place by late 2008. As of late November, design recommendations were being finalized by the Advisory Group. (See table 7.2.)

- Regional Greenhouse Gas Initiative (RGGI)—Comprising the states of Connecticut, Delaware, Maine, Maryland, Massachusetts, New Hampshire, New Jersey, New York, Rhode Island and Vermont, RGGI's first allowance auction took place in September 2008 (see table 7.2).

Canada projects carbon prices to rise from C$25/tonne in 2010 to C$65/tonne in 2018.

ABOUT CARBON MARKETS
Who Are the Players?

The complexity of emissions trading has given rise to an army of professionals in the carbon finance world. Figure 7.4 illustrates how these interact to deliver carbon financial instruments.

Table 7.2: Regional Emissions Trading Mechanisms in North America

	Western Climate Initiative (WCI)	Midwestern Greenhouse Gas Reduction Accord (MGGA)	Regional Greenhouse Gas Initiative (RGGI)
Emissions Trading Mechanism	• cap-and-trade to begin in 2012 (threshold of 25,000 $MtCO_2e$) • recognition of other fiscal measures (e.g., carbon tax on transport fuel) in participating jurisdictions • initial regional cap equal to the sum of the partner jurisdictions allowance budgets in 2012 • flexible, coordinated approach to allowance distribution; a minimum of 10% of each jurisdiction's allowances to be auctioned in 2012, growing to 25% or higher in 2020	• cap-and-trade (threshold of 10,000, 25,000 or 100,000 $MtCO_2e$ [TBA]) • cap-and-trade to be complemented by other GHG-reduction policies in participating states and province • allowances to be based primarily on current absolute emissions in baseline year, but other considerations will play a role (e.g., emissions per capita, reward for early action)	• cap-and-trade to begin in 2009 (threshold of 25,000 $MtCO_2e$) • initial cap is 4% above annual average regional emissions 2000–2004 • allowances to be auctioned by participating states, with proceeds from the sale used to fund state programs that promote energy efficiency and projects for clean renewable energy, such as solar and wind power
Scope/Sector Focus	• economy-wide, but caps on specific sectors: • electricity generation and importation • industrial process emissions • residential, industrial, commercial fuel combustion • transportation fuel (gas and diesel) combustion	• electricity generation and importation • industrial combustion sources • industrial process sources • residential, industrial, commercial fuels • transportation fuels combustion	• fossil-fuel-fired power producers >25 MW
Target	• aggregate reduction of 15% below 2005 levels by 2020 • annual, declining caps • three-year compliance periods through 2020	• by 2020: aggregate reduction of 15%, 20% or 25% (TBA) below 2005 levels • by 2050: aggregate reduction of 60%–80% below 2005 levels • three-year compliance periods	• by 2018: reduction of 10% relative to stabilized levels in 2009 • emissions to be stabilized from 2009 to 2014 • 2.5%/year reduction from 2015 to 2018 • three-year compliance periods

Compliance Mechanisms	• emissions trading, allowance banking • inclusion of offsets, but limited to no more than 49% of total emissions reductions achieved • early action recognition is one of several options open to participating jurisdictions in how they manage revenues from auctioning • no borrowing	• emissions trading, allowance banking, and "borrowing" • early action • inclusion of offsets—limited to 10%–50% of compliance target	• baseline period of 2006-07-08 • recognition of early action for period (2003-04-05) • offsets limited to 3%–10% of compliance obligation, depending on occurrence of CO_2 price trigger events (set at $7 and $10/tonne CO_2) • possibility of extensions to compliance period • allowance retirement for early voluntary renewable energy purchases • banking, but no borrowing
Point of Regulation	• point of emission for industrial sources • first jurisdictional deliverer for electricity • point of distribution for transportation and residential fuel combustion	• point of emission for industrial sources and industrial combustion • first jurisdictional deliverer for electricity • point of distribution for transportation and residential fuel combustion	• as per U.S. EPA requirements in 40 CFR Part 75, Acid Rain Program, etc.
Measurement, Monitoring and Reporting Mechanisms	• mandatory measurement and monitoring; reporting to the initiative every two years beginning in 2011; reporting threshold of 10,000 Mt	• to be announced; it is being modeled after the WCI system	• U.S. EPA 40 CFR Part 75-based monitoring and measurement
Current Status	• all measures at final recommendation stage	• information here was reviewed by the GHG Advisory Group in November 2008; draft model rule to be tabled in Aug 2009.	• a second auction of CO_2 emissions allowances took place in late December 2008
Business Implications	• because it is economy-wide, will have significant economic effect beyond sectors subject to emissions caps • subject to federal and state/provincial law; as the governments' position on GHG reduction is not yet established, this is a significant source of uncertainty	• not yet as advanced as the WCI, leaving greater uncertainty • subject to federal and state/provincial law; as the governments' position on GHG reduction is not yet established, this is a significant source of uncertainty	• of limited applicability, i.e., electricity generation sector

Adapted from Kapoor and Ambrosi, 2008

How Big Is It?

Table 7.3 illustrates the volume and value of GHG transactions on the largest markets in the world from 2006 to 2008. In-depth analyses were not available for some 2008 data at the time of publication.

Table 7.3: Carbon Transaction Volumes and Values 2006 to 2008 (* = estimated)

Adapted from Hamilton et al., 2008 and New Carbon Finance, 2009

Markets	Volume (MtCO₂e)			Value (US$ million)		
	2006	2007	2008	2006	2007	2008
EU ETS	1,044	2,061	unavailable	24,436	50,097	94,276
Primary CDM (CERs)	537	551	381	5,804	7,426	5,883
Secondary CDM (CERs)	25	240	unavailable	445	5,451	14,083*
Joint Implementation (ERUs)	16	41	unavailable	141	499	2,237*
New South Wales	20	25	unavailable	225	224	269
Total Regulated Markets	1,642	2,918	unavailable	31,051	63,697	116,748
Voluntary OTC market	14	42	unavailable	59	258	unavailable
Chicago Climate Exchange	10	23	unavailable	38	72	316
Total—Voluntary Markets	25	65	unavailable	97	331	499*
Total—Global Market	1,667	2,983	4,000 (approx.)	31,148	64,028	117,563

The data indicate the following:

- relative importance of the regulated markets, when compared to the voluntary
- domination of the global market for GHG emissions credits by the EU ETS (the volumes strongly reflect constraints placed on the fossil fuel-fired energy industry there)
- significance of trades between developed and developing economies through the Clean Development Mechanism
- growth in volumes and value of the regulated market, particularly the EU ETS, the secondary CDM and the JI markets
- relative importance of the over-the-counter (OTC) trade in GHG offsets, when compared to those made through the Chicago Climate Exchange, in 2006 and 2007

The total global value of carbon trading in 2008 exceeded US$115 billion.

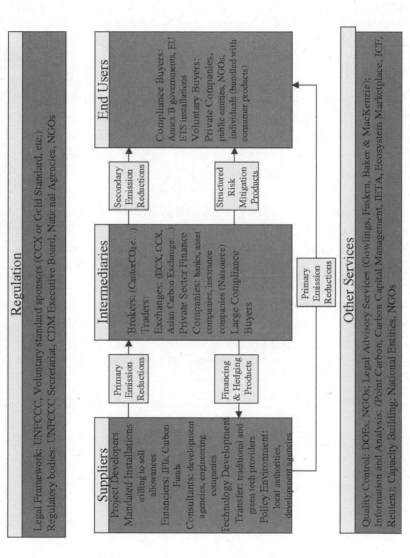

Figure 7.4: Players and Institutions in the Carbon Market

Regulation

Legal Framework: UNFCCC, Voluntary standard sponsors (CCX or Gold Standard, etc.)
Regulatory bodies: UNFCCC Secretariat, CDM Executive Board, National Agencies, NGOs

Suppliers

Project Developers
Mandated Installations
willing to sell
allowances
Financiers: IFIs, Carbon
Funds
Consultants: development
agencies, engineering
companies
Technology Development
Transfer: traditional and
green tech providers
Policy Environment:
local authorities,
development agencies

Intermediaries

Brokers: (CantorCO₂e . .)
Traders:
Exchanges: (ECX, CCX,
Asian Carbon Exchange.)
Private Sector Finance
Companies: banks, asset
companies, insurance
companies (Natsource)
Large Compliance
Buyers

End Users

Compliance Buyers:
Annex B governments, EU
ETS installations
Voluntary Buyers:
Private Companies,
public entities, NGOs,
individuals (bundled with
consumer products)

Primary Emission Reductions

Secondary Emission Reductions

Financing & Hedging Products

Structured Risk Mitigation Products

Primary Emission Reductions

Other Services

Quality Control: DOEs, NGOs; Legal Advisory Services (Gowlings, Fasken, Baker & MacKenzie);
Information and Analysis: (Point Carbon, Carbon Capital Management, IETA, Ecosystem Marketplace, ICF,
Reuters); Capacity Building: National Entities, NGOs

The Voluntary Carbon Market (VCM)

The VCM includes participants not covered by national GHG allocations or as-yet unaffected industrial sectors, either because they anticipate eventually being affected by regulation and want to achieve early gains, or they want to improve their corporate green image. This market started out much smaller than the regulatory markets, but has grown significantly. It is composed of the following:

- trades made through the Chicago Climate Exchange (CCX), a voluntary cap-and-trade scheme with members making voluntary but legally binding commitments to meet specified annual emissions reduction targets; holders of surpluses can trade with those seeking allowances to comply
- a larger volume of trades made through a fragmented OTC market, not driven by emissions caps

Buyers may purchase Verified Emission Reductions (VERs), of which there is a growing variety, subject to a proliferation of standards. The standards aim to achieve specific criteria sought by the marketplace, such as SD gains.

The OTC trade accounted for 42.1 million tonnes CO_2e in 2007, compared to 22.9 million tonnes CO_2e through the CCX, representing a tripling of volume over 2006 in the OTC trade and a doubling of CCX trade (table 7.3). Predictions for continued growth for 2008 and beyond in the VCM appear to be borne out by early results on 2008 market value. Volumes are predicted to reach 340 $MtCO_2$e by 2010 and almost 1,400 $MtCO_2$e by 2020. However, when taking future U.S. regulation into consideration, this could be an overestimate as growth is expected to level off after 2012.[24]

Price of Carbon

The various forces pushing and pulling on the price of carbon (or the price of a tonne of carbon dioxide equivalent) are summarized in table 7.4.

Table 7.4: Factors Affecting the Price of Carbon

Bullish Signals	Bearish Signals
Colder-than-expected winters; warmer-than-expected summers	Warmer-than-expected winters; colder-than-expected summers
Widening spark and dark spreads (especially in Germany and UK baseload) due to either rising gas/oil prices or rising electricity demand	Thinning of spark/dark spreads, or lower gas/oil prices
Tightening of supply of European Emission Allowances from NAPs	Relaxation of emissions controls from governments
Tightening of supply of carbon credits via Linking Directive	Loosening of restrictions on use of Kyoto credits for ETS compliance
Heightened political commitment to cutting GHGs after 2012	Softening of political will to extend Kyoto or relaxed efforts to cut GHG emissions
U.S. support for domestic GHG emissions restrictions and cap-and-trade legislation	Distancing of U.S. from Kyoto, GHG emissions control and market-based GHG legislation

Labatt & White, 2007

In the regulated market of the European Union, it is forecast that prices will increase towards €38/tonne by 2012, owing principally to insufficient liquidity in the market because of delays in issuance of Certified Emission Reductions from CDM projects and constraints in the supply of natural gas.[25]

The volume weighted price of credits transacted in the OTC offset market in 2007 ranged from $4.1/tCO$_2$e to $6.1/tCO$_2$e. On the CCX, the (weighted) average price was nearly half the OTC figure at $3.15/tCO$_2$e.

The prices of credits vary based upon the type of project. Projects involving afforestation/reforestation were some of the highest priced project types in 2006 and 2007, with weighted average prices of $6.80 to $8.20/ tCO$_2$e. Methane projects also continue to be valued highly, with weighted average prices in 2007 of around $6/ tCO$_2$e, as do renewable energy projects with prices of around $7–$8/ tCO$_2$e. The lowest priced credits originated from geological sequestration ($2.50/ tCO$_2$e).

Credit Supply and Demand in EU

While by far the largest regulatory emissions market is the European Union—with EU allowances accounting for 2 billion tonnes of emissions worth more than US$94 billion in 2008—other regulatory markets exist or are in the process of being established in Canada, Japan and New Zealand as well as the regional markets in North America described earlier. It is worth noting that emissions credited in the developing world represented 791 million tonnes in 2007 (see table 7.3).

The 2006 data from the EU ETS show that total actual CO_2 emissions from the twenty-five participating countries were slightly less (2%) than the total amount of (free) allocated emissions allocated to each of the countries at the outset of the year. In 2007, this gap between allocated emissions and actual emissions diminished to 0.4%, or 7.5 million tonnes CO_2 for the 11,300 installations included in the trading scheme at that time. Total CO_2 emissions in the EU climbed slightly in 2007, as the carbon market collapsed at one point, with the value of an allowance close to zero euro. Approximately 2,050 million allowances (2,050 tonnes CO_2) were allocated for free by all participating countries in each of 2006 and 2007.

Countries running the largest allocation deficits (emitting more than their allocations) in 2006 and 2007 were the UK, Italy and Spain. Countries with the largest allocation surpluses were Poland, France and Germany. Industrial sectors with the two highest allocation surpluses were iron and steel and oil and gas refining. Combustion (power generation) was the sector running the largest allocation deficit.

It is expected that the European coal-fired electricity generation sector will be hard hit by emissions allowance allocations in the EU after 2012, as power utilities will have to bid in auctions for them instead of receiving them free as they did from 2005. Companies in other sectors will continue to receive their permits free while auctioning is phased in. The EU's plans have stimulated more companies to examine carbon capture and sequestration.

> Morgan Stanley has said that EU companies with large numbers of coal-fired stations would suffer "a large decrease in post-2012 earnings" as the result of the ETS program.

Is It All Worth It?

It should be stated that despite the international consensus behind the work of the UNFCCC and the authority of the Kyoto Protocol, and the ensuing trading schemes that form part of national climate change policies in participating countries, there is an active and vocal opposition to the principle of emissions trading. This opposition argues that emissions trading is essentially ineffective, when compared to command and control regulation and direct forms of emissions control, and that it has implications for social inequity, especially in developing economies. In *Climate Fraud and Carbon Colonialism: The New Trade in Greenhouse*

Gases, the deficiency of trading schemes is described by author H. Bachram as follows: "By its very nature, an emissions credit entitles its owner to dump a certain amount of greenhouse gases into the atmosphere. Control of such credits effectively leads to control of how the atmosphere, perhaps the last global commons, is used. The Kyoto Protocol negotiations have not only created a property rights regime for the atmosphere. It has also awarded a controlling stake to the world's worst polluters, such as the European Union, by allocating credits based on historical emissions."[26]

Data from the EU ETS GHG verified allowance retirement registries for 2006 and 2007 show net GHG emissions increases of 0.3% and 0.68%, respectively. When viewed in comparison to average GDP growth of 3% and 2.8% in the EU during these two years, emissions seem at least to have been decoupled from economic growth. However, these data suggest that absolute reductions have yet to be achieved, thereby lending some legitimacy to the arguments against the use of emissions trading to mitigate climate change. There is also, without doubt, some legitimacy to claims that offset projects in developing countries have undesirable environmental and social side effects, in the same way that international aid programs can be misguided.

Businesses should be aware of these facts and, wherever possible, scrutinize the trade mechanisms at work on their behalf and lobby for environmental effectiveness and social justice in the trading processes.

THE FUTURE OF TRADING

An industry perspective on the future of trading was provided in late 2008 by Henry Derwent, chief executive of the International Emissions Trading Association (IETA), while commenting on the Australian government's green paper on a proposed emissions trading framework: "The issue of the future is not going to be 'why add costs to your exports?,' but 'don't expect exports without carbon pricing to get in free.'...Carbon pricing is meant to be a cold bath—a shock to the economic system. Not such as to induce heart failure, so it must be eased in to some degree. But when the complaints really start flying, the government—and those who can see that a low-carbon revolution offers as many opportunities as the digital revolution—must keep its nerve, because all the alternatives, including making sure the price is so low that it has no real effect for many years, are worse."

Further Development and Expansion of GHG Market Mechanisms

The World Business Council on Sustainable Development believes that international GHG markets will continue to play a role in a revised framework, directing energy investment capital in favor of low- and zero-GHG emissions projects. The market will be used to provide an outlet for project reduction units and link together national and international sector programs.

Such national and sector programs need not be based exclusively on emissions trading. GHG emissions can be decreased through programs to promote energy efficiency, more use of renewables, the expansion of nuclear energy, performance targets, offsets, carbon taxes, regulation or technology funds. To introduce additional flexibility in achieving national or sector objectives, these programs could link to international emissions trading markets provided they meet certain criteria for entry.[27]

The commitment period for the Kyoto Protocol ends in 2012. The post-2012 period is increasingly on the minds of the community currently involved in emissions trading, as there is an absence of clear price signals, owing to uncertainty over international consensus on a global emissions trading scheme. At the time of writing, there was clearly a need for an integrated carbon market.

As noted earlier, there were suggestions in early 2008 that the U.S. carbon trading market will be worth $1 trillion by 2020 under a domestic trades-only scenario, with carbon prices ranging around US$40/tonne as early as 2015.[28] This speculation was supported by all of the proposed bills before the U.S. Congress (although the most significant of these, Lieberman-Warner, has since been defeated). There is a consensus that restricting trades to the confines of the U.S., and eliminating access to a significant source of inexpensive credits from outside, would push carbon prices upward. It would also adversely impact the offsets market and the economies of developing countries.

The U.S. Climate Action Partnership (USCAP), composed of many of America's largest industrial corporations (e.g., Alcoa, Dow Chemical, DuPont, General Electric, General Motors) and prominent NGOs (e.g., Pew Center on Global Climate Change, Natural Resources Defense Council, World Resources Institute), has since contradicted this view, advocating linkages from an eventual U.S. trading scheme to other trading schemes internationally.[29]

In the short term, the obvious growth in carbon trading is expected to continue despite the uncertain economic climate, with some projections of global market value to be in the order of US$150 billion by the end of 2009.

Future of the Voluntary Carbon Market

The Voluntary Carbon Market is expected to continue to grow at a rapid pace. The CCX was expected to reach 80 $MtCO_2e$ traded in 2008 and growth in the OTC market was expected to exceed its 2007 growth rate. With more and more companies establishing offset strategies and preparing for inevitable carbon legislation in countries where federal legislation does not yet exist, traded volumes in 2008 were expected to exceed the 150 $MtCO_2e$ level. Although 2008 volume data were unavailable at the time of publication, estimated value of the VCM was US$499 million. In parallel with increased transactions, key stakeholders are expected to continue to build market infrastructure, such as standards and registries. In 2008, suppliers' top choices were the Voluntary Carbon Standard, the Gold Standard, the VER+, and the Climate, Community, and Biodiversity (CCB) Standards.

CHAPTER 7 TAKE-AWAYS

New trade commodity—Just as the price of a barrel of oil is transforming the world economy, the effect of the price of a tonne of CO_2 will prove to be just as profound. Both work to stimulate low-carbon economies and technologies at the expense of fossil-fuel use. While businesses could not afford to ignore the warning signs of this transformation just a few years ago, they are living its effects now. Fortunately, the path to competitive positioning in the carbon-constrained economy has become clearer because of the initiatives of pioneers in several industrial sectors (refer to chapter 6). In parallel, market mechanisms for global trade in a new commodity—GHG emissions—have taken shape, following the precedent set by the Kyoto Protocol.

Emissions trading—Emissions trading is a market-based form of pollution control and has become an essential part of the global fight to mitigate climate change. While an international framework such as the Kyoto Protocol and legislative action by governments are necessary for it to function optimally, it is strongly advocated by business as it allows GHG emissions to be reduced at optimal cost across national boundaries and industrial sectors.

Status of emissions trading in Europe and North America—The European Community's Emission Trading Scheme has been operational since 2005 and is the largest emissions trading scheme in the world. In North America, regional initiatives such as the Western Climate Initiative, the Regional Greenhouse Gas

Initiative and the Midwestern Greenhouse Gas Reduction Accord have moved faster than federal or state/provincial governments in designing and implementing emissions trading schemes, with the intent of guiding government policy. However, these are still subject to government approval or modification and as such, they cannot yet provide the regulatory certainty needed by business. While the final impact of regulations and emissions trading schemes in Canada and the U.S. are not expected for at least another two years, voluntary trades have been underway for some time. The domestic offsets market in Canada is expected to emerge in late 2009.

Business strategy—A specific business's position vis-à-vis emissions trading is a function of exposure to carbon risk and opportunity. While a company's climate policies will be affected by stakeholder expectations and standards for social responsibility, it must treat climate change as a business problem and not solely as a corporate social responsibility issue. "The effects of climate on company operations are now so tangible and certain that the issue is best addressed with the tools of the strategist, not the philanthropist."[30] Companies in regulated industrial sectors, such as energy, mining, metallurgy, chemical, and oil and gas, already know this, and emissions trading is just one of the tools at their disposal to mitigate, or capitalize on, the cost of carbon.

Extent of CO_2 cost impact—The actions of any jurisdiction or grouping of jurisdictions with capped emissions, such as those participating in regional GHG emissions control initiatives, will have significant economic effect beyond the sectors subject to these caps. Every business that purchases products and services from capped sectors will incur additional costs.

Government role—Regulated industries are already within the scope of reporting obligations in Canada (e.g., large final emitters) and as such are lobbying. And reporting obligations are on the radar in the U.S. under the December 2007 House Appropriations Bill, for which the U.S. federal government will proceed with regulations for mandatory reporting of GHG emissions above appropriate thresholds in all sectors of the U.S. economy.[31] The regulations are expected to be final in mid-2009. If the regional schemes proceed, industries in the states and provinces participating in the Western Climate Initiative face mandatory reporting of 2020 GHG emissions in 2011, subject to legal adoption by each jurisdiction.

Opportunities outside of regulated sectors—Non-regulated industries should interpret the intent of the federal or state/provincial governments for GHG emissions regulation in order to anticipate when they may be impacted by a lowering of the regulatory limit for (a) reporting and (b) meeting reduction targets. If there are no anticipated compliance issues, they can consider the possibility of offering GHG offsets to a trading regime, by reviewing the potential to generate offsets from projects or improvements to operations, nationally and internationally, and checking

- the current and future price of CO_2
- under which trading regimes these would be recognized (as these may not be the same for Kyoto Annex I countries (e.g., Canada) or other (e.g., U.S.)
- eligibility criteria.

NOTES

1 John E. Thornes and Samuel Randalls, "Commodifying the Atmosphere: 'Pennies from Heaven'?" *Geogr. Ann.,* 89 A (4),. 2007, 273–285.

2 New Carbon Finance, "Economic Researchers Predict $1 Trillion US Carbon Trading Market by 2020," February 2008, http://www.newcarbonfinance.com.

3 Per-Anders Enkvist, T. Nauclér and J. Rosander, "A Cost Curve for Greenhouse Gas Reduction," *McKinsey Quarterly,* no. 1, 2007.

4 International Strategy for Disaster Reduction, "Disaster Risk and Climate Change," 2008, http://www.unisdr.org/eng/risk-reduction/climate-change/climate-change.html.

5 World Health Organization, "Climate and Health," 2008.

6 Nicholas Stern, *The Economics of Climate Change: The Stern Review* (Cambridge: Cambridge University Press, 2007).

7 W.A. Kurz et al., "Mountain Pine Beetle and Forest Carbon Feedback to Climate Change," *Nature,* vol. 452, 2008, 987–990.

8 UNEP/GRID-Arendal, "Arctic Sea Ice Minimum Extent in September 1982 and 2008," 2008, http://maps.grida.no/go/graphic/arctic-sea-ice-minimum-extent-in-september-1982-and-2008.

9 NASA, "Arctic Sea Ice News and Analysis. National Snow and Ice Data Centre," 2008, http://nsidc.org/arcticseaicenews.

10 Ceres, "Investors Achieve Major Company Commitments on Climate Change," August 20, 2008, http://www.ceres.org/NETCOMMUNITY/Page.aspx?pid=928&srcid=705.

11 Michael Porter and Forest L. Reinhardt, "A Strategic Approach to Climate," *Harvard Business Review,* October 2007.

12 Jonathan Lash and Fred Wellington, "Competitive Advantage on a Warming Planet," *Harvard Business Review on Green Business Strategy,* 2007, 125–148.

13 World Business Council for Sustainable Development, "Establishing a Global Carbon Market—A Discussion on Linking Various Approaches to Create a Global Market," 2008.

14 New Carbon Finance, "Fundamentals Point to Higher Carbon Prices," May 23, 2008, http://www.newcarbonfinance.com.

15 McKinsey and Company, "The Carbon Productivity Challenge: Curbing Climate Change and Sustaining Economic Growth," *Perspective,* 2008.

16 T.H. Tietenberg, *Emissions Trading: Principles and Practice,* 2nd ed., (Washington: RFF Press, 2006).

17 Julia Reinaud and Cédric Philibert, "Emissions Trading: Trends and Prospects," Organization for Economic Cooperation and Development and International Energy Agency, 2007.

18 UNCTAD, 2003 UNEP, UCCE and UNCTAD, "A Guide to Emissions Trading," 2002.

19 UNFCCC, Kyoto Protocol. http://unfccc.int/kyoto_protocol/items/2830.php.

20 Ibid.

21 Enkvist, Nauclér and Rosander, "A Cost Curve for Greenhouse Gas Reduction."

22 O. Lomas, "Climate Change and Emissions Trading—A European Perspective," presentation given on behalf of Allen & Overy, at the International Environmental Lawyers Network Conference entitled "Current Environmental Issues: An International Perspective," 2008.

23 Skip Willis, Eighth Annual Workshop on Greenhouse Gas Emissions Trading, Country Roundtable: Canada, Carbon Capital Management, 2008.

24 Katherine Hamilton et al., "Forging a Frontier: Fate of the Voluntary Carbon Markets 2008," *New Carbon Finance and Ecosystem Marketplace*, July 18, 2008.

25 New Carbon Finance, "Fundamentals Point to Higher Carbon Prices."

26 Heidi Bachram, "Climate Fraud and Carbon Colonialism: The New Trade in Greenhouse Gases," *Capitalism Nature Socialism*, V. 15, no. 4, 2004.

27 World Business Council for Sustainable Development, "Establishing a Global Carbon Market."

28 New Carbon Finance, "Economic Researchers Predict $1 Trillion US," 5.

29 Leora Falk, "Business Partnership Offers Guidelines for International Emissions Reductions," United States Climate Action Partnership, July 23, 2008, http://www.us-cap.org.

30 Porter and Reinhardt, "A Strategic Approach to Climate."

31 Beverage & Diamond, P.C., "Mandatory U.S. Carbon Reporting Announced," 2008, http://www.bdlaw.com/news-271.html.

CHAPTER EIGHT

MANAGING HUMAN RESOURCES TO NURTURE A CULTURE OF INNOVATION

An issue that can make or break a company's strategy for embedding environmental issues in its plans, operations and supply chain is the "people factor." How will companies find the talent needed to spur innovation and to address, manage and implement strategies that respond to the complexities of growing energy demand, climate change, resource depletion, elimination of hazardous chemicals in products, etc.? Attracting and retaining qualified personnel is already a significant challenge for most corporations because of the changing demographics of the developed economies, highlighted by declining birth rates, strong cultural and linguistic barriers to freer global mobility among workers and the growing influence of members of Generation Y working alongside graying baby boomers, whose substantial contributions to growth of the modern corporation will soon disappear. A key ingredient to overcoming the challenge, and to gauging a company's potential for achieving a competitive edge in the market for human capital, appears to be its environmental position, i.e., whether it is a leader or a latecomer to the green rush, as today's talent is strongly attracted by strong environmental values.

Human capital is the key resource issue of the coming decades and its recruitment, its development, its deployment and its retention all determine a company's potential. Unfortunately, most companies, large and small, are often ill-equipped to effectively manage talent. The reality is that it is a seller's market.

Key strategic challenges for the corporate human resources function today include[1]

- greater integration with core business functions—this need stems from HR's perceived status as tactical, lacking influence and not sufficiently analytical

- better management of "demographic risk"—a term used to describe the challenges posed by employee population dynamics, i.e., the pool of available talent in North American companies is currently split between a senior group and a junior group, and the latter is now more mobile, more informed and arguably more fickle than in the past; these characteristics pose challenges for recruitment and retention
- leadership development—must handle environmental and social issues in an increasingly complex world, and engage with different communities outside of the organization, as well as those internal to it
- talent management—must ensure that recruitment, development and talent retention activities are aligned with business strategy, and that performance against these criteria is measured and rewarded
- maintaining a learning organization—by understanding the learning needs of different employee groups and implementing a strategy to meet these effectively; conventional training programs can only provide a small piece of the puzzle

In this chapter, innovation in business related to environmental issues is discussed within the context of HR management in order to highlight the risks and opportunities which it presents, as well as best practices observed. A business summary of 3M activities, which highlights best practices in addressing employee diversity, retention strategies and nurturing a culture of innovation, is presented at the end of this chapter.

A FRAMEWORK FOR DISCUSSION

In the recent book entitled *The Necessary Revolution*,[2] three learning characteristics are identified that allow companies to be innovative in their efforts to achieve sustainable development: seeing systems, collaborating across boundaries, and creating desired outcomes. These three elements of learning provide an interesting lens through which examples of innovation can be reviewed, particularly from the angle of human resource management, i.e., building a value system, talent recruitment, satisfying the needs of the work environment, talent retention and stimulation, etc.

1. **Seeing systems**—Leaders need to look beyond the normal management framework in which their businesses function, owing to the growing interdependencies between businesses and their various stakeholders, and the environmental and social impacts of their operations. As the limits

of earth's capacity to provide the finite resources needed for growth or to regenerate those resources are reached, it becomes obvious that these "externalities" have become limiting factors to business. The challenge is to discover creative methods of instilling this viewpoint within the organization.

2. **Collaborating across boundaries**—Once it is understood that systems extend beyond the organization, how do organizations learn to work with these outside entities? This is a formidable challenge, as collaboration requires the formation of partnerships of individuals and groups that are otherwise adversaries or competitors in many cases. Hence, a key skill set to nurture within organizations are those that can be used to engage stakeholders and build partnerships. Sometimes called "open market innovation," this collaboration must be effected through teams, networks and associations. Multinational companies such as Coco-Cola, GE, DuPont and Nike, for example, have found collaboration with the NGO world to be indispensable, both for the input of ideas and understanding the needs of other stakeholders, but also for mitigating risks to corporate reputation. The scale and growing importance of this element is illustrated by the growth in the number of NGOs as civil society evolves around causes; current estimates range around three hundred thousand NGOs worldwide, up from forty-four thousand ten years ago.

3. **Creating desired outcomes**—The third characteristic is the need to envision desired outcomes or future states, as distinct from reacting to, and correcting, present problems. This is consistent with methods used by organizations such as The Natural Step in building action plans for sustainability, where it is essential to "backcast" from a vision of a future condition to set short- and medium-term objectives today. A key ingredient in creating desired outcomes is visioning from a systemic perspective, so that seemingly diverse elements of a problem such as environmental sustainability (which encompasses an array of issues from air and water contamination, to energy choices, to wealth distribution) are, in fact, interconnected.

EVOLUTION OF THE TALENT PROBLEM

It is perhaps useful to understand how the current challenges to human capital management (HCM, previously known as human resources or personnel) in companies came to be. The successes and failures of HCM have paralleled those of the modern corporation, given that fundamentally, the function is there to support business in its quest to be profitable. Table 8.1 summarizes some of the key milestones in talent management in the past fifty years, while figure 8.1 illustrates its impact on perceived value within the company.

Table 8.1: Evolution of Corporate Talent Management

Period	Phenomenon	Reason
1950s–1960s	• internal development, executive coaching, 360-degree feedback, etc.	• limits to internal growth not yet reached
1970s	• dormancy of talent management	• economic downturn and outdated assumptions of growth
1980s	• white-collar layoffs • demise of lifetime employment • dismantling of talent management hierarchy	• recession and corporate restructuring
Early 1990s	• outside hiring	• large pool of laid-off talent
Late 1990s	• stealing talent from competitors • further reduction in talent development • end of outside hiring • aggravated retention problems	• economic growth • cost savings of theft versus talent development (cheaper to steal than to develop) • prohibitive cost of headhunters • headhunted newcomers blocking ascension of internal talent
Current	• little talent management activity	• unstable, highly competitive business environment, with rapid changes in customer demands • absence of talent pipelines because of earlier erosion • 10% executive turnover rate • scrutiny on costs

Adapted from Capelli, 2008

Most companies are currently looking for a workable solution, in the absence of tried-and-true ones, as the old models are not applicable today. Some writers are proposing talent management approaches based on supply chain management principles, i.e., just-in-time = talent-on-demand, whereby demand forecasts for products are matched by forecasts for personnel. This means that companies retain less talent than they perhaps need and make up the difference by hiring from outside (the costs of recruiting being less than the costs of retention). It also implies that uncertainty in demand for human resources (reflecting uncertainty in demand for company product) can be managed by shortening training and development programs, and sharing talent pools with other units of the company.

Figure 8.1: Human Capital Management Value Triangle

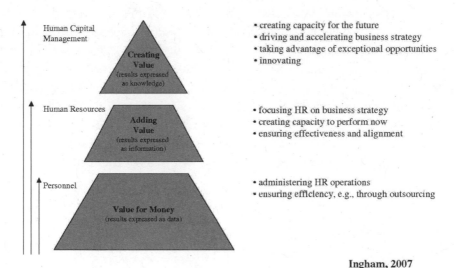

Human Capital Management

Creating Value
(results expressed as knowledge)

- creating capacity for the future
- driving and accelerating business strategy
- taking advantage of exceptional opportunities
- innovating

Human Resources

Adding Value
(results expressed as information)

- focusing HR on business strategy
- creating capacity to perform now
- ensuring effectiveness and alignment

Personnel

Value for Money
(results expressed as data)

- administering HR operations
- ensuring efficiency, e.g., through outsourcing

Ingham, 2007

Another concern, given the uncertainty in the contemporary business environment, is keeping a lid on talent development costs, as the turnover rate is high. Some firms are inviting employees to share the costs of development, as they may represent vital opportunities to the individual's career development within or outside of the company. Similarly, companies are retaining links to ex-employees, as they represent investments already made in individuals who can still contribute much.

Finally, perhaps the key element in talent management is recognition that the responsibility for where talent goes is shared between employer and employee. Companies have an interest in providing opportunities, but not at any cost. And in a seller's market, employees will go where their personal values are best served.

It should be noted that the above discussion on costs is incomplete, in that it does not take into account the value of intangible benefits that are realized through successful talent development, as suggested by the top of the triangle in figure 8.1. There is a growing body of literature that indicates companies have a greater capacity to innovate when environmental sustainability is embedded within a company's culture.

What can companies do to have the talent on hand when they need it? One idea is to ensure employee access to all of the space within the four walls, by looking to recruit inward. Dow Chemical, for example, halved its turnover rate by putting positions on internal job boards that would otherwise have been advertised externally.

Another idea, particularly related to environmental sustainability, is to understand today's definition of "meaningful work." As is noted further below in the discussion on Generation Y, civilization's contemporary challenges are not lost on most people, especially not on highly educated performers. People seek to have coherence between their personal and work lives, especially in terms of values and beliefs, and they naturally aspire to situations that provide continuity between the two. Companies that invest in environmental issues are looking after their own interests, by providing an environment where the most talented will thrive. Tim Brown, the CEO of IDEO (an innovation and design firm) best summarized this in the following statement: "People want to work on things they believe in."[3]

> Tomorrow's company will need to take innovation to the next level, by expanding its boundaries and working with more outside stakeholders. It will rely on human capital management functions to enable this change.

SUSTAINABILITY AND HUMAN CAPITAL MANAGEMENT

Implementing environmental sustainability initiatives in companies is about visioning, brand enhancement and protection of reputation, attracting and developing talent, raising awareness, learning new concepts and changing behavior to prevent environmental impact—all of which rely on human capital management, or HR processes.

How can typical HR processes support the deployment of an environmental sustainability vision within an organization? Table 8.2 summarizes the results of two different studies:

1. Research conducted on three industrial companies implementing sustainability: a government-owned electric utility, a publicly held metal manufacturer and a diversified science company. Grossly simplified, the research aimed at understanding what sustainability meant to different players within the companies, and the potential role for HR.
2. Survey of nine prominent multinationals with well-known sustainability profiles, probing where HR facilitated sustainability in the corporations at three different levels.

In the first study, one of the surveyed companies' HR representatives offered the following comment in reference to new skill sets that need to be built, given the challenges posed by environmental degradation: "Over a twenty-year time frame, you can build whatever core competencies you want. If food, water and energy are going to be the things that are really important to the planet [twenty] years from now, and people are going to be looking to companies to help us out of the bind that we are getting ourselves into, why couldn't we play a big role there?"

Table 8.2: Sustainability and Implications for Human Resource Processes

Key HR Processes	HR Process Roles as They Relate to Sustainability
Organizational Effectiveness/Change Management	• participate in strategy development • drive dialogue on sustainability among senior executives and levels of managers to build consensus on what sustainability means to the organization • develop the communication/enrollment processes to develop linkages between functional work of all divisions and sustainability • inculcate values
Strategic Human Resource Planning	• focus HR strategy content to support business directions influenced by sustainability initiative • provide leadership development opportunities • align human and organizational capital to the sustainability vision and the business strategies • develop HR staffing plans to support divestiture and acquisition of new businesses
Talent Management/ Staffing	• integrate sustainability intent and objectives into recruitment and selection processes to seek fit and build commitment in new hires • identify critical talent/job groups to support current sustainability intent objectives • build pool of human capital (knowledge, skills) toward sustainability-framed strategies to help create new business opportunities from the inside out
Training and Development	• develop leadership capacity toward sustainability alignment objectives—"role of leaders" • infuse development processes (mentoring, career development) with sustainability intent to give context to future capability building • focus skill-building to support sustainability-framed business objectives

Adapted from Colbert and Kurucz, 2007 and Wirtenberg, Harmon and Fairfield, 2007

Successful application of the HR processes described in table 8.2 leads to the question of the types of competencies that would be sought in individuals to carry a sustainability vision forward in their work. Table 8.3 provides a set of personnel characteristics developed from the experience of embedding sustainability within a global aluminum company.[4]

TYPES OF WORKERS

"Y": A Challenging Generation for HR

The tail end of Generation Y, individuals born between 1970 and the late 1990s, will soon be entering the workplace. They currently represent 12% of the U.S. workforce.[5] They have already transformed it profoundly through (and pardon the stereotypes) their ease with technology, their quest for a balanced lifestyle and flexibility in work arrangements, a hunger for stimulating work and less emphasis on the company loyalty standards set by their predecessors. This distinctive behavior has naturally created workplace challenges. It is a preoccupation for HR professionals and employers to grapple with the whims of Generation Y.

So what does Generation Y want? Everything and right away. Members of Generation Y pose a conundrum for the Baby Boom Generation and the intervening generations because they are indifferent to the values presented to them. They are in search of themselves and they value authority, hierarchy, security and performance differently.

What is important about Generation Y, for present purposes, is that it represents the young adults who are taking control of the economies of developed countries and whose foibles and eccentricities must be engaged, if not indulged, to ensure a smooth transition. A distinguishing feature of Generation Y is the premium it places on the environmental and social ethics of employers, so much so that it has become a key ingredient in talent recruitment and retention. As noted above, companies that can demonstrate action in support of espoused principles such as sustainability, and provide the time for their employees to contribute to these programs, will have a competitive edge in recruiting.

The Knowledge Worker: Another Challenge

More than one-third of the 140 million workers in the U.S. are considered knowledge workers and it is the fastest-growing segment of the workforce. More important still is that they can be more profitable for employers and require less supervision. However, the profits that employers show in knowledge-intensive sectors are highly variable, suggesting that the key to effective management of this segment of the workforce is elusive. Knowledge workers like Generation Y need and expect a

Table 8.3: Human Resources Sustainability Competencies

APPROACH			
Systems Thinker	**Manages Complexity**	**Forward-looking**	**Informed**
Works along the full value chain, uses life cycle assessment, considers "cradle to cradle" issues related to products and processes	Works in both the short and long term simultaneously, deals with interests of multiple stakeholders, examines a broad set of interrelated issues	Develops scenarios, considers implications of emerging trends, in addition to direct linkages examines indirect, secondary connections	Is aware of issues on a broad geographic basis (global considerations) and on a breadth of topics

STYLE			
Entrepreneurial	**Innovative**	**Creative**	**Motivated**	**Good with Change**	**Risk Taking**
Is accustomed to working in areas that are not typically well defined, creates new options, seeks alternative methods	Considers nontraditional issues, explores atypical or uncommon connections between ideas as well as with different people and roles	Tries different approaches (not tied to only using existing practice), uses imagination, is resourceful	Has personal conviction that there is a broad range of possible value, tangible (financial) and intangible, for both the company and for others; has desire to contribute to society while succeeding in the company	Supports exploring new approaches, questions current practice, seeks improvement on an ongoing basis	Is prepared to challenge accepted practice, questions assumptions, tries new approaches

METHOD			
Networker	**Teamworker**	**Collaborative**
Fosters a diverse network, contributes to and draws benefit from internal and external colleagues and partners	Engages with others to accomplish own tasks and also supports efforts of others	Places priority on sharing information and expertise, leverages capabilities of others, aligns interests to achieve mutual benefit

VALUES			
Ethical	**Accountable**	**Has Integrity**
Appreciates inequities inherent in society and strives to achieve exemplary conduct in all aspects of work and life	Recognizes value of transparency in determining performance, delivering on stated commitments and clearly accepting responsibility	Understands the importance of reputation and trust for the individual and the organization, strives for truthful and balanced conduct and representation in all activities

Nielsen, 2006

lifelong learning experience in the workplace well past the age of fifty, which chal-lenges companies' HR and infrastructure capacities.

The Green Worker: In Demand

From the environmental regulatory agenda of federal, state and provincial gov-ernments to boardroom discussions on sustainability or CSR, many drivers are forcing companies to seek expertise to help them manage environmental issues. Examples of areas that require skilled personnel and managers include

Classic positions:
- environmental management systems (EMSs)
- facility level monitoring and reporting programs (air emissions, wastewa-ter discharges, waste generation, recycling, etc.)
- pollution control equipment (air, wastewater and waste streams)
- site assessment and decommissioning
- spill prevention, response and cleanup
- life cycle assessment
- toxicology related to chemicals present in products and released into the environment
- SD programs, including CSR
- energy conservation programs
- site inspections and audits (e.g., environmental compliance, EMS, energy conservation, CSR)
- information technology to manage environmental issues
- alterative energy—solar thermal, solar PV, wind systems, geo-exchange systems and hydrogen power systems
- energy storage—fuel cells and batteries
- water treatment/desalination

Newer positions (having emerged in last few years):
- alternative energy—concentrated solar power (CSP) systems and tidal power
- IT systems that integrate all aspects of environment with business proc-esses and systems
- product management with backgrounds in design for environment
- advanced testing of products for presence of elaborate hazardous ingre-dients

- GHG measurement, reporting and certification
- carbon sequestration systems
- carbon trading/offsets
- green/cleantech investment funds
- hybrid and electric vehicles
- biofuel technology (e.g., enzymes, crop yield) and production
- bioplastic technology and production
- innovative energy storage—ultra capacitors, methane batteries
- green buildings design and construction and LEED certification
- stakeholder engagement
- technology/equipment to adapt to climate change
- emergency/disaster response planning related to climate change

Most important are new or changing regulations, such as REACH (refer to appendix A for additional information), which produced a sudden demand for toxicologists and chemists for exporters to the European market. In the 1990s, a similar phenomenon was seen with the arrival of ISO standards, such as ISO 9001 quality management systems and 14001 EMS, which created a protracted demand for experts in the field, as tens of thousands of companies sought certification. The growth in demand for product life cycle assessment and design for the environment, as well as GHG auditing, are also governed by ISO standards, and require specialist expertise. Companies seeking expertise on emissions trading and adaptation to climate change have created thousands of new jobs in Europe and will drive job growth significantly in North America, once regulations are in place.

Fully 3% of the Canadian labor force, or five hundred thirty-three thousand workers, are considered "environmental."[6] The UN estimates that approximately 2.3 million people worldwide work in alternative energy. While these figures are impressive, the growth in demand will continue, contributing to an already significant recruiting challenge, placing a strain on companies' ability to manage requirements and seize growth opportunities, and forcing the curricula of educational institutions (universities need a minimum of five to seven years before being able to graduate experts in new fields).

HR PROCESSES ON THE SUPPLY CHAIN

As noted in chapter 5, with the growth of outsourced functions and extension of the supply chain to include numerous players and a variety of environmental requirements, chief procurement officers are looking beyond the existing tool set of design specifications, environmental policies, periodic sampling of supplied product and auditing of suppliers to more proactive methods of engagement. Chief among these are knowledge sharing, training of buyers and suppliers, supplier capacity building and other techniques aimed at enhancing the supplier's knowledge of requirements and the management methods to ensure compliance to these requirements.

There is a growing disconnect between the standards set by western multinationals that their Asian suppliers are expected to meet and the reality that these suppliers face on the ground.[7] One representative of a U.S. apparel company relayed a comment on this issue by one of his Bangladeshi suppliers: "His sustainability strategy is to stop supplying to Western markets. Instead, he plans to sell to Indian and Chinese companies—where the demand is growing and where standards are less stringent."

Clearly, it is in the interests of companies to effectively engage their suppliers—to ensure closer alignment through HR functions such as partnering with suppliers, retailers and distributors to coordinate training/capacity building. This can provide fertile grounds for innovation.

An illustrative example of what may be possible is that of Unilever's black tea leaf suppliers in Kenya, who are largely small landowners. Their output is 40% lower than that of the larger estates, the reasons being poor husbandry practices, the high cost of farm inputs, low farmer morale and limited access to government field officers. To remedy the situation, Unilever worked with the Kenyan Tea Development Agency to establish farmer field schools, at which Unilever's sustainable tea guidelines were rolled out. The level of effort is substantial: five years of preparation, including the hiring of experienced trainers, with funding from the UK Department for International Development, followed by three-year deployment of the program. Results since establishment of the first field schools in 2006 are promising in terms of the potential for generating higher income.

In this instance, the capacity building successfully combined locally relevant initiatives and partners with the benefits of scale and reach. The example suggests that conventional supply chain management may not need new or additional tools beyond those that have already been described here and in chapter 5 to improve its environmental performance. The tools for gathering information and ensuring adaptability, agility and alignment—from supplier to customer—already exist.

Instead, the challenge is one of enabling a type of mindset and intelligence that works to transfer insights, learning and opportunities to create new value. Environmental risks and opportunities need to be identified and tracked. This typically involves linking up big-picture thinking (seeing systems), regularly undertaken at a corporate level, between the office of the CPO and the suppliers themselves to ensure that the correct criteria and triggers for discussion and innovation are in place. It often requires collaborative efforts to partner with suppliers in building capacity (collaborating across boundaries), driven by a collective business case.

> Ultimately, successful innovation is about satisfying people's needs—internal to the company, among stakeholders (including customers) and along the supply chain.

INNOVATE OR DIE

What is innovation? Peter Drucker's definition is "change that creates a new dimension of performance." He cites seven key sources of innovation,[8] four originating within the company and three outside:

1. The unexpected—unexpected successes or failures or external events
2. The incongruity—identification of a discrepancy between reality and what is generally assumed
3. Innovation based on process need—spotting weak links in processes
4. Changes in industry or market structure—opportunities arising from fundamental changes in markets or industries
5. Demographics—changes in population indicators, such as size, age or education levels
6. Changes in perception, mood and meaning—general changes in society's attitude and beliefs
7. New knowledge—important technological or other advances

This suggestion in the "do or die" proverb, that innovation is critical to corporate survival, based on one of Drucker's theorems, has been well documented in the literature. A survey of two hundred global senior executives conducted in 2002 (a time of global recession) rated innovation as one of the top three priorities for achieving company success. The survey also indicated that 91% believed that increasing their company's capacity for innovation was "critical to creating future competitive advantage and earning profits."[9]

Successful innovating companies are capable of seeing beyond the boundaries of their own organizations and recognizing the need to collaborate, particularly through their supply chain. Companies that collaborate with outsiders on their R&D reap a higher percentage of their total sales from new products than companies that don't collaborate.

The five conditions under which this type of "open market innovation" is a favorable option are[10]

1. High intensity of innovation (industries where new products are introduced with high frequency)
2. High economies of innovation (low capital requirements)
3. High need for cumulative innovations (when products are interdependent)
4. High applicability of innovations across companies or industries (there are many downstream potential beneficiaries of the innovation that do not pose competitive threats)
5. High market volatility

To this list can be added "distributed co-creation," a recent term in open innovation, which allows participants up and down the value chain to use the Web as a participatory platform for product development.[11] The most used example is software development, where firms such as IBM collaborate with online developers to develop some of their products using open source software. Wikipedia is an extreme example where the product, the online encyclopedia itself, has assumed a life of its own, as it is continuously built and expanded by participants everywhere.

Studies from the UK on the link between HR and innovation suggest that while innovation is considered by most organizations in the manufacturing, utility, financial and service industries to be critically important, it is not consistently managed, in terms of recruitment, training and performance management.[12]

INNOVATION'S RETURN ON INVESTMENT

While most executives across a range of industries worldwide continue to view innovation as one of their top three priorities, the returns on such investments can be elusive—at least at the time of this book. Innovation finds funding, but it is not always effectively managed and measured to show ROI through metrics, such as time to market and return on innovation investment. A recent Boston Consulting Group study[13] shows that:

- The measurement of time to market and ROI on innovation investment were only tracked by 18% and 22% of executives surveyed, respectively.
- Nearly all the executives surveyed (92%) were more concerned with innovations for existing customers than with breaking through in new markets.
- The biggest obstacles to innovation? Risk-averse, foot-dragging cultures.
- The industries most satisfied with their innovations are technology, telecom and travel. Least satisfied: financial services and retail.
- Most aggressive with their innovation dollars are the automotive industry (76% of automotive companies said they'll increase such spending), entertainment and media (73%), energy (71%), and health care and manufacturing (70%).
- Executives named Apple as the world's most innovative company, followed by Google, Toyota, General Electric, Microsoft and Procter & Gamble.

It is worthwhile to note that in the case of certain segments of the automotive industry, and several of the companies named as "most innovative," many of their activities are related to environmental issues, e.g., hybrid cars (Toyota), expansion of business offerings related to cleantech (GE).

Innovation is supposed to pay the innovating company. But how and when? The answers to these questions are not simple, because innovation, by its very nature, is expected to present risks to an organization and to take it out of its management comfort zone, in the hope of creating a competitive advantage through a new product or service. The disappointment expressed by executives worldwide on their returns from investment expenditures (cited above) is evidence of the less than predictable nature of these returns.

In Figure 8.2, two curves (generic and iPod) show the variation in cash flow associated with the three phases of product development innovation in the private sector: idea generation, commercialization and realization. Four factors produce variations in cash payback:

1. Startup costs or pre-launch investment—often referred to as the hole dug for itself by the innovating company. It is critical for companies to track the size of this investment, as it will determine the size of the required payback.

Figure 8.2: Innovation Cash Curve

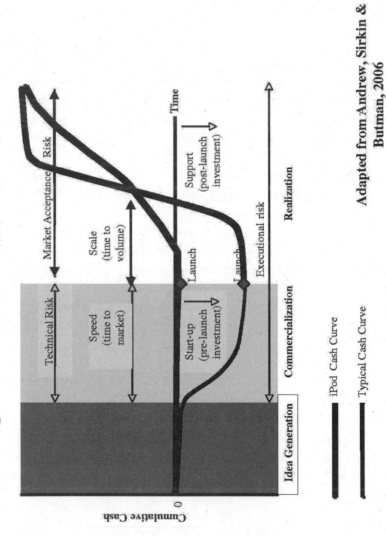

Adapted from Andrew, Sirkin & Butman, 2006

iPod Cash Curve

Typical Cash Curve

2. Speed—can increase payback if time to market is short, as a larger market share at a higher price may be captured. But if the time to market is too quick, this can raise the costs of development and risk the quality of the innovation.

3. Scale—referring to the time needed for a product to achieve volume production on the scale planned and to generate cash. The innovating company can control production and seeding the market, but it cannot dictate market acceptance. A steep slope is ideal; however, too steep may strain production capacity.

4. Support costs—or post-launch development, a function of the innovation business model, i.e., how much investment the company makes in the product, once it is in the marketplace.

Technical risk and market acceptance risk characterize the commercialization and realization phases, respectively.

The typical cash curve in figure 8.2 is contrasted by the (estimated) curve for the Apple iPod, which exhibits no dip in cash reserves for Apple, and immediate payback once in the marketplace. The iPod's reputation is a good indicator of how anomalous its cash curve is. Most innovations exhibit cash payback curves that indicate bigger pre-realization investments (a deeper hole), with or without eventual returns. For others, the upward slope is less steep. Companies must be cognizant of what to expect from their innovations, lest they induce financing problems. Companies who understand innovation's risks and opportunities know that besides cash, there are indirect benefits that, although not as readily measurable as cash, may continue to position the company favorably, enhance its brand or its relationships with suppliers, or have positive organizational impacts, such as the ability of the company to attract top talent.

Unfortunately, there is little hard data in the available literature on cash payback to innovators in environmental product and services innovation, other than general statements on impact reduction and benefits realized by stakeholders. This is a data gap that needs to be closed in the coming years for environmental innovation to truly take hold globally.

Nonetheless, what has been said thus far on both human capital management and innovation shows that human capital management is a vital link in the product or service value chain of companies. Old ways of managing this facet of business have been fundamentally changed due to demographics, external factors such as environmental sustainability, and the expectations of the current generation of knowledge workers. Companies have to be creative in attracting talent and they have to devote more resources to developing it from within. The number and quality of opportunities for innovation can be important forms of payback from successful execution of a strategy based on talent development. The following section contains information that is particularly illustrative of this connection between human capital management and innovation.

CHAPTER 8 TAKE-AWAYS

Thinking outside the box—The time has come for companies to understand that the conventional business formulas of the past decades are no longer as viable as they once were. The environmental imperatives for business, created by our collective overuse of the natural resource base, emissions of contaminants, and waste discharges must now be addressed and innovation within this new context is the key to success. Failure to grasp this reality and act upon it will be obvious to new employees, as it will be to other stakeholders. Companies have to understand their relationships with all stakeholders and the larger issues of environmental sustainability, because embedded in these relationships are the business risks and opportunities of tomorrow. This understanding will entail new types of collaboration and long-term vision. Fortunately, many companies are already on this path (perhaps unconsciously), through their recognition that much of their capitalization is tied to intangible values such as their reputation, their culture, their compliance management systems, their environmental/SD/CSR policies, or the way they manage their supply chains.

May the (labor) force be with you—The business case for enriching the company's stock of human capital has been made. Understanding the underlying motivations of tomorrow's workforce is essential to successful recruiting and, ultimately, creating the capacity to innovate. A set of incontestable values, i.e., a clear corporate direction, built on recognition of the environmental and social challenges, and backed up by concrete action, is a virtual guarantee of success in today's workforce marketplace. It will generate returns in recruitment and talent retention.

Growing role for HR—The HR function is currently in a state of flux, owing to an absence of stable models that cost-effectively frame talent recruitment, retention and development. Cost control pressures, demographic challenges and uncertainties in the business environment underlie the problem. But the burgeoning opportunities for more effective management of environmental issues in all businesses beg for greater control, ownership and management of talent and knowledge across the value chain. The importance of HR and the competitive advantage it can offer are likely to grow.

Selling virtue—Companies that are advancing their environmental agendas already recognize what a magnet this is for well-educated and well-informed recruits. They need to market this actively in the increasingly competitive and fickle talent marketplace.

Innovation culture club—The culture needed to innovate successfully must embody elements of vision, risk-taking and financial sturdiness, and be based on partnerships between R&D, IT and marketing, sales, product development and other business stakeholders. Success or failure is not black and white; there are many shades of gray, just as there are cash paybacks and indirect, less tangible, benefits of innovation. If an organization has no stomach for making mistakes, even costly ones, it will not be able to innovate.

CASE STUDY

This chapter concludes with an example of a corporation that has a demonstrated record of innovation as well as considerable evidence of having created a culture around environmental sustainability, an ethic which lends itself to innovation—3M.

3M CASE STUDY: PART 1

- worldwide sales of $24.4 billion
- 76,000 employees worldwide
- operations in more than sixty countries
- more than thirty-five business units

Key Innovations

3M's Pollution Prevention Pays (3P) program celebrated its 30th anniversary in 2005. Over the last thirty-three years, the program has prevented more than 2.7 billion pounds of pollutants and saved nearly $1.2 billion based on aggregated data from the first year of each 3P project. The 3P program helps prevent pollution at the source in products and manufacturing processes. When 3P was launched in 1975, the concept of applying pollution prevention on a company-wide basis and documenting the results was an industry first.

The 3P program was updated in 2002 to provide more opportunities for participation by research and development, logistics, transportation, and packaging employees with the addition of new award categories and criteria.

3P is a key element of 3M's environmental strategy and in moving towards sustainability. 3P seeks to eliminate pollution at the source through

- product reformulation
- process modification
- equipment redesign
- recycling and reuse of waste materials

3M employees worldwide have completed over 6,800 3P projects. Projects must meet three criteria to receive formal recognition:

1. Eliminate or reduce a pollutant
2. Benefit the environment through reduced energy use or more efficient use of manufacturing materials and resources
3. Save money—through avoidance or deferral of pollution control equipment costs, reduced operating and materials expenses or increased sales of an existing or new product

The 3P program depends directly on the voluntary participation of 3M employees. Innovative projects are recognized with 3P Awards. A 3P Coordinating Committee representing 3M's engineering, manufacturing and laboratory organizations—and the Environmental, Health and Safety group—administers the program.

Sample Projects

- The 3P project team from the Valley, Nebraska, facility reduced the inherent waste (waste inherent to the product design and process) from Red Dot Resting Electrodes, adhesive electrodes used in electrocardiogram or EKG applications, by redesigning the electrode. The team changed the configuration of the electrodes on the card, which reduced silver coating weight, adhesive coating weight and the overall size of the electrode. The project prevented nearly 11 tons of waste and saved nearly $1,000,000 in its first year of implementation.

- The Traffic Safety Systems Division invented a new prismatic reflective signing product that uses less energy, reduces process and design waste, and emits fewer volatile organic compound emissions during production than 3M's existing beaded signing products. For every square yard of new signing product produced, 3M saves 10,587 BTUs of energy and reduces process waste (including solvent emissions and landfill waste) by more than 65%. The new product was invented and rolled out in just under three months and met or exceeded existing solvent-based product specifications. This new product has been well received by customers and will allow 3M to grow its beaded sign business while improving the business's environmental footprint.

3M CASE STUDY: PART 2

HR/People Culture Attributes

The people of 3M are considered the company's most valuable resource. 3M's culture emphasizes integrity and fairness alongside innovation and excellence, and helps employees develop their diverse talents. Achieving an inclusive culture at 3M includes advancing the diversity of its U.S. operations to reflect its customer base and the communities in which the company operates.

In the U.S., 3M employs a full-time Director of Workforce Diversity to provide direction and support to enhance the recruitment and retention of diverse candidates for student and career employment. The strategy is to drive diversity and inclusion in all human resource and business processes. Workforce Diversity provides counsel to business and HR leaders on improvement opportunities and approaches. 3M engages members of the Employee Resource Groups to participate in recruiting activities.

U.S. Supplier Diversity Initiative

The following are examples of initiatives that support environmental activities.

- The company has a worldwide reputation for innovative, high-quality products. Value placed on science and innovation, a combination that attracts the best and the brightest in the fields of technology and science
- 3M gives people room to innovate, exemplified by the "15% rule," which encourages people to spend 15% of their own time on projects of their own choosing and initiative.
- Researchers can apply for Genesis Grants. The grants provide significant funding to individuals or teams to pursue embryonic new product ideas or concepts.
- The key to innovation is coupling 3M's highly diversified and differentiated technology to high-growth market space opportunities to create new-to-the-world product platforms.
- New Product Forums are regularly held, where divisions can share their latest products and developers can solicit support for a new product, idea or technology.

- Employee input is valued and leaders are expected to foster a work environment that supports employee engagement through open communication and building trust with employees. It is this work environment that encourages both employee engagement and innovation that makes 3M a favored place to work, a claim consistently supported by the company's Standard Opinion Survey process. Emphasis is on innovation, reputation in the marketplace, competitive compensation and a fair-minded, friendly culture.
- In the industry, 3M has an enviable track record of employee retention.
- 3M has a "promote from within" culture, where individuals can achieve career development and advancement consistent with their initiative and work contributions. Movement within the company is encouraged and expected.
- Autonomy is an important part of the 3M culture and is reflected in a wide variety of mechanisms, including the dual ladder structure that allows technical and professional people to develop their careers without sacrificing their focus on research and other professional interests.
- The company encourages a leadership open door policy, and one-to-one communication with management in connection with the company's performance appraisal system.
- Employee opinions are routinely measured with a biennial Leadership Survey, business unit organizational survey (administered to all sites worldwide) and other survey mechanisms. Employee input weighs heavily in management actions.
- 3M has programs in all business operations that support open communication such as Let's Talk It Over, Between Us, and various internal and external help lines.

NOTES

1 Rainer Strack, video commentary on strategic HR challenges, Boston Consulting Group, 2008, http://cdn.bcg.com/odaptor/cpa_video_a.html.
2 Peter Senge et al., *The Necessary Revolution* (New York: Doubleday, 2008).
3 Lenny T. Mendonca and Hayagreeva Rao, "Lessons from Innovation's Front Lines—An Interview with IDEO's CEO," McKinsey Quarterly, McKinsey & Company, November 2008.
4 Ron Nielsen, "Human Resources Sustainability Competencies Summary—Draft," 2006.
5 Matthew Guthridge, Asmus D. Komm and Emily Lawson, "Making Talent a Strategic Priority," McKinsey Quarterly, McKinsey & Company, January 2008.
6 Greg McMillan, "The Greening of the Jobscape," *Globe and Mail*, November 14, 2008.
7 SustainAbility, UNEP and The Global Compact, "Unchaining Value: Innovative Approaches to Sustainable Supply," 2008.
8 Peter Drucker, "The Discipline of Innovation," *Harvard Business Review*, August 2002.
9 Darrell Rigby and Chris Zook, "Open Market Innovation," *Harvard Business Review*, October 2002.
10 Ibid.
11 Jacques Bughin, Michael Chui and Brad Johnson, "The Next Step in Open Innovation," McKinsey Quarterly, McKinsey & Company, June 2008.
12 Rosalind H. Searle and Kirstie Ball, "Supporting Innovation Through HR Policy: Evidence from the UK," *Creativity and Innovation Management*, vol. 12, no. 1, 2003, 50–62.
13 Boston Consulting Group and World Federation of Personnel Management Associations, "Creating People Advantage: How to Address HR Challenges Worldwide Through 2015," 2008.

CHAPTER NINE

ROAD MAP FOR THE FUTURE

TRENDS/FORECASTS

The discussion of environmental costs and liabilities in corporate boardrooms is not new. Examples from the past four decades include

- 1970s and 1980s—legislation related to the control of air emissions and wastewater discharges from heavy industry
- 1980s and 1990s—Superfund legislation (and associated litigation) related to contaminated sites
- mid-1980s to early 2000s—lawsuits with regard to asbestos-related respiratory diseases

What is new? The discussion of environmental issues within the context of "monetary impact on brand," "fiduciary duty," "energy strategy" and "business opportunities." No longer are environmental issues viewed exclusively as a cost of doing business but are now seen as opportunities for revenue generation and cost reduction. As a result, board members at all types of organizations are now discussing the environment—whether on their own initiative or driven by the concerns of financial institutions, shareholders or customers. Unfortunately, the discussion is often motivated by public relations concerns with a focus on generating cosmetic environmental solutions, i.e., implementing superficial changes to protect brand and equity. This is changing, however, as companies understand and quantify the business risks and opportunities related to environmental issues, especially those related to the presence of hazardous substances in consumer products, resource scarcity (especially water shortages), prices and options available for energy generation, mismanagement of environmental issues along the supply chain, and measures to adapt to the changing climate.

Safe Trends

Mark Twain once aptly described the predicament faced by forecasters, which is particularly relevant in the current economic climate: "The art of prophecy is very difficult, especially with respect to the future." Nevertheless, there is consensus on the following "safe" trends, which will significantly impact business activities.

- **Electricity**—Rates in North America will continue to rise at a rate above inflation as more states and provinces switch from coal and oil to natural gas, and government legislation related to cap-and-trade schemes for GHG emissions and carbon taxes come into effect. The increase in rates will result in the tipping point being reached for some alternative energy sources.
- **Energy conservation**—Increasing energy costs will trigger renewed interest in energy conservation activities (similar to the conservation drives following the 1974 and 1981 spikes in oil prices). The intensity of conservation activities will be a function of the rate at which energy costs increase; historically, a gradual price increase has generated only minor interest whereas sudden increases trigger a flurry of activity, including changes in consumer lifestyle.
- **Global energy demand**—Both renewable and nonrenewable alternative energy sources must be leveraged to meet growing global demand in the next twenty years. The use of renewable energy sources alone cannot meet this demand for a variety of reasons—resources, supply chains, absence of infrastructure, political agendas/will, etc. The question becomes: what is the right mix for a particular company or jurisdiction that makes economic sense, minimizes environmental impact and ensures energy security?
- **Water**—The United Nations estimates that by 2025, two-thirds of the world's population will face periodic and often severe water shortages. In the U.S. alone, water managers for thirty-six states are predicting significant shortfalls within the next decade. These shortages will significantly drive the demand for investment and new technologies.[1]
- **Consumer products**—Only the tip of the iceberg of issues associated with hazardous ingredients in consumer products has been visible in the last couple of years. The new EU REACH legislation will highlight the extent

of this issue because of its disclosure requirements about both ingredients and related toxicity and trigger substantial activity on the part of industry to green their product lines.

- **Increased Fuel efficiency**—New/proposed legislation related to fuel efficiency standards and MBI for hybrid/electric vehicles as well as market demand and advancement in technology will drive increases in vehicle fuel efficiency.
- **Protection of brand**—Failure to address environmental issues can result in damage to a company's brand and thus impact its bottom line and share price. Issues may take many forms: exploitation/destruction of natural resources; degradation of the environment during exploration/production; or presence of hazardous materials in a product (especially those used by children). Companies will continue to invest in supply chain screening, product life cycle management (PLM) and climate change initiatives that support/protect their brands.
- **Supply chain**—Brands/retailers recognize that the mismanagement of environmental issues by suppliers creates cost inefficiencies that can significantly impact their bottom line. Companies are asking suppliers to reduce packaging, trim emissions, reduce energy costs and ensure the absence of hazardous materials in products. There is a significant push, albeit in most cases *ad hoc*, towards eco-design and green procurement.
- **Corporate metrics**—Corporations, governments, NGOs and investment companies are beginning to leverage quantitative financial data to reinforce the benefits of improved corporate sustainable development (SD) performance. Individuals/groups driving SD need to use the language of business and be able to translate progress into financial terms—discounted cash flow (DCF), price to cash flow per share ratio (P/CFPS) and economic value added (EVA).[2]
- **Business Risk/Opportunity Assessments**—More and more organizations are conducting detailed business risk and opportunity assessments and leveraging this information to influence strategic, tactical and operational activities. Typically these types of assessments include scenarios to address areas of uncertainty, e.g. timing of proposed cap and trade legislation associated pricing of GHG gases.
- **Increase Reporting**—Recent guidance from U.S. SEC, Ontario Securities Commission as well as pressure from shareholder groups and SD rating organizations are triggering a significant increase in the disclosure of

environmental issues and associated business risks. This will continue and expand over time as regulators/investors realize that it is not just climate change, but also a wrath of other issues that they should also be worried about.

Short-term Energy Costs

Significant uncertainty exists in predicting short-term energy costs because of the ongoing effects of the 2008 recession and its impact on markets.

Petroleum—There are numerous predictions about the cost of a barrel of oil over the next couple of years made by well-known analysts and government agencies. Typically, they fall into three camps:

Scenario 1: $40–$60/barrel due to the 2008 recession and the successful implementation of various conservation activities and new technologies that reduce exploration costs

Scenario 2: $90–$110/barrel due to a reduction in output by OPEC (as they prop up prices during the recession) and sluggish production growth

Scenario 3:   >$150/barrel due to inflationary pressure on the commodity market and a reduction in the value of the U.S. dollar stemming from the U.S. bailout

Note that the values quoted above are for West Texas Intermediate (WTI), which is an underlying commodity of the New York Mercantile Exchange's oil futures contracts.

Natural gas—Short-term gas prices will most likely fluctuate because of their historical tie to oil prices, new horizontal drilling and hydraulic fracturing technologies and completion of several large LNG plants overseas that could bring a glut of natural gas to the U.S. market. The historical oil-gas relationship is approximately a 7.5:1 ratio of a barrel of oil to 1,000 cubic feet (mcf) natural gas. This means that when oil is at $100/barrel (WTI price), natural gas should be about $13.00/mcf (as traded at the Henry Hub in Louisiana) after an appropriate lag time.

Long-term Energy Costs

Long-term forecasts for the price of petroleum products and electricity vary significantly because of uncertainty in the following areas:

Growing demand—IEA reports predict that a significant increase in demand will occur over the next thirty years, especially in rapidly developing countries like China and India as they will not allow the western nations' preoccupation with "greening the world" to hinder their growth.

New reserves—The exploration and development of petroleum reserves off the coast of Brazil and the United States, in national parks/wildlife reserves in North America and on the Arctic Ocean floor would substantially increase reserves. The 2008 U.S. Comprehensive American Energy Security & Consumer Protection Act ended a decades-old moratorium on offshore oil and gas drilling. Drilling in wildlife reserves and the Arctic will face significant protest from a variety of stakeholders, and Arctic Ocean deposits may require substantial investment because of challenging conditions.

Role of NOCs/IOCs and investment—National oil companies (NOCs) play a significant role in the petroleum market. In countries like Venezuela, Iran, Russia and China, governments use them as vehicles to dictate policy. Some NOCs want to drive their countries' domestic production, while others see oil in the ground as a future high value revenue stream. Investment by both international oil companies (IOCs) and NOCs in existing deposits and the development of new deposits significantly influence the supply side of the equation. This investment has been lacking in the last ten years.

War, political unrest and terrorists—Several key producing countries are either at war, may be at war or are politically unstable. As with any other business activity, there is always the risk of terrorist activities that may disrupt a portion of the energy supply chain, thereby influencing the immediate situation and imposing additional controls/costs going forward.

Conservation activities—As seen during previous spikes in petroleum prices, companies and individuals are willing to conserve when it comes to their pocketbook and prices are changing rapidly. However, the level of conservation is more limited when companies are faced with gradual price increases.

Weather—Climate change may trigger more frequent and stronger hurricanes in the Gulf of Mexico. These events may significantly impact on ongoing production from this area.

Some general trends:

Petroleum—The fundamental reasons for increasing price above $150 a barrel are still in place:

- inadequate investments by NOCs and IOCs: in general, NOCs are not willing to invest, as they believe that "oil in the ground is worth more than money in the bank," while IOC investment in the industry comes second to shareholder returns[3]
- global peak oil (when maximum rate of global petroleum extraction is reached) may be achieved within the next ten to twenty years because of geological limitations, environmental concerns, political instability and absence of investment (as mentioned above)
- increasing costs related to government action, including carbon sequestration and storage, carbon taxes and carbon trading programs

The U.S. EIA recently predicted that prices will continue to rise, costing $130 per barrel by 2030 ($189 per barrel adjusted for inflation).

Natural gas—The fundamental reasons that will push natural gas prices to above $20/mcf include the following:

- increase in demand due to the ongoing shift from coal-fired generating facilities to natural gas in many jurisdictions (Ontario may build twenty new facilities in the next decade), as well as an increase in ethanol production (many ethanol plants run on natural gas)
- lower production from new gas wells, less new drilling and depletion of older wells[4]
- as the price of crude oil increases, some industries switched to natural gas; many developed this dual fuel capability when gas prices skyrocketed in 2001[5]
- liquefied natural gas (LNG) will become in high demand in coastal areas of the U.S. (in particular California and New England) once terminals are constructed
- prices should fall when new major gas pipelines are built connecting new gas fields in Alaska and the Northwest Territories; however, that is likely

more than six years away (reports also suggest that virtually all of this northern gas may be used to extract oil from the oil sands in Northern Alberta)[6]

The wild card, in terms of price, will be new drilling technology that has allowed a number of new high-volume fields across the U.S.

Public Willingness

In general, the public willingness to do the right thing or pay additional fees related to improving the environment is somewhat proportional to media reports (e.g., hazardous material in consumer products, melting of ice sheets, impacts on polar bears) and unusual weather events (e.g., severe droughts, heat waves, hurricanes). That willingness has a price point, though, especially with regards to petroleum/electricity, and history shows that consumers will pay a slight increase for the greater good but will not accept significant increases due to government green policies, especially during times of sudden increases in energy price or economic recession.

Government Influence

The key issue for government is to find the right balance between Market-based Instruments (MBIs) that are enacted today (and hence hit consumers' pocketbooks) and the protection of both the environment and the requirements in terms of access to energy of future generations. Also coming into play are factors such as the opportunity to create green jobs (governments are linking subsidies to local job creation); the introduction of both regulated and voluntary GHG reductions, the need to ensure national or state/province energy independence and the desire by government leaders and citizens to be perceived as green. Some countries and states (e.g., Germany, Denmark, California and, more recently, the United Arab Emirates and provinces of Ontario and Quebec) are aggressively positioning themselves as green centers of excellence.

The overriding issue: Government leaders that accept the findings of the 2006 Stern Report on climate change are putting together well-thought-out action plans while those that remain skeptical are postponing action, citing short-term impact on the economy.

What are the key commitments of North American governments?

United States

As indicated in chapter 6, the current administration has committed to[7]

- help create 5 million new jobs by strategically investing $150 billion over the next ten years to catalyze private efforts to build a clean energy future
- within ten years, save more oil than the U.S. currently imports from the Middle East and Venezuela combined
- put 1 million plug-in hybrid cars that can get up to 150 miles per gallon on the road by 2015—cars that they will work to make sure are built in America
- ensure 10% of U.S. electricity comes from renewable sources by 2012, and 25% by 2025
- implement an economy-wide cap-and-trade program to reduce GHG emissions 80% by 2050

The National Renewable Energy Laboratory of the U.S. Department of Energy has stated the following U.S. national goals:[8]

- biofuels: reduce gasoline usage by 20% in ten years
- wind: provide 20% of total energy by 2030
- solar: be market competitive by 2015 for photovoltaics (PVs) and 2020 for concentrated solar power (CSP)

President Obama's quick action on pushing forward fuel economy standards and the U.S. government's allocation of $58 billion worth of spending and tax cuts for alternative energy and energy conservation in the U.S. stimulus package sends a clear message on their commitment to clean energy and green jobs.

Canada

Canada established a national target of an absolute 20% reduction in GHGs from 2006 levels by the year 2020 by leveraging the following initiatives:[9]

- put in place large-scale carbon capture and storage and other innovative green technologies
- generate 90% of Canadian power from sources that do not emit GHGs
- increase electricity from renewable sources like wind and wave power by 20 times

- cut GHG emissions from coal by more than 50%
- increase average fuel efficiency in new cars by 20%
- improve Canada's energy efficiency by 20%

The populist 2009 Federal budget did provide $2 billion related to renewable energy (Green Energy Fund and Green Infrastructure Fund); however, a clear national green energy strategy is required to play catch-up with many other nations and allow Canada to emerge as a center of green-technology (and thus green jobs).

Trends in Government Influence

Government actions are following these trends:

- **energy conservation**—key opportunity to reduce GHG emissions
  - more stringent fuel economy standards (>40 miles per gallon), as California, China, Japan and the EU have implemented new legislation that will have a ripple effect on other jurisdictions (refer to appendix A for the list of current/proposed standards)
  - more stringent energy efficiency standards for appliances and adaptation of these standards by developing nations, e.g., China and India; the EU has established the Global Energy Efficiency and Renewable Energy Fund to provide some 80 million euros, spread over four years, for energy efficiency and renewables in developing and transition economies
  - greater adaptation of premium fees for "peak time" electricity use by utilities and use of "smart meters"
  - adaptation of green building standards (e.g., LEED) making it a mandatory component of building codes, government procurement and funding policies (e.g. new San Francisco green building codes that will be phased in over a number of years)
- **alternative renewable energy activities**
  - expansion of state/province renewable portfolio standards (RPS) and eventual adaptation of national RPS in U.S. and Canada
  - continued, but more focused, subsidies and R&D grants to accelerate the development and demonstration of innovative technology
  - continuation of investment and renewable energy production tax credits, as well as an increase in residential rebate programs and feed-in-tariffs (e.g. Ontario proposed 53.9 to 80.2 cents/kWh for solar PV, depending on size of installation and location); the tax credits for a

particular type of alternative energy will continue to vary considerably as governments try to level the playing field
- investment in smart grid and expansion of transmission lines for de-centralized power systems in jurisdictions that are strongly supportive of renewable alternatives
- **increased product labeling/prohibitions**
  - trend towards standardization of labels for "green" or "eco" products
  - adaptation of key components of EU REACH legislation by other juris-dictions, resulting in greater disclosure of ingredients and toxicity
  - increase in extended producer responsibility legislation, mandatory recycling (including take-back programs) and waste disposal fees (primarily an instrument to reduce at source) that will trigger renewed emphasis on proper eco-design
  - greater discussions/debate on the toxicity of ingredients by NGOs with potential impairment to corporate brands
  - growing interest in potential hazards associated with nanotechnology
  - adaption of C2C concept in new government policies and guidance documents
- **cap-and-trade schemes**
  - the careful introduction of mandatory cap-and-trade schemes or carbon taxes related to significant GHG emission sources (coal and natural gas fired generating plants, refineries, tar sands projects, etc.); governments must proceed down this path, but with due caution based upon the fragility of the economy
  - in states/provinces, as indicated in chapter 7, seven states and four Canadian provinces have joined together under the Western Climate Initiative (WCI), which is creating a regional GHG control and offset trading environment; WCI's goal is to achieve an aggregate reduction of 15% below 2005 levels by 2020 (the plan calls for the first compli-ance initiatives to start in 2012 and apply to electricity sector, plus emissions from big industry such as smelters and refineries)[10]
  - at the U.S. federal level, President Obama is carrying through with his election platform—New Energy for American Plan—with a 2010 budget that commits to $150 billion over 10 years toward seeking more energy independence. The goal is to double the production of renew-able energy in three years, via tax breaks and loan guarantees for the industry. The budget also includes a cap-and-trade on carbon emis-sions, which is expected to generate $646 billion revenue during the

first eight years of carbon-capping program (presumes that a U.S. law to limit carbon emissions will be in place by 2012). According to Point Carbon, a provider of independent analysis and services for global power markets, the budget presumes a price for U.S. carbon allowances at about $13.70.

- at the Canadian federal level, at this point in time, the government is not putting forward a definitive plan of action, other than regulations aimed at achieving emissions based on emissions intensity; it is anticipated that eventually Canada will adopt a system similar to the U.S. for economic reasons—"common environmental standards and energy-development plans"

Greenhouse gas emitters need a clear signal of the potential cost of a ton of CO_2 (either by a cap-and-trade program or carbon tax) in order to make informed investment decisions.

BUSINESS OPPORTUNITIES

As with the gold rush of the late nineteenth century, some entities will prosper significantly during the green rush, while others will not, for a number of reasons. Following the 2008 credit crunch, the market's slow shift from a "momentum play" to a "value play" was accelerated. Consolidation is occurring, especially in the project-intensive side of the market (wind farms, solar PVs), as companies struggle to get funding and lose the attractiveness of their investment tax credits. Innovators continue to emerge on the technology side, especially those bringing forward technology to improve energy efficiency or drive down the cost of renewable energy sources.

The current state of affairs is best summarized by William Ambrose, president and CEO of Emerging Energy Research:

The global financial crisis is taking the steam out of the new energy boom, with a slowdown in new project spending expected in 2009. But the long-term fundamentals remain in place—the globe is still warming, the earth's fossil fuel resources are still being depleted, and the developing world's demand for energy will continue to grow in leaps and bounds…. A whole lot of weak projects and weak technologies will get pushed to the back of the line where they rightly belong. The more bankable projects will get done. The stronger players—led by solvent utilities, cash-rich oil and gas companies, the larger industrial manufacturers, and the smarter and more successful new-energy competitors—will survive and will have opportunties to reap competitive advantage in a rationalizing market.[11]

The poster company for these new green opportunities is GE, which reported revenues from its ecomagination portfolio of energy-efficient and environmentally beneficial products and services exceeding $14 billion in 2007, and an order book surpassing $70 billion. GE also increased the number of ecomagination-certified products by 38%, to a total of sixty-two products in 2007. The company's own cleantech fund also passed $1 billion for the first time.[12]

Not far behind GE is Mitsubishi Electric Corp., which announced plans to accelerate its push into the cleantech market. The company plans to achieve sales of $13.3 billion in 2016. Key areas to be addressed include solar systems, heat pumps and energy-efficient power devices.[13] The change in the market has been described by Vinod Khosla:

> The new green is about engines (large market), it is about lighting, appliances, batteries, it is about gasoline, diesel and jet fuel, and cement, water and glass, it is not about clean tech, it is about main tech. We should keep that in mind if we're going to find climate change solutions, it's going to be about main tech, about the infrastructure of our society and our daily lives.[14]

Over time the environmental market has shifted from a momentum play to a value play. Companies must establish strong differentiators to compete.

In the longer term, a new technological revolution is required. The following is an excerpt from *Break Through: From the Death of Environmentalism to the Politics of Possibility.*[15]

Overcoming global warming demands not pollution control but rather a new kind of economic development. We cannot tear down the old energy economy before building the new one. The invention of the Internet and microchips, the creation of the space program, the birth of the European Union—those breakthroughs were only made possible by big and bold investments in the future. The kind of technological revolution called for by energy experts typically does not occur via regulatory fiat. We did not invent the Internet by taxing telegraphs nor the personal computer by limiting typewriters. Nor did the transition to the petroleum economy occur because we taxed, regulated or ran out of whale oil. Those revolutions happened because we invented alternatives that were vastly superior to what they replaced and, in remarkably short order, became a good deal cheaper. The highest objective of anyone concerned about global warming must be to bring down the real prices of clean energy below the price of dirty energy as quickly as possible—most importantly, in places like China.

The following table presents a summary of the key areas of opportunity and critical hurdles to growth. In the majority of the cases, work is underway to resolve these hurdles—the key questions being timing, costs and trajectory (the direction at which the cost curve is changing as capacity increases).

Table 9.1: Key Areas of Growth and Critical Hurdles

Category	Opportunity	Critical Hurdles to Growth
1. Alternative Electricity Production	Provide clean energy to satisfy growing demand, which is being driven by climate change, peak oil and growth in developing countries	All Alternatives Sources—need oil/natural gas prices to stay high and/or legislation on GHG emissions, as well as access to capital Wind—high capital cost, absence (to date) of cost-effective energy storage and growing NIMBY opposition PV Solar—absence (to date) of efficient, low-cost cells and energy storage units; new PV cells show promise Thermal Solar—high installation costs and fragmented market (a lot of small providers) Tidal—lack of history with tidal stream projects; however, investment increasing significantly Geothermal—investment in ESG and initial cost of geo-exchange (heating/cooling) systems Nuclear—high capital cost and public perception of risks Clean Coal—unproven technology and high costs
2. Energy Efficiency & Conservation	Substantially reduce demand side of energy	General—need elevated energy prices to drive cultural changes and improve project ROIs Creativity—inability of companies to unleash employee creativity regarding conservation and efficiency
3. Emissions and Carbon Markets	Services/products to track, trade and reduce emissions	Legislation—several years away from mandatory cap-and-trade program for carbon equivalents in North America; therefore influencing decisions, but not deciding them Economy—during downturns companies spend less on voluntary programs

4. Transportation	Gain competitive advantage against companies leveraging old technology	General—need petroleum prices to stay high (else gradual repeat of 1974/1981) or substantial ongoing environmental degradation due to climate change; eventually, avoided costs/system efficiencies will drive solution Electric—need low-cost, reliable and replaceable batteries (or quick recharge using ultra capacitors) and associated infrastructure; for global adaptation, need to reduce overall cost Hybrid—need low-cost, reliable batteries; for global adaptation need to reduce overall cost Biofuel—availability of low-cost feedstock with small carbon footprint and efficiency of production processes Hydrogen Fuel Cells—high cost of producing hydrogen, safety concerns and infrastructure costs Natural Gas—competition (and hence price) for natural gas from electricity generation Clean Diesel—increasing cost of diesel
5. Green Consumer Products (excludes energy efficiency)	Provide products that are safe and easily recycled	Priority Ranking—green is nice, but safety and price of products are equally if not more important Green Products—no longer good enough to be green; also must be similar cost and improved performance Reformulate Costs—cost to reformulate some products is very high Supply Chain—inability to manage/win over supply chain as perceived as increasing costs
6. Water Treatment and Conservation	Provide clean, low-cost water for both domestic and industrial use	Pricing—current prices, especially for agricultural use, do not promote conservation activities in many areas; prices may need to rise to reflect cost to obtain additional water as reserves are diminished Costs—cost of technology for desalinization and wastewater treatment Capital—availability of capital, especially when government is funding a project
7. Adaptation to Changing Climate	Products/services related to adaptation not mitigation	Events—call to action sometimes requires numerous events before public/government motivated Economy—during economic downturns focus is on short-term activities to boost economy or infrastructure to boost mid-term revenue; prevention is a more difficult sell

One of the critical factors is the price of petroleum and natural gas. Low prices make alternative energy projects, under existing pricing, either very unprofitable or almost a token gesture of good environmental faith. Similarly, low petroleum prices significantly alter the cost equation for consumers to switch to hybrids and

Figure 9.1: Trajectory of Cost Curves

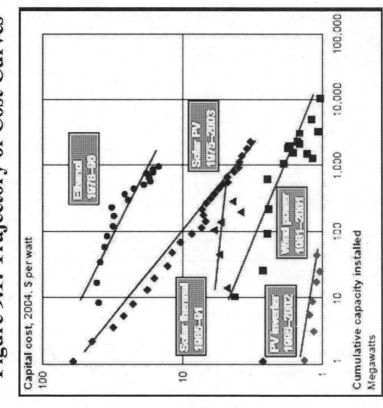

Capital cost, 2004. $ per watt

Cumulative capacity installed
Megawatts

UC Berkeley Energy Resources Group: Navigant Consulting

electrical vehicles and reinforce the role of high-mileage gasoline-powered engines, clean diesel and natural gas cars.

As discussed in chapter 3, two other critical factors are avoided costs and systems efficiencies, examples of which include the following: reduction in lost employee workdays due to air pollution, reduced spending on roadway infrastructure due to digitally controlled vehicles (i.e. smart highways), and distributed power generation allowing utilities to avoid the costs of new centralized power plants.[16]

Figure 9.1 presents information, albeit somewhat dated, on the different trajectories of key alternative technologies. Updated data points for these technologies indicate that the trajectories are continuing on similar paths, thus reinforcing the belief that ethanol (as biofuel), solar PVs and wind power show good scalability, whereas solar thermal and PV inverters (where the inverter converts low voltage DC into higher voltage AC) do not.

How big are the opportunities? A report released by the Carbon Trust entitled *Climate Change: A business revolution?* outlines the impact of climate change on six sectors that are worth a total of $7 trillion. The report, based on analysis by McKinsey & Co., found "that the deep emissions reductions necessary to tackle climate change and put us on a path to a low carbon economy, will create significant business opportunities and risks. Companies' futures will be highly dependent on how well prepared they are for the move, which will create large upsides and downsides for business." The report went on to indicate that "well positioned and proactive, forward thinking businesses could increase company value by up to 80%. Conversely, poorly positioned and laggard companies run the greatest risk of destroying value. The groundbreaking research found that as much as 65% of company value was at risk in some sectors."[17]

Table 9.2 provides a summary of areas of potential growth for both technology and productive assets (capital intensive) opportunities in the seven categories of broad environment issues related to the North American market. The allocation of a particular opportunity to the various growth categories is subjective and based upon available market research and does not address individual companies' performance. The term "uncertain growth" relates to areas that may undergo large shifts due to a variety of reasons: e.g., NGO activity, political, technology. Key areas of risk include financial markets and credit concerns, potential changes in government incentives/subsidies and uncertainty in petroleum prices during the next few years.

It is important to note that that information presented is only for the North American market. There are substantial opportunities around the globe to export technology/services related to all of the categories mentioned. In addition, nano technology was not included as a separate item as it is driving products in numerous categories, e.g., batteries, solar PVs, building materials. In the following section, highlights of areas that will potentially experience rapid growth are discussed.

Before discussing the areas of growth, it is worth mentioning (see table 9.3) some of the myths about GHG abatement as presented in a McKinsey report entitled *The Carbon Productivity Challenge: Curbing Climate Change and Sustaining Economic Growth.*[18]

Table 9.2: Examples of Areas of Growth in the North American Environmental Market

Category	Rapid Growth	Good Growth	Uncertain or Okay Growth
1. Alternative Electricity Production	- onshore wind projects if NIMBY concerns are managed properly: equipment, construction and operation (primarily along backbone of U.S./Canada and northern coast lines) - next generation dye-sensitive thin film (DSC) and organic PV (OPV) solar cells. - geo-exchange (heating and cooling) units - transmission lines - "run of the river" hydro operations in Canada - LNG plants/co-generation equipment and construction - carbon sequestration pilots (especially petroleum) - energy storage (batteries, ultra capacitors, compressed air energy storage and hydraulic storage) for wind/solar - solar PV where fuel cost high (Hawaii) or good feed-in-tariffs (proposed Ontario)	- superconductor transmission (question of cost and wide-scale use) - CSP plants in southwestern U.S. - solar PV in southwestern U.S. (grid parity anticipated in 2012 because of new PV cells) - solar thermal (predominantly in EU, but good potential in south-eastern U.S.) - hydroelectric at existing dams in U.S. - nuclear power equipment and construction - fuel cells for specialty applications - coal and biomass co-firing	- operations of nuclear power plants (ongoing PR risks) - clean coal via carbon sequestration (technology and cost issues) - hydrogen (research is promising, but still significant uncertainties) - lighter than air turbines (question of technical/market acceptance) - tidal power facilities (need results of pilot projects before proceeding) - fusion (require technical leap to get to commercialization)
2. Energy Conservation and Efficiency	- smart grid technology - technology to improve efficiency and conservation - software for grid balancing, logistics and buildings - processes and technology to increase efficiency at existing coal plants - IT hardware with reduced energy usage - "solid state" lighting products that rely on silicon thin film process	- green (LEED certification) buildings* - low E glass blocks (to reduce heating and cooling loads) - CFLs - intelligent HVAC systems - building-integrated photovoltaics - SMART Meter (refer to Google "Power Meter")	- CO_2 neutral cement (promising, but need to move to full commercialization and obtain approval for use of cement)
3. Emissions and Carbon Markets	- carbon offsets (from WWF Gold Standard certified) - conducting risk assessments of GHG financial exposure	- software to manage emissions/GHG credits - assessment/verification of emissions - emissions trading brokerage and legal services	- carbon-neutral cement (need to validate full-scale production and price point) - non-gold standard carbon offsets

4. Transportation	- batteries (lithium ion, ceramic) for maintaining speed and electrical systems and ultra capacitors for acceleration - technology (enzymes, processes, crop yield) for biofuel operations - next generation biofuel plant: equipment, construction and operation - electric and plug-in hybrid vehicles - mass transit (e.g., high-speed trains) - research on SMART highways	- videoconferencing - natural gas vehicles and conversions - clean diesel - biodiesel (scalability issue) - specialty use of fuel cells, e.g., forklifts - high-speed trains - hybrid buses (if battery issue is resolved), or else clean diesel - energy-efficient aircraft (engines, wing design, etc.)	- biofuels from food crops (political and costly) - hydrogen cars (unless hydrogen can be produced cheaply)
5. Green Consumer Products (excludes energy efficiency)	- PLM, GRC and supply chain software; note that GRC software is applicable to all types of companies - advanced systems to detect chemicals in consumer products - e-paper and associated systems - C2C consulting	- software to automate compliance with EHS legislation - bottled water with vitamins, minerals and antioxidants - recycling technologies and equipment - new methane batteries for electronic equipment - e-waste good, but shift to nonhazardous ingredients should reduce steam	- genetically modified (GM) crops (ongoing NGO and consumer backlash in many countries) - bottled water (NGO/consumer backlash) - bioplastics (several issues emerging: use of GM crops as feedstock; competition with food crops; and when they end up in landfill sites, they degrade without oxygen, releasing methane)
6. Water Treatment and Conservation	- water treatment and desalination equipment and facilities - technology to reduce cost of desalination facilities - assessment/reduction of "Virtual" water	- upgrade existing water treatment infrastructure - low-cost water treatment devices	- sales of Canadian water to U.S. (political backlash)
7. Adaptation to Changing Climate	- unfortunately, government and most companies will wait until significant event(s) occurs before undertaking major projects during depressed economic times	- emergency/disaster response planning - coastal and civil engineering to enhance existing infrastructure - technology to influence weather	- infrastructure for marine traffic and winter roads in Canadian North (potentially a bit early)

Table 9.3: Myth vs. Reality for GHG Abatement

Myth	Realities
Abatement opportunities are concentrated in the industry and power sectors.	Industry and power represent less than half the total 2030 abatement potential.*
Limited number of low-cost opportunities in industrial countries.	Negative cost-abatement potential represents 35% to 45% of the total in industrialized countries.
Abatement opportunities are concentrated in industrialized countries and China.	Developing world excluding China represents >40% of the total 2030 abatement potential.*
We can only achieve the required abatement through new technology.	Some 70% of the 2030 abatement potential* is not dependent on new technology.
Addressing GHG emissions will significantly strain the economy.	Reaching 450 ppmv (ppm per volume) could cost as little as 0.6% of GDP if all low-cost opportunities are efficiently addressed.

* below 40/tonne of CO_2 equivalents

Renewable Energy Production

According to the 2008 Clean Edge report, the renewable energy component of the cleantech market is approximately $104 billion, growing to $467 billion in 2017.[19] The IEA *World Energy Outlook 2008* report forecast that the world needs to invest $5.5 trillion (in 2007 dollars) in renewable energy sources between 2007 and 2030 to meet growing demand.[20] On a country-specific basis, the mix of alternative energy sources will be driven by the availability of natural resources; the level of citizens' concerns about the environment; the economics of individual projects and the viability of the country's economy; access to technology; and politicians with vision and the tenacity to execute.

In North America, no single alternative energy source is emerging as a clear winner for large-scale projects. Instead, several may fulfill regional niches. Note that a detailed discussion of each type of energy source, its benefits and/or issues, is presented in chapter 6. Rapid growth areas include the following:

Onshore wind power for the backbone of the U.S. and Canada. We still need to resolve the storage issue during periods of low or excessive wind (getting closer), improve energy capture, decrease installation/operating costs and do a better job of interacting with stakeholders (avoiding the NIMBY syndrome).[21] Without cost reductions, ongoing government incentives or new legislation related to carbon taxes or cap-and-trade programs are required to be competitive with other sources of electricity. T. Boone Pickens's exploits in Texas are reinvigorating this sector and demonstrating that good returns are achievable.

Solar PV is currently driven primarily by government incentives, the regional cost of electricity and, to a much lesser extent, the solar intensity of a particular location. Jefferies & Company forecasts that solar PVs will become more competitive on a broad scale by 2012, based on cost-reduction opportunities and rising metered electricity prices, including the cost of financing the installation.[22] The up-front investment may substantially decrease in the coming years as low-cost concentrated PVs made with cadmium telluride and silicon and next-generation dye-sensitive thin film (DSC) and organic PV (OPV) solar cells come onto the market, increasing durability as well as increasing cell conversion efficiencies.

Geo-exchange (heating and cooling) is described as the dark horse of renewable energy, and can be leveraged in most areas of North America. Geothermal heating uses heat pumps for efficient water and space heating in buildings and uses the earth as the heat exchanger. Installation costs are high compared to conventional fossil-fuel-fired furnaces. Payback can vary between four years (commercial) and eight years (residential). In order to accelerate adaptation, changes in building codes, reduction in price of equipment and/or additional government/ utility subsidies are required.

Hydroelectricity in Canada will continue to grow rapidly. Forecasts of untapped rivers indicate an additional 34 to 100 GW of technically feasible power is available in Canada. Work on the lower Churchill River in Labrador will begin in 2009, further expanding the country's reliance on hydroelectric generation.

A key limiting factor for all renewable sources (that are not used off-grid) is the ability to connect to the grid via transmission lines. This particular issue has significant impact on the location of facilities and project ROI, as high-voltage transmission lines are expensive. Some jurisdictions (e.g., Texas and Ontario) recognize this weakness and have committed substantial monies to establish transmission lines for alternative energy sources.

We are approaching the tipping point for some alternative renewable energy sources. However, if petroleum prices stay low, the incentives to conserve and invest in alternative energy will be diminished unless carbon tax or cap-and-trade systems are imposed, substantial government MBI put in place, or significant system efficiencies can be achieved.

Energy Storage

Energy storage options being assessed include

- batteries (electrochemical)—low-cost, minimal hazardous material; quick recharge and ability to retain charge for longer periods are required for a variety of products
- ultra-capacitors, also known as supercapacitors—made from carbon aerogel, carbon nanotubes or highly porous electrode materials; unlike batteries, ultra-capacitors can completely absorb and release charges at high rates and in a virtually endless cycle with little degradation, but the amount of energy storage is low compared to batteries
- ultra battery—combines an ultra-capacitor and a lead acid battery in a single unit; originally developed to power hybrid electric vehicles, it also promises to be an efficient and cost-effective way to store renewable energies such as solar and wind power
- compressed air energy storage—trapping of energy generated by a windmill in the form of compressed air that is stored in a reservoir beneath the earth (influences location of project)
- fluid transfer—use of molten salt or other medium to store energy from CSP thermal facilities
- hydraulic storage—leveraging expertise gained from petroleum and hydroelectric operations for use in solar/wind systems

Energy Conservation and Efficiency

As discussed in previous chapters, numerous activities are underway at companies to ensure energy efficiency considerations are included in the design, manufacture and transportation of their products. This approach is also being applied to the entire supply chain as companies realize the waste (energy inefficiencies) is costing them money.

SMART Grid technology—This is software and hardware that allows utilities to better optimize grid loading—provides communications infrastructure. Smart grid refers to a two-way system that monitors and automatically optimizes the operation of the interconnected elements of the power system—from the generator through the high-voltage network and distribution system, to the end-use consumer and their thermostats, appliances and other household devices. Research is underway to optimize these systems and, in doing so, allow greater input of decentralized alternative energy sources.

Hydro One, former transmission unit of Ontario Hydro, has emerged as a leader in the implementation of smart grid technology. According to Hydro One's publications they are in the process of redesigning their system architecture to allow the layering of additional applications on top of the technology so that they can use two-way communications for emerging conservation and demand management tools, like smart thermostats and in-home displays, distribution station monitoring and automation, real-time outage management, safety monitoring, mobile work dispatch and asset security.

Working closely with other large Canadian utilities, Hydro One was able to get the Federal government to allocate 30 MHz of spectrum to be use exclusively for the purpose of deploying systems for the operations, maintenance and management of the electric supply across Canada. The systems will rely on WiMAX (Worldwide Interoperability for Microwave Access).

Funding for smart grid has increased significantly over the last few months with U.S. economic stimulus plan allocating $4.5 billion US and Ontario Government announcing a $5 billion investment as part of its proposed Green Energy Act.

Logistics software—This software enables companies to better optimize the shipment of goods from suppliers and to customers. The key issue is reduction in transportation costs while ensuring on-time delivery. Refer to examples of savings in logistics in chapter 5.

Computerized building energy optimization tools—New software tools are being developed to assist with the design of zero-energy buildings, i.e., buildings that produce as much energy on-site as they consume on an annual basis. The tools provide an approach to building design and operation that can achieve 70%–80% reductions in load coupled with careful integration of on-site renewable energy supplies as well as thermal and electrical storage.[23]

Coal plant efficiency—Current estimates are that there are approximately 900 billion tons of coal worldwide and at current production rates this will last for 155 years. The United States has approximately 29% of the global reserves. By improving the operations of conventional coal plants, currently at 32%–38% efficiency, significant reductions in emissions can occur for the same amount of electricity generated. Research and pilot projects are underway around the globe.

IT hardware—In 2006, datacenters consumed 1.5% of all electricity in the U.S. This is projected to increase to 2.5% by 2011. Recent research from analyst Forrester has predicted that the global market for green IT will peak at US$4.8 billion in 2013, and then decline thereafter, as businesses reach peak efficiency.[24] The majority of IT hardware brands/manufacturers are offering energy-efficient systems. Refer to the Dell case study at the end of chapter 5.

Solid state lighting (SSL) products—SSL is a new technology that has the potential to far exceed the energy efficiencies of incandescent and fluorescent lighting. It uses LEDs for illumination. The term "solid state" refers to the fact that the light in an LED is emitted from a solid object—a block of semiconductor—rather than from a vacuum or gas tube, as in the case of incandescent and fluorescent lighting. Currently the life ownership cost is roughly two times higher than incandescent lamps and roughly ten times higher than CFLs. This type of light requires significantly less energy than CFLs. Performance improvements and reductions in the unit cost will have to be in place before they are widely accepted.[25]

Emissions and Carbon Markets

The key issue regarding emissions in North America is uncertainty over government action—when will legislation be passed that establishes a mandatory cap-and-trade system, and what will be the carbon price? Without this legislation, market growth will be significantly slower, especially during an economic downturn. If the 2010 U.S. budget is passed, the market will take off, creating significant opportunities related to pollution control (carbon sequestration), alternative energy and the monitoring/auditing and trading of credits. Without a clear understanding of the potential cost of a ton of CO_2 it will be difficult to make informed decisions on carbon sequestration.

Emissions trading—A report released by New Carbon Finance estimates that the U.S. will be home to a carbon market worth in excess of $1 trillion by 2020, more than twice the size of the EU ETS. The forecast assumes that the U.S. will implement an economy-wide cap-and-trade system within four to five years, and that the system will be confined to domestic trading. The report forecast is based on an estimated carbon price of $40 per tonne as early as 2015. A price of $40 per tonne is expected to raise energy costs: electricity costs by 20%, gasoline by 12% and natural gas by 10%.[26] As indicated previously, the 2010 U.S. budget is expected to generate $646 billion in revenue from carbon capping program and is based upon a price for U.S. carbon allowances at about $13.70.

It is important to note, especially given the role of complex financial instruments during the onset of the financial crisis in 2008, that artificial securities linked to emissions trading and carbon hedging mechanisms must be put in place carefully, ensuring stability of the markets, in order to avoid another EU Emission Trading Scheme Phase I or a revisit of the asset-backed commercial paper fiasco.

Carbon offsets—One part of the market that has grown rapidly is carbon offsets—both for individual consumers, as well as by companies packaging these with their offerings (e.g., airlines, and in one case an automotive company). There are currently more than 140 organizations that sell carbon offsets online, which has caused NGOs and consumers to start asking a lot more questions on the "realness" of the claimed positive environmental impact of the credits. As a result, there most likely will be a push for the use of an acceptable certification process, e.g., World Wildlife Foundation Gold Standard, or consumer legislation, with some current providers of carbon offsets coming under scrutiny or even being discredited.

Carbon capture and sequestration (CCS)—Projects are underway to assess carbon sequestration at coal-fired generation plants, petroleum production operations for offshore reserves, and oil sands development. The Alberta Saline Aquifer Project at oil sands projects is the largest project to date in North America. As part of a report entitled *Policy Drivers and Instruments to Accelerate Deployment of Clean Technologies,* the EU has agreed to support twelve large-scale CCS demonstration plants by 2015, aiming for near-zero emissions by 2020.[27] Both the U.S. and Canadian 2009 stimulus packages include monies for CCS.

Transportation

In 2008, global sales of cars and other light vehicles will hit 70 million vehicles and within a decade, as emerging countries such as India and China inevitably embrace an automobile culture, sales will soar to more than 91 million vehicles.[28] The combination of clean and sustainable energy and rising demand are triggering a catalyst for massive change in a market that is ripe for technological disruption.

In its *Annual Energy Outlook 2009* report, the U.S. Energy Information Administration (EIA) predicted that hybrid vehicle sales in the U.S. will jump from current levels to 38 percent in 2030. They also predicted that plug-in hybrids will account for 2 percent of all new car sales.

Batteries and ultra-capacitors—A significant amount of research is going into batteries (e.g., lithium ion and ceramic) for maintaining vehicles' speed and electrical systems, and ultra-capacitors for acceleration and recharging. The key issues include reduction of unit costs, reducing recharge time (need to be equivalent to time to refill car with gasoline), improving reliability and extending duration of charge.

Biofuels—Renewed focus on second-generation biofuels such as cellulosic ethanol technologies that rely on the non-edible parts of plants, and third-generation biofuels derived from algae. Numerous facilities are currently producing second-generation biofuel. The first biodiesel algae plant went on line in 2008 in Texas and produces approximately 4.4 million gallons of algal oil and 110 million pounds of biomass per year off a series of saltwater ponds spanning 1,100 acres.[29]

As low-cost/low-carbon footprint feedstocks are obtained and commercial-scale facilities increase the efficiency of their processes, biofuel prices should decrease significantly. Vinod Khosla is predicting a substantial reduction: "I personally believe in two or three years, the production cost of cellulosic ethanol will be around a-buck-twenty-five a gallon, and in within ten years you'll see a-dollar-ninety-nine a gallon ethanol in every Wal-Mart in America."[30]

Biotechnology—New bacteria/enzymes and processes to reduce the cost of creating ethanol from cellulosic material and biodiesel from algae are being developed by several companies. Another area for rapid growth is improving crop yields, where significant research is underway. Over the past thirty years, new hybrid varieties of corn have increased yields from 90 to nearly 150 bushels per acre. Scientists are predicting that 200-bushel-per-acre yields will be achieved in the next few years.[31]

Smart Highways (Research)—Still in its infancy stage, smart highways are starting to emerge. Examples of systems currently in place include:

- dynamic toll system based on the flow of vehicles into and out of the city. A derivation of this is "high-occupancy or toll" (HOT) expressways that have networks of limited-access express lanes open to high-occupancy vehicles for free and to other vehicles for a toll that varies depending on traffic flow.

- sensor-based traffic-management system that allows emergency vehicles to take control of traffic lights while en route to reduce delays.

The real goal in the not-too-distant future will be smart highways: networks of sensors connected to satellite links controlling collision-detection computers onboard the vehicles. Cars will become nodes in a worldwide network delivering information to that network and getting information from it. Ultimately, the technology will do all the driving. According to Carnegie Mellon researchers, today's typical highway lane accommodates 2,000 vehicles per hour, but with networking and automation, that capacity could be expanded to 6,000.

Green Consumer Products (Excludes Energy Efficiency)

"Green products and services" are now a mainstay of business—they have become ubiquitous—and are no longer considered inferior to their traditional non-green competitors. Consumers are expected to double their spending on green products and services in 2008, totaling an estimated $500 billion annually or $43 billion per month.[32]

Product lifecycle management (PLM)—PLM software is software that assists organizations to manage the full life cycle of a product and thereby minimizes issues related to complex regulatory compliance, avoidance of hazardous ingredients for consumer products and concerns related to take-back initiatives. More and more the process, and thus the software capability, must extend to collaboration across company's supply chain.

Detection of chemicals in products—Spurred on by the rash of product recalls and security concerns at international borders, as well as growing demand by brands to eliminate SVHC, a new wave of analyzers are coming to market to screen goods for the presence of hazardous chemicals. Companies are also offering services by which they will statistically sample goods manufactured overseas and assess the presence of hazardous chemicals that may be in violation of either legislation or company policies.

E-paper—E-paper is a portable, reusable storage and display medium that looks like paper but can be repeatedly written on (refreshed) by electronic means thousands or millions of times. Potential applications for e-paper include e-books, electronic newspapers, portable signs and foldable and rollable displays. Information to be displayed is downloaded through a connection to a computer or a cell phone, or created with mechanical tools such as an electronic pencil. Full-scale use of this technology is not expected for several years; however, its impact, once it reaches the market, will be substantial.[33]

Water Treatment and Conservation

Blue is the new green. Global Water Intelligence is predicting that the market for water purification and desalination will reach $95 billion by 2012.[34] A Calvert Research report forecasts that "to provide enough water for all uses through 2030, the world will need to invest as much as $1 trillion a year on applying existing technologies for conserving water, maintaining and replacing water-related infrastructure, and constructing sanitation systems."[35]

A recently released CERES report indicates that too few businesses and investors are taking into consideration the potential for economic upheaval if water resources become as scarce as predicted. The report singles out eight sectors that should re-assess the risk associated with water use: electric power, high tech, beverage and agriculture, apparel, biotechnology/pharmaceuticals, forest products and metals/mining.

Desalination facilities—According to the 2008–2009 edition of the *International Desalination Association Desalination Yearbook* published by Global Water Intelligence, global contracted (planned) capacity grew by 43% in 2007, enough to supply potable water to more than 50 million people. The yearbook also reports that the number of contracted desalination plants worldwide totaled 13,869 as of June 30, 2008, up from 13,080 the prior year. Many of these very large facilities are being constructed in the Middle East region. Large-scale desalination facilities are also being planned in the U.S. because of the increased scarcity of water.[36]

Desalination technology—Large-scale desalination typically uses large amounts of energy as well as specialized, expensive infrastructure, making it very costly. The large energy reserves of many Middle Eastern countries, along with their relative water scarcity, have led to extensive construction of desalination plants in this region. Several companies are actively involved in the development of new technology for desalination, which uses 50% less energy than existing systems.

Virtual Water—Several forward-thinking companies are starting to assess "virtual" water, i.e., amount of water used in the production and use of a product. This approach allows them to better document usage and prepare a more holistic reduction strategy.

Adaptation to Changing Climate

Numerous opportunities exist to assist organizations to adapt to changing climate conditions; however, until there is a significant event(s), it is doubtful that North American governments or most companies will invest much in this area. Organizations will, however, spend money on disaster and emergency response plans, as well as try to mitigate the potential impacts of climate change when undertaking new infrastructure projects, e.g., adding height to sea walls.

> Information Technology is taking on a significant role in the battle to address environmental issues. Key examples include:
>
> - green IT energy conservation initiatives
> - software for product life cycle management, supply chain collaboration and governance, risk and compliance
> - advancement in the design and charging of electric vehicles
> - "smart grid" and emerging "smart traffic" technology

CHAPTER 9 TAKE-AWAYS

Assess business risks and opportunities—Most organizations have not adequately assessed the business risks and opportunities associated with environmental issues (climate change, hazardous ingredients in products, water shortages/cost, etc.). As such, their activities tend to be reactive, disjointed, inefficient and, most importantly, detrimental to their bottom line. A business risk and opportunity assessment should be conducted and rolled into the company's strategic planning process to allow the company to move from "cosmetic environmentalism" to better manage the business side of the environment and improve brand.

Build flexible plans—The credit crunch of 2008 has taught us that strategic plans need to be flexible and revisited with changing market conditions. No longer can we confidently predict key market influencers—e.g., petroleum prices—with any degree of certainty. It is therefore critical that various scenarios be leveraged in the planning process and that the strategic plans and targets reflect these scenarios.

Focus on main tech not cleantech—As per a Vinod Khosla quote, the market is primarily about main tech, not cleantech. There are countless opportunities to capitalize on this via changes to product design (energy efficiency, elimination of hazardous ingredients, elimination of waste, improved take-back, etc.) that will affect the daily lives of North Americans.

Pay attention to Business 101—The environmental market has moved from a momentum play to a value play. There are a great number of well-intentioned individuals who lack business acumen who have created or are in the process of creating new green products and services. Key attributes that apply in this sector, as in all others, include

- a business model that is both defensible and scalable
- a proven and experienced management team that is committed
- financial strength (growth, earnings, liquidity, capitalization, access to funds) appropriate to stage of company
- technology, intellectual property and control/robustness of supply chain
- thorough understanding of current and proposed changes to environmental legislation and government incentives

Two common pitfalls are a management team that lacks hands-on experience and inadequate commercialization strategy/financing—"if you build it, they may not come!"

The latter point is critical as in many cases companies create a business plan that does not examine the risk of changing government (local, federal and regional) policies.

Develop a sustainable development/energy strategy—Whether as part of a business risks and opportunities assessment, or a separate activity, an energy/SD strategy needs to be developed and integrated into the company's business plan—not as a separate "add-on" exercise because it is fundamental to most company's growth. The analysis should enable visualization of the company and the society in which it will operate for the next twenty years, as well as the company's role within the value chain.

Manage the supply chain—Regardless of whether you produce a product at your own facilities or leverage third parties, you need to manage potential environmental mismanagement in the supply chain, as it will affect the company's bottom line (via increased costs) as well as impair corporate brand. More and more companies are morphing into sales/marketing organizations that may only assemble their finished products and rely on thousands of suppliers to do manufacturing and in some cases design. It is critical that clear rules are set and adherence to these rules monitored on a regular basis, and that systems are in place to ensure collaboration and ongoing compliance with rapidly changing global legislation.

AUTHORS' COMMENTS

We are experiencing changes of a magnitude that we have not seen before—in both the natural and business environments. Sector after sector will face increased pressure to adapt their business to address these changes. Companies that proactively identify key business risks and opportunities and act upon them will accelerate growth, while those that choose to ignore the wave of change will become the twenty-first century dinosaurs. To quote a Native American proverb, we do not inherit the earth from our ancestors; we borrow it from our children. We need to carefully manage it so that they (and our companies) can be around for a long time.

Table 9.4: Additional Sources of Reference for the Environmental/Energy Market

www.cleanedge.com—leading research and publishing firm helping companies, investors and governments understand and profit from clean technologies

www.cleantech.com—forum for information on the cleantech sector and investments

www.eia.doe.gov/steo—United States Energy Administration Short-Term Energy Outlook

www.environmentalleader.com—provides executive daily briefing on the environmental market

www.globe-net.com—weekly guide to information on business of the environment

www.greenbiz.com—update on green initiatives

www.investeco.com—information on green public and private investments managed by a Canadian fund manager

www.sdtc.ca—Sustainable Development Technology Canada

www.treehugger.com—information on green consumer products

NOTES

1 Adam Bluestein, "Blue Is the New Green," *Inc. Magazine*, November 2008.
2 Yachnin & Associates, "The SD Effect: Translating Sustainable Development into Financial Valuation Measures," 2006.
3 Susanna Wood, "Oil Prices Likely to Hit $200 a Barrel," August 11, 2008, http://news.icm.ac.uk/business/utilities/oil-prices-likely-to-hit-200-a-barrel/607.
4 Energy Shop, http://www.energyshop.com/es/homes/gas/gaspriceforecast.cfm.
5 Ibid.
6 Ibid.
7 Kevin Tuerff, "U.S. Says It Will Cut GHG At Least 50% by 2050," Environmental Leader, December 11, 2008, www.environmentalleader.com/2008/12/11/us-says-it-will-cut-ghg-at-least-50-by-2050.
8 Dan E. Arvizu, "Alternative Energy: Solar, Wind, Geothermal," Milken/Sandia Energy Workshop for Financial and Capital Market Leaders, October 23, 2008.
9 Environment Canada, "Turning the Corner: Taking Action to Fight Climate Change," March 2008, http://www.ec.gc.ca/doc/virage-corner/2008-03/brochure_eng.html.
10 Eric de Place, "Inside WCI Delay," 2008, http://www.worldchanging.com/archives//008345.html.
11 William Ambrose, "EER Research Update Q3—Renewable Power Generation," Emerging Energy Research, 2008, http://www.emerging-energy.com/user/category_docs.aspx?ll=2&catid=test1102483685&docid=/user/test1102483685_reg/RPG3QResearchUpdate.pdf&cattype=AdvisoryServices.
12 "GE's 'ecomagination' Business Grows to $14 billion; Revenue Target Raised to $25 billion as Orders Top $70 billion," Domain-b, May 29, 2008, http://www.domain-b.com/companies/companies_g/ge/20080529_harvest_grows.html.
13 "Mitsubishi Targets Sales of $13.3 B from Cleantech Products," Environmental Leader, November 7, 2008, http://www.environmentalleader.com/2008/11/07/mitsubishi-targets-sales-of-133-b-from-cleantech-products.
14 "Vinod Khosla: It's About Main Tech, Not Clean Tech," Zdnet.com, September 17, 2008, http://blogs.zdnet.com/BTL/?p=10072.
15 Michael Shellenberger and Ted Nordhaus, *Break Through: From the Death of Environmentalism to the Politics of Possibility* (Boston: Houghton Mifflin Co., 2007).
16 Michael Hollinshead, Craig Eastman and Thomas Etsell, "Forecasting Performance and Market Penetration of Fuel Cells in Transportation," 2005.
17 Business Wire, "Climate Change: The Trillion Dollar Wake Up Call," September 22, 2008, http://www.marketwatch.com/news/story/climate-change-trillion-dollar-wake/story.aspx?guid=%7B8E1752A2-EDD7-432D-BF4E-0B0626F7EC18%7D&dist=hppr.
18 McKinsey Global Institute, "The Carbon Productivity Challenge: Curbing Climate Change and Sustaining Economic Growth," June 2008, http://www.fypower.org/pdf/MGI_Carbon_Productivity.pdf.
19 Joel Makower and R. Pernick, C. Wilder, "Clean Energy Trends," 2008, http://www.cleanedge.com.
20 IEA, "World Energy Outlook 2008 Fact Sheet: Oil Demand. What Are the Prospects for Oil Consumption to 2030?", 2008.
21 Arvizu, "Alternative Energy: Solar, Wind, Geothermal."

22 Jefferies & Company Inc., "Clean Technology Primer," June 2008.

23 "Energy Analysis and Tools," National Renewable Energy Laboratory, 2008, http://www.nrel.gov/buildings/energy_analysis.html.

24 Alex Serpo, "Green Your Datacentre or It May Go Dark," April 4, 2008, http://www.zdnet.com.au/insight/software/soa/Green-your-datacentre-or-you-may-get-fired/0,139023769,339286821,00.htm.

25 Solid State Lighting, "Frequently Asked Questions," 2008, http://lighting.sandia.gov/XlightingoverviewFAQ.htm#ssl.

26 Energy Shop, http://www.energyshop.com/es/homes/gas/gaspriceforecast.cfm.

27 IEA, "Policy Drivers and Instruments to Accelerate Deployment of Clean Technologies," 2008, http://www.iea.org/Textbase/work/2007/learning/Tulej.pdf.

28 "All Roads Lean Toward the Eco-Car," *Globe and Mail*, May 13, 2008.

29 Clayton Cornell, "First Algae Biodiesel Plant Goes Online: April 1, 2008," March 29, 2008, http://gas2.org/2008/03/29/first-algae-biodiesel-plant-goes-online-april-1-2008.

30 SFGate, "On the Record with Vinod Khosla," May 11, 2008, http://www.sfgate.com/cgi-bin/article.cgi?f=/c/a/2008/05/10/BUD010IHPC.DTL.

31 Bio Technology Industry Association, "Increasing Crop Yield and Commercializing Cellulosic Biofuels Are Key to Meeting Demand for Feed," December 28, 2006, http://www.bio.org/news/newsitem.asp?id=2008_0612_01ber and Transportation Fuels.

32 Cohn & Wolfe, "*Consumers Will Double Spending on Green*," news release on research by Cohn & Wolfe, Landor Associates and Penn, Schoen & Berland Associates, September 2007.

33 Search Mobile Computing, "e-paper," 2008, http://searchmobilecomputing.techtarget.com/sDefinition/0,,sid40_gci535038,00.html.

34 ITT, "ITT's Place in the Cycle of Water—Everything but the Pipes," 6th edition, http://ittfluidbusiness.com/media/ITT_WTRBK_v6_download.pdf.

35 Calvert, "Calvert Launches Global Water Fund, Issues Report on Opportunities in $1 Trillion Annual Worldwide Investment in Water Technology and Services," 2008, CSR Wire, http://www.csrwire.com/News/13655.html.

36 Waterworld, "Report Shows Global Water Crisis Promotes Desalination Boom," October 16, 2008, http://ww.pennnet.com/display_article/342890/41/ARTCL/none/none/1/Report-shows-global-water-crisis-promotes-desalination-boom.

BIBLIOGRAPHY

Abbott, Rob. "The Risk Universe." Green Business, March 2008. http://www.green-business.ca. Also available in print.

About.com. "The History of Electric Cars." http://inventors.about.com (accessed March 2008).

AccountAbility and Consumers International. *What Assures Consumers on Climate Change? Switching on Citizen Power.* 2007.

Advertising Standards Authority. "ASA Adjudications: Toyota (GB) plc." http://www.asa.org.uk/asa/adjudications/Public/TF_ADJ_42615.htm.

Agriculture Canada. "ecoAgriculture Biofuel Capital Initiative (ecoABC)." http://www4.agr.gc.ca/AAFC-AAC/display-afficher.do?id=1195672401464&lang=e.

Ambrose, William. "EER Research Update Q3—Renewable Power Generation." Emerging Energy Research. November 11, 2008. http://www.emerging-energy.com/user/category_docs.aspx?l1=2&catid=test1102483685&docid=/user/test1102483685_reg/RPG3QResearchUpdate.pdf&cattype=AdvisoryServices.

American Chemistry Council. "Responsible Care." http://www.americanchemistry.com/s_responsiblecare (accessed in September 2008).

American Wind Energy Association. "Legislative Affairs." http://www.awea.org/legislative/.

Anasta, Paul, and John Warner. *Green Chemistry: Theory and Practice.* New York: Oxford University Press, 1998.

Andrew McAfee Blog. http://andrewmcafee.org/blog/.

Andrew, James P., Harold L. Sirkin and John Butman. *Payback: Reaping the Rewards of Innovation.* Boston: Harvard Business School Press, 2006.

Arvizu, Dan. E. "Alternative Energy: Solar, Wind, Geothermal." Milken/Sandia Energy Workshop for Financial and Capital Market Leaders, October 23, 2006. Available at http://www.nrel.gov/director/presentations_speeches.html.

Assadourian, Erik, Gary T. Gardner, Bill Baue, Thomas Prugh and Linda Starke. "State of the World 2008." Worldwatch Institute, The Worldwatch Institute Staff.

AutoblogGreen Blog. http://www.autobloggreen.com/.

Bach, Hubert. "Nuclear Power Gets Green Sheen." *Montreal Gazette*, June 15, 2008.

Bachram, H. "Climate Fraud and Carbon Colonialism: The New Trade in Greenhouse Gases." *Capitalism Nature Socialism* 15, no. 4 (2004).

Bailey, R., "Obama's Fuel Economy Follies", January 27, 2009. http://www.reason.com/news/show/131279.html

Barents Observer, "Gazprom to Sell Shtokman LNG to Canada," May 16, 2008. http://www.barentsobserver.com/gazprom-to-sell-shtokman-lng-to-canada.4482345-91228.html.

Barrett, Jane, and John Davies. "Building an Electric Car Nation with Shai Agassi." AMR Research, November 2, 2007. http://www.amresearch.com.

Baskind, Chris. "5 Reasons Not to Drink Bottled Water." June 19, 2007. http://lighterfootstep.com/.

Battery Council International. "Battery Recycling." http://www.batterycouncil.org/LeadAcidBatteries/BatteryRecycling (accessed in March 2007).

Bayer. "Bayer Sustainable Development Policy." http://www.bayer.com/en/sustainable-development-policy.aspx.

BBC. "BBC World News and Synovate Survey Reveals a Shift in Attitudes to Climate Change." 2008.

———. "Q&A: Reach Chemicals Legislation." November 28, 2007. http://news.bbc.co.uk.

Bedard, Roger, Des McGinnis and Justin Klure. *White Paper Submitted to Western Governors Association Clean and Diversified Energy Advisor Committee: Ocean Wave Energy Conversion Technology*. Electric Power Research Institute, 2005. http://oceanenergy.epri.com/attachments/ocean/reports/WGA_Ocean_Energy_White_Paper_12-15-05.pdf.

Belli-Bivar, Eric, and Lana Finney. "OSC Staff Notice 51-716 Environmental Disclosure must be improved says the Ontario Securities Commission." April 1, 2008. http://74.125.95.104/search?q=cache:4nXCOr1XUmgJ:www.davis.ca/publication/OSC-Staff-Notice-51-716-Environmental-disclosure-must-be-improved-says-the-Ontario-Securities-Commission.pdf+Ontario+Securities+Commission+published+Notice+51-716+in+2008+on+Environmental+Reporting+stated+that+company+disclosure+on+environmental+li&hl=en&ct=clnk&cd=1.

Bensimon Byrne. *Consumerology Report. The Impact of Environmental Issues*, 2008.

Benzie, Robert, and Debra Black. "Darlington to Get Two New Reactors." *Toronto Star*, June 17, 2008.

BEP, CPI, and WBCSD. *Driving Success: Human Resources and Sustainable Development*. 2nd ed. 2008.

Berthon, Bruno, Jim Grimsley, Peter Lacey and David Abood. "Achieving High Performance: The Sustainability Imperative." Accenture. 2008.

Beverage & Diamond, P.C. "Mandatory U.S. Carbon Reporting Announced." 2008. http://www.bdlaw.com/news-271.html.

Bio Technology Industry Association. "Increasing Crop Yield and Commercializing Cellulosic Biofuels Are Key to Meeting Demand for Feed." December 28, 2006. http://www.bio.org/news/newsitem.asp?id=2008_0612_01ber and Transportation Fuels.

Birol, Fatih. "Transcript: Interview with IEA Chief Economist." By Ed Crooks and Javier Blas. *Financial Times*. November 7, 2007. http://www.ft.com/cms/s/0/3c8940ca-8d46-11dc-a398-0000779fd2ac.html?nclick_check=1.

Bishop, S. "Don't Bother with the 'Green' Consumer." *Harvard Business Review*, 2008. http://www.hbrgreen.org/2008/01/dont_bother_with_the_green_con.html.

Blackwell, Richard. "Solar Power Heats up with New Ontario Projects." *Globe and Mail*, January 22, 2008, Report on Business.

Bluestein, Adam. "Blue Is the New Green." *Inc.*, November 2008.

Boston Consulting Group and World Federation of Personnel Management Associations. "Creating People Advantage: How to Address HR Challenges Worldwide Through 2015." 2008.

Boswell, Randy. "WWF Slams Shell Game." *Montreal Gazette*, August 14, 2008.

Boudreau, J.W., and P.M. Ramstad. "Talentship, Talent Segmentation, and Sustainability: A New HR Decision Science Paradigm for a New Strategy Definition." Human Resource Management 44, no. 2 (2008).

Boyd, Neil. "Opening the C-Suite: Chief Sustainability/Energy Officer—Key to a Defined Energy Strategy." Presentation to Energy Matters Summit, April 1, 2008.

BP. "Greenhouse Gas Emissions—Detailed Data from 2007." http://www.bp.com/sectiongenericarticle.do?categoryId=9023665&contentId=7043739.

———. BP Statistical Review of World Energy June 2008. http://www.bp.com/liveassets/bp_internet/globalbp/globalbp_uk_english/reports_and_publications/statistical_energy_review_2008/STAGING/local_assets/downloads/spreadsheets/statistical_review_full_report_workbook_2008.xls#'Primary Energy - Consumption'!A1.

Brenner, Aaron, Barry Eidlin and Kerry Candaele. "Wal-Mart Stores Inc." Paper presented at conference on Global Companies—Global Unions—Global Research—Global Campaigns, Cornell University, February 2006.

Breyfogle, Forrest. "Plan Do Check Act (PDCA) as Part of Lean Six Sigma Project Execution Roadmap in Improve Phase." June 23, 2008.

Brody, Paul, and Mondher Ben-Hamida. "12 Steps to a Greener Supply Chain." *Environmental Leader,* November 30, 2008. http://www.environmentalleader.com/2008/11/30/12-steps-to-a-greener-supply-chain/.

Bruno, Kenny, with Jed Greer. *The Greenpeace Book of Greenwash.* Greenpeace International. 1992. http://research.greenpeaceusa.org/?a=view&d=4588.

Bryner, Michelle. "Agricultural Biotech: Vying for More Ground." *Chemical Week* (June 2, 2008).

Buckler, Grant. "Clean Power Comes In with the Tide." *Globe and Mail,* October 20, 2008.

Bughin, J., Michael Chui and M. and B. Johnson. "The Next Step in Open Innovation." *McKinsey Quarterly* (June 2008).

Business Dictionary.com. http://www.businessdictionary.com (accessed in September 2008).

Business Wire. "Kleiner Perkins and RockPort Capital, Two Leading U.S. Cleantech Investors, Launch Joint Venture with Norwegian Electrical Vehicle Company Think OSLO, Norway & PASADENA, Calif." April 21, 2008.

Byrne, John A. "The Fast Company Interview: Jeff Immelt." Issue 96, July 2005. http://www.fastcompany.com/node/53574.

Calvert. "Calvert Launches Global Water Fund, Issues Report on Opportunities in $1 Trillion Annual Worldwide Investment in Water Technology and Services." CSR Wire, 2008. http://www.csrwire.com/News/13655.html.

Canada. Alberta. "Alberta Surges Ahead with Climate Change Action Plan." July 8, 2008. http://www.alberta.ca/home/NewsFrame.cfm?ReleaseID=/acn/200807/23960039FB54D-CC21-7234-31C3E853089A1E6C.html.

Canadian Chemical Producers Association. "Responsible Care®." http://www.ccpa.ca/ResponsibleCare/ (accessed in April 2008).

Canadian Embassy. "Canada-US Energy Relations." http://geo.international.gc.ca/can-am/washington/trade_and_investment/energy-en.asp (accessed in September 2008).

Canadian Geothermal Energy Association. http://www.cangea.ca/ (accessed in September 2008).

Canadian Standards Association. *ISO 14025:2006. Environmental labels and declarations—Type III environmental declarations—Principles and procedures.* 2007.

———. *National Standard of Canada CAN/CSA-ISO 14021-00. Environmental labels and declarations—Self-declared environmental claims (Type II environmental labeling).* 2004.

———. *Plus 14021—Environmental Claims: A Guide for Industry and Advertisers.* 2008.

Canadian Wind Energy Association. http://www.canwea.ca/ (accessed in September 2008).

Canwest News Service. "Montreal Climate Exchange begins Trading in Emission Credit Futures." *Financial Post,* May 31, 2008.

Cap Gemini Consulting. "Global CIO Survey 2008. The Role of the IT Function in Business Innovation." 2008.

Capelli, P. "Talent Management for the 21st Century." *Harvard Business Review,* March 2008.

Carbon Market Data Ltd. "Carbon Market Data Publishes Key Figures on the European Emissions Trading Scheme for the Year 2007." 2008.

———. "Carbon Market Data Publishes Key Figures on the European Emissions Trading Scheme for the Year 2006." 2007.

Carbon Trade Watch. "Hoodwinked in the Hothouse—The G8, Climate Change and Free-market Environmentalism." Transnational Institute briefing series no. 2005/3, 2005.

Carbon Trust. *Climate Change: "The Trillion Dollar Wake Up Call."* September 22, 2008. http://www.carbontrust.co.uk/News/presscentre/shareholder-value-report.htm.

———. *Cutting Carbon in Europe: The 2020 Plans and the Future of the EU ETS.* 2008.

Carlton, S. "Sustain that Sense of Ownership." *Human Resources* (November 2007).

Carol, Allain. "Génération Y. L'enfant-roi devenu adulte." *Les Éditions logiques* (2005).

Caye, J.M., and I. Marten. "Talent Management: Nurturing the Egg." Boston Consulting Group, 2007.

CBC News. "Canadians Ready to Pay to Deal with Climate Change, Says Suzuki." April 20, 2007. http://www.cbc.ca/canada/story/2007/04/20/suzuki-baird.html.

Ceres. "Investors Achieve Major Company Commitments on Climate Change." 2007. http://www.ceres.org/NETCOMMUNITY/Page.aspx?pid=928&srcid=705.

Chafkin, Max. "The Companies of Elon Musk: How the Entrepreneur of the Year Does Business and Makes Waves." December 2007. http://www.inc.com.

Challick, Rowan. "China's Carbon Output Tops US." *The Australian,* June 21, 2007.

Chamberlain, Adam. "Canada: Climate Change and the Electricity Sector. The Provincial-Federal Challenge for Canada." Bordner Ladner Gervais, on Mondaq.com, 2008. http://www.mondaq.com/article.asp?article_id=63964&lk=1.

Charter, Martin, and Anne Chick. "Welcome to the First issue of the Journal of Sustainable Product Design." *The Journal of Sustainable Product Design* (April 1997).

Childs, Dana. "Core Ethanol Crisis Looming Says Watchdog." Cleantech. January 8, 2007. http://www.cleantech.com.

Cleantech. "Fuel Cell Market Size Soon $8.5 billion, Says Report." July 20, 2007. http://media.cleantech.com/1504/fuel-cell-market-size-soon-8-5-billion.

———. "Israel's SDE Plans 100MW of Wave Energy for Africa." November 13, 2008. http://www.cleantech.com/news/3871/israels-sde-plans-100mw-wave-energy-africa.

Clifton, R., and J. Simmons, eds. *Brands and Branding.* London: Profile Books, 2003.

Climate Group. "Reducing Emission, DuPont Case Study." 2008. http://theclimategroup.org/.

Climate Progress. "Is 450 ppm Possible? Part 5: Old Coal's Out, Can't Wait for New Nukes, So What Do We Do Now?" 2008. http://climateprogress.org/2008/05/08/is-450-ppm-possible-part-5-old-coals-out-cant-wait-for-new-nukes-so-what-do-we-do-now/.

———. "McCain Calls for 700+ New Nuclear Plants (and Seven Yucca Mountains) Costing $4 Trillion." 2008. http://climateprogress.org/2008/05/04/mccain-calls-for-700-new-nuclear-plants-and-7-yucca-mountains-costing-4-trillion/.

Climate Savers. "2008 Update: Highlights from Climate Savers Companies." February 2008. http://209.85.215.104/search?q=cache:8UG9MgY0G1cJ:generazioneclima.wwf.it/pdf/cs_update08_final.pdf+Sony+savings+in+energy+consumption+due+to+logistics+optimization&hl=en&ct=clnk&cd=1.

ClimateChangeCorp.com. *Special Report: The Climate Change Industry Takes Root.* November 2008.

Clinton Global Initiative. "Virgin's $3 Bill. Commitment to Renewable Energy Initiatives 2006." July 7, 2008 update. http://commitments.clintonglobalinitiative.org/projects.htm?mode=view&rid=42976.

CNN.com. "Mattel CEO: 'Rigorous Standards' After Massive Toy Recall." November 15, 2008. http://www.cnn.com/2007/US/08/14/recall/index.html.

Cohen, David. "What's New at the Tar Sands." January 2, 2008. http://www.aspo-usa.com/index.php?option=com_content&task=view&id=291&Itemid=91.

Cohn & Wolfe. "Consumers Will Double Spending on Green." Released by Cohn & Wolfe, Landor Associates and Penn, Schoen & Berland Associates, September 2007.

Colbert, B.A., and E. Kuricz. "Three Conceptions of Triple Bottom Line Business Sustainability and the Role for HRM." *Human Resource Planning* 20 (2007).

Collins, Jim. *Good to Great.* New York: HarperCollins, 2001.

Competitive Enterprise Institute. "Corporate Social Concerns: Are They Good Citizenship, Or a Rip-Off for Investors?" Fred. L. Smith Debate in *Wall Street Journal,* December 5, 2005.

Cooke, Kristina. "Americans Pick Print Books Over Electronic Contenders." Reuters, May 30, 2008. http://www.reuters.com/article/vcCandidateFeed2.

Cooperative Bank, The. *The Ethical Consumerism Report.* 2007.

Cornell, Clayton. "First Algae Biodiesel Plant Goes Online: April 1, 2008." March 29, 2008. http://gas2. org/2008/03/29/first-algae-biodiesel-plant-goes-online-april-1-2008/.

Crawford, Tiffany. "Schools Take Aim at Bottled Water in Vending Machines." *Montreal Gazette*, June 23, 2008.

Davies, J. "Big Green: IBM and the ROI of Environmental Leadership." AMR Research. 2007.

DAVIS LLP Blog. http://www.davis.ca/en/blog/.

Davis, Valerie. "Dow Chemical Ties Energy-efficiency to Cash Savings." December 10, 2008. Environmental Leader. http://www.environmentalleader.com/2008/12/10/dow-chemical-ties-energy-efficiency-to-cash-savings/.

de Place, Eric. "Inside WCI Delay." 2008. http://www.worldchanging.com/archives//008345.html.

Del Chiaro, Bernadette, Sarah Payne and Tony Dutzik. "Solar Thermal Power and the Fight Against Global Warming." 2008. Environment America. http://www.environmentamerica.org/uploads/0f/jZ/0fjZtsJDnQCqGKdr9a7Hjg/On-The-Rise.pdf.

Dell Corporation. *Values in Action: Dell Sustainability Report & Fiscal Year 2007 in Review*. 2007.

Deloitte. *Making the Difference: Putting Supply Chain Strategy to Work*. 2007.

Department for Environment, Food and Rural Affairs (United Kingdom). "Green Claims: Practical Guidance. How to Make a Good Environmental Claim." 2003.

———. "A Shopper's Guide to Green Labels." January 2007.

Derwent, Henry. "Crucial for Our Future." *The Age*, August 20, 2008. http://www.theage.com.au/opinion/crucial-for-our-future-20080819-3y89.html?page=-1.

Dills, Jim. "Supply Chain Data Exchange for Material Disclosure Solving One of the Most Difficult RoHS-Related Problems for Small-to-Medium Sized Enterprises." Presentation to NIST, October 6, 2005.

domain-b. "GE's 'Ecomagination' Business Grows to $14 Billion; Revenue Target Raised to $25 Billion as Orders Top $70 Billion." *domain-b*, May 29, 2008. http://www.domain-b.com/companies/companies_g/ge/20080529_harvest_grows.html.

Dorn, Jonathan. "Solar Thermal Power Coming to a Boil." Earth Policy Institute, July 22, 2008. http://www.earth-policy.org/Updates/2008/Update73.htm.

Drucker, Peter. "The Discipline of Innovation." *Harvard Business Review*, August 2002.

———. *The Practice of Management*. New York: Harper & Row Publishers, 1954.

Duplantier, F.R. "Global Warming Is Greatest Hoax Ever." America's Future. http://www.americasfuture.net/1997/nov97/97-1123a.html.

DuPont. "About DuPont." http://www.dupont.com (accessed in July 2008).

Dutton, Gail. "How Nike Is Changing The World, One Factory At a Time." *Ethisphere*, March 26, 2008. http://ethisphere.com/how-nike-is-changing-the-world-one-factory-at-a-time/.

Earthling Angst Blog. http://earthlingangst.blogspot.com/.

Eco Pragmatists. "Private Energy International." November 2007.

Ecocoach. "The Cost of Building Green Is Less than You Think." August 22, 2007. http://ecocoach.wordpress.com/2007/08/22/cost-of-building-green-is-less-than-you-think/.

Economist, The. "Creditworthy: A New Rating Agency Aims to Separate Emissions Reductions from Hot Air." 2008. http://www.economist.com/finance/displaystory.cfm?story_id=11637782.

———. *Under the Spotlight: The Transition of Environmental Risk Management*, 2008. http://www.towersperrin.com/tp/getwebcachedoc?webc=HRS/USA/2008/200805/EIU_Under_the_spotlight_FINAL.pdf.

Ecos Corporation. 2006. http://www.ecoscorporation.com.

EEM inc. "A Paper Buyer's Guide to Forest Certification Schemes." Markets Initiative, 2006. http://marketsinitiative.org/index.php?page=paper-buyers-guide-certification-schemes.

———. Sustainable Business brochure.

Ehrlich, David. "Another Cellulosic Powerhouse Formed." May 14, 2008. http://cleantech.com/news/2837/another-cellulosic-powerhouse-is-formed.

Ellison, Jesse. "Save the Planet, Lose the Guilt." *Newsweek*, July 7–14, 2008.

Emerging Markets Online. "Biodiesel 2020: Global Market Survey." 2nd ed. http://www.emerging-markets.com/biodiesel/.

Energy Bible. "Renewable Energy News." http://www.energybible.com/default.html (accessed on July 31, 2008).

Energy Information Administration. "Biofuels in the U.S. Transportation Sector." 2008. http://www.eia.doe.gov/oiaf/analysispaper/biomass.html.

———. "Energy Overview." 2008. http://www.eia.doe.gov/emeu/mer/overview.html.

———. *Oil Market Basics: Demand*. January 2008. http://www.eia.doe.gov/pub/oil_gas/petroleum/analysis_publications/oil_market_basics/demand_text.htm.

Energy Justice. "Fact Sheet: 'Clean Coal' Power Plants (IGCC)." *Energy Justice*, 2008. http://www.energyjustice.net/coal/igcc/factsheet.pdf.

Energy Shop. http://www.energyshop.com/es/homes/gas/gaspriceforecast.cfm? (accessed in September 2008).

Enkvist, Per-Anders, T. Nauclér and J. Rosander. "A Cost Curve for Greenhouse Gas Reduction." *McKinsey Quarterly*, no. 1 (2007).

Environment California. "Million Solar Roofs." 2008. http://www.environmentcalifornia.org/energy/million-solar-roofs.

Environment Canada. "Canada's Offset System for Greenhouse Gases." Presentation to the GHG Offsets for the Electricity Sector Workshop, 2008.

———. "Turning the Corner: Taking Action to Fight Climate Change." March 2008. http://www.ec.gc.ca/doc/virage-corner/2008-03/brochure_eng.html.

Environmental Capital Blog. http://blogs.wsj.com/environmentalcapital/.

Environmental Leader. "BP Tops Greenpeace in Green Brands Survey." *Environmental Leader*, March 26, 2008. http://www.environmentalleader.com/2008/03/26/bp-tops-greenpeace-in-green-brands-survey/.

———. "Green Building Could Hit $140 Billion by 2013." *Environmental Leader*, November 20, 2008. http://www.environmentalleader.com/2008/11/20/green-building-could-hit-140-billion-by-2013/.

———. "Mitsubishi Targets Sales of $13.3 B from Cleantech Products." *Environmental Leader*, November 17, 2008. http://www.environmentalleader.com/2008/11/07/mitsubishi-targets-sales-of-133-b-from-cleantech-products/.

———. "Toyota Second to None in Green Brands Survey." *Environmental Leader*, March 31, 2008. http://www.environmentalleader.com/2008/03/31/toyota-second-to-none-in-green-brands-survey/.

Environmental Protection. "DuPont to Pay Record Fine in PFOA Case." *Environmental Protection*, December 1, 2008. http://www.eponline.com/articles/53881/.

Esty, Daniel, and Andrew Winston. *Green to Gold*. London: Yale University Press, 2006.

Euroactiv.com. "Chemicals Policy Review (REACH)." 2007.

Euromonitor International. "Are Central and South American Consumers Getting Greener?" 2007.

EUROPA. "Emissions Trading: 2007 Verified Emissions from EU ETS Businesses." Press release. 2008. http://ec.europa.eu/environment/climat/emission/press_en.htm.

———. "What Is Integrated Product Policy?" 2008. http://ec.europa.eu/environment/ipp.

European Chemical Agency. "New Alert: ECHA Publishes an Updated Intermediate List of Pre-Registered Substances." ECHA/PR/08/40. November 7, 2008.

European Lamp Company Federation. "Industry Commitment to Phasing Out Inefficient Lighting Products in the Home." February 26, 2007. http://www.iea.org/textbase/work/2007/cfl/Verhaar.pdf.

Everything2. "Geothermal Power." 2008. http://everything2.com/title/geothermal%2520power.

Falk, L. "Business Partnership Offers Guidelines for International Emissions Reductions." United State Climate Action Partnership. 2008. http://www.us-cap.org/.

Fehrenbacher, Katie. "Better Place to Build First U.S. Electric Vehicle Network in Bay Area." *earth2tech*, November 20, 2008. http://earth2tech.com/2008/11/20/better-place-to-build-first-us-electric-vehicle-network-in-bay-area/.

———. "Shai Agassi: Note to Next President, Better Place for U.S. Would Cost $100B." *earth2tech*, October 17, 2008. http://earth2tech.com/2008/10/17/shai-agassi-note-to-next-president-better-place-for-us-would-cost-100b/.

Fishman, Ted. "King Coal." *National Geographic*, May 2007.

Fournier, Pierre. "One Way or Another, the Oil Sands Will Play." *Globe and Mail*, October 20, 2008.

Fox, James. "The Cost of Noncompliance: Nine Ways RoHS Can Impact Your Company's Bottom Line." *Green SupplyLine*, August 26, 2006. http://www.greensupplyline.com.

Franken, Al. *Lies (And the Lying Liars Who Tell Them)*. New York: Dutton, 2003.

Futerra Sustainability Communications. "The Greenwash Guide." 2008.

Gelinas, Johanne. "Corporate Environmental Responsibility: Good Governance, Plain and Simple." *The Green Tourism Business Scheme*, September 2007. http://www.green-business.com.

General Electric. "Our Company." http://www.ge.com/company/index.html (accessed in September 2008).

———. *GE 2007 Citizen Report*. 2008. http://www.socialfunds.com/csr/reports/GE_2007_Citizenship_Report.pdf.

———. GE Amended Report (10-K/A) SEC Filing. January 19, 2007. http://sec.edgar-online.com/2007/01/19/0000040545-07-000007/Section12.asp.

Gizmag. "The LifeStraw Makes Dirty Water Clean." 2008. gizmag. http://www.gizmag.com/go/4418/.

Glitnir Geothermal Research. *United States Geothermal Energy Market Report*, 2007. http://docs.glitnir.is/media/files/Glitnir_USGeothermalReport.pdf.

Global Commerce Initiative and Cap Gemini. "2016 Future Supply Chain." 2008.

Global Market Information Database. "Climate Confidence Index an Indicator of Consumer Greenness." Blogtracker. 2007.

Global Reporting Initiative. "Disclosure on Sustainability Performance Has Become the Norm for Large Companies Globally: New Survey." October 2008. http://www.globalreporting.org/NewsEventsPress/PressResources/Pressrelease_28_Oct_2008.htm.

Global Solar Center. "Solar Industry Statistics." http://www.globalsolarcenter.com/solar_industry_statistics.html.

Globe and Mail. "All Roads Lean Toward the Eco-Car," May 13, 2008.

———. "Clean Diesels Are on the Way," May 13, 2008.

———. "Clear the Air on Financial Risks: Report," November 5, 2008.

———. "Energy Rich Western Provinces Boost Conservation and Clean Power Efforts," December 10, 2008, Special Information Supplement.

Globe-Net. "Oil and Gas Invest Billions in Environment." 2008. http://www.globe-net.com.

GoinGreen. "The New G-Wizi. The Next Level in Performance." 2008. http://www.goingreen.co.uk.

Gorrie, Peter. "A Dying Industry Turns to Volt." *Toronto Star*, November 22, 2008.

———. "Homes with Solar Panels to Get Subsidy." *Energy Refuge*, 2008. http://www.energyrefuge.com/archives/Solar_panel_subsidy.htm.

Government of Canada. "Canada's New Government Announces Targets to Tackle Climate Change and Reduce Air Pollution." Press release. April 2007. http://www.ecoaction.gc.ca/news-nouvelles/20070426-9-eng.cfm.

———. *Canada Wind Sector Overview*. Prepared by Investor Services Division, Invest in Canada Bureau. March 28, 2007. http://www.dk-mining.com/media/Candian_Wind_Sector_Overview_March_28_2007_edi.pdf.

Granros, Rory. "Risky Business." *Quality Digest Magazine*, January 23, 2007. http://qualitydigest.com.

Grant, John. *The Green Marketing Manifesto.* West Sussex: John Wiley & Sons, 2007.

Gray, Tara. "Canadian Response to the U.S. Sarbanes-Oxley Act of 2002: New Directions for Corporate Governances." 2005. http://www.parl.gc.ca/information/library/PRBpubs/prb0537-e.htm.

Greenbiz. "Building CSR into the Supply Chain." August 5, 2008. GreenBiz.com. http://www.greenbiz.com/news/2008/08/05/building-csr-supply-chain.

———. "Survey of S&P 100 Identifies Best Practices for Sustainability Communications." October 16, 2008. http://www.greenbiz.com/news/2008/10/16/survey-sp-100-identifies-best-practices-sustainability-communications.

Greenfacts. "Conclusions and Main Findings of Millennium Ecosystem Assessment Report." http://www.greenfacts.org/en/ecosystems/#10.

Greenpeace International. "Tasty News from Apple." May 2, 2007. http://www.greenpeace.org/international/news/tasty-apple-news-020507.

———. *Cleaning up Our Chemical Homes, Changing the Market to Supply Toxic-free Products.* 2nd ed. February 2007. http://www.greenpeace.org.uk/toxics/chemicalhome.

Griscom Little, Amanda. "Coal Position." December 3, 2004. http://www.grist.org/news/muck/2004/12/03/little-coal/.

Grobbel, C., J. Maly, and M. Molitor. "Preparing for a Low-Carbon Future." *McKinsey Quarterly*, no. 4 (2004).

Gulyas, Carol. "15–25% Return. T. Boone Pickens Says Peak Oil Reached, Plans World's Largest Wind Farm." June 8, 2008. Wind Energy. http://cleantechnica.com/2008/06/08/t-boone-pickens-says-peak-oil-reached-plans-worlds-largest-wind-farm/.

Gunther, Marc. "The Green Machine." *Fortune Magazine*, August 7, 2006.

Guthridge, M., A.D. Komm and E. Lawson. "Making Talent a Strategic Priority." *McKinsey Quarterly* (January 2008).

Guthridge, M., and A.D. Komm. "Why Multinationals Struggle to Manage Talent." *McKinsey Quarterly* (May 2008).

Hadekel, Peter. "Oil Sands Firms Take Heat on Environmental Impact." *Montreal Gazette*, June 27, 2008.

Hagerty, John, Jim Murphy and Mark Hillman. "From Tactical to Strategic to Holistic: AMR Research's GRC Maturity Model." December 14, 2006. AMR Research. http://www.amrresearch.com/content/View.asp?pmillid=20065.

Halko, Lisa. "California's Attorney General Acknowledges Prop 65 Abuse." *Legal Backgrounder* 22, no. 29 (July 27, 2007).

Hamilton, K., et al. "Forging a Frontier: Fate of the Voluntary Carbon Markets 2008." New Carbon Finance and Ecosystem Marketplace, 2008.

Hamilton, Tyler. "Earful on Oil." *Toronto Star*, August 29, 2008.

———. "Quebec Lands New Silicon Plant," *Toronto Star*, August 26, 2008. http://www.thestar.com/comment/columnists/article/485413.

Hard, G. and E. Evans, "Obama puts greenhouse gases on the front burner," January 29, 2009. http://blogs.consumerreports.org.

Harper, Tim. "Bush Signs Nuclear Deal with India." *Toronto Star*, December 19, 2006.

Hart, Martyn. "Green Outsourcing Changes IT for All." October 8, 2008. http://www.zdnetasia.com/insight/business/0,39051970,62046723,00.htm.

Hawken, Paul, Amory Lovins and L. Hunter Lovins. *Natural Capitalism: Creating the Next Industrial Revolution.* New York: Little, Brown and Company, 1999.

Hawken, Paul. *Ecology of Commerce: A Declaration of Sustainability.* New York: HarperBusiness, 1992.

Health Canada. "List of Prohibited and Restricted Cosmetic Ingredients (The Cosmetic Ingredient 'Hotlist')." 2008. http://www.hc-sc.gc.ca/cps-spc/person/cosmet/info-ind-prof/_hot-list-critique/prohibited-eng.php.

Hendrickson, Barbara. "Canada: Emissions Trading and Climate Change Bulletin: Western Climate Initiative." McMillan, on Mondaq.com. 2008. http://www.mondaq.com/article.asp?article_id=64646&lk=1.

Herrera, Tilde. "Navigating the Wilderness of Green Business Certifications." GreenBiz. July 14, 2008. http://www.greenbiz.com/print/26094.

Hersch, D., A. Bergman and M. Heintz. "Emissions Trading: Practical Aspects." In *Global Climate Change and U.S. Law*, edited Michael B. Gerrard, chapter 18. Chicago: American Bar Association, 2007.

Hiemstra, Glen. *Turning the Future into Revenue*. New Jersey: John Wiley & Sons, 2006.

Hoffman, A.J. "Getting Ahead of the Curve: Corporate Strategies that Address Climate Change." Prepared by the University of Michigan for the Pew Center on Global Climate Change. 2006.

Hojlo, Jeffrey, and Michael Burkett. "PLM Top Business Drivers for 2008." AMR Research. January 25, 2008.

Holliday, Chad. "An Expanded Commitment: DuPont and Sustainable Growth." DuPont speech, 2006. Available on http://www.dupont.com.

Hollinshead, Michael, Craig Eastman and Thomas Etsell. "Forecasting Performance and Market Penetration of Fuel Cells in Transportation." *Fuel Cells Bulletin*, 2005.

Holmes, Stanley. "Nike Goes for the Green." Business Week, September 25, 2006.

Horne, M. "Cap and Trade: Reducing Pollution, Inspiring Innovation." The Pembina Institute. 2008.

Hybrid Car Review. "Slow Down in Hybrid Car Sales Expected in 2008." February 1, 2008. http://hybridreview. blogspot.com/.

IBM. "Climate Protection." 2008. http://www.ibm.com/ibm/environment/climate/.

Infor. "Product Lifecycle Management (PLM)." http://www.infor.com/solutions/plm/.

Information Week Blog, The. http://www.informationweek.com/blog/main/.

Intentblog. http://www.intentblog.com/.

Interface. "Who We Are." 2008. http://www.interfaceinc.com/who/founder.html.

Intergovernmental Panel on Climate Change. *Climate Change 2007: Synthesis Report*, November 17, 2007. http://www.ipcc.ch/ipccreports/ar4-syr.htm.

International Energy Agency. *Energy Technology Perspectives*, 2008. http://www.iea.org/Textbase/techno/etp/index.asp.

———. *Policy Drivers and Instruments to Accelerate Deployment of Clean Technologies*, 2008. http://www.iea.org/Textbase/work/2007/learning/Tulej.pdf.

———. *Renewable Energy Markets: Past and Future Trends*, 2005. http://64.233.169.104/search?q=cache:peS3AuVb29YJ:www.iea.org/textbase/work/2005/Biofuels/Biofuels_Sellers_Paper.pdf+IEA+future+hydroelectric+generation+markets&hl=en&ct=clnk&cd=1.

———. *World Energy Outlook 2008, Fact Sheet: Oil Demand. What Are the Prospects for Oil Consumption to 2030?* 2008.

———. *Worldwide Trends in Energy Use and Efficiency*, 2008. http://www.iea.org/Textbase/publications/free_new_Desc.asp?PUBS_ID=2026.

International Federation of Automotive Engineering Societies. "Honorary Committee: Chad O. Holliday Jr." http://www.fisita.com/about/honorary?id=19.

International Organization for Standardization. *ISO 14024. Environmental labels and declarations – Type I environmental labeling – Principles and procedures*. 1999.

International Strategy for Disaster Reduction. "Disaster Risk and Climate Change." 2008. http://www.unisdr.org/eng/risk-reduction/climate-change/climate-change.html.

Internet Time Blog. http://www.internettime.com/.

Investeco Newsletter. "Governments Move Ahead with Carbon Pricing." June 2008. http://www.investeco.com/uploads/file/0608newsletter.pdf.

Investor Environmental Health Network. "Investor Group Calls for More Disclosure of Market Risks." February 28, 2008. http://www.iehn.org/news.press.MutualNeglect.php.

ITT. *ITT's Place in the Cycle of Water—Everything but the Pipes*. 6th ed. http://ittfluidbusiness.com/media/ITT_WTRBK_v6_download.pdf.

Jaccard, M., J. Nyboer and B. Sadownik. *The Cost of Climate Policy*. Vancouver, B.C.:UBC Press, 2002.

Jacobson, Simon. "Environmental Compliance: Initiatives Broaden, Budgets Up—Complete Apps Still Few in Number." June 14, 2008. http://www.environmentalleader.com/2008/06/14/environmental-compliance-initiatives-broaden-budgets-up-complete-apps-still-few-in-number/.

Jacobson, Simon, and Colin Masson. "Laying the Foundation for Sustainability with Environmental Compliance." http://www.osisoft.com/Resources/Articles/Laying+the+Foundations+for+Sustainability+with+Environmental+Compliance.htm.

Jeanneau, M., and P. Pichant. "The Trends of Steel Products in the European Automotive Industry." http://74.125.95.104/search?q=cache:i1OqgJ7n6xUJ:www.revue-metallurgie.org/articles/metal/pdf/2000/11/p1399.pdf+625+million+cars+and+vehicles+on+the+road+globally&hl=en&ct=clnk&cd=2.

Jefferies Equity Research. "Clean Technology Primer." June 2008.

Jha, Alok. "Drax's £50m Renewables Project Throws Biomass into the Coal Mix." *Guardian* (UK), May 19, 2008. http://www.guardian.co.uk/environment/2008/may/19/biofuels.fossilfuels.

Joel Makower Blog. http://makower.typepad.com/joel_makower/.

Johnson, Eric, and Russel Heinen. "Biofuels Face a Carbon Certification Challenge." *Chemical Week*, April 2008.

Jolly, A., ed. *Managing Climate Risk*. London: Thorogood Publishing, 2008.

Juneau Daily News. "Court Slashes Judgment in Exxon Valdez Disaster," June 25, 2008.

Kachan, Dallas. "Green Grid Joined by Climate Savers Initiative from Google & Intel." Cleantech Group. 2007. http://media.cleantech.com.

Kanellos, Michael. "Elon Musk on Rockets, Sport Cars and Solar." February 15, 2008. http://news.cnet.com/Elon-Musk-on-rockets,-sports-cars,-and-solar-power/2008-11389_3-6230661.html.

Kapoor, K., and P. Ambrosi. "State and Trends of the Carbon Market 2008." The World Bank. May 2008.

Kasriel, Daphne. "Are Emerging Market Consumers Engaging with the Green Bandwagon?" *Euromonitor International*, October 4, 2007.

Keenan, Greg. "GM Could Cut Almost 2,000 U.S. Dealerships." *Globe and Mail*, December 3, 2008.

Keizai, Fuji. "Cleantech: Current Status and Worldwide Outlook." Report Linker. www.reportlinker.com/p077393/2008/02/Cleantech-Current-Status- and-Worldwide-Outlook.html.

Kenney, Brad. "Green Spot: 3P at 3M." 2008. http://www.industryweek.com/ReadArticle.aspx?ArticleID=16131.

Kho, Jennifer. "U.S. Solar Could Surpass German Market by 2011." Greentech Media, 2008. http://www.greentechmedia.com/articles/us-solar-market-could-surpass-germany-by-2011-1148.html.

Khosla, Vinod. "Biofuels: A Case Study." 2008. http://www.khoslaventures.com.

Kiley, David. "Big Oil's Big Stall on Ethanol." *Business Week*, October 1, 2007.

Kleanthous, A., and J. Peck. "Let Them Eat Cake—Abridged. Satisfying the New Consumer Appetite for Responsible Brands." World Wildlife Fund. 2007.

Kunzig, Robert, and Wallace S. Broecker. *Fixing Climate*. London: Profile Books, 2008.

Kurz, W.A., et al. "Mountain Pine Beetle and Forest Carbon Feedback to Climate Change." *Nature* 452 (2008).

La Hamaide, Sybille. "Global Biofuel Output to Soar in Next Decade: Report." Reuters, May 29, 2008. http://www.reuters.com/article/GCA-Agflation/idUSL2930418620080529.

Labatt, Sonia, and Rodney White. *Carbon Finance: The Financial Implications of Climate Change*. New Jersey: John Wiley & Sons, 2007.

Lash, J., and F. Wellington. "Competitive Advantage on a Warming Planet." *Harvard Business Review on Green Business Strategy*, 2007.

Lisi, Anna. "Chemistry & Sustainability." *American Chemistry* (March/April, 2007).

Logomasini, A. "Europe's Global REACH: Chemical Regulations in Europe Promise Worldwide Costs." Competitive Enterprise Institute. January 4, 2006. http://.cei.org/.

Lomas, O. "Climate Change and Emissions Trading—A European Perspective." Presentation given on behalf of Allen & Overy, at the International Environmental Lawyers Network Conference entitled "Current Environmental Issues: An International Perspective," Montreal, September 12, 2008.

Lovins, Hunter. "The Economic Case for Climate Action." Presidential Climate Action Project. 2007. http://www.natcapsolutions.org/publications_files/PCAP/PCAP_EconomicCaseForClimateProtection_04xii07.pdf.

Macalister, Terry. "Biofuels: Brazil Disputes Cost of Sugar in the Tank." *Guardian* (UK), June 10, 2008.

MacMillan, Douglas. "The Issue: Immelt's Unpopular Idea." *Business Week*, March 4, 2008.

Makower, Joel. *Strategies for the Green Economy: Opportunities and Challenges in the New World of Business*. New York: McGraw-Hill, 2008.

Makower, Joel, R. Pernick and C. Wilder. "Clean Energy Trends." Clean Edge. 2008.

Management Institute for Environmental Business. "Competitive Implications of Environmental Regulation in the Paint and Coatings Industry." 1994.

Markatos, Dennis. "What Can Record Coal Prices Do to US Electricity Prices?" May 26, 2008. http://www.igloo.org/dmarkatos/whatcanrec.

Marketing Green. "Bottled Water Backlash." 2008. http://marketinggreen.wordpress.com.

Mathers, J., and M. Manion. "Cap-and-Trade Systems." Catalyst 4, no. 1. 2005. Union of Concerned Scientists. http://www.ucsusa.org/.

Mattel. "8-K SEC Filing." January 31, 2008. http://sec.edgar-online.com/2008/01/31/0001193125-08-015787/Section9.asp.

———. "Press Release: Mattel Reports 2007 Financial Results." 2008. http://www.shareholder.com/mattel/news.

———. *2007 Global Citizenship Report*. http://www.mattel.com/about_us/Corp_Responsibility/Mattel_07GCReport.pdf.

———. *2007 Global Reporting Initiative*. http://www.mattel.com/about_us/Corp_Responsibility/MATTEL_2007_GRI_REPORT.pdf.

Maung, Z. "Green Marketers Smarten Up." ClimateChangeCorp. July 29, 2008. http://www.climatechangecorp.com/content.asp?contentid=5558.

McCarthy, Shawn. "Global Warming: Province Against Province?" *Globe and Mail*, March 14, 2008.

———. "Renewable Power Firms Weather the Storm." *Globe and Mail*, October 27, 2008.

McKenna, Barrie. "The Oilman's New Stripes." *Globe and Mail*, July 10, 2008.

McKinsey and Company. "How Companies Think about Climate Change." McKinsey Global Survey. 2008.

———. "The Carbon Productivity Challenge: Curbing Climate Change and Sustaining Economic Growth." 2008. http://www.fypower.org/pdf/MGI_Carbon_Productivity.pdf.

McLaughlin, Brant. "Nuclear Power Rise to the Occasion." Values derived from Nuclear Energy Institute. August 28, 2007. http://www.associatedcontent.com/article/360531/nuclear_power_rises_to_the_occasion.html.

McMillan, G. "The Greening of the Jobscape." Globe and Mail, November 14, 2008.

McPherson, J.R., and L.T. Mendonca. "The Challenge of Hiring and Retaining Women: An Interview with the Head of HR at eBay." *McKinsey Quarterly*, no. 4 (2008).

Melnbardis, Robert. "Hydro-Quebec Approves 2,004 MW of Wind-power Farms." Reuters, May 5, 2008.

Mendonca, L.T., and H. Rao. "Lessons from Innovation's Front Lines – An Interview with IDEO's CEO." *McKinsey Quarterly* (November 2008).

Milford, Edward. "Record Growth for Wind: What Comes Next?" Renewable Energy World. August 27, 2008. http://www.renewableenergyworld.com/rea/magazine/story?id=53436.

Milmo, Dan, and David Adam. "Branson Pledges $3bn Transport Profits to Fight Global Warming." *Guardian* (UK), September 22, 2006.

Mintz, Jack, and Nancy Olewiler. *A Simple Approach for Bettering the Environment and the Economy: Restructuring the Federal Fuel Excise Tax.* Ottawa: University of Ottawa, 2008.

Molley, Lawrence. "Glitnir Market Study on Geothermal in North America, 2007." http://northofthehotzone.com/2007/glitnir-market-study-on-geothermal-in-north-america/.

Montagne, Renee, and Adam Davidson. "Mattel Recalls 9 Million Toys Made in China." August 14, 2007. http://www.npr.org/.

Monticello, Mike. "New & Future Cars: Tesla Builds a 4-Door." *Road & Track*, December 2008. http://www.roadandtrack.com/article.asp?section_id=10&article_id=7201.

Montreal Gazette "The Alternative Race Heats Up," February 26, 2007.

———. "What's Green and What's Not?" April 22, 2008.

Moore, Lynn. "New Wind Power Would Cost More." *Montreal Gazette*, October 3, 2007.

Morris, Helen. "Black, White & Green All Over." *Montreal Gazette*, April 25, 2008.

MSNBC. "Wal-Mart to Reduce Mercury in CFLs. Agreement by Suppliers Reflects a Little-known Downside to Light Bulbs." May 10, 2008. http://www.msnbc.msn.com/.

Munro, Margaret. "Biofuel Salvation of Perdition." Green Life, May 3, 2008. http://www.canada.com/montrealgazette/features/greenlife/story.html?id=fde9f701-9002-4c1f-ada1-e1722be7e6d5&p=2.

NASA. "Arctic Sea Ice News & Analysis. National Snow and Ice Data Centre." 2008. http://nsidc.org/arcticseaicenews/.

National Biodiesel Board. *Biodiesel as a Greenhouse Gas Reduction Option.* 2008. http://www.biodiesel.org/resources/reportsdatabase/reports/gen/20040321_gen-332.pdf.

National Energy Board. "Current Market Conditions October–November 2008." http://www.neb.gc.ca/clf-nsi/rnrgynfmtn/prcng/lctrct/crrntmrktcndtn-eng.html.

National Renewable Energy Laboratory. "Energy Analysis and Tools." 2008. http://www.nrel.gov/buildings/energy_analysis.html.

National Resources Defense Council. "Coal in a Changing Climate." February 2007. http://www.nrdc.org/globalwarming/coal/coalclimate.pdf.

National Safety Council. "Lead Poisoning Happens More Than You Think." n.d. http://ncs.org.

Natural Step, The. "The ABCD Approach." http://www.thenaturalstep.org/en/abcd-process (accessed in 2008).

Nelder, Chris. "Tar Sands: The Oil Junkie's Last Fix, Part 1: Tar Sands' Profitability Questionable, Energy Capital." August 24, 2007.

New Carbon Finance. "Fundamentals Point to Higher Carbon Prices." May 23, 2008. http://www.newcarbonfinance.com.

Nielsen, Ron. "Human Resources Sustainability Competencies Summary—Draft." 2006.

Nike. *Innovate for a Better World.* 2007. http://www.nike.com/nikebiz/nikeresponsibility/pdfs/color/Nike_FY05_06_CR_Report_C.pdf.

North Rizza, Mickey. "Lean and Clean with Green Purchasing." AMR Research Alert article, April 17, 2008.

Nuclear Energy Institute. "Facing Facts—Remarks by Frank L. Bowman, President and CEO NEI at the Nuclear Energy Assembly." May 5, 2008.

Obama, Barack. "New Energy for America." 2008. http://my.barackobama.com/page/content/newenergy.

Office of Climate Change. 2008. http://www.occ.gov.uk/activities/eu_ets/analysis-euets-options.pdf.

Office of the Federal Environmental Executive. http://www.ofee.gov/.

Offset Quality Initiative. "Ensuring Offset Quality—Integrating High-Quality Greenhouse Gas Offsets into North American Cap and Trade Policy." 2008.

Ottman, J. "Don't Greenwash Your Marketing." *Advertising Age*, March 4, 2008.

———. "Eco-logos: A Double-edged Sword?" *Sustainable Life Media*. Not dated.

———. *Green Marketing: Opportunities for Innovation in the New Marketing Age*. 2nd ed. Charleston, S.C.: BookSurge Publishing, 2008.

Ottman, J., E.R. Stafford and C.L. Hartman. "Avoiding Green Marketing Myopia." *Environment* 48, no. 5 (2006).

Panja, Tariq. "British Tycoon Branson Offers $25 Million Prize to Fight Climate Change," *USA Today*, February 9, 2008. http://www.usatoday.com/tech/science/2007-02-09-branson-climate-prize_x.htm.

Paris, Jerome. "Peak Oil: BP, Conoco CEOs Say It's Here—Also IEA's Fatih Birol Really Freaks Out." The Oil Drum. November 11, 2007. http://www.theoildrum.com/node/3226.

Paris, Jerome. "Shell Energy Futures." The Oil Drum. January 25, 2008. http://www.theoildrum.com/node/3548.

Paulsson, Lars, and Paul Dobson. "Offshore Wind Projects Hit the Doldrums." *Globe and Mail*, May 15, 2008.

Peck, J. "Carbon Offsetting: Forgive My Carbon Sin?" *The Ecologist* (June 2008).

Penn, Schoen & Berland Associates. "Environment a Fair-Weather Priority for Consumers." June 3, 2008. http://www.psbresearch.com/press_release_Jun3-2008.htm.

Pepsico. "Environmental News." 2008. http://www.pepsico.com/Purpose/Environment/Articles/PepsiCo-Honored-Energy-Partner-Of-Year.aspx.

———. *Environmental Sustainability Report*. 2007. http://www.pepsico.com/PEP_Citizenship/sustainability/environmental_v11d.pdf.

Perkins Cole and Fasken Martineau. "Regional Climate Change Initiatives: An Overview." 2008.

Pollution Probe Foundation. "Emissions Trading Primer." 2003.

———. *The Canadian Green Consumer Guide*. 1989.

Porter, M., and F.L. Reinhardt. "A Strategic Approach to Climate." *Harvard Business Review*, October 2007.

Porter-Novelli. "Greenfluencers." 2008.

Potter, Mitch. "The Low-Carbon Diet." *Toronto Star*, September 27, 2008.

Project Better Place. http://www.betterplace.com/an-innovative-company/who-we-are/ (accessed in September 2008).

Public Citizen. "Nuclear Giveaways in the Energy Bill Conference Report." 2008. http://www.citizen.org/documents/energybillnukeconfreport.pdf.

Rand, Tom. "Forget the Russians—The CANDU Can Do It." *Globe and Mail*, April 10, 2008.

Rapier, Robert. "The 2008 IEA WEO—Renewable Energy." The Oil Drum. December 3, 2008. http://www.theoildrum.com/node/4798.

Reed, John. "Tesla to Raise $250m for Electric Cars." *Financial Times*, February 17, 2008.

Reinaud, J., and C. Philibert. "Emissions Trading: Trends and Prospects." Organization for Economic Cooperation and Development and International Energy Agency. 2007.

Reingold, Jennifer. "Hondas in Space." FastCompany.com, issue 91 (February 2005).

Renewable Energy Corporation ASA. "REC ASA—Invests NOK 13 Billion in Singapore." June 17, 2008. http://www.recgroup.com/default.asp?V_ITEM_ID=611&xml=/R/136555/PR/200806/1228877.xml.

Reuters. "Canadians Cynical About 'Green' Marketing: Survey." 2008.

———. "Monsanto Settles PCB Case in Alabama." Environmental Working Group, August 20, 2003. http://www.ewg.org/node/15680.

Rigby, D., and C. Zook. "Open Market Innovation." *Harvard Business Review*, October 2002.

Ritch, Emma. "LED Global Market Should Keep Getting Brighter and Brighter." *American Business* Daily, January 14, 2008. http://www.mlive.com/business/ambizdaily/bizjournals/index.ssf?/base/abd-3/120029640599480.xml.

———. "MIT Unlocking Carbon Capture and Storage." *Cleantech*, November 17, 2008. http://cleantech.com/news/3888/mit-carbon-capture-research-shows-greenhouse-emissions.

Roberts, Paul. "Tapped Out." *National Geographic* (June 2008).

Romn, Joseph. "Why We Never Need to Build Another Polluting Power Plant Coal? Natural Gas? Nuke? We Can Wipe Them All Off the Drawing Board by Using Current Energy More Efficiently. Are You Listening, Washington?" *Salon*, July 28, 2008. http://www.salon.com/news/feature/2008/07/28/energy_efficiency/.

Roner, Lisa. "Runaway Ecomagination Is Not Enough for GE." Ethical Corp. June 2008. http://www.ethicalcorp.com.

Rosales, J. "Values for a Post-Kyoto Discourse." *Climatic Change* 88, no. 2 (2008).

Rowell, Andy. "Climate Risk Set to Impact Oil Sands Development." Oil Exchange International. 2008. http://priceofoil.org/2008/09/16/climate-risk-might-scupper-oil-sands-development/.

Rubens, Craig. "Primer: What You Need to Know About Brazilian Biofuels." Earth2Tech. May 7, 2008. http://earth2tech.com/2008/05/07/primer-brazilian-biofuels/.

Schmidt, A., and H. and S.J. Freeman. "Corporate Social Performance and Attractiveness as an Employer to Different Job Seeking Populations." *Journal of Business Ethics* 28, (2000).

Schneider, Andrew. "W.R. Grace to Pay Record Superfund Fine." *Seattle Post*, March 12, 2008.

Scott, Norval. "Statoil Deals New Blow to Oil Sands." *Globe and Mail*, December 5, 2008.

Search Mobile Computing. "e-paper." 2008. http://searchmobilecomputing.techtarget.com/sDefinition/0,,sid40_gci535038,00.html.

Searle, R.H., and K. Ball. "Supporting Innovation through HR Policy: Evidence from the UK." *Creativity and Innovation Management* 12, no. 1 (2003).

Senge, Peter, Bryan Smith, Nina Kruschwitz, Joe Laur and Sara Schley. *The Necessary Revolution*. New York; Doubleday, 2008.

Serpo, Alex. "Green Your Datacentre or It May Go Dark." April 4, 2008. http://www.zdnet.com.au/insight/software/soa/Green-your-datacentre-or-you-may-get-fired/0,139023769,339286821,00.htm.

SFGate. "On the Record with Vinod Khosla." May 11, 2008. http://www.sfgate.com/cgi-bin/article.cgi?f=/c/a/2008/05/10/BUD010IHPC.DTL.

Shell. "Shell Global Scenario." http://www.shell.com/home/content/aboutshell/our_strategy/shell_global_scenarios/dir_global_scenarios_07112006.html (accessed in September 2008).

Shellenberger, Michael, and Ted Nordhaus. *Break Through: From the Death of Environmentalism to the Politics of Possibility*. New York: Houghton Mifflin Co., 2007.

Silicon Valley Toxics Coalition. "Toxics in Electronics." 2008. http://www.etoxics.org.

Silke Carty, Sharon. "Loans for Automakers Near Approval." *USA Today*, September. 25, 2008.

Simmons, Matt, and Aage Figenschou. "A Peak-Oiler, but Still in the Closet? IEA's 2008 Report." ASPOU USA, 2008. www.aspousa.org/index.php/2008/11/a-peak-oiler-but-still-in-the-closet-iea/.

Smith, Grant, and Jim Kennett. "There's No More Easy Oil." *Montreal Gazette*, May 19, 2008.

Smith, Rebecca. "Lightening the Load." *Wall Street Journal Online*, October 6, 2008. http://online.wsj.com/article/SB122305854616202945.html.

Smith, S., and J. Swiersbinski. "Assessing the Performance of the UK Emissions Trading Scheme." *Environmental and Resource Economics* 37 (2007).

Snyder, N.T. "Innovation at Whirlpool: Embedment and Sustainability." *Human Resource Planning* 29 (2006).

Solar Development. "Solar Energy Fact Sheets." http://www.solardev.com/SEIA-makingelec.php (accessed December 10, 2007).

Solar Energy Industry Association. "Congress Extends Federal Solar Energy Tax Credits Through End of 2008." December 9, 2006.

Solid State Lighting. "Frequently Asked Questions." 2008. http://lighting.sandia.gov/XlightingoverviewFAQ.htm#ssl.

SolveClimate Blog. http://solveclimate.com/blog/.

Sony. "20-F SEC Filing." EDGAR Online, June 28, 2002. http://sec.edgar-online.com/2002/06/28/0000950109-02-003508/Section4.asp.

———. CSR Report 2003. http://www.sony.net/SonyInfo/Environment/issues/report/2003/.

———. CSR Report 2007. http://www.sony.net/SonyInfo/Environment/issues/report/2007/.

Souder, Elizabeth. "Will Wal-Mart Sell Electricity One Day?" RedOrbit, January 28, 2007. http://www.redorbit.com/news/science/817594/will_walmart_sell_electricity_one_day/index.html.

Spencer-Cooke, Andrea. "Hero of Zero." Tomorrow: Global Sustainable Business X, no. 6 (November–December 2000).

Speth, James. The Bridge at the Edge of the World: Capitalism, the Environment, and Crossing the Crisis of Sustainability. London: Yale University Press, 2008.

Squatiglia, Chuck. "Hydrogen Cars Are Here. Now We Just Need a Fueling Infrastructure." March 12, 2008.

Stern, Nicholas. The Economics of Climate Change: The Stern Review. New York: Cambridge University Press, 2007.

Steward, Gillian. "It's Not Just About 500 Dead Ducks," Toronto Star, May 11, 2008.

Strack, R. Video commentary on strategic HR challenges. Boston Consulting Group. 2008. http://cdn.bcg.com/odaptor/cpa_video_a.html.

Subsea World. "LNG: Powering the Future—A $106 Billion Market 2008–2012." August 2, 2008. http://www.subseaworld.com/industry/lng-powering-the-future-v-a-106-billion-market-2008-2012-02276.html.

SustainAbility, UNEP, and The Global Compact. "Unchaining Value: Innovative Approaches to Sustainable Supply." 2008.

Terrachoice. "The 'Six Sins of Greenwashing.' A Study of Environmental Claims in North American Consumer Markets." 2007.

TerraPass Blog. http://www.terrapass.com.

Tertzakian, Peter. A Thousand Barrels a Second. New York: McGraw-Hill, 2006.

Tesco. www.tescoplc.com (accessed in September 2008).

Tesla Motors Blog. http://www.teslamotors.com/.

Thornes, J.E., and S. Randalls. "Commodifying the Atmosphere: 'Pennies from Heaven?'" Geografiska Annaler: Series A, Physical Geography 89, no. 4 (December 2007).

3M. "Pollution Prevention Pays." http://solutions.3m.com/wps/portal/3M/en_US/global/sustainability/management/pollution-prevention-pays/.

Tidal Electric. "Technology: History of Tidal Power." http://www.tidalelectric.com/History.htm.

Tietenberg, T.H. Emissions Trading. Principles and Practice. 2nd ed. Washington: RFF Press, 2006.

Tingström, Johan. "Product Development with a Focus on Integration of Environmental Aspects." Doctoral Thesis, Division of Engineering Design, Department of Machine Design School of Industrial Engineering and Management, Royal Institute of Technology Stockholm, 2007.

Toronto Star. "Morning Briefing—Retail, 2008. Stores to Reduce Energy Use," August 27, 2008

Totenberg, Nina. "Supreme Court Weighs Exxon Valdez Damages." February 27, 2008. http://www.npr.org/templates/story/story.php?storyId=48308288.

Trudel, Jean-Sébastien. "Arrêtons de Pisser dans de l'eau embouteillée." Éditions Transcontinental. 2007.

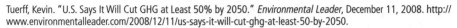

Tuerff, Kevin. "U.S. Says It Will Cut GHG at Least 50% by 2050." *Environmental Leader*, December 11, 2008. http://www.environmentalleader.com/2008/12/11/us-says-it-will-cut-ghg-at-least-50-by-2050.

U.S. Army. "Lean Six Sigma." 2008. http://www.army.mil/.

U.S. Department of Energy. "Energy Efficiencies and Renewable Energy." 2008. http://www1.eere.energy.gov/geothermal/powerplants.html.

U.S. Green Building Council. "LEED Rating System." 2008. http://www.usgbc.org/DisplayPage.aspx?CategoryID=19.

———. http://www.usgbc.org/DisplayPage.aspx?CMSPageID=222 (accessed in September 2008).

U.S. Securities and Exchange Commission. "Paypal SEC 10-K." December 31, 2001.

U.S. White House. "Energy Independence and Security Act Fact Sheet." December 2007.

———. http://www.whitehouse.gov/infocus/environment/ (accessed in September 2008).

UNEP, UCCE, and UNCTAD. "A Guide to Emissions Trading." 2002.

Unilever. "Sustainable Development 2007: An Overview." 2008. http://www.unilever.com.

United Nations Environmental Programme. "The Global Compact and Utopies, 2005. Talk the Walk. Advancing Sustainable Lifestyles Through Marketing and Communications."

United Nations Framework Convention on Climate Change. "Kyoto Protocol." 2008. http://unfccc.int/kyoto_protocol/items/2830.php.

UPS. http://www.ups.com (accessed in September 2008).

USA Today. "Venture Capitalist Khosla Joins in Effort to Save the Planet," December 25, 2007.

Voutsinos, Cosmos. "Using Nuclear Energy to Get the Most Out of Alberta's Tar Sands. A White Paper for Discussion." January 2007. http://www.computare.org/Support%20documents/Guests/Cosmos%20Voutsinos/Getting%20the%20most.htm.

Wal-Mart. "Wal-Mart Is Taking the Lead in Logistics." http://walmartstores.com/media/factsheets/fs_2314.pdf (accessed in September 2008).

WaterWorld. "Report Shows Global Water Crisis Promotes Desalination Boom." October 16, 2008. http://ww.pennnet.com/display_article/342890/41/ARCHI/none/BUSIN/1/Report-shows-global-water-crisis-promotes-desalination-boom/.

Weeren, Silvio, and Hans Wendschlag. "TED—The Eco Declaration Standard." 2007. http://www.ecma-international.org/memento/tc38-tg3-2007-001.pdf.

Weir, Fred. "Has Russian Oil Output Peaked?" *Christian Science Monitor*, May 28, 2008. http://www.csmonitor.com.

Welch, David. "GM Live Green or Die." *Business Week*, May 26, 2008.

Wenzel, Elsa. "Bill Clinton: Green Buildings Key to Fighting Climate Change." *cnet news*, November 7, 2007. http://news.cnet.com/8300-11128_3-54-90.html.

Whitaker, D. "Are Sustainability and Human Capital Management so Different?" *Personnel Today*. 2007.

Whoriskey, Peter. "There Will Be No Newspapers in 10 Years: Ballmer." *Washington Post*, published in *Montreal Gazette*, June 9, 2008.

Wigder, D. "Getting Smart About Green Targeting." *GreenBiz.com*, 2008. http://www.greenbiz.com.

Wikipedia. "Clean Coal Technology." http://en.wikipedia.org/wiki/Clean_coal (accessed in August 2008).

———. "Electricity Generation." Answers.com. http://www.answers.com/hydroelectricity#Electricity_generation (accessed in April 2008).

———. "Emissions Trading." http://en.wikipedia.org/wiki/Emissions_trading (accessed in August 2008).

———. "Energy Use." http://en.wikipedia.org/wiki/Energy_use_in_the_United_States (accessed in July 2008).

———. "Environmental Effects of Wind Power." http://en.wikipedia.org/wiki/Environmental_effects_of_wind_power (accessed in July 2008).

————. "Fuel Cells." http://en.wikipedia.org/wiki/Fuel_cell (accessed in July 2008).

————. "Government Procurement." http://en.wikipedia.org/wiki/Government_procurement (accessed in September 2008).

————. "Solar Thermal." http://en.wikipedia.org/wiki/Solar_thermal_energy (accessed in 2008).

————. "Strategic Service Management." http://en.wikipedia.org/wiki/Strategic_Service_Management (accessed in September 2008).

————. "Tidal Power." http://en.wikipedia.org/wiki/Tidal_power (accessed in July 2008).

Wilder, Clint. "Our New Greatest Generation Opportunity." Clean Edge, 2008. http://www.cleanedge.com/views/index.php?id=5382.

Willard, Bob. The Next Sustainability Wave. Gabriola Island, BC, Canada: New Society Publishers, 2005.

Williams, E. "CSR Europe's Green Marketing Guide. 4 Ps for 3 Ps." CSR Europe. 2008.

Willis, E. "Canada's Green Plan and Its Implications for Trading." Presentation to Environmental Finance Conference, Toronto, 2007.

————. "Eighth Annual Workshop on Greenhouse Gas Emissions Trading, Country Roundtable: Canada." Carbon Capital Management. 2008.

Wilson, A., G. Lenssen and P. Hind. "Leadership Qualities and Management Competencies for Corporate Responsibility." European Academy of Business in Society. 2006.

Wirtenberg, J., J. Harmon and K.D. Fairfield. "HR's Role in Building a Sustainable Enterprise: Insights from Some of the World's Best Companies." HR Planning 30, no. 1 (2007).

Wise, Peter. "EdP Buys Horizon for $2.9 Bn." Financial Times, March 28, 2008.

Wood, R.C., and G. Hamel. "The World Bank's Innovation Market." Harvard Business Review, November 2002.

Wood, Susanna. "Oil Prices Likely to Hit $200 a Barrel." August 11, 2008. http://news.icm.ac.uk/business/utilities/oil-prices-likely-to-hit-200-a-barrel/607/.

Woody, Todd. "PG&E Gives Away 1 Million Energy Efficient Light Bulbs." Green Wombat, October 3, 2007. http://www.greenwombat.com.

World Business Council for Sustainable Development. "Establishing a Global Carbon Market – A Discussion on Linking Various Approaches to Create a Global Market." 2008.

————. "Meeting Changing Expectations." ISBN No. 2-94-0240-03-5. http://www.wbcsd.org/DocRoot/hbdf19Txhmk3kDxBQDWW/CSRmeeting.pdf.

————. "Policy Directions to 2050: A Business Contribution to the Dialogues on Cooperative Action." 2007.

World Health Organization. "Climate and Health." 2008. http://www.who.int/mediacentre/factsheets/fs266/en/index.html.

World Nuclear Association. "The Economics of Nuclear Power." 2008. http://www.world-nuclear.org/info/inf02.html.

WorldNetDaily. "Congress Bans Incandescent Bulbs: Massive Energy Bill Phases Out Edison's Invention by 2014." December 19, 2007. http://www.worldnetdaily.com/news.

Yachnin & Associates. "The SDEffect™: Translating Sustainable Development into Financial Valuation Measures." 2006.

Yakabuski, Konrad. "McGuinty Is Wrong-Headed on Nuclear." Globe and Mail, July 10, 2008.

Yezza, Islem. "Global Market for Bioplastics." Helmut Kaiser Consultancy. 2008.

ZDNet Blog. http://news.zdnet.com/.

ZFacts.com. "Crude Price in Today's Dollars." http://zfacts.com/p/196.html (accessed November 24, 2008).

————. "Regular Gasoline Price in Today's Dollars." http://zfacts.com/p/35.html (accessed November 24, 2008).

EXAMPLES OF ECO-DESIGN AND GREEN PROCUREMENT LEGISLATION/POLICY

Eco-design and green procurement legislation consider the following topics:

- eco-design requirements
- prohibition of chemicals in products
- registration of substances/chemicals
- hazard labeling and material safety data sheets (MSDS)
- energy usage and associated labeling of products
- fuel efficiency and use of renewable fuels
- type and quantity of packaging materials
- consumer products safety (including drugs and food)
- air emissions, wastewater discharge and waste during production of goods
- government green procurement requirements
- take-back and end-of-life

Note that in addition to these key areas, other legislation relating to product rebates (e.g., purchase of hybrid vehicles or energy-saving appliances), worker health and safety, resource conservation and extraction fees, and trade (import/export) must be considered. In the following section, examples of more recent legislation in each area are presented. A detailed assessment of all pertinent legislation is beyond the scope of this book.

ECO-DESIGN

There is no comprehensive legislation in the United States and Canada relating to eco-design. Instead, there is legislation relating to particular aspects of eco-design, such as energy usage, labeling of products and fuel efficiency.

The EU adopted its Eco-design of Energy-using Products (EuP) Directive in 2005. It establishes an overall framework under which manufacturers of energy-using products will be obliged to reduce the energy consumption and other negative environmental impacts that occur throughout the product life cycle at the design stage. The directive makes provision for the introduction of so-called implementing measures, which can be Minimum Energy Performance Standards (MEPS) or other mechanisms. The directive very broadly defines an energy-using product as "a product, which is dependent on energy input (electricity, fossil fuels and renewable energy sources) to work as intended." Under the EuP, designers are expected to consider and reduce the cradle-to-grave environmental impacts of their products, including[1]

- use of raw materials and natural resources
- negative contributions towards climate change (for example, GHGs)
- energy consumed during the extraction of raw materials, transportation, production, sale, use (including stand-by) and disposal
- waste generation
- release of hazardous substances

Andris Piebalgs, commissioner of the EU Energy Commission, summarized the goals of the EuP as follows:

The CO_2 emissions saving potential through Ecodesign requirements for energy-using products is of the order of magnitude of 180 Mt of CO_2—the equivalent to one quarter of the reduction target of "20% by 2020"—out of which about 15 Mt could be achieved through switching to more efficient light bulbs in households. Ecodesign measures thus play an important role in reducing CO_2 emissions, increasing our security of supply and ensuring cost-savings to consumers.[2]

Information on EU legislation and policies related to eco-design can be obtained from www.europa.cu.

PROHIBITIONS OF CHEMICALS IN PRODUCTS

Numerous pieces of legislation prohibit the use of chemicals; examples include regulations relating to

- global ozone depleting substances
- polychlorinated biphenyls (PCBs)
- Restrictions of Hazardous Substances (RoHSs)

It is important to note that the U.S. EPA has only banned five chemicals since 1976. The hurdles are so high for the agency that it has not even been able to ban asbestos, which is widely acknowledged as a likely carcinogen and is barred in more than thirty countries. Instead, the EPA relies on industry to voluntarily cease production of suspect chemicals.[3] In the case of asbestos, restrictions on its use are significantly influenced by civil lawsuits.

California recently enacted a law that gives its Department of Toxic Substances Control the power to set up a framework for dealing with chemicals of concern, instead of on a substance-by-substance basis (which often leads to contentious legislation or litigation).

The EU RoHS legislation was considered one of the first pieces of environmental legislation that significantly affected the supply chain for electronic parts manufacturers. The legislation prohibits six chemicals from being in electrical and electronic equipment: lead, mercury, cadmium, hexavalent chromium, polybrominated biphenyls (PBBs) and polybrominated diphenyl ethers (PBDEs).

EU Emergency Legislation on Phthalates

In 1999, the EU parliament passed emergency legislation to ban six phthalates from toys for children under three years of age that were designed to be put in the mouth. The ban became permanent in 2005: the EU banned DEHP, DBP and BBP phthalates from use in all toys and childcare articles, while other DINP, DIDP and DNOP phthalates were banned in toys and childcare articles that can be put in the mouth. The legislation allowed manufacturers one year to put systems in place before the ban took effect.[4]

New China RoHS

The Chinese RoHS, called Management Methods for Controlling Pollution by Electronic Information Products, is mandatory for electrical and electronic products being sold into China. Manufacturers, importers and distributors must ensure that their products meet the declaration and labeling (the CCC mark—China Compulsory Certificate) requirements of China. The list of prohibited chemicals is the same as the EU RoHS. It is important to note that testing/certification is a prerequisite (Chinese lab test results only) for this legislation.[5]

Korean RoHS/Waste Electrical & Electronic Equipment (WEEE)

The Act for Resources Recycling of Electrical/Electronic Products and Automobiles, commonly referred to as "Korea RoHS," combines the concepts of EU RoHS, EU WEEE, and EU End-of-Life. Many of the concepts are similar to the related EU directives, but the Korean RoHS Enforcement Ordinance and Regulation differ in implementation and application.[6]

U.S. RoHS Status

There has been a proliferation of individual state laws related to RoHS that have conflicting requirements. U.S. industry wants one law that supersedes state law to make compliance easier. Current proposals call for federal legislation that mirrors parts of California's Electronic Waste Recycling Act (California's RoHS).

Canada RoHS Status

Nova Scotia has proposed an amendment to its Solid Waste-Resource Management Regulations that would require producers to implement design for the environment (DfE) measures restricting use of the six EU RoHS substances. This amendment is still under discussion, however, and other provinces have not as yet put forward any similar plans.[7]

REGISTRATION OF SUBSTANCES

Several countries and regions have put in place legislation to ensure that they have sufficient information on chemicals that are imported, manufactured or exported within their jurisdictions. Key jurisdictions include the U.S., Canada, Europe, China, Japan, Korea, Philippines, Australia and New Zealand. Typically, a country will have a National Inventory List (NIL) for "existing" chemicals. Substances that are not listed on the NIL are considered "new" and are subject to notification and approval by the authorities.

New EU REACH

The EU regulation on Registration, Evaluation, Authorisation and Restriction of Chemical substances (REACH) came into force on June 1, 2007. Key objectives of this legislation include

- a registration system for approximately thirty thousand new and existing chemical substances manufactured or imported into the EU in quantities greater than 1 tonne per year
- reverse burden of proof—manufacturers or importers of substances are responsible for demonstrating they are safe
- improved supply chain communication—downstream users to provide use and risk management measures information
- authorization procedure for most hazardous substances
- greater transparency and openness for the public by providing easier access to information on chemicals

In December 2008 the European Chemicals Agency (ECHA) published a list of pre-registered substances. The list contains about 150,000 substances that were pre-registered by 65,000 companies between June 1 and December 1, 2008.

Key business implications of this legislation include that it

- affects substances already in the marketplace, hence it may significantly impact what substances are purchased and sold
- requires companies to work together to prepare submissions to ECHA, therefore issues of competitive information will emerge that will need to be addressed
- imposes bi-directional flow of information along the supply chain, requiring revamping of IT systems and processes
- ensures that companies cannot manufacture or supply substances that are not registered—no data, no market!

The European Commission has estimated that REACH will cost industry between €2.8 billion and €5.2 billion over eleven years. Other estimates put the figure as high as €12.8 billion. The commission also calculates that REACH will save Europe €54 billion over thirty years because fewer people will become ill as a result of exposure to chemicals.[8] Recent statements by the EC indicate that this value may be higher. Examples of key activities that will drive "direct" REACH costs are listed below.

- preparation of substance inventory information related to pre-registration
- supply chain communication of uses

- testing where insufficient information exists
- identification of appropriate exposure scenarios and assessment of risk management measure based upon uses
- revision of Material Safety Data Sheets (MSDSs) to address new classifications, exposures scenarios and risk management measures
- generation of chemical safety assessments and registration dossiers

Examples of indirect costs include

- price increase or discontinuation of raw materials, reformulation and new approvals
- negative impact on corporate brand if a company does not comply or hazardous substances are identified in products being used for consumer goods
- NGOs may publicize presence of Substances of Very High Concern (SVHC) in products
- downstream users in the EU will only purchase registered products and scrutinize the use of SVHC

EU Genetically Modified (GM) Organisms

In 2001, the EU passed a directive related to the deliberate release into the environment of genetically modified organisms. They followed this up in 2003 and 2004 with detailed rules for the application for authorization of new genetically modified food and feed, the notification for existing products and adventitious or technically unavoidable presence of genetically modified material, which has benefited from a favorable risk evaluation. Key features of these regulations are these:[9]

- Safety assessment of biotech crops is carried out by an independent European authority, the European Food Safety Authority (EFSA), and is a continuous process that remains in place even after a product is authorized, through careful monitoring and the requirement to renew the approval of biotech products every ten years.
- The tracing and labeling of biotech crop–derived ingredients are required throughout the food chain for maximum transparency for consumers aimed at guaranteeing freedom of choice.

- A set of European-level recommendations (known as coexistence guidelines) on how to cultivate biotech crops alongside conventional and organic crops exist in order to ensure that there is no discrimination against any type of agriculture.
- Competent authorities in member states are fully involved in the safety assessment of biotech crops.

California Chemical Information Call-in for Nanotechnologyy

According to Alston & Bird LLP February 2009 *Toxic Tort Advisory,* the California Department of Toxic Substances Control has issued a "chemical information call-in" broadly requiring carbon nanotube manufacturers and importers to submit data regarding analytical test methods, fate and transport in the environment and other relevant information.

Proposed Canadian Nanotechnology Legislation

Alston and Bird LLP report also advised that Canada may become the first nation in the world to require companies to detail their use of engineered nanomaterials and target companies and institutions that manufactured or imported a total quantity greater then 1 kg of a nanomaterial during he 2008 calendar year.

LABELING/MSDS FOR PRODUCTS

Labels serve as the first alert that there may be hazards associated with using a product and indicate what precautions to take when using the product. In many countries they also inform the person reading the label that a MSDS is available. Typically, three types of labels are regulated by government agencies.

1. Chemical product labels that provide information to workers on how to properly handle the material
2. Consumer labels that provide information, usually using less technical jargon, to consumers on the proper handling of the material
3. Specialized labels that address types of products (medical, pesticides) and are sometimes a combination of the chemical product and consumer label requirements

California Proposition 65 requires that substances on the list of "chemicals known to cause cancer or birth defects" (about 850 substances) and those listed as "probable animal carcinogens" are properly labeled. Failure to label these may result in litigation.

Canadian Food and Drugs Act proposed changes **(Bill C51)**, whose stated purpose is to protect and promote the health and safety of the public, and to encourage accurate and consistent product representation. The proposed changes to the FDA will significantly change the regulation of drugs and other FDA-regulated products in Canada by introducing a new "progressive licensing" regime, life-cycle monitoring and testing post-market, by increasing adverse reaction reporting and by introducing new recall powers for the Minister of Health.

EU REACH requires companies to notify recipients of the chemical name(s) and how the product can be used safely if an SVHC is present above 0.1% based upon weight (w/w).

An MSDS, referred to as a Safety Data Sheet (SDS) in the EU and parts of the Pacific Rim, must be prepared and supplied with each regulated material used or manufactured in a workplace, and in many cases must accompany the actual shipment. Depending upon the jurisdiction, the document may have to be in the local language; contain specific information, e.g., contents of the product and safe handling requirements; and require periodic update.

A key component of MSDS and chemical product labels is the classification of the material. The United Nations has produced a new Globally Harmonized System (GHS) for classification and labeling of chemicals. The GHS was supposed to harmonize the rules and regulations related to classification of hazardous goods; some countries (e.g., Japan and South Korea) are adding further requirements to the general principles, thus significantly reducing the harmonization benefits.

ENERGY USAGE AND LABELING

Most governments have put forward legislation/programs to address energy usage on two complementary paths:

- energy labeling of household appliances
- Minimum Energy Performance Standards (MEPS)

Examples of legislation include these:[10]

- In the U.S., there are two voluntary endorsement-labeling programs. The Department of Energy (DOE) supports a voluntary office equipment program called ENERGY STAR, which is a joint effort with the EPA. In addition, since 1992, a nonprofit organization called Green Seal has implemented a voluntary ecolabel—the Green Seal of Approval—which endorses energy-efficient products. The National Energy Conservation Policy Act (NECPA) also requires the U.S. Federal Trade Commission to mandate labels for appliances that indicate their energy consumption.

- The Energy Policy Act directs the DOE to establish MEPS for nine categories of energy- and water-consuming commercial sector products, electric motors, lighting products, plumbing products and office equipment. It also provides for application to additional products if technically feasible and economically justified.
- The 2007 U.S. Energy Independence and Security Act (EISA) required all general-purpose lighting in federal buildings to use ENERGY STAR products or products designated under the Energy Department initiatives by 2013 and new MEPS.
- Canada has adopted the International ENERGY STAR program but also recognizes the criteria and logo established under the U.S. scheme. Canada has established MEPS regulation under the Energy Efficiency Act (EEA) for a wide range of products. Note that the federal legislation does not apply to goods manufactured and sold within a province; however, provinces have their own energy-efficiency regulations, which may differ from the federal regulations or may apply to other classes of equipment.
- The European Community ENERGY STAR Programme is a voluntary energy-labeling program for office equipment. The EU has also issued directives regarding the labeling and standard product information about the consumption of energy and other resources by household appliances,[11] and a Directive on the Eco-design of Energy-using products (EuP) that addresses energy use. Refer to Eco-Design discussion.

Additional information on the different eco-labeling programs is presented in chapter 4.

FUEL EFFICIENCY AND RENEWABLE FUEL

Legislation on fuel economy has been in place for several years. The following table presents examples from various countries. It is important to note that the 1908 Ford Model T got 25 miles per gallon (mpg)—9.41 liters for 100 km.[12]

Table A.1: Global Fuel Economy Requirements

Country	Current Requirements	Future Requirements
United States	2.75 mpg (car) CAFE Standard*	35 mpg CAFE Standard by 2020 with phase in to begin in 2011*
California	25 mpg†	35.7 mpg by 2016† and 42.5 mpg by 2020 with fifteen other states adopting California rules‡
Canada	27 mpg (cars and light trucks)§	BC and Quebec are proposing that the California standard be adopted§
China	36 mpg†	43 mpg by 2009 and to be announced for 2011†
European Union	40 mpg†	48.9 mpg by 2012†
Japan	40 mpg†	48.9 mpg proposed for 2015†

CAFE = Corporate Average Fuel Efficiency
* Hard and Evans, 2009
† Next Big Future, 2008
‡ Bailey, 2009
§ Grist.org, 2008

U.S. Legislation

EISA legislates both the use of alternative fuel sources by setting a mandatory Renewable Fuel Standard for biofuels and a new national fuel economy standard of 35 mpg by 2020. This is the first statutory increase in fuel economy standards for automobiles since 1975.

Canada

The Canadian government passed a bill in May 2008 to ensure that gasoline contains 5% ethanol by 2010. The bill also provides for diesel to contain 2% renewable fuels by 2012. In order for this to occur, the approximate 1 billion liters of ethanol and biodiesel that is forecast to be processed at Canadian facilities in 2007 must climb to 3 billion liters a year.[13]

Most provincial governments have established RFS, with Manitoba being the most stringent—has mandated 8.5 percent ethanol content in gasoline since 2007. Other provinces have either 5 percent or higher renewable content in gasoline (Alberta, British Columbia, New Brunswick, Ontario and Saskatchewan) or are proposing it (Quebec).

In 2008 the British Columbia government introduced a carbon tax on gasoline and diesel fuels that was based upon carbon dioxide emissions. The starting price of the program was $10 per tonne of carbon dioxide and increases by $5 per tonne on an annual basis until it reaches $30 per tonne in 2012. The tax is suppose to be revenue neutral in that money collected is suppose to go back to the public in the form of tax cuts to individuals and businesses.

Europe

In 2006, the UK government ordered petrol stations to source 5% of their fuel from renewable energy by 2010. Germany also put in place a law that required a minimum of 10% of petrol be "plant" sourced by 2009 and 17% by 2020. In the last six months, EU lawmakers are reassessing this legislation in light of the biofuel debate.

Note that in addition to regulating fuel efficiency and the role of renewable fuel, federal and state/provincial governments are also providing consumers with tax credits related to the purchase of hybrid vehicles. These range in value, but can be several thousand dollars.

The key question is who will have the competitive advantage—the automakers who take the lead and provide vehicles for the more stringent markets, or those that reactively respond once their market share is significantly eroded in the U.S.? Additional information is available in chapter 1 (information on the biofuel debate), chapter 3 (information on the state of green automobiles) and chapter 6 (discussion of biofuels and fuel cells).

PACKAGING MATERIAL AND AMOUNTS

There are numerous pieces of legislation dictating what can be in packaging material, especially related to "food contact" materials and recycling requirements. As international commerce, Internet sales and the trend towards products with short life spans continue to develop, the volume of goods placed on the market (and subsequent waste from these products and their packaging) has increased dramatically, often faster than waste disposal capacity.

Packaging constitutes a growing waste stream in many countries, particularly those undergoing rapid socio-economic change, such as Eastern Europe. In North America and Western Europe, the per-capita consumption of packaging is also increasing. One important factor is the growing proportion of single-person households, which favor smaller retail units, single-portion packs and other convenience items over economy-size packages and bulk goods.[14] The goal of new extended producer responsibility legislation is to drive reductions in the amount of packaging at source via the redesign of packaging material.

California and New York Plastic Bag Law

In 2006, California required stores over a certain size to provide bins for the collection of plastic bags brought back by customers for recycling. The store is responsible for the collection, transportation and recycling of the plastic bags. New York City introduced similar legislation in 2008.

Canada

The provinces of Quebec and Ontario have regulated product stewardship by putting in place a cost recovery fee structure applicable to printers, publishers and the packaging industry to recover the costs of municipal recycling programs. The laws mandate fees to ensure 50% product recovery. Several municipalities have also prohibited plastic bags or mandated a fee be charged.

EU Packaging Regulations

The EU has had a packaging and packaging waste directive since 1994. The aim of the directive was to harmonize the management of packaging waste in the EU and tackle the impact that packaging and packaging waste have on the environment. Although the primary objective is to increase the recovery and recycling of packaging waste in a consistent way in all member states of the EU (so as to avoid barriers to trade), priority is also given to reducing the amount of packaging used and increasing the reuse of packaging. A revised Packaging Directive was published in February 2004. It sets new recovery and recycling targets, as a percentage of all packaging waste, to be met by December 31, 2008.[15]

Table A.2: EU Packaging Waste Targets

New Targets	Percentage
Minimum Recovery	60%
Recycling	55%–80%
Of Which Minimum Material-specific Recycling Targets Include	
Glass	60%
Paper/board	60%
Metals	50%
Plastics	22.5%
Wood	15%

CONSUMER PRODUCTS SAFETY (INCLUDING DRUGS/FOOD)

A significant amount of legislation exists around the world related to consumer products—the majority of which addresses food and drugs.

New U.S. Amendment to Consumer Product Safety

Responding to public concern arising from a wave of defective toys and other goods, the U.S. is overhauling the country's consumer product laws and strengthening the beleaguered safety agency that oversees the marketplace. Congress has not adopted major consumer product legislation in eighteen years, and this legislation is in response to the explosive growth of foreign imports, particularly from countries with few significant safety standards. It requires the creation of a public database of complaints and permits the attorney general to seek court injunctions if products endanger residents and the federal government is not acting. It makes mandatory many toy safety standards that are now voluntary and, as part of that change, requires that toys be tested in compliance with a comprehensive set of rules. The legislation also increases the possible maximum penalty for violations to $20 million, from the current $1.25 million. It also makes it a crime for a company to sell a product that has been recalled.

Canadian Hazardous Products Act (HPA)

Consumer Product Safety of Health Canada establishes and enforces safety standards for consumer products. The overall mandate is to control/eliminate danger to the health and safety of the public by regulating both the presence of hazards in products and their design, construction or contents. Key components related to consumer products include the following lists:

- items that are banned from import, sale and advertisement in Canada
- products that must meet specific regulations in order to be imported, sold or advertised in Canada
- voluntary standards that may apply to some products, negotiated between industry and government
- products that are not regulated but are of concern and hence should be carefully reviewed by industry

Proposed Canadian Consumer Product Safety Act

The proposed legislation will replace Part 1 of the HPA and is designed to protect consumers from unsafe products and tainted food and drugs. The legislation imposes a blanket prohibition against the import and sale of products that are dangerous to human health or safety. It also reverses the onus onto the manufacturer or seller of the product to show how they abide by the rules. The legislation allows the health minister to ban any product with an "existing or potential hazard," even if the exposure has a chronic adverse effect many years later. If a dangerous product does end up on the shelves, the minister can order companies to provide information proving that the products are safe as well as order mandatory recalls of the product. More importantly, companies will have to report any adverse incidents to the minister within two days, as well as keep track of where their products are sold. If companies do not comply with the new law, they can receive fines up to $1 million that could increase to $5 million if there is a conviction in court, as compared with the current maximum fine of $5,000.[16]

EU General Products Safety Directive (GPSD)

The GPSD, which came into force in 2004, aims at ensuring that only safe consumer products are sold in the EU. In general, the GPSD applies in a complementary way to products and/or risks covered by sector-specific product safety legislation. A structured list of legislation relevant to specific sectors has been drafted by the Directorate-General for Enterprise and Industry. This list is known as the Pink Book, and it is updated annually to incorporate legislative developments.[17]

RELEASES DURING PRODUCTION OF GOODS

There exist numerous federal, state/provincial and local regulations that address the release of chemicals during the production of goods. In terms of eco-design, it is important to understand the impact that hazardous chemicals may have on facility permits (air emissions, wastewater and waste) and key stakeholders (government, public, NGOs and customers) via reporting obligations under various pieces of legislation (e.g., United States Tier II and Form R and Canadian National Pollutant Release Inventory). For existing sources, the introduction of very hazardous chemicals into production may trigger renewed interest in the facility/company, while for new sources, the release of "additional" emissions in a nonattainment area will most likely trigger a review.

The City of Toronto recently became the first Canadian city to require businesses to provide information on their releases of harmful chemicals. The disclosure requirement, known as the "right to know" bylaw, will require companies to provide information on 25 hazardous substances, which the City will make available on the Internet. This approach is similar to Environment Canada's NPRI program and has been used by U.S. cities to encourage companies to reduce pollutants voluntarily.

GOVERNMENT GREEN PROCUREMENT

There are numerous government programs for green procurement that are known under other names:

United States:
- Affirmative Procurement (also called Green Procurement)—required by federal agencies
- Environmentally Preferable Purchasing (EPP) Program—EPA
- Green Procurement Program (GPP)—Department of Defense

Canada:
- Guidelines for the Integration of Environmental Performance Considerations in Federal Government Procurement—Office of Greening Government Operations (OGGO)

United States

The Office of the Federal Environmental Executive oversees federal greening initiatives. Government green purchasing includes the acquisition of recycled content products, environmentally preferable products and services, bio-based products, energy- and water-efficient products, alternative fuel vehicles, products using renewable energy, and alternatives to hazardous or toxic chemicals. The White House Task Force on Waste Prevention and Recycling, in conjunction with the EPA and the U.S. Department of Agriculture, assists federal agencies to promote the acquisition of recycled content, environmentally preferable and bio-based products; non-ozone depleting substances; and products containing alternatives to certain priority chemicals. The U.S. Department of Energy and EPA assist agencies to implement the energy-related purchasing requirements, including the purchase of alternative fuel vehicles and alternative fuels. The General Services Administration and the Defense Logistics Agency, as the central source for supplies key to making the federal green purchasing program successful.[18]

Table A.3 presents examples of U.S. government rules related to green procurement.

Table A.3: Examples of U.S. Government Green Procurement

Federal Acquisition Regulation (FAR)

Subpart FAR23.2 prescribes policies and procedures for acquiring energy- and water-efficient products and services, and products that use renewable energy technology. Amended to include provisions for implementation Executive Order 13423 requirement to purchase EPEAT-registered products.

FAR Subpart 23.4 prescribes policies and procedures for acquiring EPA-designated products through AP programs required by the Resource Conservation and Recovery Act of 1976 and Executive Order 13101.

FAR Subpart 23.7 prescribes policies and procedures for acquiring energy-efficient, water conserving and environmentally preferable products/services.

Code of Federal Regulation (CFR), Title 40, Part 247

The CFR is a publication established by Act of Congress (44 U.S.C. § 1510). It represents a compilation of all the regulations issued by federal administrative agencies that have "general applicability and legal effect." As a consequence, the contents of the CFR cover a wide range of subjects, including recycling and AP.

EPA

CPG Items lists fifty-four items that can be purchased with recycled content paper, re-refined oil, flyash in concrete, etc. The agency must require that 100% of purchases meet or exceed CPG. A written justification/waiver is required for noncompliance.

Executive Orders

Executive Order 13101 requires federal agencies to incorporate waste prevention and recycling into daily operations and to increase the use of recovered materials by instituting procurement preferences for these products.

Executive Order 13221 requires federal agencies to purchase products that use no more than 1 watt in their standby power-consuming mode. DOE's Federal Energy Management Program program develops lists of recommended products that meet this requirement.

Executive Order 13150 establishes programs providing incentives for federal employees to use mass transportation and vanpools.

Executive Order 13149 requires the federal government to reduce petroleum consumption through improvements in fleet fuel efficiency and the use of alternative fuel vehicles and alternative fuels.

Executive Order 13148 requires federal agencies to establish environmental management systems, implement compliance audits and pollution prevention programs, meet the legal requirements of the Emergency Planning and Community Right-to-Know Act, reduce the use of toxic and hazardous substances, reduce ozone depleting substance use and implement sustainable landscaping practices.

Executive Order 13134 requires USDA, DOE and other agencies to work together to promote the development and use of bio-based products and bio-energy in an environmentally sound manner.

Executive Order 13123 requires federal agencies to reduce GHG emissions and energy use caused by facility operations, expand renewable energy use, reduce the use of petroleum in facilities and reduce water consumption in facilities.

Canada

The Canadian government has adopted the Policy on Green Procurement, which seeks to reduce the environmental impacts of government operations and promote environmental stewardship by integrating environmental performance considerations in the procurement process.

Green procurement is set within the context of achieving value for money. It requires the integration of environmental performance considerations into the procurement process, including planning, acquisition, use and disposal. In this context, value for money includes the consideration of many factors, such as cost, performance, availability, quality and environmental performance. Green procurement also requires an understanding of the environmental aspects and potential impacts and costs associated with the LCA of goods and services. Under the Policy on Green Procurement, deputy heads are required to ensure that the objectives of green procurement are realized. Requirements of the policy include setting green procurement targets as appropriate, with the assistance of Public Works and Government Services Canada.

Take-back/End-of-life

Take-back legislation holds manufacturers responsible for the environmentally safe recycling or disposal of their end-of-life products. Manufacturers are expected to provide a financial or physical plan to ensure that such products are collected and processed. The European Union and Japan were among the first to introduce such legislation. In North America, most take-back legislation has focused on the recycling of bottles and cans.

Expanding volume, short life cycles, and an ever-growing waste stream are three key reasons that environmental regulations have targeted electronics and electrical equipment. New types and improved models of electronic devices, telecommunications equipment and electrical appliances are flooding the marketplace. Cell phones, computers, DVD players, televisions, GPS finders...with the speed at which new technology is developed, last year's model is frequently discarded in favor of the latest features. The impact on waste disposal resources—both landfills and incinerators—is a practical concern for many governments.[19]

As a result, Europe enacted Waste Electrical and Electronic Equipment (WEEE) and End-of-Life Vehicles (ELV) Directives. Key aims of the WEEE Directive include

- reducing waste from electric and electronic equipment
- increasing recovery and recycling rates
- improving the environmental performance of all operators involved throughout the life cycle of electric and electronic equipment
- implementing producer responsibility

Expanding U.S. E-waste Legislation

Twelve states (increasing soon) plus New York City have passed laws creating state-wide e-waste recycling programs. There are two basic models: Producer Responsibility (manufacturer pays) and Advanced Recovery Fee (ARF; consumer pays). All except California are "producer responsibility" laws, requiring manufacturers to pay for recycling. Additional information on e-waste in the U.S. can also be obtained from the Electronic Manufacturer's Coalition for Responsible Recycling, a group of companies that have come together out of a belief that ARF is the best approach to financing management of end-of-life electronics at the state and national levels. Coalition companies include major manufacturers in the consumer electronics sector for televisions, as well as personal computer and monitors.

Expanding Canada WEEE

Five provinces have enacted legislation similar to EU WEEE. Environment Canada estimates state that more than 140,000 tons of computer equipment, phones, televisions, stereos, and small home appliances accumulate in Canadian landfills each year. For a listing of requirements by province, see www.greensupplyline. com. Additional information on e-waste in Canada can be obtained from the Electronics Product Stewardship Canada (EPSC), an industry-led organization that is developing a national electronics end-of-life program. For additional information on EPSC, refer to www.epsc.ca.

Existing EU ELV

Europe's End-of-Life Vehicles Directive sets recovery targets for recycling of vehicles and components, encourages manufacturers to design their vehicles with part reuse and recycling in mind, and restricts the use of certain heavy metals in new vehicle manufacturing processes. Waste prevention is the priority objective of the directive. To this end, it stipulates that vehicle manufacturers and material and equipment manufacturers must[20]

- endeavor to reduce the use of hazardous substances when designing vehicles
- design and produce vehicles that facilitate the dismantling, reuse, recovery and recycling of end-of-life vehicles
- increase the use of recycled materials in vehicle manufacture
- ensure that components of vehicles placed on the market after July 1, 2003, do not contain mercury, hexavalent chromium, cadmium or lead, except in the applications listed in Annex II; the Council or the Commission may amend the Annex where scientific and technical progress make it possible to avoid using these substances

NOTES

1   European Council for an Energy Efficient Economy, "The Eco-design Directive for Energy Using Products," http://www.eceee.org/european_directives/Eco_design.
2   Europa, "Energy Efficiency," 2008, http://europa.eu/scadplus/leg/en/s14003.htm.
3   Lyndsey Layton, "Chemical Law Has Global Impact," Washington Post, June 12, 2008, www.washingtonpost.com/wp-dyn/content/article/2008/06/011/AR2008061103569.
4   Greenpeace, "Tasty News for Apple," May 2, 2007, http://www.greenpeace.org.
5   Tom Valliere, "China RoHS Overview," iNEMI Life After EU ROHS Forum, Chicago, September 28, 2006.
6   RoHS International, 2008.
7   Foresite.org, Regulatory Compliance Canada – RoHS, 2008, http://www.foresite.org.
8   BBC, "Q&A: Reach Chemicals Legislation," November 28, 2005, http://news.bbc.co.uk.
9   Europa, "Energy Efficiency Requirements for Light Bulbs and Other Energy-using Products on Track for Adoption," June 22, 2007.
10 National Resource Council, "II. The Process and Institutional Context for Energy Efficiency Standards and Labels in Each Country," 2008, http://oee.nrcan.gc.ca.
11 Europa, "Energy Efficiency."
12 Mark Truby, "Sierra Club Ads May Dim Ford Party," Detroit News, June 4, 2003.
13 Margaret Munro, "BioFuel Salvation or Perdition?", Montreal Gazette, May 3, 2008.
14 Department of Environmental Quality, "International Packaging Regulations," 2005.
15 Department for Environment, Food and Rural Affairs, "Producer Responsibility Obligations (Packaging Waste)," January 2006.
16 Sarah Schmidt, "New Consumers' Bill Pledged," Montreal Gazette, April 9, 2008.
17 Europa, "The General Products Safety Directive," 2008, http://ec.europa.eu/consumers; Europa, "What Is Integrated Product Policy?," 2008, http://ec.europa.eu/environment/ipp.
18 Office of the Federal Environmental Executive, 2008, http://www.ofee.gov.
19 Christine Murner, "Plastics, Electronic & the Environment: How New Global Regulations Affect Material Choices," Plastics Technology, October 2006.
20 Europa, "Management of End of Life Vehicles," 2008, http://europa.eu/scadplus.

LIST OF ACRONYMS

AAU	assigned amount units
ACE	automated commercial environment
APU	auxiliary power units
ARF	advanced recovery fee
ART	advanced renewable tariff
ASA	Advertising Standards Agency
BFR	brominated fire retardants
BR&OA	business risk and opportunity assessment
BSC	balanced scorecard
BSR	business for social responsibility
BU	business units
CAES	compressed air energy storage
CAFE	corporate average fuel efficiency
CARB	California Air Resources Board
CBP	Customers and Border Protection
CCB	climate, community, and biodiversity
CCPA	Canadian Chemical Producers Association
CCPI	clean coal power initiative
CCS	carbon capture and sequestration
CCX	Chicago Climate Exchange
CDM	centralized data management
CDM	clean development mechanism
CdTe	cadmium telluride
CEO	Chief Executive Officer
CER	certified emission reduction
CFC	chloro-fluorcarbons
CFL	compact fluorescent light
CFR	Code of Federal Regulation
CHEMTREC	chemical transportation emergency center
CIGS	copper indium gallium selenide
CMR	carcinogens, mutagens, reproductive
CNM	customer needs management
CO_2	carbon dioxide
CPG	consumer product goods
CPO	Chief Procurement Officer
CPV	concentrated PV
CRM	customer relationship management
CSA	Canadian Securities Administrators
CSCI	Climate Savers Computing Initiative
CSP	concentrated solar power
CSR	corporate social responsibility
DCF	discounted cash flow
DEFRA	Department for Environment, Food and Rural Affairs
DfE	design for environment
DJSI	Dow Jones sustainability index
DMS	direct material sourcing
DoD	Department of Defense
DOE	designated operational entity
DNA	Designated National Authorities
DSC	dye-sensitive thin film
DSSC	dye-sensitized solar cell
DU	downstream users
EAM	enterprise asset management
ECHA	European Chemical Agency
ECPA	Electric Consumers Protection Act
EEA	Energy Efficiency Act
EFSA	European Food Safety Authority
EGS	enhanced geothermal systems
EHS	environmental, health and safety
EIA	environmental impact assessments
EIA	Economist Intelligence Unit
EICC	electronics industry code of conduct
EISA	Energy Independence and Security Act
EMCCR	Electronic Manufacturer's Coalition for Responsible Recycling
EMS	environmental management systems
EPA	Environmental Protection Agency
EPI	Earth Policy Institute
EPP	environmental product policy
EPP	environmentally preferable purchasing
EPP	environmental preferred purchasing
EPSC	Electronic Product Stewardship Canada
ERCB	Energy Resources and Conservation Board
ERP	enterprise resource planning
ERU	emission reduction units
ETS	emissions trading schemes
EU	European Union
EuP	Eco-Design Directive
EV	electric vehicle
EVA	economic value added
FIT	feed-in tariff
FSC	Forest Stewardship Council
GEI	GREENGUARD Environmental Institute
GeSI	global e-sustainability initiative
GHG	greenhouse gas
GHS	globally harmonized system
GPSD	General Products Safety Directive
GW	giga watts
GM	genetically modified
GMO	genetically modified organism
GNP	gross national product

GPP	green procurement program	POEMS	product-oriented environmental management systems
GRC	governance, risk, and compliance	PTC	protection tax credits
GRI	global reporting initiative	PV	photovoltaic
GSN	green supply network	PVC	polyvinyl chloride
HCM	human capital management	PWSCG	Public Works and Government Services Canada
HPA	Hazardous Products Act		
HR	human resources	R&D	research and development
IEA	International Energy Agency	R&O	risks & opportunities
IEC	International Electrotechnical Commission	REACH	registration, evaluation and authorization of chemicals
IEHN	Investor Environmental Health Network		
IETA	International Emissions Trading Association	REC	renewable energy certificates
IGCC	integrated gasification combined cycle	RFS	renewable fuel standards
IOC	independent oil companies	RGGI	regional greenhouse gas initiative
IPCC	Intergovernmental Panel on Climate Change	RoHS	restriction of hazardous substances
IPP	integrated product policy	RPS	renewable portfolio standard
IT	information technology	SD	sustainable development
ITC	investment tax credits	SDS	safety data sheet
ISO	International Organization for Standardization	SEC	Securities and Exchange Commission
		SFI	sustainable forestry initiative
LCA	life cycle assessments	SMARTER	specific, measurable, acceptable to those working to achieve them, realistic, timely, extending the capabilities of those working to achieve them, and rewarding
LCI	life cycle inventory analysis		
LED	light-emitting diodes		
LEED	leadership in energy and environmental design		
LNG	liquefied natural gas	SME	small to medium size enterprises
MA	millennium ecosystem assessment	SOP	standard operating practices
MBI	market-based instruments	SO_2	sulfur dioxide
MD&A	management discussion and analysis	SOX	Sarbanes-Oxley
MDM	master data management	SRI	socially responsible investing
MEG	multiple exciton generation	SSL	solid state lighting
MGGA	Midwestern Greenhouse Gas Reduction Accord	SVHC	substances of very high concern
		SVC	sustainable value networks
MRFS	mandatory renewable fuel standard	SWOT	strengths, weaknesses, opportunities and threats
MSDS	material safety data sheets		
MW	mega watts	TBL	triple bottom line
NAP	national allocation plans	TFT	Tropical Forest Trust
NECPA	National Energy Conservation Policy Act	3P	pollution prevention pays
NGOs	non-government organizations	TNC	transnational corporations
NIL	national inventory list	Transcaer	transportation community awareness and emergency response
NOC	national oil companies		
NPDL	new product development and launch	UN	United Nations
NRDC	National Resource Defense Council	UNFCC	United Nations framework convention on climate change
OFFE	Office of the Federal Environmental Executive		
OGGO	Office of Greening Government Operations	USCAP	US Climate Action Partnership
OPV	organic PV	VCM	voluntary carbon market
OTC	over the counter	VER	verified emission reductions
P/CFPC	price to cash flow per share ratio	VGF	Virgin green fund
PBB	project better place	VOC	volatile organic carbon
PBB	polybrominated biphenyls	vPvP	very persistent and very bioaccumulative
PBDE	polybrominated diphenyl ethers	WBCSD	World Business Council for Sustainable Development
PBI	performance-based incentive		
PBT	persistent, bioaccumulative and toxic	WCI	Western Climate Initiative
PEFC	program for the endorsement of forest certification scheme	WEEE	waste electrical and electronic equipment
		WWF	World Wildlife Fund
PLM	product life cycle management	ZEV -	zero emission vehicle

INDEX